PATENTS, COPYR
TRADEMARKS AND LITER
Course Handbook
Number 148

Legal and Business Aspects of the Advertising Industry 1982

Felix H. Kent
Elhanan C. Stone
Cochairmen

G4-3705
Practising Law Institute

Library of Congress Catalog Card Number: 82-80182

FOREWORD

This course handbook is one of about 150 published each year by the Practising Law Institute.

Its primary function is to serve as an educational supplement to each program. It may also be used as a reference manual by attorneys and related professionals unable to attend the sessions.

The method of reproduction utilized has been chosen to insure that registrants receive these materials as quickly as possible in the most usable form practicable.

The Practising Law Institute wishes to acknowledge its debt and extend its sincere appreciation to the authors who have rendered this valuable service. They exemplify the finest tradition of our profession by sharing their expertise with their colleagues.

Prepared for distribution at the
LEGAL AND BUSINESS ASPECTS OF THE
ADVERTISING INDUSTRY
Program
April 22-23, 1982
New York City

CONTENTS

RD

1

THE ADVERTISER/AGENCY RELATIONSHIP

Felix H. Kent

March 11, 1982

The Advertiser/Agency Relationship

I. Historical Development of Relationship Between Advertiser and Agency:

(a) Agency originally acted as agent for media and obtained commissions from them.

(b) Use of "Agency" is probably a misnomer. In the legal sense, most activities carried out by Agency are not under direct control of Advertiser. The question frequently arises to what extent the Agency may bind the client in dealing with third parties. The question also has sales tax implications.

(c) The evolvement of "a la carte" agencies and house agencies and the return to full service agencies.

II What do Agreements Provide? (Sample Agreement Attached - Exhibit "A".)

1. Appointment of Agency. Is it the sole Agency? Handling of additional products. Problems of competitive products.

2. Nature of Services:

(a) Study of product or services and competitive products and services.

(b) Creation and planning of advertising and marketing program.

(c) Research - question of compensation

beyond copy research.

(d) Media analysis, plans and purchases.

(e) Production of print advertising.

(f) Production of broadcast commercials.

(g) Program contracts, talent contracts and securing of music and literary rights.

(h) Collateral services - brochures, reports, convention, dealer meetings, etc.

(i) Checking, billing, follow-up on contracts.

3. Compensation of Agency:

(a) Commission System:

(i) 15% on gross amount (17.65% on net) of media expenditures.

(ii) Commission on production (art work engravings, type compositions, etc.)

(iii) Commission on broadcast programs, talent, etc.

(b) Fee System: Agency receives set amount of annual or monthly fees; Media commissions are applied or rebated to advertiser. Periodic reconciliations.

(c) Variations: Guaranteed Profit or Guaranteed Commission contracts; share of profits from sales; cost plus contracts and other variations.

(d) Out-of-pocket expenditures.

(e) Special work: research, promotional, permit-of-sale, booklets, etc.

(f) Outdoor advertising.

(g) Cash discounts - generally passed on to client, provided there is no overdue indebtedness.

(h) Prompt payment of invoices.

4. Contracts with Suppliers

(a) Must obtain competitive bids

(b) Must disclose dealings with controlled or affiliated companies.

5. Rights on Termination:

(a) Notice period - generally 60 or 90 days.

(b) Agency has right to commissions on advertising media whose closing or broadcasting dates fall within notice period.

(c) Assumption of Agency's liabilities under media and talent contracts. Note problems with talent and unions if commercials are used by advertiser or other agency without payment of residuals.

(d) Ownership of advertising material?* Was it used? Was it paid for? Is there a difference based on whether Agency was on Commission or Fee basis?

*See Brown v. Molle Co., 20F.Supp. 135 (S.D.N.Y. 1937)

6. Indemnity for Claims:

Should contract include indemnity clause? When should Agency indemnify Advertiser and *vice versa*? Should Agency be responsible to defend trademark infringement actions? Governmental proceedings? Claims arising from comparative advertising? Practical effect with respect to coverage under advertising liability policy.

7. Handling of Competitive Products:

Agency is generally restricted. Problems with respect to multi-product advertisers.

8. Appointment of Master Agency for the large advertiser:

Division of functions, master agency commission.

III. Liability to Media:

1. There are conflicting cases on whether Advertiser is automatically liable for media commitments of Agency. The preponderance of authority imposes liability on Advertiser:

See Clarke v. Watt, 83 Misc. 404, 145 N.Y.S. 145 (App. Div., 1913). American Broadcasting-Paramount Theatres v. American Manufacturers Mutual, 42 Misc.2d 939, 249 N.Y.S.2d 481 (Sup. Ct. 1963), aff'd 251 N.Y.S.2d 906; aff'd 17 N.Y.2d 849 (1966); cert den. 385 U.S. 931 (1967). But also see Huntington Pennysaver v. Tire Supply, 59 Misc.2d 268, 298 N.Y.S.2d 824 Dist. of Suffolk Cty (1969) in which Agency alone was held liable to newspaper; and Washington Broadcasting Co. v. Goozh Gifts, Inc., 118 A.2d 392 (Mun. Ct. of Appeals, D.C. 1955) where there was no contract. The court held that since all dealings were with the Agency, there was clearly no intent on the part of the station to hold the Advertiser. Similarly, a buying service was not entitled to recover from the Agency when the Advertiser went bankrupt (See Atwood Richards, Inc. v. Clyne Maxon, Inc., N.Y. Law Journal, June 26, 1975.) The case of Columbia Broadcasting System, Inc. v. Stokely-Van Camp, Inc., 522 F.2d 369 (1975) was decided in favor of the Advertiser but special circumstances existed.

The Institute of Broadcasting Financial Management

has proposed a compromise clause (Exhibit "B") under which Advertiser becomes liable only when it is notified that Agency is in default.

2. In case of advertiser's failure to pay Agency, the Agency generally still has to pay the media; however, there may be a distinction between liability to print media and to broadcast media. "Sole Agency Liability" continues to prevail with print media.

3. Liability to suppliers other than media generally rests with Agency, but, increasingly, agencies seek to protect themselves against liability if they are not paid by clients.

IV. <u>Contracts for "A la Carte" Services</u>:

Growth in the '70s of "boutiques" and media buying services:

1. Contract with separate creative organization; generally on fee basis and with short notice of termination period; difficult to tie compensation to advertising placement.

2. <u>Contracts with Media Buying Services</u>:

(a) Different types of buying services;

(b) Extent of control over purchases.

(c) Liability to media in case buying services

fail to make payment has not been settled conclusively. Question how Agency and Advertiser can protect against claims resulting from buying services failure to pay.

EXHIBIT "A"

Date:

TO:

Gentlemen:

You have retained us and we hereby agree to serve as your advertising agency in accordance with and subject to the following terms and conditions:

1. Assignment

Our assignment shall relate to the following product(s) or service(s):________________________________

During the term of this agreement we shall be the sole company charged with the responsibility of preparing and placing advertising with respect to such product(s) or service(s). You may assign additional products or services to us from time to time, subject to our ability to handle same. If additional products or services are assigned to us and we agree to handle same, all terms and conditions hereof shall apply in the same manner as with respect to the originally assigned product(s) or service(s).

2. Nature of Services

We shall perform the following services for you in connection with the planning, preparing and placing of advertising for your product(s) or service(s):

(a) Study your products or services;

(b) Analyze your present and potential markets;

(c) Create, prepare and submit to you for approval, advertising ideas and programs;

(d) Employ on your behalf, our knowledge of available media and means that can be profitably used to advertise your products or services;

(e) Prepare and submit to you for approval, estimates of costs of these recommended advertising programs;

(f) Write, design, illustrate or otherwise prepare your advertisements, including commercials to be broadcast, or other appropriate forms of your message;

(g) Order the space, time or other means to be used for your advertising, endeavoring to secure the most advantageous rates available;

(h) Properly incorporate the message in mechanical or other form and forward it with proper instructions for the fulfillment of the order;

(i) Check and verify insertions, displays, broadcasts or other means used, to such degree as is usually performed by agencies;

(j) Audit invoices for space, time, material preparation and services.

3. Compensation

The basis of our compensation shall be as follows:

(a) On all space and facilities purchased and talent engaged by us on your behalf, we shall bill you at the published card rates or negotiated rates, as may be applicable, for space and facilities and at the authorized engagement rate for talent, plus any taxes, insurance, pension and welfare fund contributions, etc., applicable thereto. You recognize that we are a signatory to collective bargaining agreements with Screen Actors Guild and American Federation of Television and Radio Artists and that the hiring of talent by us on your behalf will be subject to the terms of such agreements.

(b) If no agency commission is granted or allowed to us on any purchases of space or facilities or on any engagement of talent, you agree that we may invoice you an amount which, after deduction of our cost, will yield us fifteen (15%) percent of such amount as agency commission.

(c) On art work, engravings, type compositions and any and all art and mechanical expenses incurred by us, pursuant to your authorization, we shall invoice you an amount which, after deduction of our cost, will yield us fifteen (15%) percent of such amount as agency commission.

(d) If we undertake, at your request, special assignments such as market, product or distribution research, or other research (with the exception of research for copy development testing purposes), or special assignments such as market counseling or sales meeting presentations, the charges made by us will be agreed upon in advance whenever possible. If no agreement was made, we shall charge you at our standard rates for the work performed by us. In addition, for materials or services purchased from outside sources under your authorization, we shall invoice you an amount which, after deduction of our cost, will yield us fifteen (15%) percent of such amount as agency commission.

(e) You agree to reimburse us for such cash outlays as we may incur, such as forwarding and mailing, telephoning, telegraphing and travel, in connection with services rendered in relation to your account.

4. <u>Billing and Payment Procedures</u>

(a) We shall invoice you for all media costs sufficiently in advance of our payment date to media to permit prepayment by you to enable us to take advantage of all available cash discounts.

(b) The cost of production materials and services shall be billed by us upon completion of the production job, or - if cash discounts are earnable - upon receipt of supplier invoice.

(c) On all outside purchases other than for

media, we shall attach to the invoice proof of billed charges from suppliers.

(d) All cash discounts on agency purchases including but not limited to media, art, printing and mechanical work, shall be passed on to you provided our billing terms are complied with and there is no overdue indebtedness at the time of payment to the vendor.

(e) Rate or billing adjustments shall be credited or charged to you on the first billing date after we have been invoiced or as soon as otherwise practical.

(f) All invoices shall be rendered on or about the first day of each month and will be payable the 10th day of the month.

(g) Invoices shall be submitted in an itemized format.

5. Commitments to Third Parties

(a) All purchase of space and facilities and all engagement of talent with respect to the advertising of your products shall be subject to your prior approval.

(b) If you should direct us to cancel or terminate any previously authorized purchase or project, we shall promptly take all appropriate action, provided that you will hold us harmless with respect to any costs incurred by us as a result thereof.

(c) We warrant and represent to you that in purchasing any materials or services for your account, we shall exercise due care in selecting suppliers and make every effort to obtain the lowest price for the desired quality of materials or services. Wherever possible, we shall obtain competitive bids. In no event shall we purchase any materials or services from any supplier which is a subsidiary or affiliated company or which is known to us to be owned or controlled by any of the directors or officers of this company, without making full disclosure to you of any such relationship.

(d) We warrant and represent that if at any time we shall obtain discounts or rebates from any supplier, whether based on volume or work given to such supplier by us or otherwise, then and in such event, we shall remit to you within a reasonable time after our receipt of such discount or rebate, such proportion thereof as the volume of work given by us to such supplier on your behalf bears to the total volume of work given by us to such supplier from all of our clients during the pertinent period to which the discount or rebate is applicable.

6. Inspection of Books

We agree that any and all contracts, correspondence, books, accounts and other sources of information relating to your business upon reasonable prior notice shall be available for inspection at our office by your authorized representatives during ordinary business hours.

7. Safeguarding of Property

(a) We shall take all reasonable precautions to safeguard any of your property entrusted to our custody or control, but in the absence of negligence on our part or willful disregard by us for your property rights, we shall not be responsible for any loss, damage, destruction, or unauthorized use by others of any such property.

(b) We shall not be responsible for the return of engravings after their use in publications, unless you specifically request their return before they are sent to the publication.

8. Term of Agreement

The term of this agreement shall commence on ____________________ and shall continue in full force and effect until terminated by either party upon written notice of such intention given ninety (90) days in advance, provided that in no event may this agreement be terminated effective prior to the expiration of twelve (12) months from the commencement of the term. Notices shall be deemed given on the day of mailing or in case of notice by telegram, on the day it is deposited with the telegraph company for transmission.

The rights, duties and responsibilities of this agency shall continue in full force during the period of notice, including the ordering and billing of advertising in print media whose closing dates fall within such period and the ordering and billing of advertising in broadcast media where the air dates fall within such period.

9. Rights Upon Termination

(a) At the termination, you agree that any advertising, merchandising, packaging and similar plans and ideas prepared by us and submitted to you (whether submitted separately or in conjunction with or as part of other material) but not used by you, shall remain our property unless it was either mutually agreed in writing that any such plan or idea became your property, or specific payment of the cost of its development was agreed upon and made by you. You agree to return to us any copy, art work, plates or other physical embodiment of the creative work relating to any such ideas or plans, which may be in your possession upon termination.

(b) Upon termination of this contract, we shall transfer, assign and make available to you, or your representative, all property and materials in our possession or control belonging to and paid for by you.

We also agree to give all reasonable cooperation toward transferring with approval of third parties in interest, all contracts and other arrangements with advertising media or others, for advertising space, facilities and talent, and other materials yet to be used, and all rights and claims thereto and therein, upon being duly released from the obligation thereof. You recognize that talent contracts with members of certain labor unions or guilds generally cannot be assigned except to signatories to the collective bargaining agreements governing the services rendered by such talent.

(c) Upon termination, no rights or liabilities shall arise out of this relationship, regardless of any plans which may have been made for future advertising, except that any uncancellable contracts made on your authorization and still existing at termination hereof, which contracts were not or could not be assigned by us to you or someone designated by you, shall be carried to completion by us and paid for by you in the manner described in Paragraph 3. above.

10. Governing Law

This agreement shall be interpreted in accordance with the laws of the State of New York.

If the above accords with your understanding and agreement, kindly indicate your consent hereto by signing in the place provided below.

Very truly yours,

By:____________________________
Title:

ACCEPTED AND AGREED:

____

By:____________________________
Title:

EXHIBIT "B"

IBFM/BCA RECOMMENDED LIABILITY CLAUSE

Agency is acting as agent for a disclosed principal, the Advertiser named on the face hereof ("Advertiser"), including, so long as Agency is not insolvent, as Advertiser's agent for making payment on all billings hereunder. However, Agency shall be liable for the payment of sums due hereunder and Company shall look solely to Agency for the payment thereof, unless and until Agency becomes insolvent, at which time, without relieving Agency of liability until Company is paid in full, Advertiser shall be liable to Company and not to Agency on all unpaid billings for services rendered by Company hereunder (excluding advertising agency commissions), but only to the extent that Advertiser has not theretofore made payment to the Agency thereon, and/or to the extent that Advertiser has theretofore made payment to the Agency thereon (i) while knowing that Agency had entered into an agreement or arrangement purporting to assign or pledge to a third party monies which may be or become payable by Advertiser to Agency, or that Agency was in danger of becoming insolvent; or (ii) after receiving notice (together with a current statement of account) from Company that Agency is seriously delinquent under this or any other agreement(s) between Company and Agency acting on behalf of Advertiser by failing to make payment on billings within 45 days after the end of the month in which service is provided thereunder.

NOTES

2

BASIC COPY RULES

Elhanan C. Stone

March 11, 1982

BASIC COPY RULES

Use of Names, Photographs, etc.

Applicable laws in New York and virtually all other states prohibit the use of the names and likenesses of living persons in advertising without written permission. See New York Civil Rights Law, Section 50 and 51.

Generally, privacy does not survive the grave so the use of the names of the deceased should not be a problem. However, certain jurisdictions give rights to heirs in this area and this must be considered. The other side of the privacy coin, however, is the right of publicity which in some jurisdictions has been considered a property right. That is if during his lifetime a performer has exploited his right of publicity, it is decendible and assignable as is any other property right. See Factors Etc., Inc. v. Pro Arts Inc., 579 F.2d 215 (2d Cir. 1978), cert. denied, 440 U.S. 908 (1979); but see Memphis Development Foundation v. Factors, 616 F.2d 956 (6th Cir.), cert. denied, 101 S.Ct. 358 (1980) for a contrary view based on state law. See also Law Makes Distinctions in Use of Look-Alikes by Elhanan C. Stone; Advertising Age November 9, 1981.

Naming or depicting buildings in advertising is generally not a problem. However, Section 397 of the New York General Business Law gives protection in this area to those buildings of non-profit, religious, benevolent, educational, fraternal and similar organizations. You just can't use Lincoln Center, St. Patrick's Cathedral, Columbia University, etc. for advertising purposes without written permission.

Use of Titles and Excerpts from Literary Material

Titles

For the most part, copyright may not be claimed in a title. However, relief may be available to an aggrieved party under a theory of unfair competition. If a title acquires a secondary meaning, its unauthorized appropriation may be actionable. But Compco Corporation V. Day-Brite Lighting, Inc. 376 U.S. 234 (1964) and Sears Roebuck & Company V. Stiffel Company 376 U.S. 225 (1964) raise serious questions as to whether any protection is available under theories of unfair competition where it is not otherwise available by patent or copyright protection. Also see American Broadcasting Company Merchandising, Inc. V. Button World Manufacturing, Inc. 151 U.S. P.Q. 361 (N.Y. Supreme Court 1966).

Excerpts From Literary Materials

Traditionally, a troublesome area because "fair use", the defense generally raised to copyright infringement actions of this nature, constitutes an issue of fact and is so flexible as virtually to defy definition. Considerable research is recommended, starting with "Nimmer On Copyright", 1979 Matthew Bender, Section 13.05 and following and the cases cited therein.

Imitations

Generally, the law does not protect style and advertisers have imitated famous performers without too much difficulty. However, certain jurisdictions recognize property rights in the unique styles and mannerisms of some performers and have afforded relief on this basis. For an interesting discussion of the area see "Style And Performance" by Anthony Liebig, Bulletin of the Copyright Society, Vol. 17 No. 1 (1969). However, a recent case involving the Marx Brothers and the imitation of their style and performance in a theatrical production entitled A Day In Hollywood A Night In The Ukraine indicates that courts might recognize some right of publicity in a style of performance. Groucho Marx's Productions Inc., etc. al., USDC SDNY Number 80 Civ. 2310 Slip Opinion October 2, 1981.

Use Of:

"New"

All advertised merchandise should be new unless full disclosure to the contrary is made. Also, FTC is inclined to question use of any claim that a product is "new" for a period of time longer than six months. However, in a bona fide test marketing of a new product which does not cover more than 15% of the population and does not exceed six months in duration, the six month rule does not apply until the test period has ended.

"Free"

The FTC Guide provides that:

All terms, conditions and obligations of the "free" offer should be set forth clearly and conspicuously at the outset so as to leave no reasonable probability that its terms might be misunderstood.

In a given trade area, (1) a single size of a product or a single kind of service should not be advertised with a "Free" offer for more than six months in any twelve month period, (2) at least thirty days should elapse before another such offer is promoted, (3) no more than three such offers should be made in any twelve month period, and (4) in such period, the offeror's sale of the product in the size promoted with a "Free" offer should nto exceed 50 percent of the total volume of his sales of the product, in the same size.

In the case of introductory offers, no "Free" offer should be made and no representation may be made that the price is for one item and that the other is "Free", unless the offeror expects, in good faith, to discontinue the offer after a limited time and to commence selling the product or service promoted, separately, at the same price at which it was promoted with a "Free" offer.

Offers of free merchandise or services which may be deceptive for failure to meet the Guide's provisions may not be corrected by substituting other similar words or terms which tend to convey the impression to consumers that an article or service is free.

"Cents-Off"

The FTC's regulations forbid "cents-off" offers to be made unless:

- The commodity has recently and regularly been sold at a customary price in the promotional trade area.

- The packager's or labeler's selling price is reduced by at least the amount of the stated "cents-off".

- The package of label is clearly marked:

  Regular Price..................
......................Cents-Off
You Pay.......................

- Any additional "cents-off" representation is limited to the phrase ".........cents-off the regular retail price".

- In a given trade area, the packager or labeler (1) does not initiate more than three "cents-off" promotions of any single size commodity within a twelve month period, (2) allows at least thirty days to lapse between such promotions of any particular size commodity, and (3) does not sell any single size so labeled for more than six months within any twelve month period.

"Cents-off" sales do not account for more than fifty percent of the packager's or labeler's total sales volume of any single size commodity during any twelve month period.

"Guarantee"

Too extensive for coverage here - See FTC Guides on subject.

Deceptive Advertising of Guarantees

16 CFR 239; adopted April 26, 1960.

§ 239.0 Determining violations.

In determining whether terminology and direct or implied representations concerning guarantees, however made, i.e., in advertising or otherwise, in connection with the sale or offering for sale of a product, may be in violation of the Federal Trade Commission Act, the following general principles will be used:

§ 239.1 Guarantees in general.

In general, any guarantee in advertising shall clearly and conspicuously disclose—

(a) *The nature and extent of the guarantee.*

This includes disclosure of—

(1) What product or part of the product is guaranteed,

(2) What characteristics or properties of the designated product or part thereof are covered by, or excluded from, the guarantee,

(3) What is the duration of the guarantee,

(4) What, if anything, any one claiming under the guarantee must do before the guarantor will fulfill his obligation under the guarantee, such as return of the product and payment of service or labor charges; and

(b) *The manner in which the guarantor will perform.*

This consists primarily of a statement of exactly what the guarantor undertakes to do under the guarantee. Examples of this would be repair, replacement, refund. If the guarantor or the person receiving the guarantee has an option as to what may satisfy the guarantee this should be set out; and

(c) *The identity of the guarantor.*

The identity of the guarantor should be clearly revealed in all advertising, as well as in any documents evidencing the guarantee. Confusion of purchasers often occurs when it is not clear whether the manufacturer or the retailer is the guarantor. (Guide 1.)

§ 239.2 Prorata adjustment of guarantees.

(a) Many guarantees are adjusted by the guarantor on a prorata basis. The advertising of these guarantees should clearly disclose this fact, the basis on which they will be prorated, e.g., the time for which the guaranteed product has been used, and the manner in which the guarantor will perform.

(b) If these guarantees are to be adjusted on the basis of a price other than that paid by the purchaser, this price should be clearly and conspicuously disclosed.

Example: "A" sells a tire with list price of $48 to "B" for $24, with a 12 months guarantee. After 6 months use the tire proves defective. If "A" adjusts on the basis of the price "B" paid, $24, "B" will only have to pay one-half of $24, or $12, for a new tire. If "A" instead adjusts on the basis of list price, "B" will owe one-half of $48, or $24, for a new tire. The guarantor would be required to disclose here the following: That this was a 12 months guarantee, that a list price of $48 would be used in the adjustment, that there would be an adjustment on the basis of the time that the tire was used, and that he would not pay the adjusted amount in cash, but would make an adjustment on a new tire.

NOTE: Guarantees which provide for an adjustment based on a fictitious list price should not be used even where adequate disclosure of the price used is made. (Guide 2.)

§ 239.3 "Satisfaction or Your Money Back" representations.

(a) "Satisfaction or Your Money Back", "10 Day Free Trial", or similar representations will be construed as a guarantee that the full purchase price will be refunded at the option of the purchaser.

(b) If this guarantee is subject to any conditions or limitations whatsoever, they shall be set forth as provided for in § 239.1.

Example: A rose bush is advertised under the representation "Satisfaction or Your Money Back". The guarantor requires return of the product within 1 year of purchase date before he will make refund. These limitations, i.e., "return" and "time" shall be clearly and conspicuously disclosed in the ad. (Guide 3.)

§ 239.4 Lifetime guarantees.

If the words "Life", "Lifetime", or the like, are used in advertising to show the duration of a guarantee, and they relate to any life other than that of the purchaser or original user, the life referred to shall be clearly and conspicuously disclosed.

Example: "A" advertised that his carburetor was guaranteed for life, whereas his guarantee ran for the life of the car in which the carburetor was originally installed. The advertisement is ambiguous and deceptive and should be modified to disclose the "life" referred to. (Guide 4.)

§ 239.5 Savings guarantees.

(a) Advertisements frequently contain representations of guarantees that assure prospective purchasers that savings may be realized in the purchase of the advertiser's products.

(b) Some typical advertisements of this type are "Guaranteed to save you 50%", "Guaranteed never to be undersold", "Guaranteed lowest price in town".

(c) These advertisements should include a clear and conspicuous disclosure of what the guarantor will do if the savings are not realized, together with any time or other limitations that he may impose.

Example: "Guaranteed lowest price in town" might be accompanied by the following disclosure:

"If within 30 days from the date that you buy a sewing machine from me, you purchase the identical machine in town for less and present a receipt therefor to me, I will refund your money".

NOTE: The above guarantees may constitute affirmative representations of fact and, in this respect, are governed by § 239.7. (Guide 5.)

§ 239.6 Guarantees under which the guarantor does not or cannot perform.

(a) A seller or manufacturer should not advertise or represent that a product is guaranteed when he cannot or does not promptly and scrupulously fulfill his obligations under the guarantee.

(b) A specific example of refusal to perform obligations under the guarantee is use of "Satisfaction or your money back" when the guarantor cannot or does not intend promptly to make full refund upon request. (Guide 6.)

§ 239.7 Guarantee as a misrepresentation.

Guarantees are often employed in such a manner as to constitute representations of material facts. If such is the case, the guarantor not only undertakes to perform under the terms of the guarantee, but also assumes responsibility under the law for the truth of the representations made.

Example 1: "Guaranteed for 36 months" applied to a battery is a representation that the battery can normally be expected to last for 36 months and should not be used in connection with a battery which can normally be expected to last for only 18 months.

Example 2: "Guaranteed to grow hair or money back" is a representation that the product will grow hair and should not be used when in fact such product is incapable of growing hair.

Example 3: "Guaranteed lowest prices in town" is a representation that the advertiser's prices are lower than the prices charged by all others for the same products in the same town and should not be used when such is not the fact.

Example 4: "We guarantee you will earn $500 a month" is a representation that prospective employees will earn a minimum of $500 each month and should not be used unless such is the fact. (Guide 7.)

Nothing contained in these Guides relieves any party subject to a Commission cease and desist order or stipulation from complying with the provisions of such order or stipulation. The guides do not constitute a finding in and will not affect the disposition of any formal or informal matter before the Commission.

Use Of:

Money

Printed illustrations of paper money, checks, negotiatable instruments and other obligations and securities of the U.S. are not permitted for advertising purposes. The reproduction of coins in advertising is allowed. TV commercials which are produced on tape as opposed to film may utilize paper money inasmuch as there is no negative and the basic Treasury Department regulations, which are primarily concerned with counterfeiting, are not violated. It is best, however, to consult with the local U.S. Attorney if considering this since some have been known to object to the use of paper money even on tape.

Flags

While there is no federal law prohibiting the use of the U.S. Flag in advertising, a Joint Resolution of the Congress from 1942 stipulates that "...the flag should never be used for advertising purposes in any manner what so ever".

In addition to the above, all states as well as the District of Columbia have statutes prohibiting the use in advertising of their own flag as well as the U.S. Flag.

It is worthy of note that the use prohibited is a flagrant use and not an incidental use, i.e., a print ad with Fifth Avenue in the background with flags flying on various buildings should not violate normal flag sanctions.

FTC can get into the act if the use of flags, incidental or otherwise could be construed to imply foreign origin of a U.S. made product.

The use of foreign flags in advertising depends upon existing diplomatic relations between the U.S. and the country whose flag is desired. Inquiries should be directed to the applicable embassy. However, it should be noted that the use of the Swiss flag or coat of arms as an advertisement or insignia for trade or commercial purposes is punishable under U.S. statute by fine or imprisonment (Title 18, PAR. 708 U.S. Criminal Code).

Stamps

The basic rule is quite simple. Neither illustrations nor facsimilies of stamps, cancelled or uncancelled, may be used for advertising purposes. Use in books, journals, newspapers or albums, for philatelic, educational, historical, and newsworthy purposes is permitted under certain conditions, but this should be checked with Postal and/or Treasury Department authorities.

III. Use of Trademarks

A. What is a trademark?

A trademark describes the origin of goods. It is not a proper noun which describes the goods themselves, it is properly used only as an adjective.

B. To whom does it belong?

A trademark must be used to have any proprietary right attached to it. Shipment of goods in commerce to which the mark is attached is the sine qua non of registration. Use of a proposed trademark in advertising does not confer a right to apply for registration on the Principal Register.

Registration provides prima-facie evidence of the registrant's ownership and the registrant's exclusive right to use the mark.

C. Deceptive use of trademarks

The trademark describes only origin of goods. Care must be used that the mark not be used in a manner which might be deceptive. The FTC proposed cancellation of the trademark Outgro for a medicine designed to alleviate pain from ingrown toenail. An FTC complaint charged that the registered trademark Helps Build Strong Bodies Twelve Ways for Wonder Bread was part of a deceptive claim.

The Lanham Act 15 USCA 1051-11 27 provides an affirmative defense to an infringement action if the mark has been used to violate the antitrust laws.

D. When does a trademark become generic?

An application for cancellation of a trademark may be filed on grounds that the mark has become generic. At one time escalator, cellophane, thermos bottle and aspirin were all trademarks. If marks commonly are used or allowed to be used generically, loss of the mark may occur.

E. Use of the trademark of others

The general rule is that there is no infringement if a competitor's trademark is used in a nondeceptive manner. Caveat. If a suit for unfair competition is filed in a comparative advertising case, there might well be an additional count for trademark infringement. Trademarks are not like copyrights in that they may be reproduced provided there is no passing off. viz. The trademark affixed to a prop automobile is reproduced in an advertisement for another product.

Testimonial Advertising

a) What is a testimonial?

b) Who may give one?

c) Special Problems:

1. Children

2. Drugs

d) How do you get testimonials?

e) FTC tesimonial guides

A testimonial advertisement is generally defined as one in which a reader or viewer receives the impression that the advertisement conveys the opinion of the person giving the testimonial and not that of the advertiser. However, the opinion contained in the testimonial must be capable of being substantiated by the advertiser. For instance, a consumer may truly believe that consumption of aspirin will prevent stomach cancer. The consumer's true belief does not permit the advertiser to use that opinion in an advertisement. The testimonial must also reflect the giver's true experience with the product. In the case of an expert, the expert must have exercised his expertise in coming to the conclusion set forth in the advertisement.

Except for testimonials given by well-known "name talent", any consideration given for the testimonial is a material fact which must be disclosed in the advertising. In order to avoid such disclosure, no consideration should be given in the testimonial itself. Any consideration should only be for the use of the testimonial or the appearance of the person giving a testimonial in the advertising. Even the promise to use the testimonial in advertising could be interpreted as consideration for the testimonial.

¶ 39,038 Final Guides Concerning Endorsements and Testimonials in Advertising

16 CFR 255; §§ 255.0, 255.3 and 255.4, effective May 21, 1975; §§ 255.1, 255.2 and 255.5, effective January 18, 1980; *45 Federal Register* 3870, January 18, 1980.

FINAL GUIDES

The Commission has adopted as final three proposed guidelines on the use of endorsements and testimonials in advertising. These guides were proposed May 21, 1975 (40 FR 22146). The new final guides, 16 CFR 255.1, 255.2, and 255.5 complement the three other guides previously adopted by FTC in May 1975, 16 CFR 255.0, 255.3, and 255.4 (40 FR 22127).

In addition to promulgating these three new final Guides and their accompanying examples, the FTC modified one example to Final Guide O, "Definitions," adopted in May, 1975.

§ 255.0 Definitions.

(a) The Commission intends to treat endorsements and testimonials identically in the context of its enforcement of the Federal Trade Commission Act and for purposes of this part. The term "endorsements" is therefore generally used hereinafter to cover both terms and situations.

(b) For purposes of this part, an "endorsement" means any advertising message (including verbal statements, demonstrations, or depictions of the name, signature, likeness or other identifying personal characteristics of an individual or the name or seal of an organization) which message consumers are likely to believe reflects the opinions, beliefs, findings, or experience of a party other than the sponsoring advertiser. The party whose opinions, beliefs, findings, or experience the message appears to reflect will be called the endorser and may be an individual, group or institution.

(c) For purposes of this part, the term "product" includes any product, service, company or industry.

(d) For purposes of this part, an "expert" is an individual, group or institution possessing, as a result of experience, study or training, knowledge of a particular subject, which knowledge is superior to that generally acquired by ordinary individuals.

Example 1: A film critic's review of a movie is excerpted in an advertisement. When so used, the review meets the definition of an endorsement since it is viewed by readers as a statement of the critic's own opinions and not those of the film producer, distributor or exhibitor. Therefore, any alteration in or quotation from the text of the review which does not fairly reflect its substance would be a violation of the standards set by this part.

Example 2: A TV commercial depicts two women in a supermarket buying a laundry detergent. The women are not identified outside the context of the advertisement. One comments to the other how clean her brand makes her family's clothes, and the other then comments that she will try it because she has not been fully satisfied with her own brand. This obvious fictional dramatization of a real life situation would not be an endorsement.

Example 3: In an advertisement for a pain remedy, an announcer who is not familiar to consumers except as a spokesman for the advertising drug company praises the drug's ability to deliver fast and lasting pain relief. He purports to speak, not on the basis of his own opinions, but rather in the place of and on behalf of the drug company. Such an advertisement would not be an endorsement.

Example 4: A manufacturer of automobile tires hires a well known professional automobile racing driver to deliver its advertising message in television commercials. In these commercials, the driver speaks of the smooth ride, strength, and long life of the tires. Even though the message is not expressly declared to be the personal opinion of the driver, it may nevertheless constitute an endorsement of the tires. Many consumers will recognize this individual as being primarily a racing driver and not merely a spokesman or announcer for the advertiser. Accordingly, they may well believe the driver would not speak for an automotive product unless he/she actually believed in what he/she was saying and had personal knowledge sufficient to form that belief. Hence they would think that the advertising message reflects the driver's personal views as well as those of the sponsoring advertiser. This attribution of the underlying views to the driver brings the advertisement within the definition of an endorsement for purposes of this part

Example 5: A television advertisement for golf balls shows a prominent and well-recognized professional golfer hitting the golf balls. This would be an endorsement by the golfer even though he makes no verbal statement in the advertisement.

[Guide O]

§ 255.1 General Considerations.

(a) Endorsements must always reflect the honest opinions, findings, beliefs, or experience of the endorser. Furthermore, they may not contain any representations which would be deceptive, or could not be substantiated if made directly by the advertiser. [*See* Example 2 to Guide 3 (Section 255.3) illustrating that a valid endorsement may constitute all or part of an advertiser's substantiation.]

(b) The endorsement message need not be phrased in the exact words of the endorser, unless the advertisement affirmatively so represents. However, the endorsement may neither be presented out of context nor reworded so as to distort in any way the endorser's opinion or experience with the product. An advertiser may use an endorsement of an expert or celebrity only as long as it has good reason to believe that the endorser continues to subscribe to the views presented. An advertiser may satisfy this obligation by securing the endorser's views at reasonable intervals where reasonableness will be determined by such factors as new information on the performance or effectiveness of the product, a material alteration in the product, changes in the performance of competitors' products, and the advertiser's contract commitments.

(c) In particular, where the advertisement represents that the endorser uses the endorsed product, then the endorser must have been a bona fide user of it at the time the endorsement was given. Additionally, the advertiser may continue to run the advertisement only so long as he has good reason to believe that the endorser remains a bona fide user of the product. [*See* Section 255.1(b) regarding the "good reason to believe" requirement.]

Guide 1, Example 1: A building contractor states in an advertisement that he specifies the advertiser's exterior house paint because of its remarkable quick drying properties and its durability. This endorsement must comply with the pertinent requirements of Guide 3. Subsequently, the advertistr reformulates its paint to enable it to cover exterior surfaces with only one coat. Prior to continued use of the contractor's endorsement, the advertiser must contact the contractor in order to determine whether the contractor would continue to specify the paint and to subscribe to the views presented previously.

Example 2: A television advertisement portrays a woman seated at a desk on which rest five unmarked electric typewriters. An announcer says "We asked Mrs. X, an executive secretary for over ten years, to try these five unmarked typewriters and tell us which one she liked best."

The advertisement portrays the secretary typing on each machine, and then picking the advertiser's brand. The announcer asks her why, and Mrs. X gives her reasons. Assuming that consumers would perceive this presentation as a "blind" test, this endorsement would probably not represent that Mrs. X actually uses the advertiser's machine in her work. In addition, the endorsement may also be required to meet the standards of Guide 3 on Expert Endorsements.

[Guide 1]

§ 255.2 Consumer Endorsements.

(a) An advertisement employing an endorsement reflecting the experience of an individual or a group of consumers on a central or key attribute of the product or service will be interpreted as representing that the endorser's experience is representative of what consumers will generally achieve with the advertised product in actual, albeit variable, conditions of use. Therefore, unless the advertiser possesses and relies upon adequate substantiation for this representation, the advertisement should either clearly and conspicuously disclose what the generally expected performance would be in the depicted circumstances or limited applicability of the endorser's experience to what consumers may generally expect to achieve. The Commission's position regarding the acceptance of disclaimers or disclosures is described in the preamble to these Guides published in the *Federal Register* on January 18, 1980.

(b) Advertisements presenting endorsements by what are represented, directly or by implication, to be "actual consumers" should utilize actual consumers, in both the audio and video or clearly and conspicuously disclose that the persons in such advertisements are not actual consumers of the advertised product.

(c) Claims concerning the efficacy of any drug or device as defined in the Federal Trade Commission Act, 15 U. S. C. § 55, shall not be made in lay endorsements unless (a) the advertiser has adequate scientific substantiation for such claims and (b) the claims are not inconsistent with any determination that has been made by the Food and Drug Administration with respect to the drug or device that is the subject of the claim.

Guide 2, Example 1: An advertisement presents the endorsement of an owner of one of the advertiser's television sets. The consumer states that she has needed to take the set to the shop for repairs only one time during her 2-year period of ownership and the costs of servicing the set to date have been under $10.00. Unless the advertiser possesses and relied upon adequate substantiation for the implied claim that such performance reflects that which a significant proportion of consumers would be likely to experience, the advertiser should include a disclosure that either states clearly and conspicuously what the generally expectable performance would be or clearly and conspicuously informs consumers that the performance experienced by the endorser is not what they should expect to experience. The mere disclosure that "not all consumers will get this result" is insufficient because it can imply that while all consumers cannot expect the advertised results, a substantial number can expect them. [See the cross reference in Guide 2(a) regarding the acceptability of disclaimers or disclosures.]

Example 2: An advertiser presents the results of a poll of consumers who have used the advertiser's cake mixes as well as their own recipes. The results purport to show that a majority believed that their families could not tell the difference between the advertised mix and their own cakes baked from scratch. Many of the consumers are actually pictured in the advertisement along with relevant, quoted portions of their statements endorsing the product. This use of the results of a poll or survey of consumers probably represents a promise to consumers that this is the typical result that ordinary consumers can expect from the advertiser's cake mix.

Example 3: An advertisement purports to portray a "hidden camera" situation in a crowded cafeteria at breakfast time. A spokesperson for the advertiser asks a series of actual patrons of the cafeteria for their spontaneous, honest opinions of the advertiser's recently introduced breakfast cereal. Even though the words "hidden camera" are not displayed on the screen, and even though none of the actual patrons is specifically identified during the advertisement, the net impression conveyed to consumers may well be that these are actual customers, and not actors. If actors have been employed, this fact should be disclosed.

[Guide 2]

§ 255.3 Expert endorsements.

(a) Whenever an advertisement represents, directly or by implication, that the endorser is an expert with respect to the endorsement message, then the endorser's qualifications must in fact give him the expertise that he is represented as possessing with respect to the endorsement.

(b) While the expert may, in endorsing a product, take into account factors not within his expertise (e.g., matters of taste or price), his endorsement must be supported by an actual exercise of his expertise in evaluating product features or characteristics with respect to which he is expert and which are both relevant to an ordinary consumer's use of or experience with the product and also are available to the ordinary consumer. This evaluation must have included an examination or testing of the product at least as extensive as someone with the same degree of expertise would normally need to conduct in order to support the conclusions presented in the endorsement. Where, and to the extent that, the advertisement implies that the endorsement was based upon a comparison such comparison must have been included in his evaluation; and as a result of such comparison, he must have concluded that, with respect to those features on which he is expert and which are relevant and available to an ordinary consumer, the endorsed product is at least equal overall to the competitors' products. Moreover, where the net impression created by the endorsement is that the advertised product is superior to other products with respect to any such feature or features, then the expert must in fact have found such superiority.

Example 1: An endorsement of a particular automobile by one described as an "engineer" implies that the endorser's professional training and experience are such that he is well acquainted with the design and performance of automobiles. If the endorser's field is, for example, chemical engineering, the endorsement would be deceptive.

Example 2: A manufacturer of automobile parts advertises that its products are approved by the "American Institute of Science." From its very name, consumers would infer that the "American Institute of Science" is a bona fide independent testing organization with expertise in judging automobile parts and that, as such, it would not approve any automobile part without first testing its efficacy by means of valid scientific methods. Even if the American Institute of Science is such a bona fide expert testing organization, as consumers would expect, the endorsement may nevertheless be deceptive unless the Institute has conducted valid scientific tests of the advertised products and the test results support the endorsement message.

Example 3: A manufacturer of a non-prescription drug product represents that its product has been selected in preference to competing products by a large metropolitan hospital. The hospital has selected the product because the manufacturer, unlike its competitors, has packaged each dose of the product separately. This package form is not generally available to the public. Under the circumstances, the endorsement would be deceptive because the basis for the choice of the manufacturer's product, convenience of packaging, is neither relevant nor available to consumers.

Example 4: The president of a commercial "home cleaning service" states in a television advertisement that the service uses a particular brand of cleanser in its business. Since the cleaning service's professional success depends largely upon the performance of the cleansers it uses, consumers would expect the service to be expert with respect to judging cleansing ability, and not be satisfied using an inferior cleanser in its business when it knows of a better one available to it. Accordingly, the cleaning service's endorsement must at least conform to those consumer expectations. The service must, of course, actually use the endorsed cleanser. Additionally, on the basis of its expertise, it must have determined that the cleansing ability of the endorsed cleanser is at least equal (or superior, if such is the net impression conveyed by the advertisement) to that of competing products with which the service has had experience and which remain reasonably available to it. Since in this example, the cleaning service's president makes no mention that the endorsed cleanser was "chosen," "selected," or otherwise evaluated in side-by-side comparisons against its competitors, it is sufficient if the service has relied solely upon its accumulated experience in evaluating cleansers without having to have performed side-by-side or scientific comparisons.

Example 5: An association of professional athletes states in an advertisement that it has "selected" a particular brand of beverages as its "official breakfast drink". As in Example 4, the association would be regarded as expert in the field of nutrition for purposes of this section, because consumers would expect it to rely upon the selection of nutritious foods as part of its business needs. Consequently, the association's endorsement must be based upon an expert evaluation of the nutritional value of the endorsed beverage. Furthermore, unlike Example 4, the use of the words "selected" and "official" in this endorsement imply that it was given only after direct comparisons had been performed among competing brands. Hence, the advertisement would be deceptive unless the association has in fact performed such comparisons between the endorsed brand and its leading competitors in terms of nutritional criteria, and the results of such comparisons conform to the net impression created by the advertisement.

[Guide 3]

§ 255.4 Endorsements by organizations.

Endorsements by organizations, especially expert ones, are viewed as representing the judgment of a group whose collective experience exceeds that of any individual member, and whose judgments are generally free of the sort of subjective factors which vary from individual to individual. Therefore an organization's endorsement must be reached by a process sufficient to ensure that the endorsement fairly reflects the collective judgment of the organization. Moreover, if an organization is represented as being expert, then, in conjunction with a proper exercise of its expertise in evaluating the product under § 255.3 (Expert endorsements), it must utilize an expert or experts recognized as such by the organization or standards previously adopted by the organization and suitable for judging the relevant merits of such products.

Example: A mattress seller advertises that its product is endorsed by a chiropractic association. Since the association would be regarded as expert with respect to judging mattresses, its endorsement must be supported by an expert evaluation by an expert or experts recognized as such by the organization, or by compliance with standards previously adopted by the organization and aimed at measuring the performance of mattresses in general and not designed with the particular attributes of the advertised mattress in mind. (See also § 255.3, Example 5.)

[Guide 4]

§ 255.5 Disclosure of Material Connections.

When there exists a connection between the endorser and the seller of the advertised product which might materially affect the weight or credibility of the endorsement (*i.e.*, the connection is not reasonably expected by the audience) such connection must be fully disclosed. An example of a connection that is ordinarily expected by viewers and need not be disclosed is the payment or promise of payment to an endorser who is an expert or well known personality, as long as the advertiser does not represent that the endorsement was given without compensation. However, when the endorser is neither represented in the advertisement as an expert nor is known to a significant portion of the viewing public, then the advertiser should clearly and conspicuously disclose either the payment or promise of compensation prior to and in exchange for the endorsement or the fact that the endorser knew or had reasons to know or to believe that if the endorsement favors the advertised product some benefit, such as an appearance on TV, would be extended to the endorser.

Example 1: A drug company commissions research on its product by a well-known research organization. The drug company pays a substantial share of the expenses of the research project, but the test design is under the control of the research organization. A subsequent advertisement by the drug company mentions the research results as the "findings" of the well-known research organization. The advertiser's payment of expenses to the research organization need not be disclosed in this advertisement. Application of the standards set by Guides 3 and 4 provides sufficient assurance that the advertiser's payment will not affect the weight or credibility of the endorsement.

Example 2: A film star endorses a particular food product. The endorsement regards only points of taste and individual preference. This endorsement must of course comply with Section 255.1; but even though the compensation paid the endorser is substantial, neither the fact nor the amount of compensation need be revealed.

Example 3: An actual patron of a restaurant, who is neither known to the public nor presented as an expert, is shown seated at the counter. He is asked for his "spontaneous" opinion of a new food product served in the restaurant. Assume, first, that the advertiser had posted a sign on the door of the restaurant informing all who entered that day that patrons would be interviewed by the advertiser as part of its TV promotion of its new soy protein "steak". This notification would materially affect the weight or credibility of the patron's endorsment, and, therefore, viewers of the advertisement should be clearly and conspicuously informed of the circumstances under which the endorsement was obtained.

Assume, in the alternative, that the advertiser had not posted a sign on the door of the restaurant, but had informed all interviewed customers of the "hidden camera" only after interviews were completed and the customers had no reason to know or believe that their response was being recorded for use in an advertisement. Even if patrons were also told that they would be paid for allowing the use of their opinions in advertising, these facts need not be disclosed.

[Guide 5]

Sections 255.0, 255.3, 255.4 are promulgated by the Federal Trade Commission and become effective May 21, 1975. (40 *Federal Register* 22127, May 21, 1975.) Sections 255.1, 255.2, and 255.5 become effective January 18, 1980 (45 *Federal Register* 3870, January 18, 1980.)

[Explanatory material regarding Guides 0, 1, 2 and 5 begins on next page.]

Supplemental Information about Guides 0, 1, 2, and 5

SUPPLEMENTARY INFORMATION: Section 255.1 [Final Guide 1] is titled "General Considerations," and it has three subparts. Subpart (a) requires endorsements to reflect only the honest views of the endorser and states that endorsements may not contain claims that could not be supported if made directly by the advertiser. Subpart (b) prohibits presenting an endorsement out of its context in a manner that distorts it. It also permits use of celebrity or expert endorsements only so long as the advertiser has good reason to believe the endorser continues to subscribe to the views presented. Subpart (c) requires an endorser actually to use the product advertised when the advertisement so represents, and it permits the advertiser to use such an endorsement only so long as it has good reason to believe the endorser continues to use the product. Two examples illustrating application of this Guide were also adopted.

Section 255.2 [Final Guide 2] is titled "Consumer Endorsements," and it also has three subparts. Subpart (a) states that because the endorsement of product performance by a consumer or group of consumers implies that the average person can expect to obtain comparable performance, advertisers should possess substantiation for this implicit claim or clearly and conspicuously disclose what the generally expectable performance of the product would be or clearly and conspicuously inform consumers of the limited applicability of the endorsed performance. Subpart (b) states that endorsements by what are represented to be "actual consumers" should use actual consumers or disclose the fact that actors are appearing. Subpart (c) states that advertisers must have adequate support for consumers' endorsements of drugs and that such endorsements must be consistent with any determinations about the drug made by the Food and Drug Administration. Three examples to illustrate applications of this Guide were also adopted.

Section 255.5 [Final Guide 5] is titled "Disclosure of Material Connections." It requires the advertiser to disclose a connection between that advertiser and the endorser that might materially affect the weight or credibility of the endorsement.

Two material connections are highlighted that would require disclosures: compensation received prior to and in exchange for the endorsement and that the endorser knew or had reason to know that if the "right things" were said, he or she would "appear on T.V." The payment of compensation need be disclosed only when the endorser is neither a celebrity nor an expert. Three examples to illustrate application of this Guide were also adopted.

The text of the new Final Guides and their examples follow this supplementary discussion in which the Commission details the modification it has made in one example to Final Guide O and in the new Final Guides based upon the public comments received and upon its own reevaluation. At the outset, the Commission directs attention to its use of examples to illustrate various provisions of the Guides, and it emphasizes that these examples are not to be viewed as providing definitive answers on compliance with the Guides. As the Commission and the courts have repeatedly made clear, the "net impression" of an advertisement must be assessed in determining the message conveyed.[1] Examples of the type included here as an aid to interpreting the basic principles of the Guides simply are not designed to and cannot present the totality of audio/visual effects that form an advertisement's "net impression". Thus, as should be obvious, any determination as to whether a particular advertisement meets or fails to meet the requirements of these Guidelines must rest upon a review of the actual advertisement. Indeed, it is

[1] *Carter Products, Inc.* v. *FTC*. 323 F.2d 523, 528 (5th Cir. 1963); *FTC* v. *Sterling Drug, Inc.*, 317 F.2d 669, 674 (2d Cir. 1963); *Murray Space Shoe Corp.* v. *FTC*. 304 F.2d 270, 272 (2d Cir. 1962); *Charles of the Ritz Dist. Corp.* v. *FTC*. 143 F.2d 676, 679 (2d Cir. 1944); *Aronberg* v. FTC, 132 F.2d 165, 167 (7th Cir. 1942); *Porter & Dietsch*, 90 FTC 770, 873 (1977), *order modified*, 605 F.2d 294 (7th Cir. 1979).

possible that advertisements which resemble examples used herein may nonetheless, due to factors in their presentation, violate the Act.

Furthermore, the advertiser must insure that the disclosures required by these Guides are designed and presented in a manner that attracts consumers' attention *and* communicates the required information. To underscore this duty the Commission requires that disclosures made pursuant to these Guides be made in a clear and conspicuous manner. Based upon its experience from regulating advertising, the Commission believes that advertisers and their advertising agencies possess the communications expertise necessary to design clear and conspicuous disclosures and the Commission expects them to do so. Therefore, the Commission believes it unnecessary to specify the exact wording that must be used in the particular disclosure required by these guides, nor to set standards for the manner in which this information must be presented in broadcast or print.[2] In the past, the Commission provided guidelines on how affirmative disclosures might be presented in broadcast advertising,[3] and these continue in effect. However, notwithstanding those guidelines, the Commission expects advertisers to design and present disclosure of required information in a clear and conspicuous manner.

Modification to Example 4 of Final Guide O, "Definitions" (Part 255.0). The Commission has modified Example 4 to the Definitions Guide in order to clarify the distinction between use of an endorsement and use of "slice-of-life" dramatization or spokesperson, neither of which are subject to these guidelines. The example was published May 21, 1975 in 40 FR at 22127, *et seq.*

Modifications to New Final Guides 1, 2, and 5 (Parts 255.1, 255.2, and 255.5). Guide 1(a): The Commission has determined to add a cross-reference to this Guide, directing attention to Example 2 to Guide 3, section 255.3, to make clear that an endorsement may constitute all or part of the substantiation for an advertising claim. The Commission does not believe, however, that even a valid endorsement may constitute substantiation for a performance claim for an OTC drug.

Guide 1(b). The Commission has determined that obligations imposed by the "good reason to believe" requirement need not apply to consumer endorsements. It has also added language to that proposed that will advise advertisers of the factors the Commission will consider in determining whether the advertiser has "good to believe" that an expert or celebrity endorser continues to subscribe to the views presented in the advertisement. The new language suggests that the advertiser check with the endorser at "reasonable intervals" where reasonableness depends upon a number of factors that will vary with the situation. In this regard, the Commission intends to take a pragmatic view of the relation between advertisers and endorsers that considers not only the performance of the product but also the status of the endorser. The Commission has also added Example 1 to Guide 1 to illustrate one application of the principle of this subpart.

Guide 1(c). The Commission has adopted this subpart without modification, and it has adopted new Examples 2 and 3 to illustrate this subpart's application. The Commission has added a cross-reference to the "good reason to believe" requirement of subpart (b) since it intends to treat that principle the same way in this subpart, applying it to all endorsements which represent "bona fide" use. New Example 1 to Guide 1, is applicable to this subpart as well.

Guide 1, Example 1. This new example illustrates one application of the advertiser's duty to determine whether the endorser continues to

[2] Of course, the Commission has specified in particular cease and desist orders and rules that certain disclosures must contain particular language and be presented in specific ways. Advertisers under those orders and rules must comply with those particular requirements.

[3] See Commission's Statement of Enforcement Policy of October 21, 1970 regarding the use of affirmative disclosures in broadcast advertising. Vol 2 CCH Trade Regulations Reports Section 7569.09.

subscribe to the views presented in the advertisement. It purports to describe a situation where an advertiser reformulates a product previously endorsed by an expert. The advertiser should check with the endorser to determine if that product change affects his or her views of the product's performance. Contact with the endorser after reformulation may also be mandated by Guide 3 (Expert Endorsements, Section 255.3) which requires that the expert must have based his or her endorsement on an adequate "examination or testing" of the product.

Guide 1, Example 2. This example is designed to illustrate the "bona fide use" requirement of Guide 1(c). It is designed to make the point that an endorsement of a product does not necessarily require "bona fide use". In example 2, the endorser presents her views in a "blind comparison test" which is not designed to represent that the endorser is a "bona fide user" of the product. Frequently, of course, the net impression of advertisements that feature endorsements includes a representation of "bona fide use." Where that occurs, Guide 1(c) simply requires that such representation accord with the facts.

Guide 2(a). Advertisers should understand that the Commission strongly favors consumer endorsement that, in fact, depict a typical experience. However, the Commission recognizes that a consumer endorsement representing a non-typical experience with a clear disclaimer, or with a disclosure of what is typical may not be deceptive. Generally, a disclaimer alone probably will not be considered sufficient to dispel the representation that the experience is typical, but because the Commission is not prepared to hold that in every instance a bare disclaimer would be inadequate, reliance thereon will not be considered a *per se* violation of Section 5 of the Federal Trade Commission Act. In any instance where only a disclaimer is made, however, the advertiser should be certain that it is as prominent as, and integrated with, the endorsement itself and that the circumstances surrounding the endorsement minimize the message that it is a typical experience. Advertisers should also know that a simple statement that "not all consumers will get this result" or a similar disclaimer will not be considered as adequate. The advertiser should realize, further, that the net effect of the advertisement will be studied to determine if if has the capacity to deceive. If the Commission has reason to believe that such a deception is imparted by the consumer endorsement, the endorsement may be subject to a Commission challenge.

Final Guide 2(a) makes it clear that the Commission's concern is directed to endorsements that involve central attributes of the advertiser's product or service. Further, it is the Commission's experience from cases such as *Firestone*,[4] *National Dynamics*,[5] *Ford*,[6] and *Porter & Dietsch*[7] that the more central and specific the endorsed experience is, the more material its representation becomes. Commission attention to such endorsements will be focused accordingly.

Guide 2(b). The Commission has modified the disclosure required by the proposed guide to inform the public that, contrary to an advertisement's representation, actors are appearing instead of actual consumers. The proposed guide had been read to require a clear and conspicious disclosure that "professional actors" were "appearing for compensation." The purpose of the disclosure is to alert consumers that the presentation they are viewing involves professionals and should be viewed accordingly, and the Commission has determined that this purpose is satisfied by a less extensive message. The Commission agrees with comments that suggested that too extensive a

[4] *Firestone Tire & Rubber Co.*, 81 FTC 398 (1972), *aff'd* 481 F. 2d 246 (6th Cir. 1973); *cert. denied*, 414 U.S. 1112 (1973).

[5] *National Dynamics Corporation*, 82 FTC 488 (1973), *mod. in part*, 492 F. 2d 1333 (2d Cir. 1974); *cert. denied* 419 U.S. 993 (1974); *order modified* 85 F.T.C. 391 (1975); *order further modified* 85 FTC 1052 (1975).

[6] *Ford Motor Company*, Docket 9001, *Opinion and Order Remanding*, 87 FTC 756 (1976).

[7] *Porter & Dietsch, Inc.*, 90 FTC 770, 873 (1977), *order modified*, 605 F.2d 294 (7th Cir. 1979).

disclosure may imply, contrary to fact, that the substance of the views presented is not genuine.

Guide 2(c). The proposed guide banned consumers' endorsements of drug products on the grounds that consumers' experience with drugs in not acceptable evidence of how such products perform. The Commission has determined that such a prohibition is unnecessary and that adequate protection for the viewing public is achieved by (a) requiring advertisers to possess adequate scientific substantiation for the claims made by the endorser; and (b) assuring that no claims contained in the endorsement are inconsistent with any determination made by the Food and Drug Administration with respect to the drug or device.

Guide 2, Example 1 and 2. The Commission has replaced the two proposed examples to Guide 2 with three new ones. The first two examples are designed to illustrate Guide 2(a). Example 1 purports to show one type of endorsement presentation that will be interpreted as a claim that a substantial proportion of consumers will experience results similar to the endorser's. The example also discusses the reasons why a particular disclaimer would be insufficient. Example 2 is designed to illustrate that certain presentations of consumer endorsements of performance based on personal judgment may also represent a promise that the viewer should expect similar results.

Guide 2, Example 3. In response to the comments, the Commission has developed an example designed to illustrate an implicit representation that "actual consumers" are presenting their spontaneous, honest views about the advertised product. This example to Guide 2(b) purports to demonstrate that such a representation can be conveyed even though the real people appearing are not named or words such as "hidden camera" are not used.

Guide 5. The Commission has made modifications in the text of the guide. The first modification makes clear that, to be material, compensation must be paid or promised "in exchange for" the giving of the endorsement. Comments suggested that the proposed guide could be read to require the disclosure of compensation unrelated to the endorsement itself, such as payment to participate in a blind comparison test. The Commission has also determined that when consumer endorsers knew or had reason to know or believe that they would be featured in advertising if the "right things" were said about the product, this fact should be disclosed as well.

Examples to Guide 5. Comments on proposed Example 1 criticized it as inconsistent with the final guides on expert and organizational endorsements (§ 255.3 and § 255.4). The example had described the "findings" of a well-known research organization based on a study commissioned by a drug company/advertiser. The example stated that the advertisement in which the "findings" were represented should include a disclosure of the fact that the advertiser commissioned the test. The Commission agrees with comments that the Expert and Organizational endorsements guides' provisions for adequate exercise of expertise as a basis for endorsement would ordinarily provide sufficient protection for consumers in such situations, and it has modified this example accordingly. Because proposed Example 2 adds nothing substantive not already covered in modified Example 1, the Commission has deleted it.

Proposed Example 3 (which now appears as Example 2) has been retained in its original form. It is designed to illustrate that an advertisement featuring a celebrity endorsement that meets the other requirements of the Guides need not contain a disclosure of the fact that the celebrity was compensated for his/her appearance.

The Commission has modified proposed Example 4 which appears now as Example 3. This example is designed to better illustrate the application of Guide 5 to the endorsements of actual consumers. It illustrates the principle that even if a consumer's endorsement is truthful, an advertiser can, through his recruitment of the endorser, create a situation—an expectation on the endorser's part—that may materially affect the weight or credibility of the endorsement. The example also illustrates that compensation to a consumer endorser promised only after the securing of an endorsement need not be disclosed.

Acquisition of Music

a) What rights are acquired?

b) Reservation of small performing rights

c) Synchronization licenses

d) Performing rights of societies

d) Typical Acquisition of Music Agreement

The rights acquired are generally divided into so-called dramatic or grand performing rights, and nondramatic or small performing rights. If the music is used in such a way as to contribute to the "telling of a story", then grand performing rights should be acquired. A composer often requires the reservation to himself of the right to license small performing rights in order to be eligible to receive royalties from performing rights societies, such as ASCAP and BMI. When music is acquired for use in television, a so-called synchronization license should also be obtained in order to permit the use of the music in conjunction with pictures. This synchronization license is an addition to the right to perform although both may be contained in a single document.

Ted Bates new york / advertising
1515 Broadway · New York, New York 10036, U.S.A.
Phone 212 869-3131 · Cable: Batesword, New York

M U S I C

WORK-FOR-HIRE AGREEMENT

Re: Music Entitled

Dear

The following constitutes our agreement by Ted Bates & Company, Inc. on behalf of our client, ______________________________, (the "Client").

1. You have created and written a certain "work" which is the ___ music ___lyrics ___arrangement (check which is applicable) of a musical jingle, a copy of which is annexed hereto.

2. The said work (or "works") and all other works produced and supplied by you pursuant to this agreement shall be considered a "work for hire" under the copyright law. Our Client shall be the sole proprietor of all rights in such work, except for the right of non-dramatic public performance of the composition which is reserved to the writer for licensing through the performing rights' society indicated below in accordance with its rules and regulations including, but not limited to, all copyrights and any renewals thereof. We, on behalf of our Client, alone may license, sell, assign or otherwise exploit the rights in such work, except those rights of public performance. Further, it is specifically understood that we have the right to alter, expand, adapt and make any arrangements of said work, and we shall have the sole right to decide whether and in what manner said work shall be published, advertised, publicized, or exploited by us, our successors or assigns. We shall have the further right to secure a statutory copyright therein anywhere in the world in the name(s) of such persons, firms or corporations as we may elect, and we or our designees will have the right to secure extensions and renewals of such copyright registrations. Finally, you hereby assign to us, on behalf of our Client, the copyright and all other rights for existing and future media in and to all material created, produced and/or supplied by you pursuant to this agreement to the extent that such material is not otherwise owned by us as a work made for hire.

3. We agree to pay you and you agree to accept in full consideration for all services and materials provided by you pursuant to this agreement, the sum of $__________.

Continued...

4. You represent and warrant to us that:

    (a) The work created by you is original.

    (b) It does not and will not infringe upon or violate the copyrights or any other rights whatsoever of any person or entity.

    (c) No adverse claim exists with respect to it.

    (d) It has not heretofore been published or exploited in any form anywhere in the world.

    (e) You have the full and exclusive right and authority to enter into this agreement.

5. You will indemnify and save harmless us, or Client and any other person, firm or corporation making use of such work from and against any and all loss, damage or expense, including reasonable attorney's fees, resulting from or by reason of the breach or alleged breach of any representation or warranty herein made by you.

Please evidence your acceptance hereof and agreement hereto by signing in the place indicated below.

Very truly yours,

TED BATES & COMPANY, INC.
As Agent for

By______________________
Mimi Wallace
Vice President
Broadcast Business Affairs

Please Check One:

☐ ASCAP

☐ BMI

ACCEPTED AND AGREED:

____

Date:______________________

Note: "Work" to be attached.

MW:pj

Ted Bates new york/advertising

Date______________________

EXHIBIT "A"

Attention:

Re: Music entitled

Dear

As copyright owner of the above-captioned work(s), we hereby grant to you a non-exclusive right to license the performance rights in and to the musical composition, lyrics and/or arrangement(s) produced by or for us hereunder but only insofar as it relates to the performance of the said musical composition, lyrics and/or arrangement(s) in our Client's commercial announcements broadcast over radio and television stations (local or network) and the right to receive directly any and all royalties as may be paid for such use(s) by any performing rights society of which you are a member and which licenses such use(s). It is understood, however, that we are under no obligation to actually perform the composition, lyrics and/or arrangement(s) in the aforesaid manner.

Please acknowledge receipt and acceptance of the foregoing by signing and returning the enclosed copies to the undersigned.

Cordially,

TED BATES & COMPANY, INC.
As Agent for

By______________________________

Check Appropriate Rights Society

ASCAP

BMI

By__________________________

NOTES

3

SWEEPSTAKES AND CONTESTS

Felix H. Kent

Reprinted from PLI's 1980 course handbook _Legal and Business Problems of the Advertising Industry_ since there have been no substantial changes in the law.

SWEEPSTAKES AND CONTESTS

I. A Sweepstakes or Contest constitutes a lottery and is illegal if the following three elements are all present:

(a) Consideration

(b) Chance

(c) Prize

In a legitimate contest, winners are selected purely on the basis of skill and not chance. If any element of chance is present, the contest would be illegal even though some skill may be involved. In a legitimate sweepstakes, there is no consideration required to enter. There is, however, a vast divergence among the states on definitions of "consideration. For instance, store visits may constitute consideration. Listening to a television or radio program generally is not consideration. Having to invite a salesman into the house and listen to his "pitch" may well be consideration. Taking a test drive may be consideration. In some states, no detriment to the consumer is required and even the remotest benefit to the advertiser can constitute consideration.

II. The FTC, FCC, Post Office Department, State Banking Commissions, State Liquor Authorities, State Insurance Departments and others have taken jurisdiction over sweepstakes and contests.

III. Federal Legislation has enabled the conduct and advertising of State-sponsored lotteries.

IV. To what extent may a state restrict mail offers to participate in sweepstakes? See Missouri v. Readers' Digest Ass'n Inc., 527 S.W.2d 355. Missouri does not recognize Federal preemption of control over mailed offers. North Carolina may be taking this same approach.

V. The Federal Trade Commission adopted a Trade Regulation Rule (16 CFR 419) applicable to games used by food retailing and gasoline industries. It requires disclosure (in addition to standard information such as number of prizes and duration of promotion) of odds of winning, geographical area and number of participating outlets. The FTC has proposed a similar Rule to cover all sweepstakes.

VI. Florida and New York require advance registration of chance promotions and the posting of cash or bonds to guarantee the awarding of prizes. Rhode Island also requires registration if retail stores participate in the promotion.

VII. Some states require special disclosures in the rules, including posting of winners names, or the awarding of prizes within a certain number of days. Other states have legislation which prohibits chance promotions in certain types of establishments, e.g., franchisees or in connection with certain products, e.g., alcoholic beverages.

NOTES

4

INDUSTRY SELF-POLICING

Elhanan C. Stone
Ronald Smithies
Marylou Jennerjahn

Reprinted from PLI's 1980 course handbook _Legal and Business Problems of the Advertising Industry_.

SPECIAL NOTE TO MATERIALS CONTAINED IN THIS CHAPTER:

As of March 10, 1982 the advertising standards of the NAB Radio and Television Codes (including guidelines, interpretations, policies, etc.) have been cancelled and enforcement thereof terminated until the conclusion of litigation in which the NAB is currently involved or until further notice. This action was taken by the NAB Executive Committee on March 10, 1982.

Industry Self-Policing

I. Code Authority - National Association of Broadcasters

a) The Codes

b) Multiple Product Announcements

c) Children's TV Advertising

d) Children's Premiums

e) Guidelines for Non-Prescription Medications

II. National Advertising Review Board

a) NAD Children's Unit

III. National Business Council
Guidelines on Advertising Substantiation

a) Charles Pfizer & Co., Inc. v FTC, CCH Trade Reg. Reporter, Transfer Binder, 1970-73, Paragraph 20,056

A. Television stations and networks are quite rigorous in their standards for acceptability in advertising. Although the NAB codes cannot be absolutely binding because of antitrust considerations, for all practical purposes almost all television stations do conform.

1. Multiple Product Announcements

The stated reason for the prohibition of multiple product announcements, unless they are in a commercial which appears to be one commercial, is to reduce clutter on television. The major problem of compliance comes in the area of "tags" appended to the ends of the commercials. Such tags may be used only for different forms or flavors of the product. Thus, it has been held that a commercial for a denture cleanser with a tag for a denture adhesive would not be allowed. A tag for a cat food appended to a commercial for dog food has been refused.

2. Children's Premiums

There has been an attempt by the FTC to restrict the advertising on television of children's premiums and currently state laws are pending to restrict premium advertising. The NAB code requires that advertising for premiums be clearly separated from the advertising for the product and that it use no more than one half of the commercial.

B. The Pfizer case sets forth the concept of "reasonable basis" for making a claim. What constitutes reasonable basis varies as to the type of claim and product. The rigor of testing for a taste claim for a 20¢ candy bar is clearly different from the rigor required for a drug product. Generally if a consumer can perceive a claim for himself and if any particular consumer could be misled but the economic harm is deminimis, then the reasonable basis for requirement is not great. In the case of comparative advertising or where consumer mispreception would lead to large economic injury, then reasonable basis becomes a much more rigorous standard.

THE ADVERTISING INDUSTRY'S NEW PROGRAM OF SELF - REGULATION
Congressional Record
(February 1, 1973)

THE ADVERTISING INDUSTRY'S NEW PROGRAM OF SELF-REGULATION

HON. GEORGE E. DANIELSON

OF CALIFORNIA

IN THE HOUSE OF REPRESENTATIVES

Wednesday, January 31, 1973

Mr. DANIELSON. Mr. Speaker, the public is increasingly calling for an end to false and misleading advertising. Today I met with representatives of the American Advertising Federation who told me about the advertising industry's new program of self-regulation.

The objective of this new program is to receive and act upon consumer complaints, and work with both Government and industry to maintain high standards of truth in advertising. Because of the deep concern my colleagues have shown for the accuracy of advertising, I am inserting the American Advertising Federation's description of this program in the RECORD.

THE SELF-REGULATORY PROGRAM

The advertising industry joined forces last year to initiate a voluntary program of self-regulation to be headed by the newly formed National Advertising Review Board. The NARB acts on consumer and industry complaints regarding truth and accuracy in national advertising. It is dedicated to providing a vehicle for continual improvement of advertising practices.

THE NARB—ITS LEADERSHIP

Charles W. Yost, former ambassador to the United Nations, was selected chairman of the NARB. Also elected to the board were 30 members representing national advertisers, 10 representing advertising agencies and 10 representing public or non-industry fields.

Emphasis on advertiser representation stems from the fact that he bears the ultimate responsibility for the advertising that is produced. At the same time, it must be recognized that the inclusion of public representatives in an industry program of self-regulation at the policy making level is unique. Few, if any, other industries or professions provide for involvement of the consumer on other than a complainant level.

SPONSORING GROUPS

The associations sponsoring the NARB are the American Advertising Federation, the American Association of Advertising Agencies, the Association of National Advertisers and the Council of Better Business Bureaus.

COMPLAINT PROCEDURES AND ENFORCEMENT

NARB is organized so that complaints are initially handled by an investigating staff, the National Advertising Division (NAD) of the Council of Better Business Bureaus, and any appeals are forwarded to the NARB. Complaints regarding truth and accuracy—the content of an ad and whether it has the capacity to mislead or deceive—may be initiated by individual consumers, representatives of consumer organizations or through the industry's own internal monitoring.

NAD evaluates the merits of the issues raised in the complaints. In most cases, this means checking the representations made in the advertising with the available information on the performance of the product under accepted standards of truth and accuracy.

In addition to handling complaints, the NAD monitors the various advertising media seeking to uncover any possible abuses before they attract broad public concern. It also renders advisory opinions in advance to advertisers and/or agencies as a way of averting future problems.

If a complaint is considered justified, the NAD works with the advertiser and/or agency to seek an appropriate change in the advertising. The emphasis is on a constructive resolution of the problem. It is up to the advertiser to establish the truth of the claims.

If, however, there is an impasse and the questioned advertising is neither altered nor withdrawn, the complaint is appealed to the NARB. To expedite this appeals process, the chairman of the NARB appoints a five-man panel to hear each specific case and reach a decision on behalf of the entire board. Each panel includes three advertisers, one agency and one public member.

The NARB panel reviews the complaint and the NAD staff findings and provides an opportunity for the advertiser or his representative to present his side of the case in a full evidentiary hearing. NARB panels normally are able to arrive at a decision within a few hours. The decision is transmitted to the advertiser at the highest corporate level.

If the advertiser still refuses to cooperate with the NARB panel or does not agree with the decision of the panel that the advertising is in violation of NARB standards, the chairman of the NARB, after exhausting all procedures, informs the appropriate government agency.

NARB publicly discloses all decisions and monthly reports are released on the status of all cases before NAD or on appeal to NARB. Advertisers in disagreement with the decision of NARB or its investigative staff are given the opportunity to submit their own statements to be incorporated in NARB's public announcements.

The party initiating the complaint is informed of the outcome of the NAD investigation and/or resolution of the NARB panel. If the complainant is dissatisfied with the outcome of the NAD investigation, he too may appeal for a hearing by an NARB panel, again evidencing the functioning role the consumer has in NARB procedures.

THE FIRST YEAR OF OPERATION—PROGRESS REPORT

The workability of the NARB self-regulatory program may be evaluated by reviewing some of the statistics issued after one year of performance. The National Advertising Division reported it had received or initiated 444 complaints against national advertising (as of December 1972). Of the total:

131 complaints were dismissed as without merit. These were cases in which, in the opinion of NAD, the advertiser provided adequate substantiation of claims.

84 complaints were found to be justified, and in all cases the advertiser agreed either to withdraw the ad or to modify it.

227 complaints were still under investigation.

Nine cases dismissed by NAD were appealed by the complainants to NARB for panel adjudication with the following results:

four complaints were not sustained.

two complaints were upheld, assured by the advertisers that the challenged ads would not be used in the future.

three more are in the process of being adjudicated.

It is significant to the self-regulatory program that:

In all cases so far the complaint was resolved before notification of a governmental enforcement agency was necessary.

The individual consumer, as a group, accounted for the largest share of the total complaints.

Virtually every NAD request to an advertiser for substantiation of claims was complied with.

NARB panel judgments are added to the extensive body of precedents dealing with advertising acceptability already developed by the Council of Better Business Bureaus and are available to assist NAD with its staff role of initial evaluation and review.

Panel rulings also serve as precedents for future panels convened to review related cases and constitute a body of information and opinion that will serve as guidelines for advertisers.

RESPONDING TO CHANGE

In evaluating the year-old program, Chairman Yost noted that NARB and NAD are providing self-regulatory machinery that did not exist previously. Further, he said that it was to be expected that procedural problems would be encountered during the program's developmental stages.

Ambassador Yost asserted that "neither NARB nor its investigative staff can be considered an apologist for questionable advertising practices nor a 'defender' of the advertising industry. They act judiciously and fairly on all matters that come before them."

To seek continual improvement of the self-regulatory machinery, the procedures of NARB/NAD have been amended to provide for public disclosure of decisions, despite the earlier judgment that confidentiality was desirable except where compliance with NARB panel findings was not voluntarily forthcoming. The over-riding public involvement and interest resulted in the adoption of the full public disclosure policy.

Also, to help decrease the amount of time between issuance of complaint and its resolution, NAD's investigative procedures are being more closely tied to the Council of Better Business Bureau's trade practices division in Washington, which has experts in a number of advertising areas giving NAD greater research capability. New personnel have been added.

ISSUES OF SOCIAL RESPONSIBILITY

Although NARB and its investigative staff, the NAD, are primarily concerned with truth and accuracy in national advertising, the NARB chairman also is empowered to appoint five-member consultive panels to review the broader questions of taste, morality and social responsibility.

NAD has received only a limited number of complaints deemed to be concerned with such matters. Procedures call for the convening of an NARB panel to review these more subjective advertising questions when the volume of such complaints warrants such action.

As opposed to truth and accuracy questions which are dealt with on a case by case basis, issues of taste and social responsibility will involve the use of "white papers" to caution against a given practice of concern.

LOCAL ADAPTATION

The development of local advertising review boards, based on the national model, is being undertaken in several cities through the efforts of the American Advertising Federation and its local ad clubs and the Better Business Bureaus.

It should be emphasized that this program is not designed to be a panacea for whatever ills exist in the marketplace. It is a conscientious and honest effort on behalf of the advertising industry to respond constructively to public complaints about specific advertising and to elevate further advertising performance.

For further information, write or call:

William Ewen, Executive Director, National Advertising Review Board, 850 Third Avenue, New York, New York 10022, (212) 832-1320.

Roger Purdon, Vice President, National Advertising Division, Council of Better Business Bureaus, 845 Third Avenue, New York, New York 10022, (212) 832-3131.

The Television Code

National Association of Broadcasters
Twenty-First Edition, January 1980

Television Code

Effective March 1, 1952
Second Edition, March 1954
Third Edition, July 1956
Fourth Edition, March 1958
Fifth Edition, March 1959
Sixth Edition, July 1960
Seventh Edition, May 1962
Eighth Edition, September 1963
Ninth Edition, April 1964
Tenth Edition, August 1965
Eleventh Edition, August 1966
Twelfth Edition, October 1967
Thirteenth Edition, August 1968
Fourteenth Edition, September 1969
Fifteenth Edition, March 1971
Sixteenth Edition, April 1972
Seventeenth Edition
First printing, April 1973
Second printing, January 1974
Eighteenth Edition, June 1975
Nineteenth Edition, June 1976
Twentieth Edition, June 1978
Twenty-First Edition, January 1980

Table of Contents

BROADCASTERS' RESPONSIBILITIES

Television is seen and heard in nearly every American home. These homes include children and adults of all ages, embrace all races and all varieties of philosophic or religious conviction and reach those of every educational background. Television broadcasters must take this pluralistic audience into account in programming their stations. They are obligated to bring their positive responsibility for professionalism and reasoned judgment to bear upon all those involved in the development, production and selection of programs.

ADVERTISERS' RESPONSIBILITIES

The free, competitive American system of broadcasting which offers programs of entertainment, news, general information, education and culture is supported and made possible by revenues from advertising. While television broadcasters are responsible for the programming and advertising on their stations, the advertisers who use television to convey their commercial messages also have a responsibility to the viewing audience. Their advertising messages should be presented in an honest, responsible and tasteful manner. Advertisers should also support the endeavors of broadcasters to offer a diversity of programs that meet the needs and expectations of the total viewing audience.

VIEWERS' RESPONSIBILITIES

The viewer also has a responsibility to help broadcasters serve the public. All viewers should make their criticisms and positive suggestions about programming and advertising known to the broadcast licensee. Parents particularly should oversee the viewing habits of their children, encouraging them to watch programs that will enrich their experience and broaden their intellectual horizons.

I. PRINCIPLES GOVERNING PROGRAM CONTENT

General goals

It is in the interest of television as a vital medium to encourage programs that are innovative, reflect a high degree of creative skill, deal with significant moral and social issues and present challenging concepts and other subject matter that relate to the world in which the viewer lives.

Television programs should not only reflect the influence of the established institutions that shape our values and culture, but also expose the dynamics of social change which bear upon our lives.

Responsibly exercised artistic freedom

To achieve these goals, television broadcasters should be conversant with the general and specific needs, interests and aspirations of all the segments of the communities they serve. They should affirmatively seek out responsible representatives of all parts of their communities so that they may structure a broad range of programs that will inform, enlighten, and entertain the total audience.

Broadcasters should also develop programs directed toward advancing the cultural and educational aspects of their communities.

To assure that broadcasters have the freedom to program fully and responsibly, none of the provisions of this Code should be construed as preventing or impeding broadcast of the broad range of material necessary to help broadcasters fulfill their obligations to operate in the public interest.

The challenge to the broadcaster is to determine how suitably to present the complexities of human behavior. For television, this requires exceptional awareness of considerations peculiar to the medium.

Accordingly, in selecting program subjects and themes, great care must be exercised to be sure that treatment and presentation are made in good faith and not for the purpose of sensationalism or to shock or exploit the audience or appeal to prurient interests or morbid curiosity.

Family viewing considerations

Additionally, entertainment programming inappropriate for viewing by a general family audience should not be broadcast during the first hour of network entertainment programming in prime time and in the immediately preceding hour. In the occasional case when an entertainment program in this time period is deemed to be inappropriate for such an audience, advisories should be used to alert viewers. Advisories should also be used when programs in later prime time periods contain material that might be disturbing to significant segments of the audience.

These advisories should be presented in audio and video form at the beginning of the program and when deemed appropriate at a later point in the program. Advisories should also be used responsibly in promotional material in advance of the program. When using an advisory, the broadcaster should attempt to notify publishers of television program listings.

Special care should be taken with respect to the content and treatment of audience advisories so that they do not disserve their intended purpose by containing material that is promotional, sensational, or exploitative. Promotional announcements for programs that include advisories should be scheduled on a basis consistent with the purpose of the advisory.

The scheduling provisions of Section I (Principles Governing Program Content) shall not apply to programs under contract to a station as of April 8, 1975, all episodes of which were then in existence, if such station is unable, despite reasonable good faith efforts, to edit such programs to make them appropriate for family viewing or to reschedule them so as not to occupy family viewing periods. This exception shall in no event apply after September 1, 1977. Any such programs excepted from scheduling provisions shall, of course, bear the required advisory notices. *(Interpretation No. 5)*

II. RESPONSIBILITY TOWARD CHILDREN

Broadcasters have a special responsibility to children. Programs designed primarily for children should take into account the range of interests and needs of children from instructional and cultural material to a wide variety of entertainment material. In their totality, programs should contribute to the sound, balanced development of children to help them achieve a sense of the world at large and informed adjustments to their society.

In the course of a child's development, numerous social factors and forces, including television, affect the ability of the child to make the transition to adult society.

The child's training and experience during the formative years should include positive sets of values which will allow the child to become a responsible adult, capable of coping with the challenges of maturity.

Children should also be exposed, at the appropriate times, to a reasonable range of the realities which exist in the world sufficient to help them make the transition to adulthood.

Because children are allowed to watch programs designed primarily for adults, broadcasters should take this practice into account in the presentation of material in such programs when children may constitute a substantial segment of the audience.

All the standards set forth in this section apply to both program and commercial material designed and intended for viewing by children.

III. COMMUNITY RESPONSIBILITY

1. Television broadcasters and their staffs occupy positions of unique responsibility in their communities and should conscientiously endeavor to be acquainted fully with the community's needs and characteristics in order better to serve the welfare of its citizens.

2. Requests for time for the placement of public service announcements or programs should be carefully reviewed with respect to the character and reputation of the group, campaign or organization involved, the public interest content of the message, and the manner of its presentation.

IV. SPECIAL PROGRAM STANDARDS

1. **Violence; conflict.**

A. Violence, physical or psychological, may only be projected in responsibly handled contexts, not used exploitatively. Programs involving violence should present the consequences of it to its victims and perpetrators.

Presentation of the details of violence should avoid the excessive, the gratuitous and the instructional.

The use of violence for its own sake and the detailed dwelling upon brutality or physical agony, by sight or by sound, are not permissible.

B. **Conflict and children.** The depiction of conflict, when presented in programs designed primarily for children, should be handled with sensitivity.

2. **Anti-social behavior; crime.** The treatment of criminal activities should always convey their social and human effects.

The presentation of techniques of crime in such detail as to be instructional or invite imitation shall be avoided.

3. Self-destructive behavior: drugs; gambling; alcohol.

A. Narcotic addiction shall not be presented except as a destructive habit. The use of illegal drugs or the abuse of legal drugs shall not be encouraged or shown as socially acceptable.

B. The use of gambling devices or scenes necessary to the development of plot or as appropriate background is acceptable only when presented with discretion and in moderation, and in a manner which would not excite interest in, or foster, betting nor be instructional in nature.

C. The use of liquor and the depiction of smoking in program content shall be deemphasized. When shown, they should be consistent with plot and character development.

4. **Sports programs.** Telecasts of actual sports programs at which on-the-scene betting is permitted by law shall be presented in a manner in keeping with federal, state and local laws, and should concentrate on the subject as a public sporting event.

5. **Mental/physical disadvantages.** Special precautions must be taken to avoid demeaning or ridiculing members of the audience who suf-

fer from physical or mental afflictions or deformities.

6. **Human relationships; sex; costume.** The presentation of marriage, the family and similarly important human relationships, and material with sexual connotations, shall not be treated exploitatively or irresponsibly, but with sensitivity. Costuming and movements of all performers shall be handled in a similar fashion.

7. **Pluralism; minorities.** Special sensitivity is necessary in the use of material relating to sex, race, color, age, creed, religious functionaries or rites, or national or ethnic derivation.

8. **Obscenity; profanity.** Subscribers shall not broadcast any material which they determine to be obscene, profane or indecent.

Above and beyond the requirements of law, broadcasters must consider the family atmosphere in which many of their programs are viewed.

There shall be no graphic portrayal of sexual acts by sight or sound. The portrayal of implied sexual acts must be essential to the plot and presented in a responsible and tasteful manner.

Subscribers are obligated to bring positive responsibility and reasoned judgment to bear upon all those involved in the development, production, and selection of programs.

9. **Hypnosis.** The creation of a state of hypnosis by act or detailed demonstration on camera is prohibited, and hypnosis as a form of "parlor game" antics to create humorous situations within a comedy setting is forbidden.

10. **Superstition; pseudo-sciences.** Program material pertaining to fortune-telling, occultism, astrology, phrenology, palm-reading, numerology, mind-reading, character-reading, and the like is unacceptable if it encourages people to regard such fields as providing commonly accepted appraisals of life.

11. **Professional advice/diagnosis/treatment.** Professional advice, diagnosis and treatment

will be presented in conformity with law and recognized professional standards.

12. **Subliminal perception.** Any technique whereby an attempt is made to convey information to the viewer by transmitting messages below the threshold of normal awareness is not permitted.

13. **Animals.** The use of animals, consistent with plot and character delineation, shall be in conformity with accepted standards of humane treatment.

14. **Game programs; contests.**

A. Quiz and similar programs that are presented as contests of knowledge, information, skill or luck must, in fact, be genuine contests; and the results must not be controlled by collusion with or between contestants, or by any other action which will favor one contestant against any other.

B. Contests may not constitute a lottery.

15. **Prizes: credits, acknowledgements.** The broadcaster shall be constantly alert to prevent inclusion of elements within a program dictated by factors other than the requirements of the program itself. The acceptance of cash payments or other considerations in return for including scenic properties, the choice and identification of prizes, the selection of music and other creative program elements and inclusion of any identification of commercial products or services, their trade names or advertising slogan within the program are prohibited except in accordance with Sections 317 and 508 of the Communications Act.

16. **Misrepresentation; deception.**

A. No program shall be presented in a manner which through artifice or simulation would mislead the audience as to any material fact. Each broadcaster must exercise reasonable judgment to determine whether a particular method of presentation would constitute a material deception, or would be accepted by the audience as normal theatrical illusion.

B. A television broadcaster should not present fictional events or other non-news material as authentic news telecasts or announcements, nor permit dramatizations in any program which would give the false impression that the dramatized material constitutes news.

17. **Applicability of Code standards.** The standards of this Code covering program content are also understood to include, wherever applicable, the standards contained in the advertising section of the Code.

V. TREATMENT OF NEWS AND PUBLIC EVENTS

General

Television Code standards relating to the treatment of news and public events are, because of constitutional considerations, intended to be exhortatory. The standards set forth hereunder encourage high standards of professionalism in broadcast journalism. They are not to be interpreted as turning over to others the broadcaster's responsibility as to judgments necessary in news and public events programming.

News

1. A television station's news schedule should be adequate and well-balanced.
2. News reporting should be factual, fair and without bias.
3. A television broadcaster should exercise particular discrimination in the acceptance, placement and presentation of advertising in news programs so that such advertising should be clearly distinguishable from the news content.
4. At all times, pictorial and verbal material for both news and comment should conform to other sections of these standards, wherever such sections are reasonably applicable.
5. Good taste should prevail in the selection and handling of news:

Morbid, sensational or alarming details not essential to the factual report, especially in connection with stories of crime or sex, should be avoided. News should be telecast in such a manner as to avoid panic and unnecessary alarm.

6. Commentary and analysis should be clearly identified as such.

7. Pictorial material should be chosen with care and not presented in a misleading manner.

8. All news interview programs should be governed by accepted standards of ethical journalism, under which the interviewer selects the questions to be asked. Where there is advance agreement materially restricting an important or newsworthy area of questioning, the interviewer will state on the program that such limitation has been agreed upon. Such disclosure should be made if the person being interviewed requires that questions be submitted in advance or participates in editing a recording of the interview prior to its use on the air.

9. A television broadcaster should exercise due care in the supervision of content, format, and presentation of newscasts originated by his/her station, and in the selection of newscasters, commentators, and analysts.

Public Events

1. A television broadcaster has an affirmative responsibility at all times to be informed of public events, and to provide coverage consonant with the ends of an informed and enlightened citizenry.

2. The treatment of such events by a television broadcaster should provide adequate and informed coverage.

VI. CONTROVERSIAL PUBLIC ISSUES

1. Television provides a valuable forum for the expression of responsible views on public issues of a controversial nature. The television broadcaster should seek out and develop with accountable individuals, groups and organizations, programs relating to controversial public issues of import to his/her fellow citizens; and to give fair representation to opposing sides of issues which materially affect the life or welfare of a substantial segment of the public.

2. Requests by individuals, groups or organizations for time to discuss their views on controversial public issues should be considered on the basis of their individual merits, and in the light of the contribution which the use requested would make to the public interest, and to a well-balanced program structure.

3. Programs devoted to the discussion of controversial public issues should be identified as such. They should not be presented in a manner which would mislead listeners or viewers to believe that the program is purely of an entertainment, news, or other character.

4. Broadcasts in which stations express their own opinions about issues of general public interest should be clearly identified as editorials. They should be unmistakably identified as statements of station opinion and should be appropriately distinguished from news and other program material.

VII. POLITICAL TELECASTS

1. Political telecasts should be clearly identified as such. They should not be presented by a television broadcaster in a manner which would mislead listeners or viewers to believe that the program is of any other character.
(Ref.: Communications Act of 1934, as amended, Secs. 315 and 317, and FCC Rules and Regulations, Secs. 3.654, 3.657, 3.663, as discussed in NAB's "Political Broadcast Catechism & The Fairness Doctrine.")

VIII. RELIGIOUS PROGRAMS

1. It is the responsibility of a television broadcaster to make available to the community appropriate opportunity for religious presentations.

2. Programs reach audiences of all creeds simultaneously. Therefore, both the advocates of broad or ecumenical religious precepts, and the exponents of specific doctrines, are urged to present their positions in a manner conducive to viewer enlightenment on the role of religion in society.

3. In the allocation of time for telecasts of religious programs, the television station should use its best efforts to apportion such time fairly among responsible individuals, groups and organizations.

IX. PRESENTATION OF ADVERTISING

1. Applicability of Code Standards.

A. This Code establishes basic standards for all television broadcasting. The principles of acceptability and good taste within the Program Standards section govern the presentation of advertising where applicable. In addition, the Code establishes in this section special standards which apply to television advertising.

B. Commercial television broadcasters make their facilities available for the advertising of products and services and accept commercial presentations for such advertising. However, television broadcasters should, in recognition of their responsibility to the public, refuse the facilities of their stations to an advertiser where they have good reason to doubt the integrity of the advertiser, the truth of the advertising representations, or the compliance of the advertiser with the spirit and purpose of all applicable legal requirements.

C. Since advertising by television is a dynamic technique, a television broadcaster should keep under surveillance new advertising devices so that the spirit and purpose of these standards are fulfilled.

2. **Sponsor identification.** Identification of sponsorship must be made in all sponsored programs in accordance with the requirements of the Communications Act of 1934, as amended, and the Rules and Regulations of the Federal Communications Commission.

3. **Safety considerations.** Representations which disregard normal safety precautions shall be avoided.

Children shall not be represented, except under proper adult supervision, as being in contact with or demonstrating a product recognized as potentially dangerous to them.

4. **Audience sensibilities: general.**

A. In consideration of the customs and attitudes of the communities served, each television broadcaster should refuse his/her facilities to the advertisement of products and services, or the use of advertising scripts, which the station has good reason to believe would be objectionable to a substantial and responsible segment of the community. These standards should be applied with judgment and flexibility, taking into consideration the characteristics of the medium, its home and family audience, and the form and content of the particular presentation.

B. Advertising messages should be presented with courtesy and good taste; disturbing or annoying material should be avoided; every effort should be made to keep the advertising message in harmony with the content and general tone of the program in which it appears.

5. **Audience perceptions of clutter.** A multiple product announcement is one in which two or more products or services are presented within the framework of a single announcement. A multiple product announcement shall not be scheduled in a unit of time less than 60 seconds, except where integrated so as to appear to the viewer as a single message. A multiple product announcement shall be considered integrated and counted as a single announcement if:

—the products or services are related and interwoven within the framework of the announcement (related products or services shall be defined as those having a common character, purpose and use); and

—the voice(s), setting, background and continuity are used consistently throughout so as to appear to the viewer as a single message.

Multiple product announcements of 60 seconds in length or longer not meeting this definition of integration shall be counted as two or more announcements under standard XIV-5 of the Code. This provision shall not apply to retail or service establishments.

6. **Audience sensibilities; children.**

A. The broadcaster and the advertiser should exercise special caution with the content and presentation of television commercials placed in or near programs designed for children. Exploitation of children should be avoided. Commercials directed to children should in no way mislead as to the product's performance and usefulness.

B. Commercials, whether live, film or tape, within programs initially designed primarily for children under 12 years of age shall be clearly separated from program material by an appropriate device.

C. Trade name identification or other merchandising practices involving the gratuitous naming of products is discouraged in programs designed primarily for children.

D. Appeals involving matters of health which should be determined by physicians should not be directed primarily to children.

E. No children's program personality or cartoon character shall be utilized to deliver commercial messages within or adjacent to the programs in which such a personality or cartoon character regularly appears. This provision shall also apply to lead-ins to commercials when such lead-ins contain sell copy or imply endorsement of the product by program personalities or cartoon characters.

Restricted or unacceptable categories

7. **Alcoholic beverages.**

A. The advertising of hard liquor (distilled spirits) is not acceptable.

B. The advertising of beer and wines is acceptable only when presented in the best of good taste and discretion, and is acceptable only subject to federal and local laws.

This requires that commercials involving beer and wine avoid any representation of on-camera drinking. *(Interpretation No. 4)*

8. **Vocational training.** Advertising by institutions or enterprises which in their offers of instruction imply promises of employment or make exaggerated claims for the opportunities awaiting those who enroll for courses is generally unacceptable.

9. **Ammunition; firearms; fireworks.** The advertising of firearms/ammunition is acceptable provided it promotes the product only as sporting equipment and conforms to recognized standards of safety as well as all applicable laws and regulations. Advertisements of fire-

arms/ammunition by mail order are unacceptable. The advertising of fireworks is unacceptable.

10. **Astrology, etc.** The advertising of fortune-telling, occultism, astrology, phrenology, palm-reading, numerology, mind-reading, character-reading or subjects of a like nature is not permitted.

11. **Personal products.** Because all products of a personal nature create special problems, acceptability of such products should be determined with especial emphasis on ethics and the canons of good taste. Such advertising of personal products as is accepted must be presented in a restrained and obviously inoffensive manner.

12. **Betting/gambling.** The advertising of tip sheets and other publications seeking to advertise for the purpose of giving odds or promoting betting is unacceptable.

The lawful advertising of government organizations which conduct legalized lotteries and the advertising of private or governmental organizations which conduct legalized betting on sporting contests are acceptable provided such advertising does not unduly exhort the public to bet.

Restricted or unacceptable advertising techniques

13. **Indirect advertising.** An advertiser who markets more than one product should not be permitted to use advertising copy devoted to an acceptable product for purposes of publicizing the brand name or other identification of a product which is not acceptable.

14. **Bait and switch.** "Bait-switch" advertising, whereby goods or services which the advertiser has no intention of selling are offered merely to lure the customer into purchasing higher-priced substitutes, is not acceptable.

15. **Pitch techniques.** The "pitchman" technique of advertising on television is inconsistent with good broadcast practice and generally damages the reputation of the industry and the advertising profession.

Sponsored program-length segments consisting substantially of continuous demonstrations or sales presentation, violate not only the time standards established in the Code but the broad philosophy of improvement implicit in the voluntary Code operation and are not acceptable. *(Interpretation No. 1)*

16. **Testimonials.** Personal endorsements (testimonials) shall be genuine and reflect personal experience. They shall contain no statement that cannot be supported if presented in the advertiser's own words.

17. **Policy regarding religious time sales.** A charge for television time to churches and religious bodies is not recommended.

X. CLAIMS: GENERAL

1. **False, misleading or deceptive advertising.** The role and capability of television to market sponsors' products are well recognized. In turn, this fact dictates that great care be exercised by the broadcaster to prevent the presentation of false, misleading or deceptive advertising. While it is entirely appropriate to present a product in a favorable light and atmosphere, the presentation must not, by copy or demonstration, involve a material deception as to the characteristics, performance or appearance of the product.

Broadcast advertisers are responsible for making available, at the request of the Code Authority, documentation adequate to support the validity and truthfulness of claims, demonstrations and testimonials contained in their commercial messages.

2. **Use of research, surveys or tests.** Reference to the results of bona fide research, surveys or tests relating to the product to be advertised shall not be presented in a manner so as to create an impression of fact beyond that established by the work that has been conducted.

3. **Fictitious exploitations.** Appeals to help fictitious characters in television programs by purchasing the advertiser's product or service or sending for a premium should not be permitted, and such fictitious characters should not

be introduced into the advertising message for such purposes.

4. **Competitive references.** Advertising should offer a product or service on its positive merits and refrain from discrediting, disparaging or unfairly attacking competitors, competing products, other industries, professions or institutions.

5. **Placement of advertising messages.** A sponsor's advertising messages should be confined within the framework of the sponsor's program structure. A television broadcaster should avoid the use of commercial announcements which are divorced from the program either by preceding the introduction of the program (as in the case of so-called "cowcatcher" announcements) or by following the apparent sign-off of the program (as in the case of so-called trailer or "hitch-hike" announcements). To this end, the program itself should be announced and clearly identified, both audio and video, before the sponsor's advertising material is first used, and should be signed off, both audio and video, after the sponsor's advertising material is last used.

XI. ADVERTISING OF MEDICAL PRODUCTS/SERVICES

1. The advertising of medical products presents considerations of intimate and far-reaching importance to consumers because of the direct bearing on their health.

2. Because of the personal nature of the advertising of medical products, claims that a product will effect a cure and the indiscriminate use of such words as "safe," "without risk," "harmless," or terms of similar meaning should not be accepted in the advertising of medical products on television stations.

3. A television broadcaster should not accept advertising material which in his/her opinion offensively describes or dramatizes distress or morbid situations involving ailments, by spoken word, sound or visual effects.

4. Commercials for services or over-the-counter products involving health consider-

ations are of intimate and far-reaching importance to the consumer. The following principles should apply to such advertising:

A. Physicians, dentists or nurses or actors representing physicians, dentists or nurses, shall not be employed directly or by implication. These restrictions also apply to persons professionally engaged in medical services (e.g., physical therapists, pharmacists, dental assistants, nurses' aides).

B. Visual representations of laboratory settings may be employed, provided they bear a direct relationship to bona fide research which has been conducted for the product or service. *(See Television Code X-2)* In such cases, laboratory technicians shall be identified as such and shall not be employed as spokespersons or in any other way speak on behalf of the product.

C. Institutional announcements not intended to sell a specific product or service to the consumer and public service announcements by non-profit organizations may be presented by accredited physicians, dentists or nurses, subject to approval by the broadcaster. An accredited professional is one who has met required qualifications and has been licensed in his/her resident state.

XII. CONTESTS

1. Contests shall be conducted with fairness to all entrants, and shall comply with all pertinent laws and regulations. Care should be taken to avoid the concurrent use of the three elements which together constitute a lottery—prize, chance and consideration.
2. All contest details, including rules, eligibility requirements, opening and termination dates should be clearly and completely announced and/or shown, or easily accessible to the viewing public, and the winners' names should be released and prizes awarded as soon as possible after the close of the contest.
3. When advertising is accepted which requests contestants to submit items of product identification or other evidence of purchase of products, reasonable facsimiles thereof should be made acceptable unless the award is based upon skill and not upon chance.
4. All copy pertaining to any contest (except that which is required by law) associated with

the exploitation or sale of the sponsor's product or service, and all references to prizes or gifts offered in such connection should be considered a part of and included in the total time allowances as herein provided. *(See Television Code XIV)*

XIII. PREMIUMS AND OFFERS

1. Full details of proposed offers should be required by the television broadcaster for investigation and approved before the first announcement of the offer is made to the public.

2. A final date for the termination of an offer should be announced as far in advance as possible.

3. Before accepting for telecast offers involving a monetary consideration, a television broadcaster should be satisfied as to the integrity of the advertiser and the advertiser's willingness to honor complaints, indicating dissatisfaction with the premium by returning the monetary consideration.

4. There should be no misleading descriptions or visual representations of any premiums or gifts which would distort or enlarge their value in the minds of the viewers.

5. Assurances should be obtained from the advertiser that premiums offered are not harmful to person or property.

6. Premiums should not be approved which appeal to superstition on the basis of "luck-bearing" powers or otherwise.

XIV. TIME STANDARDS FOR NETWORK-AFFILIATED STATIONS

The following standards for quantity and placement of non-program material are designed to serve the interests of the viewers and reflect as well consideration of the appropriate interests of broadcasters and advertisers within that public interest context.

1. **Non-Program Material Definition.** Non-program material in both prime time and all other time includes billboards, commercials and promotional announcements.

Non-program material also includes:

A. In programs of 90 minutes in length or less, credits in excess of 30 seconds per program, except in feature films. In no event should credits exceed 40 seconds in such programs.

The 40-second limitation on credits shall not apply, however, in any situation governed by a contract entered into before October 1, 1971.

B. In programs longer than 90 minutes, credits in excess of 50 seconds per program, except in feature films. In no event should credits exceed 60 seconds in such programs.

The only exclusions from the foregoing definition of non-program material are: (1) public service announcements; (2) voice-over credits program information announcements not to exceed 30 seconds; (3) scheduling information regarding unusual special news programs; (4) scheduling information presented in special programs of indeterminate length (e.g., special news, sports or other special events programs) regarding an immediately upcoming program(s) whose regular broadcast time has been affected by the indeterminate length program, and (5) promotional informational material used to fulfill time requirements of certain formats two hours in length or longer such as theatrical length motion pictures, mini-series, made-for-television movies, occasional special long-length versions of series programs. In such situations, the broadcaster may, no more than 12 times per year, and at his/her discretion, utilize promotional/informational material to fill the time requirement provided such material does not exceed an average of two minutes per hour. The limit on the amount of such material per program shall be four minutes and, when used, the material shall be generic in nature.

2. **Allowable Time for Non-Program Material.**

A. **Prime Time.**

(1) Prime time is a continuous period of not less than three consecutive hours per broadcast day as designated by the station between the hours of 6:00 PM and midnight.

(2) In prime time on network-affiliated stations, the amount of non-program material shall not exceed nine minutes 30 seconds in any 60-minute period. When deemed necessary by the broad-

caster, an additional 30 seconds per hour may be used for promotional announcements.

B. All Other Time. In all other time, non-program material shall not exceed 16 minutes in any 60-minute period.

C. Children's Programming Time. Children's programming time is defined as those hours other than prime time in which programs initially designed primarily for children under 12 years of age are scheduled.

Within this time period on Saturday and Sunday, non-program material shall not exceed nine minutes 30 seconds in any 60-minute period.

Within this time period on Monday through Friday, non-program material shall not exceed 12 minutes in any 60-minute period.

3. **Averaging Concept.** In prime time and all other time, programs of 90 minutes in length or longer, the reasonable averaging of the amount of allowable time for non-program material and/or of the number of allowable interruptions is permitted for the purpose of preserving program continuity in the interests of the viewer. In such situations, one or more 60-minute period(s) may contain more than the allowable amount of non-program material and/or more than the allowable number of interruptions providing the remaining 60-minute period(s) contains appropriately less non-program material and/or fewer interruptions so that, on average, each hour of the program is compliant with applicable Television Code standards. Additionally, when the telecast of live programs of indeterminate length, such as sports programs and on-the-spot news coverage, carries over from one time period to another (e.g., prime time to all other time), allowance will be made for the reasonable overage of non-program material in any given hour of the program providing the total amount of non-program material does not exceed the total allowed for the period of time which the program covers.

4. **Program Interruptions.**

A. Definition: A program interruption is any occurrence of non-program material within the main body of the program.

B. In prime time, the number of program

interruptions shall not exceed two within any 30-minute program, or four within any 60-minute program. Programs longer than 60 minutes shall be prorated at two interruptions per half hour.

The number of interruptions in 60-minute variety shows shall not exceed five.

C. In all other time, the number of interruptions shall not exceed four within any 30-minute program period.

D. In children's weekend programming time, as defined in Section XIV-2C, the number of program interruptions shall not exceed two within any 30-minute program or four within any 60-minute program.

E. In both prime time and all other time, the following interruption standard shall apply within programs of 15 minutes or less in length:

5-minute program——1 interruption;
10-minute program——2 interruptions;
15-minute program——2 interruptions.

F. News, weather, sports and special events programs are exempt from the interruption standards because of the nature of such programs.

5. **Consecutive Announcements.** In both prime time and all other time, no more than five non-program material announcements may be scheduled consecutively within programs by the originating Code subscriber, of which no more than four may be commercial announcements, and no more than three non-program material announcements may be scheduled consecutively during any station break.

Public service announcements are excluded from the consecutive announcement count. The consecutive announcement limitation need not apply in situations in which the number of interruptions in a program has been reduced.

6. **Prize and donor identification.** Reasonable and limited identification of prizes and donors' names where the presentation of contest awards or prizes is a necessary part of program content shall not be included as non-program material as defined above.

Aural and/or visual prize identification of up to 10 seconds duration may be deemed "reasonable and limited." Where such identification is longer than 10 seconds, the entire announcement or visual presentation will be charged against the total commercial time for the program period. *(Interpretation No. 3)*

7. **Shopping guides/service formats.** Programs presenting women's/men's service features, shopping guides, fashion shows, demonstrations and similar material provide a special service to the public in which certain material normally classified as non-program is an informative and necessary part of the program content. Because of this, the time standards may be waived by the Code Authority to a reasonable extent on a case-by-case basis.

8. **Product or service references.** Gratuitous references in a program to a non-sponsor's product or service should be avoided except for normal guest identification.

9. **Film promotion.** The presentation of commentary or film excerpts from current theatrical releases in some instances may constitute commercial material under the Time Standards for Non-Program Material. Specifically, for example, when such presentation, directly or by inference, urges viewers to attend, it shall be counted against the commercial allowance for the program of which it is a part. *(Interpretation No. 2)*

10. **Trade name identification.** Stationary backdrops or properties in television presentations showing the sponsor's name or product, the name of the sponsor's product, trade-mark or slogan should be used only incidentally and should not obtrude on program interest or entertainment.

XV. TIME STANDARDS FOR INDEPENDENT STATIONS

1. Non-program elements shall be considered as all-inclusive, with the exception of required credits, legally required station identifications, and "bumpers." Promotion spots and public service announcements, as well as commercials, are to be considered non-program elements.

2. The allowed time for non-program elements, as defined above, shall not exceed seven minutes in a 30-minute period or multiples thereof in prime time (prime time is defined

as any three contiguous hours between 6:00 PM and midnight, local time), or eight minutes in a 30-minute period or multiples thereof during all other times.

3. Where a station does not carry a commercial in a station break between programs, the number of program interruptions shall not exceed four within any 30-minute program, or seven within any 60-minute program, or 10 within any 90-minute program, or 13 in any 120-minute program. Stations which do carry commercials in station breaks between programs shall limit the number of program interruptions to three within any 30-minute program, or six within any 60-minute program, or nine within any 90-minute program, or 12 in any 120-minute program. News, weather, sports, and special events are exempted because of format.

4. Not more than four non-program material announcements, as defined above, shall be scheduled consecutively. An exception may be made only in the case of a program 60 minutes or more in length, when no more than seven non-program elements may be scheduled consecutively by stations who wish to reduce the number of program interruptions.

5. The conditions of paragraphs three and four shall not apply to live sports programs where the program format dictates and limits the number of program interruptions.

(For children's time standards on independent stations see provisions XIV-2C, 4D under Time Standards for Network-Affiliated Stations.)

GUIDELINES/INTERPRETATIONS BASED ON CODE STANDARDS

From time to time the Code Authority issues advertising guidelines and clarifications expanding on provisions of the Code. Among areas covered are acne, alcoholic beverages, arthritis and rheumatism remedies, bronchitis, comparative advertising, children's premiums and offers, children's TV advertising, disparagement, hallucinogens, hypnosis, lotteries, men-in-white, non-prescription medications, personal products, testimonials, time standards, toys, vegetable oils and margarines, and weight reducing products/services. Copies may be obtained from any NAB Code Authority office.

The following Regulations and Procedures shall obtain as an integral part of the Television Code of the National Association of Broadcasters:

I. Name

The name of this Code shall be *The Television Code of the National Association of Broadcasters.**

II. Purpose of the Code

The purpose of this Code is cooperatively to maintain a level of television programming which gives full consideration to the educational, informational, cultural, economic, moral and entertainment needs of the American public to the end that more and more people will be better served.

III. Subscribers

Section 1. Eligibility

Any individual, firm or corporation which is engaged in the operation of a television broadcast station or network, or which holds a construction permit for a television broadcast station within the United States or its dependencies, shall, subject to the approval of the Television Board of Directors as hereinafter provided, be eligible to subscribe to the Television Code of the NAB to the extent of one subscription for each such station and/or network which it operates or for which it holds a construction permit; provided, that a non-television member of NAB shall not become eligible via Code subscription to receive any of the member services or to exercise any of the voting privileges of a member.

*By-Laws of the National Association of Broadcasters, Article VI, Section 8, C: "Television Board. The Television Board is hereby authorized:—(4) to enact, amend and promulgate standards of practice or codes for its Television members, and to establish such methods to secure observance thereof as it may deem advisable:—."

Section 2. Certification of Subscription

Upon subscribing to the Code, subject to the approval of the Television Board of Directors, there shall be granted forthwith to each such subscribing station authority to use the "NAB Television Seal of Good Practice," a copyrighted and registered seal to be provided in the form of a certificate, a slide and/or a film, signifying that the recipient thereof is a subscriber in good standing to the Television Code of the NAB. The seal and its significance shall be appropriately publicized by the NAB.

Section 3. Duration of Subscription

Subscription shall continue in full force and effect until 30 days after the first of the month following receipt of notice of written resignation. Subscription to the Code shall be effective from the date of application subject to the approval of the Television Board of Directors; provided, that the subscription of a television station going on the air for the first time shall, for the first six months of such subscription, be probationary, during which time its subscription can be summarily revoked by an affirmative two-thirds vote of the Television Board of Directors without the usual processes specified below.

Section 4. Suspension of Subscription

Any subscription, and/or the authority to utilize and show the above-noted seal, may be voided, revoked or temporarily suspended for television programming, including commercial copy, which, by theme, treatment or incident, in the judgment of the Television Board constitutes a continuing, willful or gross violation of any of the provisions of the Television Code, by an affirmative two-thirds vote of the Television Board of Directors at a regular or special meeting; provided, however, that the following conditions and procedures shall apply:

A. *Preferring of Charges—Conditions Precedent:*

Prior to the preferring of charges to the Television Board of Directors concerning violation of the Code by a subscriber, the Television Code Board (hereinafter provided for) (1) Shall have appropriately, and in good time, informed and advised such subscriber of any and all complaints and information coming to the attention of the Television Code Board and relating to the programming of said subscriber, (2) Shall have reported to, and advised, said subscriber by analysis, interpretation, recommendation or otherwise, of the possibility of a violation or breach of the Television Code by the subscriber, and (3) Shall have served upon the subscriber, by Registered Mail a Notice of Intent to prefer charges, at least 20 days prior to the filing of any such charges with the Television Board of Directors. During this period the Television Code Board may, within its sole discretion, reconsider its proposed action based upon such written reply as the subscriber may care to make, or upon such action as the subscriber may care to take program-wise, in conformance with the analysis, interpretation, or recommendation of the Television Code Board.

(i) Notice of Intent

The Notice of Intent shall include a statement of the grounds and reasons for the proposed charges, including appropriate references to the Television Code.

(ii) Time

In the event that the nature of the program in question is such that time is of the essence, the Television Code Board may prefer charges within less than the 20 days above specified, provided that a time certain in which reply may be made is included in its Notice of Intent, and provided that its reasons therefor must be specified in its statement of charges preferred.

B. *The Charges:*

The subscriber shall be advised in writing by Registered Mail of the charges preferred. The charges preferred by the Television Code Board to the Television Board of Directors shall include the grounds and reasons therefor, together with specific references to the Television Code. The charges shall contain a statement that the conditions precedent, herein before described, have been met.

C. *Hearing:*

The subscriber shall have the right to a hearing and may exercise same by filing an answer within 10 days of the date of such notification.

D. *Waiver:*

Failure to request a hearing shall be deemed a waiver of the subscriber's right thereto.

E. *Designation:*

If a hearing is requested by the subscriber, it shall be designated as promptly as possible and at such time and place as the Television Board may specify.

F. *Confidential Status:*

Hearings shall be closed; and all correspondence between a subscriber and the Television Code Board and/or the Television Board of Directors concerning specific programming shall be confidential; provided, however, that the confidential status of these procedures may be waived by a subscriber.

G. *Presentation; Representation:*

A subscriber against whom charges have been preferred, and who has exercised his/her right to a hearing, shall be entitled to effect presentation of his/her case personally, by agent, by attorney, or by deposition and interrogatory.

H. *Intervention:*

Upon request by the subscriber-respondent or the Television Code Board, the Television Board of Directors, in its discretion, may permit the intervention of one or more other subscribers as parties-in-interest.

I. *Transcript:*

A stenographic transcript record shall be taken and shall be certified by the Chairperson of the Television Board of Directors to the Office of the Secretary of the National Association of Broadcasters, where it shall be maintained. The transcript shall not be open to inspection unless otherwise provided by the party respondent in the proceeding.

J. *Television Code Board; Counsel:*

The Television Code Board may, at its discretion, utilize the services of an attorney from the staff of the NAB for the purpose of effecting its presentation in a hearing matter.

K. *Order of Procedure:*

At hearings the Television Code Board shall open and close.

L. *Cross-Examination:*

The right of cross-examination shall specifically obtain. Where procedure has been by deposition or interrogatory, the use of cross-interrogatories shall satisfy this right.

M. *Presentation:*

Oral and written evidence may be introduced by the subscriber and by the Television Code Board. Oral argument may be had at the hearing and written memoranda or briefs may be submitted by the subscriber and by the Television Code Board. The Television Board of Directors may admit such evidence as it deems relevant, material and competent, and may determine the nature and length of the oral argument and the written argument or briefs.

N. *Authority of Presiding Officer; of Television Board of Directors:*

The Presiding Officer shall rule upon all interlocutory matters, such as, but not limited to, the admissibility of evidence, the qualifications of witnesses, etc. On all other matters, authority to act shall be vested in a majority of the Television Board unless otherwise provided.

O. *Films, Transcriptions, etc.:*

Films, kinescopes, records, transcriptions, or other mechanical reproductions of television programs, properly identified, shall be accepted into evidence when relevant.

P. *Continuances and Extensions:*

Continuance and extension of any proceeding or for the time of filing or performing any act required or allowed to be done within a specific time may be granted upon request, for a good cause shown. The Board or the Presiding Officer may recess or adjourn a hearing for such time as may be deemed necessary, and may change the place thereof.

Q. *Findings and Conclusions:*

The Television Board of Directors shall decide the case as expeditiously as possible and shall notify the subscriber and the Television Code Board, in writing, of the decision. The decision of the Television Board of Directors shall contain findings of fact with conclusions, as well as the reasons or bases therefor. Findings of fact shall set out in detail and with particularity all basic evidentiary facts developed on the record (with appropriate citations to the transcript of record or exhibit relied on for each evidentiary fact) supporting the conclusion reached.

R. *Reconsideration or Rehearing:*

A request for reconsideration or rehearing may be filed by parties to the hearing. Requests for reconsideration or rehearing shall state with particularity in what respect the decision or any matter determined therein is claimed to be unjust, unwarranted, or erroneous, and with respect to any finding of fact shall specify the pages of record relied on. If the existence of any newly discovered evidence is claimed, the request shall be accompanied by a verified statement of the facts together with the facts relied on to show that the party, with due diligence, could not have known or discovered such facts at the time of the hearing.

The request for rehearing may seek:

a. Reconsideration
b. Additional oral argument
c. Reopening of the proceedings
d. Amendment of any findings, or
e. Other relief.

S. *Time for Filing:*

Requests for reconsideration or rehearing shall be filed within 10 days after receipt by the respondent of the decision. Opposition thereto may be filed within five days after the filing of the request.

T. *Penalty, Suspension of:*

At the discretion of the Television Board, application of any penalty provided for in the decision may be suspended until the Board makes final disposition of the request for reconsideration or rehearing.

U. *Disqualification:*

Any member of the Television Board may disqualify himself/herself, or upon good cause shown by any interested party, may be disqualified by a majority vote of the Television Board.

Section 5. Additional Procedures

When necessary to the proper administration of the Code, additional rules of procedure will be established from time to time as authorized by the By-Laws of the NAB; in keeping therewith, special consideration shall be given to the procedures for receipt and processing of complaints and to necessary rules to be adopted from time to time, taking into account the source and nature of such complaints; such rules to include precautionary measures such as the posting of bonds to cover costs and expenses of processing same; and further provided that special consideration will be given to procedures insuring the confidential status of proceedings relating to Code observance.

Section 6. Amendment and Review

Because of the new and dynamic aspects inherent in television broadcast, the Television Code, as a living, flexible and continuing document, may be amended from time to time by the Television Board of Directors; provided that said Board is specifically charged with review and reconsideration of the entire Code, its appendices and procedures, at least once each year.

Section 7. Termination of Contracts

All subscribers on the air at the time of subscription to the Code shall be permitted that period prior to and including the earliest legal cancellation date to terminate any contracts, then outstanding, calling for program presentations which would not be in conformity with the Television Code, provided, however, that in no event shall such period be longer than 52 weeks.

IV. Affiliate Subscribers

Section 1. Eligibility

Any individual, firm or corporation, which is engaged in the production or distribution, lease, or sale of recorded programs for television presentation, subject to the approval of the Television Code Board as hereinafter provided, shall be eligible to become an affiliate subscriber to the Television Code of the NAB.

Section 2. Certification of Subscription

Upon becoming an affiliate subscriber to the Code, subject to the approval of the Television Code Board, there shall be granted forthwith to each such affiliate subscriber authority to use a copyrighted and registered seal and declaration, in a manner approved by the Television Code Board, identifying the individual firm or corporation as an affiliate subscriber to the Television Code of the NAB. Such authority shall not constitute formal clearance or approval by the Television Code Board of specific film programs or other recorded material.

Section 3. Duration of Affiliate Subscription

The affiliate subscription shall continue in full force and effect until 30 days after the first of the month following receipt of a written notice of resignation. The affiliate subscription of the Code shall be effective from the date of application subject to the approval of the Television Code Board.

Section 4. Suspension of Affiliate Subscription

Any affiliate subscription and the authority to utilize and show the above-noted seal may be voided, revoked, or temporarily suspended for the sale or distribution for television presentation of any film or other recorded material which by theme, treatment, or incident, in the judgment of the Television Code Board, constitutes a continuing, willful or gross violation of any of the provisions of the Television Code, by a majority vote of the Television Code Board at any regular or special meeting. The conditions and procedures applicable to subscribers shall not apply to affiliate subscribers.

Section 5. Representation of Affiliate Subscribers

Any affiliate subscriber or group of affiliate subscribers may authorize an individual or association to act for them in connection with their relations with the Television Code Board by filing a written notice of such representation with the Board. Such representation, however, in no way will limit the right of the Television Code Board to suspend individual affiliate subscribers in accordance with the provisions of Section 4.

V. Rates

Each subscriber and affiliate subscriber shall pay "administrative" rates in accordance with such schedule, at such time, and under such conditions as may be determined from time to time by the Television Board *(See Article VI,*

Section 8, C. Television Board (3) and (4), By-Laws of the NAB); provided, that appropriate credit shall be afforded to a television member of the NAB against the regular dues paid to NAB.

VI. The Television Code Board

Section 1. Composition

There shall be a continuing committee entitled the Television Code Board to be composed of not more than nine members, all of whom shall be from subscribers to the Television Code. They shall be appointed by the President of NAB, subject to confirmation by the Television Board, and may include one member from each of the subscribing nationwide television networks. Members of the Television Board shall not be eligible to serve on the Board. Due consideration shall be given, in making the appointments, to factors of diversification of geographical location, market size, company representation and network affiliation.

No person shall continue as a member of the Television Code Board if the station or entity he/she represents ceases to subscribe to the Television Code. In such case a vacancy occurs in the office immediately, and a successor may be appointed to serve out the unexpired term.

The first term shall be for three years. The second term shall be for two years. Each new term shall commence at the close of the annual meeting of membership following appointment.

A. *Limitation of Service:*

No person shall serve for more than two terms, consecutively, as a member of the Television Code Board; provided, however, this limitation shall not apply to network representatives.

Serving out the unexpired term of a former member shall not constitute a term within the meaning of this section.

B. *Meetings:*

The Television Code Board shall meet at least twice in each calendar year on a date to be determined by the Chairperson. The Chairperson, or the Code Authority General Manager, may, at any time, on at least five days written notice, call a special meeting of the Board.

C. *Quorum:*

For all purposes, a majority of the members of the Television Code Board shall constitute a quorum.

Section 2. Authority and Responsibilities

The Television Code Board is authorized and directed:

(1) To recommend to the Television Board of Directors amendments to the Television Code; (2) to consider, in its discretion, any appeal from any decision made by the Code Authority General Manager with respect to any matter which has arisen under the Code, and to suspend, reverse, or modify any such decision; (3) to prefer formal charges, looking toward the suspension or revocation of the authority to show the Code seal, to the Television Board of Directors concerning violations and breaches of the Television Code by a subscriber; (4) to be available to the Code Authority General Manager for consultation on any and all matters affecting the Television Code.

VII. Code Authority General Manager

Section 1. Code Authority General Manager

There shall be a position designated as the Code Authority General Manager. This position shall be filled by appointment of the President of NAB, subject to the approval of the Board of Directors.

Section 2. Authority and Responsibilities

The Code Authority General Manager is authorized and directed: (1) To maintain a continuing review of all programming and advertising material presented over television, especially that of subscribers to the Television Code of NAB; (2) to receive, screen and clear complaints concerning television programming; (3) to define and interpret words and phrases in the Television Code; (4) to develop and maintain appropriate liaison with governmental agencies and with responsible and accountable organizations and institutions; (5) to inform, expeditiously and properly, a subscriber to the Television Code of complaints or commendations, as well as to advise all subscribers concerning the attitudes and desires program-wise of accountable organizations and institutions, and of the American public in general; (6) to review and monitor, if necessary, any certain series of programs, daily programming, or any other program presentations of a subscriber, as well as to request recorded material, or script and copy, with regard to any certain program presented by a subscriber; (7) to reach conclusions and make recommendations or prefer charges to the Television Code Board concerning violations and breaches of the Television Code by a subscriber; (8) to recommend to the Code Board amendments to the Television Code.

A. *Delegation of Powers and Responsibilities:*

The Code Authority General Manager shall appoint such executive staff as is needed, consistent with resources, to carry out the above described functions, and may delegate to this staff such responsibilities as he/she may deem necessary.

SUBJECT INDEX

The Radio Code

National Association of Broadcasters
Twenty-Second Edition, January 1980

Reprinted with permission from
Code Authority
National Association of Broadcasters
1771 N St., N.W., Washington, D.C. 20036

Table of Contents

In 1937 a major segment of U.S. commercial radio broadcasters first adopted industry-wide standards of practice. The purpose of such standards then, as now, is to establish guideposts and professional tenets for performance in the areas of programming and advertising content.

Admittedly, such standards for broadcasting can never be final or complete, because broadcasting is a creative art, always seeking new ways to achieve maximum appeal and service. Therefore, its standards are subject to periodic revision to reasonably reflect changing attitudes in our society.

In 1945 after two years devoted to reviewing and revising the 1937 document, new standards were promulgated. Further revisions were made in subsequent years when deemed necessary. The objectives behind them have been to assure that advertising messages be presented in an honest, responsible and tasteful manner and that broadcasters, in their programming, tailor their content to meet the needs and expectations of that particular audience to which their programming is directed.

The growth of broadcasting as a medium of entertainment, education and information has been made possible by its commercial underpinning. This aspect of commercial broadcasting as it has developed in the United States has enabled the industry to grow as a free medium in the tradition of American enterprise. The extent of this freedom is underscored by those laws which prohibit censorship of broadcast material. Rather, those who own the nation's radio broadcasting stations operate them—pursuant to this self-adopted Radio Code—in recognition of the needs of the American people and the reasonable self-interests of broadcasters and broadcast advertisers.

THE RADIO BROADCASTER'S CREED

We Believe:

That Radio Broadcasting in the United States of America is a living symbol of democracy; a significant and necessary instrument for maintaining freedom of expression, as established by the First Amendment to the Constitution of the United States;

That its contributions to the arts, to science, to education, to commerce, and therefore to the public welfare have the potential of influencing the common good achievements of our society as a whole;

That it is our obligation to serve the people in such manner as to reflect credit upon our profession and to encourage aspiration toward a better estate for our audiences. This entails making available to them through all phases of the broadcasting art such programming as will convey the traditional strivings of the U.S. towards goals beneficial to the populace;

That we should make full and ingenious use of the many sources of knowledge, talents and skills and exercise critical and discerning judgment concerning all broadcasting operations to the end that we may, intelligently and sympathetically:

Observe both existing principles and developing concepts affecting our society;

Respect and advance the rights and the dignity of all people;

Enrich the daily life of the people through the factual reporting and analysis of news, and through programming of education, entertainment, and information;

Provide for the fair discussion of matters of public concern; engage in works directed toward the common good; and volunteer our aid and comfort in times of stress and emergency;

Contribute to the economic welfare of all by expanding the channels of trade, by encouraging the development and conservation of natural resources, and by bringing together the buyer and seller through the broadcasting of information pertaining to goods and services.

Toward the achievement of these purposes we agree to observe the following:

I. PROGRAM STANDARDS

A. News

Radio is unique in its capacity to reach the largest number of people first with reports on current events. This competitive advantage bespeaks caution—being first is not as important as being accurate. The Radio Code standards relating to the treatment of news and public events are, because of constitutional considerations, intended to be exhortatory. The standards set forth hereunder encourage high standards of professionalism in broadcast journalism. They are not to be interpreted as turning over to others the broadcaster's responsibility as to judgments necessary in news and public events programming.

1. *News Sources.* Those responsible for news on radio should exercise constant professional care in the selection of sources—on the premise that the integrity of the news and the consequent good reputation of radio as a dominant well-balanced news medium depend largely upon the reliability of such sources.

2. *News Reporting.* News reporting should be factual, fair and without bias. Good taste should prevail in the selection and handling of news. Morbid, sensational, or alarming details not essential to factual reporting should be avoided. News should be broadcast in such a manner as to avoid creation of panic and unnecessary alarm. Broadcasters should be diligent in their supervision of content, format, and presentation of news broadcasts. Equal diligence should be exercised in selection of editors and reporters who direct news gathering and dissemination, since the station's performance in this vital informational field depends largely upon them.

3. *Commentaries and Analyses.* Special obligations devolve upon those who analyse and/or comment upon news developments, and management should be satisfied completely that the task is to be performed in the best interest of the listening public. Programs of news analysis and commentary should be clearly identified as such, distinguishing them from straight news reporting.

4. *Editorializing*. Broadcasts in which stations express their own opinions about issues of general public interest should be clearly identified as editorials.

5. *Coverage of News and Public Events*. In the coverage of news and public events broadcasters should exercise their judgments consonant with the accepted standards of ethical journalism and should provide accurate, informed and adequate coverage.

6. *Placement of Advertising*. Broadcasters should exercise particular discrimination in the acceptance, placement and presentation of advertising in news programs so that such advertising is clearly distinguishable from the news content.

B. Controversial Public Issues

1. Radio provides a valuable forum for the expression of responsible views on public issues of a controversial nature. Controversial public issues of importance to fellow citizens should give fair representation to opposing sides of issues.

2. Requests by individuals, groups or organizations for time to discuss their views on controversial public issues should be considered on the basis of their individual merits, and in the light of the contributions which the use requested would make to the public interest.

3. Discussion of controversial public issues should not be presented in a manner which would create the impression that the program is other than one dealing with a public issue.

C. Community Responsibility

1. Broadcasters and their staffs occupy a position of responsibility in the community and should conscientiously endeavor to be acquainted with its needs and characteristics to best serve the welfare of its citizens.

2. Requests for time for the placement of public service announcements or programs should be carefully reviewed with respect to the character and reputation of the group, campaign or organization involved, the public

interest content of the message, and the manner of its presentation.

D. Political Broadcasts

1. Political broadcasts, or the dramatization of political issues designed to influence voters, shall be properly identified as such.

2. Political broadcasts should not be presented in a manner which would mislead listeners to believe that they are of any other character.
(Reference: Communications Act of 1934, as amended, Secs. 315 and 317, and FCC Rules and Regulations, Secs. 3.654, 3.657, 3.663, as discussed in NAB's "Political Broadcast Catechism & The Fairness Doctrine.")

3. Because of the unique character of political broadcasts and the necessity to retain broad freedoms of policy void of restrictive interference, it is incumbent upon all political candidates and all political parties to observe the canons of good taste and political ethics, keeping in mind the intimacy of broadcasting in the American home.

E. Advancement of Education and Culture

1. Because radio is an integral part of American life, there is inherent in radio broadcasting a continuing opportunity to enrich the experience of living through the advancement of education and culture.

2. Radio broadcasters, in augmenting the educational and cultural influences of the home, schools, religious institutions and institutions of higher education and other entities should:

(a) be thoroughly conversant with the educational and cultural needs and aspirations of the community served;

(b) develop programming consonant with the stations particular target audience.

F. Religion and Religious Programming

1. Religious programming shall be presented by responsible individuals, groups or organizations.

2. Radio broadcasting reaches audiences of

all creeds simultaneously. Therefore, both the advocates of broad or ecumenical religious precepts, and the exponents of specific doctrines, are urged to present their positions in a manner conducive to listener enlightenment on the role of religion in society.

G. Responsibility Toward Children

Broadcasters have a special responsibility to children. Programming which might reasonably be expected to hold the attention of children should be presented with due regard for its effect on children.

1. Programming should be based upon sound social concepts and should include positive sets of values which will allow children to become responsible adults, capable of coping with the challenges of maturity.

2. Programming should convey a reasonable range of the realities which exist in the world to help children make the transition to adulthood.

3. Programming should contribute to the healthy development of personality and character.

4. Programming should afford opportunities for cultural growth as well as for wholesome entertainment.

5. Programming should be consistent with integrity of realistic production, but should avoid material of extreme nature which might create undesirable emotional reaction in children.

6. Programming should avoid appeals urging children to purchase the product specifically for the purpose of keeping the program on the air or which, for any reason, encourage children to enter inappropriate places.

7. Programming should present such subjects as violence and sex without undue emphasis and only as required by plot development or character delineation.

Violence, physical or psychological, should only be projected in responsibly handled contexts, not used to excess or exploitatively. Programs involving violence should present the consequences of it to its victims and perpetrators.

The depiction of conflict, and of material reflective of sexual considerations, when presented in programs designed primarily for children, should be handled with sensitivity.

8. The treatment of criminal activities should always convey their social and human effects.

H. Dramatic Programming

1. In the design of dramatic programs it is in the interest of radio as a vital medium to encourage those that are innovative, reflect a high degree of creative skill, deal with significant moral and social issues and present challenging concepts and other subject matter that relate to the world in which the listener lives.

2. Radio programming should not only reflect the influence of the established institutions that shape our values and culture, but also expose the dynamics of social change which bear upon our lives.

3. To achieve these goals, radio broadcasters should be conversant with the general and specific needs, interests and aspirations of all the segments of the communities they serve.

4. Radio should reflect realistically the experience of living, in both its pleasant and tragic aspects, if it is to serve the listener honestly. Nevertheless, it holds a concurrent obligation to provide programming which will encourage positive adjustments to life.

In selecting program subjects and themes, great care must be exercised to be sure that treatment and presentation are made in good faith and not for the purpose of sensationalism or to shock or exploit the audience or appeal to prurient interests or morbid curiosity.

5. In determining the acceptability of any dramatic program, especially those containing elements of crime, mystery, or horror, consideration should be given to the possible effect on all members of the listening audience.

In addition, without sacrificing integrity of presentation, dramatic programs on radio shall avoid:

(a) the presentation of techniques of crime in such detail as to be instructional or invite imitation;

(b) presentation of the details of violence involving the excessive, the gratuitous and the instructional;

(c) sound effects calculated to mislead, shock, or unduly alarm the listener;

(d) portrayals of law enforcement in a manner which does not contribute to its proper role in our society.

I. General

1. The intimacy and confidence placed in radio demand of the broadcaster, the networks and other program sources that they be vigilant in protecting the audience from deceptive broadcast practices.

2. Sound effects and expressions characteristically associated with news broadcasts (such as "bulletin," "flash," "we interrupt this program to bring you," etc.) shall be reserved for announcement of news, and the use of any deceptive techniques in connection with fictional events and non-news programming shall not be employed.

3. The broadcasters shall be constantly alert to prevent inclusion of elements within programming dictated by factors other than the requirements of the programming itself. The acceptance of cash payments or other considerations in return for including the choice and identification of prizes, the selection of music and other creative programming elements and inclusion of any identification of commercial products or services, trade names or advertising slogans within the programming are prohibited unless consideration for such inclusion is revealed to the listeners in accordance with Sections 317 and 508 of the Communications Act.

4. Special precautions should be taken to avoid demeaning or ridiculing members of the audience who suffer from physical or mental afflictions or deformities.

5. The broadcast of gambling sequences deemed necessary to the development of plot

or as appropriate background is acceptable only when presented with discretion and in moderation, and in a manner which would not excite interest in, or foster, betting nor be instructional in nature.

6. Quiz and similar programming that is presented as a contest of knowledge, information, skill or luck must, in fact, be a genuine contest and the results must not be controlled by collusion with or between contestants, or by any other action which will favor one contestant against any other.

7. Contests may not constitute a lottery.

8. Listener contests should not mislead as to the nature or value of prizes, likelihood of winning, nor encourage thoughtless or unsafe acts.

9. No programming shall be presented in a manner which through artifice or simulation would mislead the audience as to any material fact. Each broadcaster must exercise reasonable judgment to determine whether a particular method of presentation would constitute a material deception, or would be accepted by the audience as normal theatrical illusion.

10. Legal, medical and other professional advice will be permitted only in conformity with law and recognized ethical and professional standards.

11. Narcotic addiction shall not be presented except as a destructive habit. The use of illegal drugs or the abuse of legal drugs shall not be encouraged or be presented as desirable or socially acceptable.

12. Material pertaining to fortune-telling, occultism, astrology, phrenology, palm-reading, numerology, mind-reading, character-reading, or subjects of a like nature, is unacceptable if it encourages people to regard such fields as providing commonly accepted appraisals of life.

13. Representations of liquor and smoking shall be de-emphasized. When represented, they should be consistent with plot and character development.

14. Obscene, indecent or profane matter, as

proscribed by law, is unacceptable.

15. Special sensitivity is necessary in the use of material relating to sex, race, color, age, creed, religious functionaries or rites, or national or ethnic derivation.

16. The presentation of marriage, the family and similarly important human relationships, and material with sexual connotations, should not be treated exploitatively or irresponsibly, but with sensitivity.

17. Broadcasts of actual sporting events at which on-the-scene betting is permitted by law should be presented in a manner in keeping with federal, state and local laws, and should concentrate on the subject as a public sporting event.

18. Detailed exposition of hypnosis or material capable of having an hypnotic effect on listeners is forbidden.

19. Any technique whereby an attempt is made to convey information to the listener by transmitting messages below the threshold of normal awareness is not permitted.

20. The commonly accepted standards of humane animal treatment should be adhered to as applicable in programming.

21. Broadcasters are responsible for making good faith determinations on the acceptability of lyrics under applicable Radio Code standards.

22. Guests on discussion/interview programs and members of the public who participate in phone-in programs shall be treated with due respect by the program host/hostess.

Interview/discussion programs, including telephone participation programs, should be governed by accepted standards of ethical journalism. Any agreement substantively limiting areas of discussion/questions should be announced at the outset of the program.

23. The standards of this Code covering programming content are also understood to include, wherever applicable, the standards contained in the advertising section of the Code.

24. To assure that broadcasters have the

freedom to program fully and responsibly, none of the provisions of this Code should be construed as preventing or impeding broadcasts of the broad range of material necessary to help broadcasters fulfill their obligations to operate in the public interest.

II. ADVERTISING STANDARDS

Advertising is the principal source of revenue of the free, competitive American system of radio broadcasting. It makes possible the presentation to all American people of the finest programs of entertainment, education, and information.

Since the great strength of American radio broadcasting derives from the public respect for and the public approval of its programs, it must be the purpose of each Broadcaster to establish and maintain high standards of performance, not only in the selection and production of all programs, but also in the presentation of advertising.

This Code establishes basic standards for all radio broadcasting. The principles of acceptability and good taste within the Program Standards section govern the presentation of advertising where applicable. In addition, the Code establishes in this section special standards which apply to radio advertising.

A. General Advertising Standards

1. Commercial radio broadcasters make their facilities available for the advertising of products and services and accept commercial presentations for such advertising. However, they shall, in recognition of their responsibility to the public, refuse the facilities of their stations to an advertiser where they have good reason to doubt the integrity of the advertiser, the truth of the advertising representations, or the compliance of the advertiser with the spirit and purpose of all applicable legal requirements.

2. In consideration of the customs and attitudes of the communities served, each radio broadcaster should refuse his/her facilities to the advertisement of products and services, or the use of advertising scripts, which the station has good reason to believe would be objectionable to a substantial and responsible segment of the community. These standards should be applied with judgment and flexibility, taking into consideration the characteristics of the medium, its home and family audi-

ence, and the form and content of the particular presentation.

B. Presentation of Advertising

1. The advancing techniques of the broadcast art have shown that the quality and proper integration of advertising copy are just as important as measurement in time. The measure of a station's service to its audience is determined by its overall performance.

2. The final measurement of any commercial broadcast service is quality. To this, every broadcaster shall dedicate his/her best effort.

3. Great care shall be exercised by the broadcaster to prevent the presentation of false, misleading or deceptive advertising. While it is entirely appropriate to present a product in a favorable light and atmosphere, the presentation must not, by copy or demonstration, involve a material deception as to the characteristics or performance of a product.

4. The broadcaster and the advertiser should exercise special caution with the content and presentation of commercials placed in or near programs designed for children. Exploitation of children should be avoided. Commercials directed to children should in no way mislead as to the product's performance and usefulness. Appeals involving matters of health which should be determined by physicians should be avoided.

5. Reference to the results of research, surveys or tests relating to the product to be advertised shall not be presented in a manner so as to create an impression of fact beyond that established by the study. Surveys, tests or other research results upon which claims are based must be conducted under recognized research techniques and standards.

C. Acceptability of Advertisers and Products

In general, because radio broadcasting is designed for the home and the entire family, the following principles shall govern the business classifications:

1. The advertising of hard liquor shall not be accepted.

2. The advertising of beer and wines is acceptable when presented in the best of good taste and discretion.

3. The advertising of fortune-telling, occultism, astrology, phrenology, palm-reading, numerology, mind-reading, character-reading, or subjects of a like nature, is not acceptable.

4. Because the advertising of all products and services of a personal nature raises special problems, such advertising, when accepted, should be treated with emphasis on ethics and the canons of good taste, and presented in a restrained and inoffensive manner.

5. The advertising of tip sheets and other publications seeking to advertise for the purpose of giving odds or promoting betting is unacceptable.

The lawful advertising of government organizations which conduct legalized lotteries and the advertising of private or governmental organizations which conduct legalized betting on sporting contests are acceptable provided such advertising does not unduly exhort the public to bet.

6. An advertiser who markets more than one product shall not be permitted to use advertising copy devoted to an acceptable product for purposes of publicizing the brand name or other identification of a product which is not acceptable.

7. Care should be taken to avoid presentation of "bait-switch" advertising whereby goods or services which the advertiser has no intention of selling are offered merely to lure the customer into purchasing higher-priced substitutes.

8. Advertising should offer a product or service on its positive merits and refrain from discrediting, disparaging or unfairly attacking competitors, competing products, other industries, professions or institutions.

Any identification or comparison of a competitive product or service, by name, or other means, should be confined to specific facts rather than generalized statements or conclusions, unless such statements or conclusions are not derogatory in nature.

9. Advertising testimonials should be genuine, and reflect an honest appraisal of personal experience.

10. Advertising by institutions or enterprises offering instruction with exaggerated claims for opportunities awaiting those who enroll, is unacceptable.

11. The advertising of firearms/ammunition is acceptable provided it promotes the product only as sporting equipment and conforms to recognized standards of safety as well as all applicable laws and regulations. Advertisements of firearms/ammunition by mail order are unacceptable.

D. Advertising of Medical Products

Because advertising for over-the-counter products involving health considerations is of intimate and far-reaching importance to the consumer, the following principles should apply to such advertising:

1. When dramatized advertising material involves statements by doctors, dentists, nurses or other professional people, the material should be presented by members of such profession reciting actual experience, or it should be made apparent from the presentation itself that the portrayal is dramatized.

2. Because of the personal nature of the advertising of medical products, the indiscriminate use of such words as "safe," "without risk," "harmless," or other terms of similar meaning, either direct or implied, should not be expressed in the advertising of medical products.

3. Advertising material which offensively describes or dramatizes distress or morbid situations involving ailments is not acceptable.

E. Time Standards for Advertising Copy

1. As a general rule, up to 18 minutes of advertising time within any clock hour are acceptable. However, for good cause and when in the public interest, broadcasters may depart

from this standard in order to fulfill their responsibilities to the communities they serve.

2. Any reference to another's products or services under any trade name, or language sufficiently descriptive to identify it, shall, except for normal guest identification, be considered as advertising copy.

F. Contests

1. Contests shall be conducted with fairness to all entrants, and shall comply with all pertinent laws and regulations.

2. All contest details, including rules, eligibility requirements, opening and termination dates, should be clearly and completely announced or easily accessible to the listening public; and the winners' names should be released as soon as possible after the close of the contest.

3. When advertising is accepted which requests contestants to submit items of product identification or other evidence of purchase of products, reasonable facsimiles thereof should be made acceptable. However, when the award is based upon skill and not upon chance, evidence of purchase may be required.

4. All copy pertaining to any contest (except that which is required by law) associated with the exploitation or sale of the sponsor's product or service, and all references to prizes or gifts offered in such connection should be considered a part of and included in the total time limitations heretofore provided. *(See Time Standards for Advertising Copy.)*

G. Premiums and Offers

1. The broadcaster should require that full details of proposed offers be submitted for investigation and approval before the first announcement of the offer is made to the public.

2. A final date for the termination of an offer should be announced as far in advance as possible.

3. If a consideration is required, the advertiser should agree to honor complaints indicat-

ing dissatisfaction with the premium by returning the consideration.

4. There should be no misleading descriptions or comparisons of any premiums or gifts which will distort or enlarge their value in the minds of the listeners.

The following Regulations and Procedures shall obtain as an integral part of the Radio Code of the National Association of Broadcasters:

I. Name

The name of this Code shall be the Radio Code of the National Association of Broadcasters, hereinafter referred to as the Radio Code.*

Definitions:

Wherever reference is made to programs it shall be construed to include all program material including commercials.

II. Purpose of the Code

The purpose of this Code is cooperatively to establish and maintain a level of radio programming which gives full consideration to the educational, informational, cultural, economic, moral and entertainment needs of the American public to the end that more and more people will be better served.

III. The Radio Code Board

Section 1. Composition

There shall be a continuing Committee entitled the Radio Code Board.* The Code Board shall be composed of 11 members. Members of the Radio Board shall not be eligible to serve on the above specified Board. The Chairperson and members of the Code Board shall be appointed by the President of the NAB, subject to confirmation by the Radio Board, and may include no more than two members as representatives of subscribing nationwide radio networks. Due consideration shall be given, in making such appointments, to factors of diversification, such as market size, geographical location, network affiliation, class of broadcast service, etc. The

*The Radio Board of the NAB shall have power: "to enact, amend and promulgate Radio Standards of Practice or Codes, and to establish such methods to secure observance thereof as it may deem advisable:—." By-Laws of the National Association of Broadcasters, Article VI, Section 8, B. Radio Board.

Board shall be fully representative of the radio industry. All Code Board members shall be selected from subscribers to the Radio Code. In every odd-numbered year, four members shall be appointed for two-year terms; in every even-numbered year, five members shall be appointed for two-year terms provided, however, that network representatives be rotated on an annual basis. Appointments become effective at the conclusion of the annual NAB convention of the year in which appointments are made.

A. *Limitation of Service:*

A person shall not serve consecutively as a member of the Board for more than two two-year terms or for more than four years consecutively provided, however, that appointment to fill an unexpired term shall not count toward the limitation of service as previously stated.

Network representatives on the Radio Code Board shall be limited to non-consecutive two-year terms; provided, in the first year of such representation one network member may be appointed for a one-year term and one for a two-year term. Thereafter, all network members may be appointed for two-year terms. Any one network representative may be reappointed following an interim two-year period.

A majority of the membership of the Radio Code Board shall constitute a quorum for all purposes unless herein otherwise provided.

Section 2. Authorities and Responsibilities

The Radio Code Board is authorized and directed:

(1) To recommend to the Radio Board amendments to the Radio Code; (2) to consider in its discretion, any appeal from any decision made by the Code Authority General Manager with respect to any matter which has arisen under the Code, and to suspend, reverse, or modify any such decision; (3) to prefer formal charges, looking toward the suspension or revocation of the subscription and/or the authority to use the Radio Code Audio and Visual Symbols, to the Radio Board concerning violations and breaches of the Radio Code

by a subscriber; (4) to be available to the Code Authority General Manager for consultation on any and all matters affecting the Radio Code.

A. *Meetings:*

The Radio Code Board shall meet regularly semi-annually on a date to be determined by the Chairperson. The Chairperson of the Board may, at any time, on at least five days' written notice, call a special meeting of the Board.

IV. Code Authority General Manager

Section 1. General Manager

There shall be a position designated as the Code Authority General Manager. This position shall be filled by appointment of the President of NAB, subject to the approval of the Board of Directors.

Section 2. Authority and Responsibilities

The Code Authority General Manager is responsible for the administration, interpretation and enforcement of the Radio Code. In furtherance of this responsibility he/she is authorized and directed:

(1) To maintain a continuing review of all programming and advertising material presented over radio, especially that of subscribers to the Radio Code of NAB; (2) to receive, screen and clear complaints concerning radio programming; (3) to define and interpret words and phrases in the Radio Code; (4) to develop and maintain appropriate liaison with governmental agencies and with responsible and accountable organizations and institutions; (5) to inform, expeditiously and properly, a subscriber to the Radio Code of complaints or commendations, as well as to advise all subscribers concerning the attitudes and desires program-wise of accountable organizations and institutions, and of the American public in general; (6) to receive and monitor, if necessary, any certain series of programs, daily programming, or any other program presentations of a subscriber, as well as to request recorded material, or script and copy, with regard to any certain program presented

by a subscriber; (7) to reach conclusions and make recommendations or prefer charges to the Radio Code Board concerning violations and breaches of the Radio Code by a subscriber; (8) to recommend to the Code Board amendments to the Radio Code; (9) to take such action as may be necessary to enforce the Code, including revocation of subscription as hereinafter provided in Chapter V, Section 4.

A. *Delegation of Powers and Responsibilities:*

The Code Authority General Manager shall appoint such executive staff as is needed, consistent with resources, to carry out the above described functions, and may delegate to this staff such responsibilities as he/she may deem necessary.

V. Subscribers

Section 1. Eligibility

A. Any individual, firm or corporation which is engaged in the operation of a radio broadcast station or radio network; or which holds a construction permit for a radio broadcast station within the United States or its dependencies, shall, subject to the approval of the Radio Board, as hereinafter provided, be eligible to subscribe to the Radio Code of the NAB to the extent of one subscription for each such station or network, or each station which holds a construction permit; provided, that a non-radio member of NAB shall not become eligible via Code subscription to receive any of the member services or to exercise any of the voting privileges of a member.

B. The Radio Code Board may recommend categories of affiliate subscribers as may be desired, together with applicable fees for such affiliate subscriptions.

Section 2. Certification of Subscription

Upon subscribing to the Code there shall be granted forthwith to each such subscribing station authority to use such copyrighted and registered audio and visual symbols as will be provided. The symbols and their significance shall be appropriately publicized by the NAB.

Section 3. Duration of Subscription

Subscription shall continue in full force and effect until there has been received a written notice of resignation or until subscription is revoked by action of the Code Authority, the Radio Code Board or the Radio Board of Directors.

Section 4. Revocation of Subscription

Any subscription and/or the authority to utilize the above-noted symbols, may be voided, revoked or temporarily suspended for radio programming, including commercial copy, which, by theme, treatment or incident, in the judgment of the Code Authority constitutes a continuing, willful or gross violation of any of the provisions of the Radio Code; provided, however, that the following conditions and procedures shall govern:

A. *Conditions Precedent:*

Prior to Revocation of Subscription, the Code Authority (1) Shall appropriately inform the subscriber of any and all complaints and information it possesses relating to the programming of said subscriber, (2) Shall have reported to, and advised, said subscriber by analysis, interpretation, recommendation or otherwise, of the possibility of a violation or breach of the Radio Code, and (3) Shall have served upon the subscriber by registered mail a Notice of Intent to Revoke Subscription; such Notice shall contain a statement of the grounds and reasons for the proposed revocation, including appropriate references to the Radio Code and shall give the subscriber 30 days to take such action as will satisfy the Code Authority. During this interim period the Code Authority may, within its sole discretion, reconsider its proposed action based upon such written reply as the subscriber may care to make, or upon such action as the subscriber may care to take program-wise, in conformance with the analysis, interpretation or recommendation of the Code Authority. If upon termination of the 30 day period, no such action has been taken or the subscriber has not requested a hearing, as hereinafter provided, his/her subscription to the Code shall be considered revoked.

B. *Time:*

In the event that the nature of the program in question is such that the Code Authority deems time to be of the essence, the Code Authority may limit the time in which compliance must be made, provided that a time certain in which subscriber may reply is included in the Notice of Intent, and provided further that the Code Authority's reasons therefor are specified in its Notice of Intent to Revoke Subscription.

C. *Hearing:*

The subscriber shall have the right to a hearing before the Code Board by requesting same and by filing an answer within 20 days of the date of receipt of the Notice of Intent. Said answer and request for hearing shall be directed to the Chairperson of the Code Board with a copy to the Code Authority.

D. *Waiver:*

Failure to request a hearing shall be deemed a waiver of the subscriber's right thereto. If a hearing is requested, action of the Code Authority is suspended pending decision of the Code Board.

E. *Designation:*

If hearing is requested by the subscriber, it shall be designated as promptly as possible and at such time and place as the Code Board may specify.

F. *Confidential Status:*

Hearings shall be closed; and all correspondence between a subscriber and the Code Authority and/or the Code Board concerning specific programming shall be confidential; provided, however, that the confidential status of these procedures may be waived by a subscriber.

G. *Presentation; Representation:*

A subscriber who has exercised his/her right to a hearing, shall be entitled to effect presentation of his/her case personally, by agent, by attorney, or by deposition and interrogatory.

H. *Intervention:*

Upon request by the subscriber-respondent or the Code Authority, the Code Board, in its discretion, may permit the intervention of one or more subscribers as parties-in-interest.

I. *Transcript:*

A stenographic transcript record may be taken if requested by respondent and shall be certified by the Chairperson of the Code Board to the Office of the Secretary of the National Association of Broadcasters, where it shall be maintained. The transcript shall not be open to inspection unless otherwise provided by the party respondent in the proceeding.

J. *Code Authority; Counsel:*

The Code Authority may, at its discretion, utilize the services of an attorney from the staff of the NAB for the purpose of effecting its presentation in a hearing matter.

K. *Order of Procedure:*

At hearings, the Code Authority shall open and close.

L. *Cross-Examination:*

The right of cross-examination shall specifically obtain. Where procedure has been by deposition or interrogatory, the use of cross-interrogatories shall satisfy this right.

M. *Presentation:*

Oral and written evidence may be introduced by the subscriber and by the Code Authority. Oral argument may be had at the hearing and written memoranda or briefs may be submitted by the subscriber and by the Code Authority. The Code Board may admit such evidence as it deems relevant, material and competent, and may determine the nature and length of the oral argument and the written argument or briefs.

N. *Transcriptions, etc.:*

Records, transcriptions, or other mechanical reproductions of radio programs, properly identified, shall be accepted into evidence when relevant.

O. *Authority of Presiding Officer of Code Board:*

The Presiding Officer shall rule upon all interlocutory matters, such as, but not limited to, the admissibility of evidence, the qualifications of witnesses, etc. On all other matters, authority to act shall be vested in a majority of the Code Board unless otherwise provided.

P. *Continuances and Extensions:*

Continuance and extension of any proceeding or for the time of filing or performing any act required or allowed to be done within a specific time may be granted upon request, for a good cause shown. The Code Board or the Presiding Officer may recess or adjourn a hearing for such time as may be deemed necessary, and may change the place thereof.

Q. *Findings and Conclusions:*

The Code Board shall decide the case as expeditiously as possible and shall notify the subscriber, Code Authority, and the Radio Board in writing, of the decision. The decision of the Code Board shall contain findings of fact with conclusions, as well as the reasons or bases therefor. Findings of fact shall set out in detail and with particularity all basic evidentiary facts developed on the record (with appropriate citations to the transcript of record or exhibit relied on for each evidentiary fact) supporting the conclusion reached.

R. *Disqualification:*

Any member of the Code Board may disqualify himself/herself, or upon good cause shown by any interested party, may be disqualified by a majority vote of the Code Board.

S. *Review:*

A request for review of the Code Board's decision may be filed by the subscriber with the Radio Board. Such petition for review must be served upon the Chairperson of the Radio Board within 10 days after receipt by the subscriber of the Code Board's decision.

T. *Penalty, Suspension of:*

At the discretion of the Code Board, application of any penalty provided for in the decision may be suspended until the Radio Board makes final disposition of the Petition for Review. The entire record in the proceedings before the Code Board shall be certified to the Radio Board. The review will be limited to written statements and no provision is made for further oral argument.

U. *Final Decision:*

The Radio Board shall have the discretion upon review to uphold, reverse, or amend with direction the decision of the Code Board. The decision of the Radio Board is final.

Section 5. Additional Procedures

When necessary to the proper administration of the Code, additional rules of procedure will be established from time to time as authorized by the By-Laws of the NAB; in keeping therewith, special consideration shall be given to the procedures for receipts and processing of complaints and to necessary rules to be adopted from time to time, taking into account the source and nature of such complaints; such rules to include precautionary measures such as the posting of bonds to cover costs and expenses of processing same; and further provided that special consideration will be given to procedures insuring the confidential status of proceedings relating to Code observance.

Section 6. Amendment and Review

The Radio Code may be amended from time to time by the Radio Board which shall specify the effective date of each amendment; provided, that said Board is specifically charged with review and reconsideration of the entire Code, its appendices and procedures, at least once each year.

Section 7. Termination of Contracts

All subscribers on the air shall be in compliance at the time of subscription to the Code.

VI. Rates

Each subscriber shall pay fees in accordance with such schedule, at such time, and under such conditions as may be determined from time to time by the Radio Board (*See Article VI, Section 8, B. Radio Board By-Laws of the NAB).*

SUBJECT INDEX

Code Authority
National Association of Broadcasters
1771 N St., N.W., Washington, D.C. 20036

477 Madison Ave., New York, N.Y. 10022
7060 Hollywood Blvd., Hollywood, Calif. 90028

Guidelines on

Advertising Substantiation

Report of the Sub-Council on Advertising and Promotion of the National Business Council for Consumer Affairs

This report contains the results of studies by an Advisory Committee. It does not necessarily represent the views of the Department of Commerce or any other Federal Government agency.

Honorable Peter G. Peterson
Secretary of Commerce
Washington, D.C. 20230

Dear Mr. Secretary

As part of its effort to identify positive actions which can be taken by advertisers to help anticipate and resolve problems in the area of consumer affairs, the NBCCA Sub-Council on Advertising and Promotion has examined intensively the subject of substantiation of claims.

Earlier work of the Sub-Council has resulted in publication of a statement on "Violence and the Media" and a comprehensive project report on "Corporate Policies and Procedures on Advertising and Promotion". Recognition of the particular importance of claims substantiation has prompted the Sub-Council to develop suggested specific guidelines for use by advertisers in the development of individual corporate principles and procedures relating to documentation of claims.

We are pleased to transmit this report of the Sub-Council, "Guidelines on Advertising Substantiation", for your consideration. The guidelines are intended to promote ultimate consumer satisfaction with products and services as related to consumers' understanding of claims made for them.

We should like to express our appreciation for your help during the coming weeks in distributing these guidelines widely to advertisers, advertising agencies, and the public.

Sincerely,

Robert E. Brooker

Robert E. Brooker
Chairman, National Business
Council for Consumer Affairs

Robert J. Keith

Robert J. Keith
Chairman, Sub-Council on
Advertising and Promotion

Donald S. Perkins

Donald S. Perkins
Co-Chairman, National Business
Council for Consumer Affairs

Archibald McG. Foster

Archibald McG. Foster
Vice-Chairman, Sub-Council on
Advertising and Promotion

Report on Guidelines on Advertising Substantiation

The Purpose of the Report

Much interest has been expressed in recent months concerning the importance of substantiation of certain advertising claims. Little, however, has been done to define clearly the purpose and scope of substantiation. The guidelines included in this document are intended broadly to promote ultimate consumer satisfaction with performance of products as related to consumers' understanding of claims made for those products, rather than narrowly as a means to help defend against possible future legal problems of an advertiser. The report should be of use to all interested in the subject of claims documentation and is intended to be of particular assistance to brand managers and others involved in reviewing documentation of claims about to be made.

The Importance of Advertising

The Sub-Council appreciates the indispensable role of national advertising in supporting the distribution and sales of consumer goods and services. It is essential to the operation of the Nation's economy. Without it, sellers would have to resort to much less efficient means of communicating with prospective consumers regarding the availability of goods and services, with commensurately inflated costs. From the consumer's viewpoint, advertising provides the only continuous offering of goods and services from which the individual can make the choices required to satisfy changing needs.

Consumer advertising, therefore, is important to sellers and buyers alike. It is an integral part of the supply and demand mechanism by which the national economy operates. Such advertising facilitates the optimum allocation of resources and, accordingly, is a positive competitive factor. *It is important that businessmen protect and preserve the integrity of consumer advertising.* While this statement is intended to apply primarily to traditional forms of advertising and sales promotion materials, regardless of media used, the Sub-Council urges manufacturers and packagers to apply the same standards to promotional information appearing on consumer packaging materials.

The Role of Government in Advertising

The Sub-Council recognizes the important role of government in prohibiting advertising which is not truthful. The Sub-Council, however, recommends against any government restraints on the advertiser's right of expression in commercial advertising which are not reasonably necessary to prevent fraud and deception and to protect the public health.

Government control of information contained in consumer advertising which exceeds what is necessary to achieve these commonly accepted goals would diminish the effectiveness of advertising as a legitimate competitive activity and would impose prohibitive burdens and costs, particularly on smaller advertisers. Such action would seriously impair competition and, equally important, would reduce the amount of information available to consumers.

The Responsibility of Advertisers

The Sub-Council emphasizes that if advertising is to continue to serve its beneficial function in the market process, the advertiser must insure against its misuse. Advertisers must be able to substantiate the truth and accuracy of all claims with reasonable supporting information. Claims based on opinion should be clearly identified as such. As a measure of their responsibility and dedication to this objective, advertisers must individually set up and enforce the procedures and guidelines they require for this purpose. The Sub-Council believes that self-regulation in this regard is feasible and proper. In view of the large number of advertisers and advertising material involved, it could well be the most effective and practical approach.

It is particularly important that advertisers substantiate, in advance of their use, all factual claims relating to the safety, performance, effectiveness, quality, and price of products and services. The Sub-Council urges advertisers to observe the following thirteen precautions when making claims in these areas in consumer advertisements:

- 1. *All consumer advertising claims* should be worded to communicate clearly and accurately the realistic scope of the claim.
- 2. *Factual claims* of performance, product improvement, effectiveness, quality and durability, and competitive comparisons in consumer advertising should be based on reasonable test information related to conditions of normal consumer use and should apply in the preponderance of probable consumer use situations.
- 3. *Performance demonstrations* should be closely related to claimed consumer benefits. Demonstrations, surveys, and tests should be based on recommended or normal consumer use, and artificial or biased conditions must be avoided unless clearly identified. Testimonials should be based on actual and normal use.
- 4. Consumer products should be safe for their advertised use, and *factual health and safety claims* should be supported by a high degree of test information closely related to normal consumer use.
- 5. Consumer advertising should not suggest, depict, or extol *product applications which present an unreasonable safety risk* to the consumer, taking into consideration foreseeable consumer misuse of such products.

6. *Market performance claims*, such as sales leadership, should be based on appropriate consumer research or reliable market statistics.
7. Advertisers should not suggest or imply uses for which a particular product or service has not been reasonably *tested for effectiveness* nor suggest or imply results which the product or service is not reasonably capable of producing in recommended or normal consumer use.
8. Consumer advertising of *price and price comparisons* should clearly state information sufficient to enable the average consumer to understand the price advertised and what the price includes. Price claims which are exaggerated or incapable of reasonable verification should be avoided.
9. Advertisers should avoid *exaggerated statements and demonstrations* which reasonably could be misconstrued by consumers, "dangling" comparatives, and any intentional distortion of fact, as well as unsubstantiated claims of uniqueness.
10. Considerable care must be taken when advertising claims involve *judgment or opinion* in order to avoid statements that could reasonably confuse or deceive the public.
11. *Appeals to emotions* in consumer advertising should be in good taste and reasonably related to normal consumer expectations and attitudes with respect to the product involved.
12. Extra care must be given in formulating and documenting claims that relate to *controversial issues* of current public importance, such as environmental issues.

13. Special consideration must be given to eliminate confusion when communicating claims to *special audiences*, particularly children. Every effort should be made to insure that the expectations of these consumers are not unintentionally raised above the product's ability to perform. Care must also be taken in advertising to other audiences, such as the elderly, the poor, and the educationally disadvantaged, who may be especially vulnerable to certain types of claims.

Review and Substantiation Procedures Within a Company

The Sub-Council recognizes that many consumer products or service companies have formal procedures for the review and verification of advertising claims. The Sub-Council urges all consumer advertisers who have not already done so to establish clear, written advertising substantiation procedures to insure the truth and accuracy of all factual claims and their compliance with applicable federal, state, and local laws and regulations and with special substantiation procedures set up by advertising agencies and media, and industry advertising codes.

These procedures should be approved and promulgated by top management. Thereafter, they should be distributed to brand managers and to advertising, research and development, engineering, manufacturing, legal, public relations, marketing, sales, service, and other pertinent areas of the company as well as to advertising agencies involved.

These procedures should make clear the need for required reasonable substantiation information to support all specific factual claims in consumer advertising and should require the source of all supporting information (e.g., laboratory research, consumer research, or other material) to be indicated. Substantiating information in support of important factual claims should be filed with the advertising copy or specifically identified. Approvals of factual claims should be in the form of signed statements by members of management who have the expertise which qualifies them to support the verification.

Advertisements involving claims, the accuracy of which the public reasonably can be expected to judge, should be based on consumer research as well as any other supporting information indicated by these guidelines when such consumer research is not duplicative and wasteful considering the other supporting information and the relative accuracy and effectiveness of testing methods. In conducting consumer research for the purpose of making consumer advertising claims, advertisers should exercise considerable attention to test design, projectability, sample, and reliability.

Finally, retailers and other distributors of consumer products should be entitled to rely on the factual claims of the manufacturer in preparing their own advertising, unless such distributors have actual knowledge that a specific claim cannot be substantiated. Moreover, retailers and distributors of consumer products should exercise care in the creation of their promotional activities to insure that they do not exceed the manufacturer's substantiated claims for the product.

Implementation of Guidelines

All consumer advertisers are urged to adopt these guidelines and to disseminate copies to all of their personnel responsible for preparing or reviewing consumer advertising.

In addition, the Sub-Council urges every advertiser of consumer products and services to assign responsibility to a specific official of their organization to receive, and respond to, requests for product or service information from individual consumers submitted in good faith to aid in making their personal buying decisions or to facilitate their personal use of such products or services.

Appendix

It is not practical for the Sub-Council to offer specific procedures and guidelines for all manufacturers and types of consumer products and services nor is it the Sub-Council's function to endorse particular company procedures. Illustrative samples from various companies, advertising agencies, media and industry associations, however, may be helpful to those currently operating without formal procedures. While various examples are annexed to this statement, the task of writing such procedures and guidelines, and of assuring acceptance, is the responsibility of each company. Only by such individual action will the Sub-Council's objectives be achieved.

Example A—Packaged Food Manufacturer

The advertising policy of the firm states, "Food products cannot be shown or written about in such a manner so as to exaggerate, misrepresent or in any way incorrectly show the product qualities. This applies to the depiction of the product itself, as well as the reported results of any test, experiment, or demonstration."

The advertising policy calls for the approval by 12 different departments within the company of all advertising. Among others these include the brand manager, research and development, product safety officer, consumer service, legal department, and purchasing.

The advertising policy also states, "Products which are to be photographed should be representative of those available to the consumer and should therefore be obtained in representative markets from retail shelves or trade warehouse when possible. When a new product has not yet reached the retail shelves or trade warehouse, a representative sample should be obtained from an actual production run. If a new product is not yet being produced at the plant, a laboratory sample may be used if there will be no material difference in appearance between it and the plant-production product. If a laboratory sample or early production run product is used, the Consumer Service representative having responsibility for the product will obtain a sample from a representative retail market or trade warehouse as soon as it becomes available for comparison with pictorial representation. If any material difference exists, the Brand Manager and Consumer Service representative will immediately institute a corrective change in the representation."

Regarding the preparation of products for photography, the guide states, "Products should be prepared for photography according to package directions. Any deviation from such directions must be disclosed on the label or in the ad. Implements used should be those which are readily available to the average consumer and the method of preparation should be such that it does not require any professional expertise."

Example B—Advertising Agency Guidelines

One of the country's leading advertising agencies has drawn up its own procedure manual for food advertising. It covers acquisition of food used in advertising, preparation and depiction, use of props, copy and servings.

Regarding preparation of food, the manual states, "The food is not to be washed, strained, blotted or otherwise subjected to treatment which would not occur under normal circumstances of preparation and use by the consumer. No coloring or extraneous material is to be added to the food unless clearly and conspicuously disclosed in the ad. In photographing or filming the food, techniques may not be used which would distort the size or quantity of some or all of the ingredients of the food nor any color filters or other devices be used which may distort the appearance of the food."

Props used in food advertising—plates, bowls, cups, glasses, eating utensils and the like—are, according to the manual, ". . . to be of normal size and dimension to avoid 'giantism'—i.e., making use of undersized props to exaggerate the size or quantity of the food or certain of its elements."

The agency's manual also states, "If the copy or label for the product specifies that one package or can of food product will yield X number of servings, and a serving is shown in the ad, the number of ounces in the serving shown must be consistent with the statement. If not consistent, the number of ounces in the serving shown must be clearly and conspicuously disclosed in the ad."

Example C—Automobile Manufacturer

A corporate procedure has been instituted by a major automobile manufacturer to define the responsibilities and methods related to the review and validation of the accuracy of its advertising claims.

Specific responsibilities are assigned to the company's product planning, comptroller's, engineering and research, legal, safety and quality control, advertising and sales promotion departments.

The product planning department, the procedure states, ". . . is responsible for assuring the accuracy of all product information provided to advertising agencies and for obtaining the required supporting data and for providing additional information as requested when adequate documentation is available."

Under the procedure, advertising agencies ". . . are required to identify the source of each claim contained in an advertisement, using an identification system developed by the advertising manager. When supporting documentation is not yet available this fact will be noted."

Documents used to provide a source of information for

advertising claims include engineering publications, product descriptions, product planning letters, reference photographs, trim, paint, and plastic charts, paint and trim option charts, price lists, and other published engineering data.

The procedure calls for any claim included in advertising material which has not been previously validated and documented to be highlighted in the list submitted by the agency as requiring special attention.

Example D—Laundry and Personal Product Manufacturer

At this firm the brand manager group is charged with the ultimate responsibility for the supportability of advertising. If, in the process of technical or legal clearance, a difference of opinion arises, the brand manager is responsible for resolving it by carrying the matter to higher levels of management for review and decision.

Their policy requires that each new advertising submission be forwarded to the technicians assigned to the brand for their evaluation. Principal questions to be answered are: (1) Do existing product performance data adequately support, from a technical point of view, claims made for the product in the advertising? (2) If the evidence is not on hand, can such data be developed by the technical people?

Following technical evaluation, the advertising is submitted, together with appropriate written substantiation, to the legal department for review.

Written substantiation of the supportability of each claim is prepared by the brand group, drawing on information provided by technical people as appropriate. A standard format, "Proof of Advertising Claim", is used by all brands. These statements are cleared with the technical people who review the accuracy of supporting data from their point of view and initial the document when they are satisfied.

Where support of a claim rests on market research or

technical testing for factual foundation, the proof of claim statement includes a summary of the research-testing involved which covers the date of the testing, who conducted the test, explanation of the method employed, and explanation of the results.

When completed the document is forwarded to the legal department for approval. The completed and initialed proof of claims statements are kept on file to support all future use of the claims involved.

Example E—Television Network Standards

One of the major television networks has established general advertising standards which apply to all its advertisers. Those standards state that the network ". . . reserves the right to accept or reject at any time any product offered for advertising over its facilities and to investigate the accuracy of all statements and claims made in commercial copy." The network ". . . also reserves the right to require elimination or revision of any material contrary to the public interest or inconsistent with the company's standards of truth and accuracy. Illustrations and text in demonstrations of advertisers' products on television programs shall faithfully represent the products themselves."

Regarding price and value claims, the standards state: "Statements of prices and values must be confined to specific facts. Misleading price claims and unfair comparisons tend to challenge the integrity of all advertising and must not be used."

Example F—Industry Association

The National Association of Broadcasters, composed of radio and television station owners throughout the U.S., adopted its Television Code in 1952 and has revised it periodically since. The Code outlines standards in program and advertising content to which television members of the NAB adhere.

In the section dealing with general advertising the Code states: ". . . a television broadcaster should, in recognition of his responsibility to the public, refuse the facilities of his station to an advertiser where he has good reason to doubt the integrity of the advertiser, the truth of the advertising representations, or the compliance of the advertiser with the spirit and purpose of all applicable legal requirements."

The Code also states: "The role and capability of television to market sponsors' products are well recognized. In turn, this fact dictates that great care be exercised by the broadcaster to prevent the presentation of false, misleading, or deceptive advertising. While it is entirely appropriate to present a product in a favorable light and atmosphere, the presentation must not, by copy or demonstration, involve a material deception as to the characteristics, performance, or appearance of the product."

Example G—Packaged Food Manufacturer

In its "Guidelines for Product Claim Support" one of the nation's leading packaged food manufacturers states that evidence from consumer research studies used to support a claim ". . . should be timely enough to have application to the current market situation. When market conditions dictate, more current research support will be required."

The guidelines state that in all cases the claim as stated in advertising must be supported. In addition, if there is an implied claim perceived by, or likely to be perceived by, a significant proportion of potential viewers or readers, then support must also be available for the implied claim, even if that claim is not intended.

Regarding market performance claims relating to the extent of broad usage or popularity, the guidelines require the support of accepted consumer or retail research measurements, such as Nielsen ratings, for any such claims.

Children, especially pre-schoolers, are highly dependent on the guidance and direction of the adult world around them—television included—for their individual development. Since children, especially when unsupervised by adults, may not in all situations be able to discern the credibility of what they watch, they pose an ethical responsibility for others to protect them from their own potential susceptibilities. However, broadcasters believe that advertising of products or services normally used by children can serve to inform children not only of the attributes of products/services but also of many aspects of the society and world in which they live. Everyone involved in the creation, production and presentation of such advertising to children has a responsibility to assure that such material avoids being exploitative of or inappropriate to a child's still developing cognitive abilities and sense of value.

Recognizing these special considerations the NAB Code Authority issues these Children's Television Advertising Guidelines designed to assist manufacturers, their agencies, and broadcasters in the preparation and evaluation of television commercials.

Except where hereinafter stated, or where advertising has been granted an exemption under the application of III. Adult Interpretation, these guidelines apply to advertising of products designed primarily for children, or to advertising designed primarily for children or to advertising which is telecast during programs designed primarily for children or within station breaks between such consecutive programs, designed primarily for children.

In addition to the following special guidelines, all such advertising is subject to review, where applicable, under the standards contained in the Television Code.

I. General

A. Documentation adequate to support the truthfulness and accuracy of all claims and representations contained in the audio or video of the advertisement must be made available upon request to broadcasters and/or the Code Authority.

B. The disclosure of information on the characteristics and functional aspects of a product/service is strongly encouraged. This includes, where applicable, relevant ingredient and nutritional information. In order to reduce the possibility of misimpressions being created, all such information shall be presented in a straightforward manner devoid of language or production techniques which may exaggerate or distort the characteristics or functions of the product.

C. Television advertisements shall not include presumptions that a product or service requiring material investment can be had for the asking. Children shall not be directed to purchase or to ask a parent or other adult to buy a product or service for them.

D. In order to help assure that advertising is non-exploitative in manner, style and tone, such advertising shall avoid using exhortative language. It shall also avoid employing irritating, obtrusive or strident audio techniques or video devices such as cuts of less than one second in length, a series of fast cuts, special effects of a psychedelic nature (e.g., flashing colors, flashing lights, flashing supered copy, or other effects which could overglamorize or mislead).

E. Any representation of a child's concept of himself/herself or of his/her relationship to others must be constructively handled. When self-concept claims are employed, the role of the product/service in affecting such promised benefits as strength, growth, physical prowess and growing up must accurately reflect documented evidence.

F. Advertisements shall not portray attitudes and practices inconsistent with generally recognized social values and customs.

G. Appeals shall not be used which directly or by implication contend that if children have a product they are better than their peers or lacking it will not be accepted by their peers.

H. Material shall not be used which

can reasonably be expected to frighten children or provoke anxiety, nor shall material be used which contains a portrayal of or appeal to violent, dangerous or otherwise anti-social behavior.

I. Advertisements and products advertised shall be consistent with generally recognized standards of safety Advertisements shall not include demonstrations of any product in a manner that encourages harmful use or dramatizations of actions inconsistent with generally recognized standards of safety.

J. The use of real-life authority figures/celebrities as product presenters shall not include their personal testimonials or endorsements.

K. Persons who are recognized as being identified, specifically or generically, with an advertised product's counterpart in real-life may not be used as spokespeople or endorsers. This prohibition also applies to actors representing such persons.

L. Non-prescription medications and supplemental vitamin products, regardless of how taken or administered, shall not be advertised in or adjacent to programs initially designed primarily for children under 12 years of age. (This prohibition does not apply to products which have been vitamin enriched or fortified in accordance with accepted nutritional principles.)

M. Advertisements shall not include dramatizations of any product in a realistic war atmosphere.

N. Over simplification or minimization of price such as "only" or "just" shall not be used.

Price may be employed in advertising only if it can be supported as the usual and customary price in a substantial number of retail outlets in the given trade area or areas where the advertising is scheduled.

O. Advertisements shall include audio and video disclosure when items such as batteries needed to operate a product as demonstrated in the advertising are not included.

P. Positive exposition of a product's own attributes are acceptable. However, because of their potential to encourage dissatisfaction on a child's part, competitive/comparison/superiority claims or techniques are disallowed.

Q. Advertising shall positively and clearly disclose a product's method of operation and source of power, where applicable.

R. Advertising shall disclose when a product requires assembly. There shall be no demonstration which creates the impression that a product comes fully assembled when such is not the case.

II. Products/Special Categories

A. Toys

In addition to the foregoing I. General precepts the following guidelines are applicable to all television toy advertising and to other advertising designed primarily for children which emphasizes a product's play value. Excepted are those commercials primarily designed for and directed to adults.

1. Advertising shall present the toy on its actual merit as a plaything. It shall neither exaggerate nor distort play value.

2. Audio and visual production techniques shall not misrepresent the appearance and performance of toys. Any view of a toy or any demonstration of its performance shall be limited to that which a child is reasonably capable of reproducing.

3. When a toy is presented in the context of a play environment, the setting and situation shall be that which a child is reasonably capable of reproducing.

4. The use of stock film footage, real-life counterparts of toys, fantasy and animation are acceptable if: (a) they are confined to the first one third of the commercial, (b) no child or toy appears within them and, (c) the commercial as a whole conforms to the Children's Television Advertising Guidelines.

Any other use of stock film footage, real-life counterparts, fantasy, and animation and any over-glamorization (e.g., large displays, dazzling visual effects) is not permitted.

5. The original purchase must be clearly disclosed in the body of the commercial. There shall not be any implication that optional extras, additional units or items that are not available with the toy, accompany the toy's original purchase.

In the closing five seconds of the commercial the original purchase must be disclosed by video with audio disclosure where necessary for clarification.

6. Advertising shall not employ costumes and props which are not available with the toy as sold or are not reasonably accessible to the child without additional cost.

B. Premiums and Offers

The Advertising Guidelines for Children's Premiums and Offers shall be applied to all advertising designed primarily for children which promotes premiums or offers. Excepted are those commercials which are primarily designed for and directed to adults.

1. The amount of time devoted to a premium or offer shall be a continuous segment and shall not exceed one half of the commercial or twenty seconds, whichever is less in length. If the premium/offer is related to and used with the product advertised, its incidental appearance in the product segment of the commercial will be permitted on a case-by-case basis.

2. The premium/offer shall at some time be displayed in a still visual presentation, so that it is clearly depicted.

3. In the premium/offer segment, the use of stock footage, real-life counterparts, fantasy or animation is not permitted. In order to maintain continuity, the product spokesperson may deliver a lead-in to the premium/offer segment, provided it contains no endorsement or sell copy for the premium or offer. Also for continuity, the voice-over used in the premium/offer segment may be that of the product spokesperson.

4. The number of items shown in a play situation shall not exceed two per child, or a maximum of four with two or more children, unless the possession of more by one child can be reasonably supported by the advertiser.

5. Positive disclosure of special information, such as the price or separate purchase nature of the items offered, shall be made in the audio. As deemed appropriate, supporting disclosure simultaneously in the video will be required.

6. If any conditions are attached to obtaining a "free" premium or offer, all the conditions must be clearly and conspicuously disclosed simultaneously in audio and video. The appearance of the word "free" in a video super shall not exceed in size that of the conditions disclosed.

7. Toy Advertising Guidelines and all Children's Television Advertising Guidelines shall apply where applicable to premiums and offers.

C. Food

All Children's Television Advertising Guidelines under I. General in addition to the following specific guidelines will apply to food advertising.

1. Given the importance of sound health and nutritional practices, advertisements for edibles shall be in accord with the commonly accepted principles of good eating and seek to establish the proper role of the advertised product within the framework of a balanced regimen. Any representation of the relationship between an edible and energy must be documented and accurately depicted.

2. Each commercial for breakfast-type products shall include at least one audio reference to and one video depiction of the role of the product within the framework of a balanced regimen.

3. Special, enriched foods designed to serve as a substitute for a meal may be advertised as such provided their purpose and nutritional value are featured in the advertising and supported by adequate documentation.

D. Snacks, Candy, Gum, and Soft Drinks

All Children's Television Advertising Guidelines under I. General in addition to the following guideline will apply to advertising for snacks, candy, gum and soft drinks.

1. Commercials for products such as snacks, candies, gums and soft drinks shall not suggest or recommend indiscriminate and/or immoderate use of the product.

E. Clothing

All Children's Television Advertising Guidelines, I. General, will apply to clothing advertising. In addition, where such advertising references the play value of clothing, the Toy Advertising Guidelines II. A. will also be applicable.

F. School/Educational Supplies

All Children's Television Advertising Guidelines, I. General, will apply to school/educational supply advertising. In addition, where such advertising references the play value of the product, the Toy Advertising Guidelines II. A. will also be applicable.

G. Feature Film Trailers

Feature films, other than those appropriate for a general family audience, shall not be advertised in or adjacent to programs initially designed primarily for children under 12 years of age.

III. Adult Interpretation

A. Advertising of any product covered by the foregoing categories if designed for and directed to adults, will be exempted from the application of the provisions of the Children's Television Advertising Guidelines provided:

1. The creative concept and execution of the commercial, both the audio and video, are clearly designed to appeal to adults and not primarily to children under 12.

2. Any use of a child is limited to a real-life situation and, if the child is used other than as an incidental, background character, such use is confined to a situation in which the parent/adult-child relationship is established and the parent/adult remains a principal character.

3. The broadcast schedule does not include the placing of the commercial in or adjacent to programs designed primarily for children.

4. The commercial complies with all applicable Television Code standards.

B. The advertising of any product designed primarily for use by adults shall be reviewed on a case-by-case basis to determine acceptability for telecast in or adjacent to programs designed primarily for children, taking into account safety and like considerations. Such advertising may be exempted from certain provisions of the Children's Television Advertising Guidelines (e.g., I-J, I-K, I-P).

Children's Television Advertising Guidelines History

I. Precursors

A. Toy Advertising Guidelines

1st ed.: 6/1/61 (a); 2nd ed.: 3/64 (p); Rev'd 2nd ed.: 12/65 (p) with interps. 4/70 (p), 6/70 (p), 11/70 (p) (all 2/1/71 (enlt)), 11/71 (p), 10/72 (p); Later Rev'd 2nd ed.: 1/1/75 (e).

B. Advertising Guidelines for Children's Premiums/Offers

1st ed.: 10/1/72 (e); Rev'd 1st ed.: 1/1/75.

C. Children's Advertising Statement of Principles

1st ed.: 1/1/74 (enlt); Interps.: 4/1/74 (e); 2nd ed.: 1/1/75.

II. Current Guidelines

A. 1st ed.: sec. II-G, 1/1/76 (e), other secs., 9/1/76 (e)

B. 2nd ed.: 4/77 (e), rev'd preface, sec. III-A, addl sec. III-B.

III. Annotations

A. Interp. arts. as publ'd in *Code News*, reprinted in Broadcast Self-Regulation (ref. subject index).

Key: (a)-adopted; (e)-effective; (enlt)-effective no later than; (p)-printed.

National Association
of Broadcasters
Code Authority
Advertising Guidelines-Radio

Effective September 1, 1973

Preamble

The use of illegal drugs and the abuse of legal prescription medicines, particularly among young people, are matters of grave public concern. The acts themselves and the consequences of the acts can have a most destructive effect on the lives of many individuals . . . users and non-users alike. They also have an undermining effect on many of the vital, positive aspects of our society.

Notwithstanding the scope and variety of efforts which are being made to understand and overcome the problems, there appears to be no simple explanation for and solution to the use of illegal drugs and the abuse of legal prescription medicines.

As to non-prescription medications, although no link between their advertising and drug abuse has been established, broadcasters have developed and continue to seek ways to improve upon standards governing the broadcast advertising of non-prescription medications. This reflects broadcaster awareness of and response to the continuing concern about indiscriminate use of, and undue reliance upon, chemical substances.

Responsible self-medication has played and continues to play an important role in the lives of many citizens. Sensibly pursued, it serves a constructive purpose.

The following Advertising Guidelines for Non-Prescription Medications, effective September 1, 1973, are applicable to all non-prescription medications administered internally (e.g., ingested, inhaled).

Previously promulgated guidelines covering the stimulant, calmative and sleeping-aid product categories are included hereunder with appropriate revisions.

The intent of the Guidelines is to encourage within affected advertising that which:

(a) provides factual information about the products, consistent with objective package/label information;

(b) avoids representations that a product will alter a user's mood or attitude beyond that reasonably experienced through the relief of symptoms/conditions for which the product has been proven effective;

(c) advises users to read and follow label instructions/cautions;

(d) avoids over-statements of a product's capabilities.

It is believed that the Guidelines will foster advertising approaches which will benefit the public interest.

The Guidelines are subject to extension and modification as needed.

I. General

A. Claims of product effectiveness, including comparative efficacy claims, must be substantiated by clinical, other scientific evidences or responsible medical opinion.

B. Advertisements shall contain an overt reference to the need to read and/or follow the product's labeling/directions/caution information.

C. Representations of a product's capabilities (palliative or other effects) shall not be over-stated. They shall be directed to symptoms/conditions for which the product is intended and for which substantiation has been supplied.

D. Claims of immediate relief or other immediate effects shall be confined to those products where clinical documentation supports the presentation. Before-and-after product use situations shall adequately reflect the time generally required to achieve relief of symptoms/conditions covered on labeling.

E. Audio approaches commonly associated with the "drug culture" or which imply a casual attitude toward the use of drugs and medications shall not be employed. A non-prescription medication shall not be advertised in a manner which is likely to result in its use for other than its indicated conditions, or in a manner which suggests or implies that it is other than a medicine.

F. The use of children shall not be permitted in presentations on behalf of non-prescription medications intended for adults. In advertisements for medications specifically formulated for children, the inclusion of youth or children shall be confined to situations involving responsible adult supervision. Any such presentation shall avoid audio approaches tending to capture the attention of children rather than adults.

G. Products shall be presented for occasional use only.

H. Depictions of reliance on non-prescription medications in order to deal with, or as a simplistic solution for, problems common to interpersonal relationships or other everyday problems shall not be permitted.

I. References to a non-prescription medication as "non-habit forming" or "non-addictive" shall not be permitted.

J. The use of authority figures/celebrities as product presenters shall not include their personal testimonials or endorsements.

K. The sound of pill/capsule taking shall not be permitted.

L. Specific identification of non-prescription medications by their color or over-emphasis on the color of the product shall not be permitted.

M. Advertisements for non-prescription medications shall not be scheduled in or adjacent to programs designed primarily for children.

II. Product Categories

A. Stimulants

1. If ingredients are referenced directly or indirectly, disclose common name where such exists and/or nature of principal ingredient (e.g., "contains caffeine," "equivalent to X cups of coffee").

2. The temporary nature of the product's effectiveness shall be overtly disclosed.

3. Product use to encourage the extension of one's normal abilities shall not be depicted.

4. Representations that a product will allow one to function adequately contrary to sound safety practices shall not be permitted.

5. Representations indicating that a product can provide physical energy shall not be permitted (e.g., "If simple fatigue wears you down, if you work too hard or rest too little, get pep and energy from product X").

6. Language indicating that a product will heighten one's spirits, such as "quick-lift," "more alive," "feel brighter," "pick up" shall not be permitted.

7. Direct or indirect references to or comparisons with prescription drugs shall not be permitted.

8. Contrasting "before and after" dramatizations shall not be permitted.

9. Representations of chronic conditions shall not be permitted.

10. Testimonials and endorsements shall not be permitted.

B. Calmatives

1. Reference to "tension" is acceptable only if qualified as "simple nervous tension" or its equivalent.

2. The temporary nature of the product's effectiveness shall be overtly disclosed.

3. Product use to encourage the extension of one's normal abilities shall not be depicted.

4. Representations that a product will allow one to function adequately contrary to sound safety practices shall not be permitted.

5. Language which tends to oversimplify or exaggerate the condition for which the product is used shall not be permitted (e.g., "depression," "tranquilized," "frustration," "nervous wreck," "anxiety," "up-tight").

6. Direct or indirect references to or comparisons with prescription drugs, shall not be permitted.

7. Contrasting "before and after" dramatizations shall not be permitted.

8. Representations of chronic conditions shall not be permitted.

9. Testimonials and endorsements shall not be permitted.

9. Testimonials and endorsements shall not be permitted.

C. Sleeping Aids

1. Representation of the product as a direct cause of rather than as an aid to sleep shall not be permitted.

2. Depiction of dependence on a drug or drugs in anticipation of next day's activities shall not be permitted.

3. If "tension" is mentioned as the cause of sleeplessness, it shall be qualified as "simple nervous tension" or its equivalent.

4. Direct or indirect references to or comparisons with prescription drugs shall not be permitted.

5. Representations of chronic conditions shall not be permitted.

6. Testimonials and endorsements shall not be permitted. ■

*Reprinted with permission from the National Association of Broadcasters Code Authority

National Association
of Broadcasters
Code Authority
Interpretation

Non-Prescription Medications Guidelines: Questions-and-Answers

As reported in the February issue of *Code News*, the Non-Prescription Medications Advertising Guidelines go into effect September 1, 1973.

On March 9, 1973, the Code Authority and over 30 broadcasters from the New York City area participated in an initial workshop session designed to help clarify anticipated applications of the new guidelines.

Interpretations reached at that session follow herewith in the form of representative questions and answers, and are offered to assist advertisers, their agencies and broadcasters in their review of television commercials for non-prescription medications. Advertisers are urged to take the initiative in reviewing their current commercials in order to help assure guideline-compliant treatment for schedules on and after the September 1, 1973, effective date.

Q. What products are covered by the guidelines?

A. The new guidelines are applicable to all non-prescription medications that are ingested, inhaled, or inserted. This includes medications that come in suppository form. Food supplement vitamins, toothpastes, toothpowders, denture cleansers and like products are not covered by the guidelines. Externally applied medications (e.g., dandruff and acne preparations) are also exempt from the guidelines.

Q. Do claims of product effectiveness, be they comparative or non-comparative in nature, require documentation?

A. Yes. In keeping with long-established broadcast self-regulatory policies, product effectiveness claims of any type must be substantiated by clinical, other scientific evidence or responsible medical opinion.

Q. How may an "overt reference" to the need to read and to follow the product's labeling/directions/caution information (Guideline I-B) be presented?

A. An "overt reference" may be presented in either the audio or video of the commercial.

Q. In terms of production techniques, do these groundrules cover the manner in which the "overt reference" to the need to read and/or follow the product's labeling/directions/caution information is made?

A. Yes. If the disclosure appears in the video, it must be (1) on the screen long enough (3-4 seconds) to be read easily, (2) large enough to be read easily, and (3) must be in an over-all video context that does not distract from the disclosure. These requirements apply to all affected commercials, regardless of length. If the disclosure is made in the audio, a statement unequivocally comprising an "overt reference" must be used.

Q. What type of language would satisfy the acceptable "overt reference" requirement?

A. If the product's package label/instruction sheet contains no special caution or qualifying information about the use of the product, then such clauses as "use as directed," "read label information" and "use in accordance with instructions" are acceptable. However, if the product's package label contains special caution information about the product's use, language such as "use only as directed" should be used.

Q. If a phrase such as "safe when used as directed" appears in commercial copy, is the qualifier which accompanies "safe" sufficient to meet the "overt reference" required under Guideline I-B-7?

A. No. When the qualifier is used in conjunction with the copy claim "safe," it alone does not meet the "overt reference" requirement. A separate "overt reference" is needed in audio or video.

Q. How can the symptoms/conditions for which the product is intended be determined (I-C)?

A. The symptoms/conditions for which the product is intended are listed in the label information.

Q. What is meant by the second sentence of the Non-Prescription Medications Guideline I-D: "Portrayals of before-and-after product use situations shall adequately reflect the time generally required to achieve relief of symptoms/conditions covered on labeling?

A. The statement is intended to emphasize the requirement that advertising for non-prescription medications should clearly indicate the time generally required to achieve relief of symptoms/conditions covered on labeling. The time required to achieve such relief may be established in either the audio or video of the commercial. If video, the passage of time may be indicated by various devices. However, quick dissolves or similar techniques are to be avoided because of their potential to mislead. "Before-and-after" portrayals, if used, should also avoid dramatic "after" effects such as users performing/enjoying their lives as though they had not had the need for self-medication.

A. Verbal expressions which tend to exaggerate the effects of potency of the non-prescription medication are to be avoided.

A. Facial expressions relating to post-use effects of a medication must be restrained and will be reviewed carefully.

Q. May a child appear in a commercial designed to promote the sale of a non-prescription medication in two strengths—one for children, the other for adults?

A. No. Under Guideline I-F of the Non-Prescription Medications Guidelines, "the use of children shall not be permitted in presentations on behalf of non-prescription medications intended for adults." This requirement holds precedence, even though a segment of the commercial is devoted to the promotion of a medication specifically formulated for children.

Q. What age group comprises the "children" category under the Non-Prescription Medications Guidelines?

A. "Children" shall be taken to mean those 12 years of age or younger.

Q. Does a commercial for a child's non-prescription medication which employs a parental voice-over and visuals of children at play meet the requirement of Guideline I-F that "the appearance of youth or children shall be present only in situations involving responsible adult supervision"?

A. No, it does not. In children's non-prescription medications advertisements, relationship between the youth/child and parent must be established if youth/children are used. The parent should be presented as the responsible supervisor of the situation.

Q. Guideline I-G states: "Products shall be presented for occasional use only." What is meant by "occasional use?"

A. The intent of the phrase is to disallow commercials which portray continuing, day-in, day-out use of non-prescription medications.

Q. May "occasional use" be established in either audio or video?

A. Yes.

Q. If Guideline I-G and I-H preclude the depictions of reliance on non-prescription medications to cope with everyday problems, do they necessarily also preclude the use of "slice-of-life" advertising techniques?

A. No, they do not per se preclude "slice-of-life" advertising techniques, so long as the commercial clearly shows that the use of the non-prescription medication is confined to treating the symptom/condition and not one's ability to handle these everyday problems.

National Association
of Broadcasters
Code Authority
Interpretation

Q. May "authority figures/celebrities" be used to present an ad?

A. Yes, if they do not personally endorse, or give a testimonial for the product they are presenting.

Q. What class of non-prescription medications is Guideline I-L intended to cover?

A. Guideline I-L ("Specific identification of non-prescription medications by their color or video over-emphasis on the color of the product shall not be permitted.") encompasses pills/tablets/capsules—color identification of which is sometimes associated with the "drug culture." The portion of Guideline I-L which reads: "... video over-emphasis on the color of the product shall not be permitted" applies to all affected non-prescription medications. ■

April 73 CN

More Q & A's on Non-Prescription Medications Guides

On April 6 the proprietary advertising subcommittee of the Television Code Review Board met to further discuss the newly adopted Non-Prescription Medications guidelines (*Code News*, February, March, 1973).

In the meeting, questions raised by various advertisers regarding specific applications of the guidelines were reviewed. The results are offered hereunder as an additional interpretive guide to advertisers, their agencies and broadcasters dealing with the advertising of affected non-prescription medications.

Q. Will exemptions from compliance with the Non-Prescription Medications guidelines be allowed in the case of commercials less than 10 seconds in length?

A. No. There should be no exemptions from any of the guidelines because of an ad's length.

Q. Do external rubs fall in the category of products governed by the Non-Prescription Medications guidelines?

A. The guidelines are applicable to product commercials for external rubs if the commercials contain references to/depictions of the inhalation of the vapors which may emanate from the rubs.

Q. Is minority medical opinion acceptable as documentation for an over-the-counter medication copy claim?

A. Minority medical opinion is acceptable as documentation for an OTC copy claim provided 1) the minority opinion represents responsible sources, 2) full and clear disclosure is made in the commercial regarding the minority aspect of the responsible opinion and 3) full and clear disclosure is made in the commercial regarding the existence of the majority opinion. Depending on specific circumstances, a disclaimer such as, "Contrary to the prevailing majority point of view..." could satisfy the third requirement given above.

Q. Would a video shot of appropriate language on a product's label satisfy the "overt reference" requirement I-B?

A. A video shot of appropriate language on a product's label could satisfy the "overt reference" requirement I-B. If this technique is employed, the specific "overt reference" language must be isolated from any distracting elements and must be of the type that would normally meet the disclaimer requirements of I-B. Each proposed use of this technique should be reviewed carefully to help assure compliance with the applicable guideline.

Q. Is a 60-second multiple product announcement consisting of a 30-second commercial for an adult proprietary product in which no children appear and a 30-second commercial for a children's proprietary product in which children appear—under adult supervision—acceptable under I-F?

A. Yes. Guideline I-F also does not preclude the back-to-back scheduling of a 30-second commercial for an adult proprietary product and a separate 30-second commercial for a children's proprietary product in which children appear.■

Mar 73 CN

*Reprinted with permission from National Association of Broadcasters Code Authority

children's advertising guidelines

REVISED SEPTEMBER 1977

CHILDREN'S ADVERTISING REVIEW UNIT
National Advertising Division
Council of Better Business Bureaus, Inc.
845 Third Avenue, New York, N.Y. 10022

CHILDREN'S ADVERTISING GUIDELINES

Preamble

These guidelines have been developed for the use of advertisers and advertising agencies and for the self-regulatory mechanism which they have established, the National Advertising Division, to help ensure that advertising directed to children is truthful, accurate and fair to children's perceptions.

Because trends in advertising are continually changing and because research and study are constantly shedding new light on children's development and understanding of advertising, these Guidelines have been revised and will continue to be revised periodically as circumstances dictate.

In this second revision, modifications have been made in sections D (Presentation) and E (Promotion by Program Characters etc.). Specifically, subsections D-3, 6, and 10 have been added and subsections D-8 (formerly D-6) and D-9 (formerly D-7) and E-1, 2 have been expanded. In addition, word changes, which clarify the text, have been made in several places.

Principles

Five basic Principles underlie these Guidelines for advertising directed to children:

I. Advertisers should always take into account the level of knowledge, sophistication and maturity of the audience to which their message is primarily directed. Since younger children have a limited capability for evaluating the credibility of what they watch, they place a special responsibility upon advertisers to protect them from their own susceptibilities.

II. Realizing that children are imaginative and that make-believe play constitutes an important part of the growing up process, advertisers should exercise care not to exploit that imaginative quality of children. Unreasonable expectations of product quality or performance should not be stimulated either directly or indirectly by advertising.

III. Recognizing that advertising may play an important part in educating the child, information should be communicated in a truthful and accurate manner with full recognition by the advertiser that the child may learn practices from advertising which can affect his or her health and well-being.

IV. Advertisers are urged to capitalize on the potential of advertising to influence social behavior by developing advertising that, wherever possible, addresses itself to social standards generally regarded as positive and beneficial, such as friendship, kindness, honesty, justice, generosity and respect for others.

V. Although many influences affect a child's personal and social development, it remains the prime responsibility of the parents to provide guidance for children. Advertisers should contribute to this parent-child relationship in a constructive manner.

A. Interpretation

Advertisers are reminded that the interpretation of these Guidelines should conform to and implement the Principles stated above. The intent in all cases should be to deal fairly and honestly with children, fulfilling the spirit as well as the letter of the Guidelines. Each individual commercial or advertisement should be considered in that context. Differences in the nature of broadcast media and print media should be taken into account. The Guidelines should not be regarded as prescribing rigid or inflexible rules which may deprive children and advertisers of the benefits of innovations and new approaches.

B. Scope

The clauses in these Guidelines embrace advertising designed to appeal to children eleven years of age and under. This includes children's advertising which is broadcast in children's programs and programs in which audience patterns typically contain more than 50% children. Commercials appearing in shows in which children are a substantial audience segment, but less than 50%, will be regarded as subject to these Guidelines only when they are clearly addressed to children eleven and under. Print advertising is subject to these Guidelines when it is primarily directed to or primarily read by children.

C. Social Values

Advertising should emphasize positive social and moral values and enrich the dignity of human life, and should avoid portrayals of violence, appeals to fear, or prejudice of any kind. To this end:

1. Advertisements should never portray as desirable any practices which are generally considered unacceptable from the standpoint of social, legal, moral, institutional or family

values. Social stereotyping which is demeaning or derogatory to any group should be avoided.

2. Advertisements should not reflect disdain for parents or parental judgment, nor reflect unfavorably on other generally recognized sources of child guidance.

3. Advertisements should never portray undesirable living habits. Advertising should convey respect for others and the world in which the child lives. Civility and good manners should be encouraged.

4. Advertisements should encourage good use of language. This does not preclude informal usage.

5. Advertisements should avoid the contention that, by possessing a product, a child will be more accepted by his peers, or by lacking it, he or she will be less accepted by his peers.

6. Advertisements should avoid the implication that a parent or adult who purchases a given product or service for a child is better or more generous than one who does not.

7. Advertisements should not falsely imply that purchase and use of a product will confer upon the user the prestige, skills, or other special qualities of characters appearing in the commercial or ad. Material benefits attributed to the product or service should be inherent in the use thereof.

D. Presentation

Children have vivid imaginations. Use of imagination enables a child to project himself beyond his immediate capacities and reach for his future potential. Advertisers should, therefore, always respect a child's imagination. The use of imaginative situations appropriate to the audience concerned is an acceptable and normal communications practice. Implicit in the foregoing is the concept that fantasy, including animation, is an appropriate form of communication to any audience, including the very young. However, the use of special situations and fantasy in advertising should not suggest unattainable expectations of performance. To achieve this, presentations should not exploit the child's difficulty in distinguishing between the real and the fanciful. Therefore:

1. Copy, sound and visual presentations--as well as the advertisement in its totality--should not mislead (a) on performance characteristics such as speed, method of operation, size, color, durability, nutritional benefits, noise, etc.; (b) on perceived benefits such as the acquisition of strength, popularity, growth, proficency, intelligence and the like; or (c) on the expectation of price range or cost of the product.

2. The advertisement should clearly establish what is included in the original purchase of a product. When items are to be purchased separately, the fact should

be disclosed in a way that is clear to the child audience primarily addressed. Advertising for all products sold unassembled should indicate that assembly is required. If any other product is essential in order to use the advertised product--such as batteries--this should be disclosed.

3. In general, information which requires disclosure for legal or other reasons should be in language understandable by the child audience to which the advertisement is addressed. In television advertising, audio as well as video disclosure is encouraged. In all media, disclaimers, when used, should be clearly worded, legible, and prominent.

4. A clearly depicted presentation of the complete advertised product should be shown in the advertisement. Where appropriate to help identify the product, the package may also be depicted, provided it does not mislead as to product characteristics, content, or the price range to be expected.

5. Advertising demonstrations should show the use of a product or premium in a way that can be duplicated by the child for whom the product is intended.

6. An effort should be made to establish the size of a product clearly and adequately. This is of particular importance when size claims are being used, such as "giant sized," "monster size," etc.

7. Representation of food products should be made so as to encourage sound usage of the product with a view toward healthy development of the child and the development of good nutritional practices. Advertisements representing mealtime in the home should clearly and adequately depict the role of the product within the framework of a balanced diet. Over-consumption of food products and beverages should be avoided, nor should it be implied that any one food provides all the nutrients contained in a well-designed daily food plan.

8. To ensure truthful and accurate representations of playthings in television advertisements, they should be shown in normal play environments and situations, except when the number of products to be featured exceeds what would reasonably be owned by the child or children shown in the play situation.

9. Should a whole line of toys or more toys than might reasonably be owned by the average child be featured, in a television advertisement, limbo settings (which are defined as non-representational settings with a plain background) or in-store settings are suggested. These settings might provide a better context for fair demonstration of such products to children. When representing large lines of products (in print or television) special care should be

taken to ensure that the child will understand the separate purchase requirements.

10. When toys or any other product can be purchased either individually or as a collection of related items, price representation, if any, should clearly indicate to the child that the cost of the collection is greater than the cost of the individual item.

E. Promotion by Program Character, Editorial Character or Personal Endorsement

It is recognized that very young children may not fully recognize differences between editorial and program content and advertising content. Hence, endorsement by characters on the programs or in the editorial content of a publication may confuse children. Therefore:

1. Program personalities or characters, either live or animated, on children's programs should not be used to promote products, premiums or services in or adjacent to any program(s) in which the personality or character appears. Similarly, when a product resembling the program personality or character is advertised within a program in which the person or character appears, care should be taken to clearly differentiate between the content of the advertisement and the content of the program.

2. In print media, characters and personalities associated with the editorial content of a publication should not be used to promote products, premiums or services in the same publication. Nor should elements from the editorial content be used in such a way as to prevent the child from readily distinguishing the advertisement from the editorial content.

3. Subject to paragraph (1) of this section, "product characters"--personalities live or animated who are closely associated with or identified with the product--may be used as presenters for the advertised product or service, provided they do not do or say anything to mislead children as to the product or service concerned.

4. Nationally known persons may not be used to attribute a characteristic or quality to a product (including a premium) unless they are generally recognized as qualified to speak on the subject. All personal endorsements should reflect the real experience and beliefs of the endorser.

F. Comparative Claims

It is recognized that advertising which compares the advertised product to another product may be difficult for children to understand and evaluate and may therefore be misunderstood. Therefore, advertisers are urged to present products on their merits without reference to competition.

In the event that a true and significant advantage may exist in a product which can be readily understood by children, this advantage should be clearly explained. If advertisers do develop comparative advertising to children this should be done with the following cautions in mind:

1. Comparative statements should be informational and not demeaning to other products or to previous versions of the same product.
2. Comparative statements should not suggest that the advertised product is superior to another in individual attributes or overall characteristics unless such statements can be documented.
3. Comparative statements implying overall superiority should be avoided when such statements are based on attributes in which the advertised product excels, and where the competitor's product excels in other attributes not mentioned.
4. Comparative price statements should be based on the usual and customary price paid in a substantial number of sales in the trade area where the advertising is carried. Price comparisons should be understandable to the average child for whom the product is intended.

G. Pressure to Purchase

The purpose of advertising to children is to encourage trial and repeat purchases. However, children are not as prepared to make independent decisions–or contribute to family decisions– as are adults. Accordingly, to avoid undue pressure to purchase:

1. Children should not be urged to ask parents or others to buy any products.
2. Products which by their very nature are not primarily intended for use by children should not employ advertising directed to children; nor should such products be promoted by premiums or other means directly to children.
3. All price representations should be clearly and concisely set forth in a manner so as not to exert undue pressure to purchase, and price minimizations such as "only" or "just" should not be used in any advertising directed to children.

H. Safety

For the child, imitation, exploration and experimentation are important facets of the learning process. The various media can enhance this process, as can advertising in each of the media which the child encounters. Recognizing this, advertisers should guide their advertising to contribute to the establishment of safe and sound habits in children. Moreover, children, and occasionally parents, may not be cognizant of hazards that may exist through use or abuse of products. Therefore:

1. Advertisements should not portray adults or children in

any unsafe acts, situations or conditions or in acts which are harmful to others.

2. Advertisements should avoid demonstrations or portrayals that encourage misuse, or dangerous or inappropriate use of the product which is inconsistent with generally accepted standards of safety.

3. Medications, drugs and supplemental vitamins (liquid or pills) should not be advertised to children.

I. Claim Substantiation

In accordance with the basic principle of dealing fairly and honestly with children:

1. Advertising to children should not claim or imply any product or performance characteristics which are not supportable by factual data or research which conforms to sound professional practices.

2. Puffery (defined as "flattering publicity" or "extravagant commendation") is not acceptable support for an objective product claim. Advertising claims which might be construed as literally true must be literally true.

J. Additional Guidelines for Premium Advertising

The use of premiums in advertising has potential to enhance the appeal of a product to a child. Special attention should, therefore, be paid to the use of premiums in advertising. To guard against premiums exploiting the children's immaturity:

1. Care should be taken that the child's attention is focused primarily on the product rather than the premium. Therefore, major emphasis should be given to the product and its benefits. Emphasis on the premium should be clearly secondary.

2. It is recognized that limitation of the time devoted to a premium offer within a commercial may not be sufficient to ensure primary attention to the product offer. Therefore, advertisers are urged to weigh all factors, including time, to ensure that the product message is primary.

3. When a premium offer is used, the conditions of the offer should be stated simply, in terms which a child can understand. Every effort should be made to communicate so-called "mandatory" statements and disclaimers in terms which will be understood by a child audience.

BBB

CHILDREN'S ADVERTISING REVIEW UNIT
National Advertising Division
Council of Better Business Bureaus, Inc.
845 Third Avenue, New York, N.Y. 10022

Opinion of the Commission

I. *The Proceedings.*

By Commissioner KIRKPATRICK: On July 15, 1970, the Federal Trade Commission issued its complaint alleging that Pfizer, Inc., had violated Section 5 of the Federal Trade Commission Act. Respondent Pfizer contested the allegations of this complaint and the matter was assigned to a hearing examiner for a hearing. The hearing examiner decided that the Commission's staff counsel had failed to establish that an order to cease and desist should issue. Counsel supporting the complaint have appealed the examiner's decision to the Commission. Upon consideration of the record of the proceedings before the hearing examiner, the examiner's initial decision, and the briefs and arguments of the parties, the Commission has decided that the decision of the hearing examiner should be affirmed.

II. *The Complaint.*

The Commission's staff counsel, who have the burden of proving the allegations of the complaint, challenge certain advertising by Pfizer for the product "UN-BURN," a nonprescription product recommended for use on minor burns and sunburn. The complaint cited the following radio and television advertising for Un-Burn as typical and representative:

> "New Un-Burn actually anesthetizes *nerves* in sensitive sunburned skin."
>
> "Un-Burn relieves pain *fast*. Actually *anesthetizes nerves* in sensitive sunburned skin."
>
> "Sensitive skin . . . Sunburned skin is sensitive skin . . . . Sensitive sunburned skin needs . . . UN-BURN. New UN-BURN contains the same local anesthetic doctors often use . . . . Actually anesthetizes nerves in sensitive sunburned skin. I'll tell you what I like about UN-BURN. It's the best friend a blonde ever had! . . . . I'm a blonde . . . and I know what it means to have sensitive skin. Why I'm half afraid of moon burn! That's why I'm mad about UN-BURN. It stops sunburn pain in . . . less time than it takes me to slip out of my bikini. That's awfully nice to know when you're the sensitive type . . . ."[1]

The complaint alleges that the foregoing advertising claims were not substantiated by Pfizer by "adequate and well-controlled scientific studies or tests prior to the making of such statements."

Based on these facts, complaint counsel set forth charges alleging two separate and distinct violations of Section 5 of the Federal Trade Commission Act—first, a charge of unlawful deception, and second, a charge of unlawful unfairness. The deception charge alleged that Pfizer's advertising constituted a *deceptive practice* in representing to consumers that "each of the statements respecting the pain-relieving properties of the said product has been substantiated by respondent by adequate and well-controlled scientific studies or tests prior to the making of such statements." The unfairness charge rests upon the proposition that it is an *unfair practice* to make advertising claims of this nature lacking adequate and well-controlled studies or tests.

III. *Deception.*

Section 5 of the Federal Trade Commission Act provides that deceptive acts or practices in commerce are unlawful. In Section 5 advertising cases, the requisite "acts or practices" have usually taken one of three forms: (1) advertising containing direct representations, (2) advertising containing representations which reasonably may be said to be implied by the adver-

[1] As recommended by the hearing examiner in his initial decision, during the oral argument before it the Commission observed the TV commercials being challenged, and listened to the radio tapes. (See I. D., p. 6-7, CX 4, 5, 6, 7.) These advertisements for Un-Burn contain two primary representations: (1) Un-Burn will actually anesthetize nerves in sunburned skin; (2) Un-Burn will stop sunburn pain fast.

tising, or (3) advertising which fails to disclose material facts. The Commission may utilize its accumulated "expertise" in analyzing the facts of each case to determine what direct and implied representations are contained in advertising.[2] Its expertise is also utilized in evaluating what facts are material to consumers, and thereby to determine the situations in which material facts have not been disclosed. A sufficient showing of deception is made if there exists a "capacity to deceive."[3] In evaluating the capacity of an advertisement to deceive, the net impression of the advertisement, evaluated from the perspective of the audience to whom the advertising is directed, is controlling.

It is against the foregoing regulatory framework that the deception charge in this case must be viewed.

While there were many direct representations contained in the Un-Burn advertising, they are not being challenged. Thus, unlike most deceptive advertising cases, the truth or falsity, or deceptiveness, of advertising claims such as "*New* Un-Burn," or "actually anesthetizes nerves," or "relieves pain fast" is *not* an issue in this proceeding. The complaint does charge, however, that respondent's advertising, both directly and by implication, represented that each of the statements respecting the pain-relieving properties of Un-Burn *has been substantiated* by respondent by adequate and well-controlled scientific studies or tests *prior* to the making of such statements.

Complaint counsel have not undertaken to prove explicit deception, but rather are relying solely upon the Commission's expertise to find that the implied representation is reasonably contained in the advertising, and that it has the capacity to deceive consumers.[4] Complaint counsel argue that Un-Burn's advertising *implied* that—*each* statement in advertising—respecting pain-relieving properties—has been substantiated—by respondent—by adequate—and well-controlled —scientific tests—or studies—conducted *prior* to the making of such statements. Thus, we are urged, for example, to make the following distinctions: (1) between "pain-relieving properties," and other claims of product efficacy, content, speed and method of operation; (2) between substantiation "by respondent," and substantiation which may have been "by someone else" (competitors, doctors, consumers, independent laboratories, etc.); (3) between a very precise type of substantiation ("adequate and well-controlled scientific studies or tests"), and other possible standards of substantiation (*e. g.*, adequate substantiation, usual and customary steps, reasonable basis, reliable, comprehensive, etc.); (4) between "scientific studies or tests" and other possible bases for substantiation, such as medical literature, clinical experience, consumer experience; and (5) between "prior" testing and a reasonable basis for belief, or subsequent tests.

Complaint counsel argue that respondent's advertising represented to consumers that Un-Burn is a drug which actually anesthetizes nerves in sensitive sunburned skin, and which will provide fast and total relief of sunburn pain. Complaint counsel cite the phrase "anesthetizes nerves fast" and the advertising references to doctors as statements which consumers will associate with scientific proof of the product's efficacy and as implying medical approbation of Un-Burn. In response, respondent argues that the total setting of the ad, the frivolous nature of the dialogue, the use of a bikinied model, and the general "aura of sexiness" prevent the ad, taken as a whole, from carrying the scientific overtones argued by complaint counsel.

Complaint counsel's sixth proposed finding of fact would hold that respondent represented by implication that the statements that Un-Burn anesthetizes nerves in sensitive skin and stops sunburn pain fast have been substantiated by respondent by "adequate evidence" prior to the making of such statements. Complaint counsel's seventh proposed finding of fact, on the other hand, goes further. It is there argued that by representing that they had "adequate evidence" to substantiate their advertising claims, respondent thereby impliedly represented that they possessed adequate and well-controlled scientific studies or tests which substantiated such claims. The Commission does not believe that such an implied representation can reasonably be found in respondent's advertising.

IV. *Unfairness.*

The Commission's jurisdiction to proscribe "unfair" commercial practices has been utilized frequently as an independent

[2] *FTC v. Colgate Palmolive Co.* [1965 TRADE CASES ¶ 71,409], 380 U. S. 374 (1965).

[3] See Gellhorn, *Proof of Consumer Deception Before the Federal Trade Commission,* 17 Kansas L. Rev. 559 (1969).

[4](O. A. Tr., p. 4). Complaint counsel frame their argument in the following terms:

"[I]t is obvious that (1) because respondent's advertising clearly represented that Un-Burn is a drug that will stop sunburn pain fast (Tr. 779), (2) because the public believes that an advertiser cannot make false claims about his product (Tr. 774, 776, 778), (3) because the public expects a product to work (Tr. 778, 779), and (4) because the public expects a manufacturer to have evidence that his product will work as claimed (Tr. 778, 779, 780, 781), respondent did in fact represent in its advertising that each of the statements respecting the pain relieving properties claimed for Un-Burn had been substantiated by respondent with adequate and reliable evidence and that this evidence was obtained prior to the making of such statements." (Complaint counsel's appeal brief, pp. 5 & 6.)

basis for Commission action.[5] Most often the term is coupled, perhaps in an effort to add direction and content, either to the deceptive or to the restrictive aspects of the practice in question.[6] The Commission, of course, has been delegated the power by Congress to give definition and content to the term "unfair practices."[7] The 1938 Wheeler-Lea Amendment made it clear that this jurisdiction extends to the protection of consumers:

> ". . . this amendment makes the consumer, who may be injured by an unfair trade practice, of equal concern, before the law, with the merchant or manufacturer injured by the unfair methods of a dishonest competitor."[8]

The Commission's responsibilities with regard to unfair trade practices were analyzed in its 1969 *All-State Industries* opinion:[9]

> "[T]he responsibility of the Commission in this respect is a dynamic one: it is charged not only with preventing well-understood, clearly defined, unlawful conduct but with utilizing its broad powers of investigation and its accumulated knowledge and experience in the field of trade regulation to investigate, identify, and define those practices which should be forbidden as unfair because contrary to the public policy declared in the Act. The Commission, in short, is expected to proceed not only against practices forbidden by statute or common law, but also against practices not previously considered unlawful, and thus to create a new body of law—a law of unfair trade practices adapted to the diverse and changing needs of a complex and evolving competitive system."

The recent *S & H* case sets forth a succinct confirmation of the Commission's jurisdiction over unfair practices:

> "[T]he Federal Trade Commission does not arrogate excessive power to itself if, in measuring a practice against the elusive, but congressionally mandated standard of fairness, it, like a court of equity, considers public values beyond simply those enshrined in the letter or encompassed in the spirit of the antitrust laws."[10]

In footnoting this statement, the court said:

> "The Commission has described the factors it considers in determining whether a practice which is neither in violation of the antitrust laws nor deceptive is nonetheless unfair:
>
> '(1), whether the practices, without necessarily having been previously considered unlawful, offends public policy as it has been established by statutes, the common law, or otherwise—whether, in other words, it is within at least the penumbra of some common law, statutory, or other established concept of unfairness; (2) whether it is immoral, unethical, oppressive or unscrupulous, (3) whether it causes substantial injury to consumers (or competitors or other businessmen).' 'Statement of Basis and Purpose of Trade Regulation Rule 408 [Unfair or Deceptive Advertising and Labelling of Cigarettes in Relation to the Health Hazards of Smoking].' 29 Fed. Reg. 8324, 8355 (1964)."

An unfairness analysis will take into account many basic economic facts and considerations, and will permit a broad focus in the examination of marketing practices. Unfairness is potentially a dynamic analytical tool capable of a progressive, evolving application which can keep pace with a rapidly changing economy.[11] Thus as consumers products and marketing practices change in number, complexity, variety, and function, standards of fairness to the consumer may also change.

Generally, the individual consumer is at a distinct disadvantage compared to the producer or distributor of goods in reaching conclusions concerning the reliability of product claims. Very often the price of a consumer product is sufficiently low that the cost to the consumer of obtaining relevant product information exceeds the benefits resulting from the increased satisfaction achieved thereby. In other cases, the complexity of a consumer product, and accordingly the large amount of detailed product information necessary to an informed decision, makes the costs of obtaining product information prohibitive. This problem is further magnified by the large number of compet-

[5] *Cf. All-State Industries, et al.*, Docket No. 8738 (April 1, 1969) [1970 TRADE CASES ¶ 73,112], 423 F. 2d 423 (1970), *cert. denied*, 400 U. S. 828 (1970); *FTC v. R. F. Keppel & Bros., Inc.* [1932-1939 TRADE CASES ¶ 55,042], 291 U. S. 304 (1934); *Wolf v. FTC* [1940-1943 TRADE CASES ¶ 56,326], 135 F. 2d 564 (7th Cir.) (1943); *First Buckingham Community, Inc.*, Docket 8750 (May 20, 1968); *Chemway Corporation*, Docket C-1945 (June 14, 1971).

[6] See, *e. g.*, *Topper Corporation, et al.*, Docket C-2073 (November 1, 1971).

[7] *FTC v. Sperry & Hutchinson*, Docket 8671 (June 1968), *rev'd* [1970 TRADE CASES ¶ 73,337], 432 F. 2d 146 (5th Cir. 1970), *rev'd* [1972 TRADE CASES ¶ 73,861], 405 U. S. 233 (March 1, 1972).

[8] H. R. Rep. No. 163, 75th Cong. 1st Session, p. 3 (1937).

[9] Slip opinion at p. 11.

[10] *Federal Trade Commission v. Sperry & Hutchinson Co., supra.*

[11] See *FTC v. Standard Education Society*, 86 F. 2d 692, 696 (2d Cir. 1936), *rev'd on other grounds* [1932-1939 TRADE CASES ¶ 55,170], 302 U. S. 112 (1937) (Hand, J.):

"[The Commission's] powers are not confined to such practices as would be unlawful before it acted; they are more than procedural; its duty in part at any rate, is to discover and make explicit those unexpressed standards of fair dealing which the conscience of the community may progressively develop."

ing products on the market.[12] Thus, with the development and proliferation of highly complex and technical products, there is often no practical way for consumers to ascertain the truthfulness of affirmative product claims prior to buying and using the product. When faced with a vast selection of products to choose from, the typical family unit is not sufficiently large enough, and its requirements are too varied, to allow detailed investigation of the goods to be purchased. The consumer simply cannot make the necessary tests or investigations to determine whether the direct and affirmative claims made for a product are true.

Given the imbalance of knowledge and resources between a business enterprise and each of its customers, economically it is more rational, and imposes far less cost on society, to require a manufacturer to confirm his affirmative product claims rather than impose a burden upon each individual consumer to test, investigate, or experiment for himself. The manufacturer has the ability, the know-how, the equipment, the time and the resources to undertake such information by testing or otherwise—the consumer usually does not.

[*Reasonable Basis*]

Turning to that part of the complaint which challenges respondent's marketing practices as unfair, the Commission is of the view that it is an unfair practice in violation of the Federal Trade Commission Act to make an affirmative product claim without a reasonable basis for making that claim. Fairness to the consumer, as well as fairness to competitors, dictates this conclusion. Absent a reasonable basis for a vendor's affirmative product claims, a consumer's ability to make an economically rational product choice, and a competitor's ability to compete on the basis of price, quality, service or convenience, are materially impaired and impeded. The balance of this opinion will concern itself with an analysis of the reasonable basis standard in relation to the record before us.

The consumer is entitled, as a matter of marketplace fairness, to rely upon the manufacturer to have a "reasonable basis" for making performance claims. A consumer should not be compelled to enter into an economic gamble to determine whether a product will or will not perform as represented. The economic gamble involved in a consumer's reliance upon affirmative product claims is created by the vendors' activities, and cannot be easily avoided by consumers. Taking a different analytical perspective and weighing the minimal cost and burden on vendors by requiring that there be a reasonable basis for affirmative product claims, against economic losses to consumers which can fairly be ascribed to advertising claims lacking such reasonable basis (losses which are, in a practical sense, unavoidable for the consumer), it is likewise clear that economic fairness requires that this obligation be imposed on vendors.[13] The record reflects the fact that the cost to a consumer of a visit to a dermatologist to obtain a prescription drug is sufficiently high that most persons with sunburn utilize an over-the-counter commercial preparation (Tr. 1031-1032). Thus, the consumer is to a great degree dependent on the manufacturer for information concerning products of this type.

In addition, fairness to competitors requires that the vendor have a reasonable basis for his affirmative product claims. A sale made as a result of an unsupported advertising claim deprives competitors of the opportunity to have made that sale for themselves.

This view finds direct support in the recent decision in *Leon A. Tashof v. F. T. C.*[14] There, the Commission found that a retailer falsely advertised that his products were available at discount prices. The Commission in effect ordered the respondent to stop advertising that he sold any product at a discount price unless he had a reasonable basis for such a claim. In view of this retailer's past history, the Commission prescribed a specific type of "reasonable basis" —the Commission ordered that the respondent, before advertising that he sells at discount prices, must take a statistically significant survey to demonstrate that prevailing market prices are substantially above respondent's prices. In affirming the Commission's decision, the Court expressly noted that this order subjected the respondent to civil penalties if the respondent advertises

[12] In the over-the-counter drug field, for example, it has been estimated that there are between 100,000 and 200,000 products available. (Statement of Dr. Charles C. Edwards, Commissioner, Food and Drug Administration, in Hearings Before the Subcommittee on Monopoly of the Select Committee on Small Business, 92d Congress, 1st Session, May 25, 1971, Part 1.)

[13] Compare Fletcher, *Fairness and Utility in Tort Theory,* 85 Harv. L. Rev. 537, 542 (1972).

> "Reasonableness is determined by a straightforward balancing of costs and benefits. If the risk yields a net social utility (benefit), the victim is not entitled to recover from the risk-creator; if the risk yields a net social disutility (cost), the victim is entitled to recover. The premises of this paradigm are that reasonableness provides a test of activities that ought to be encouraged and that tort judgments are an appropriate medium for encouraging them."

This balance admittedly gives more consideration to the producers' interests than does the test suggested by Adam Smith: "[T]he interest of the producer ought to be attended to only so far as it may be necessary for promoting that of the consumer." Smith, *An Inquiry Into The Nature and Causes of the Wealth of Nations,* 625 (Modern Library Edition, 1937).

[14] [1971 TRADE CASES ¶ 73,417], 437 F. 2d 707 (D. C. Cir. 1970).

discount prices without having taken the survey, *even if the advertisement is true.* The unfairness analysis in the Commission's *All-State Industries*[15] case is also directly on point.

> "*When a seller knows, but the buyer does not know,* that the debt contracted by the buyer in making a credit purchase will be assigned to a third party, *the buyer may be entering into a transaction quite different in its characteristics from the one the buyer imagines he is entering* . . . . In this circumstance, we find it palpably unfair for a seller who routinely assigns instruments of indebtedness executed by his purchasers to third parties to fail to disclose to his purchasers that such transfer is contemplated and may result in a substantial alteration of the buyer's rights and liabilities." (Emphasis added.)

In summary, the Commission concludes that the making of an affirmative product claim in advertising[16] is unfair to consumers unless there is a reasonable basis for making that claim.

This standard, it should be noted, focuses in large part on the adequacy of the underlying evidence, and is not solely a "reasonable man" test. It thus rounds out the *Kirchner* case, which suggested that an advertiser ". . . should have in his possession such information as would satisfy a reasonable and prudent businessman, acting in good faith, that such representation was true." This test evaluates both the reasonableness of an advertiser's actions and the adequacy of the evidence upon which such actions were based.

The question of what constitutes a reasonable basis is essentially a factual issue which will be affected by the interplay of overlapping considerations such as (1) the type and specificity of the claim made—*e. g.*, safety, efficacy, dietary, health, medical; (2) the type of product—*e. g.*, food, drug, potentially hazardous consumer product, other consumer product; (3) the possible consequences of a false claim—*e. g.*, personal injury, property damage; (4) the degree of reliance by consumers on the claims; (5) the type, and accessibility, of evidence adequate to form a reasonable basis for making the particular claims. More specifically, there may be some types of claims for some types of products for which the only reasonable basis, in fairness and in the expectations of consumers, would be a valid scientific or medical basis. The precise formulation of the "reasonable basis" standard, however, is an issue to be determined at this time on a case-by-case basis. This standard is determined by the circumstances at the time the claim was made, and further depends on both those facts known to the advertiser, and those which a reasonable prudent advertiser should have discovered. Such facts should be possessed *before* the claim is made.

In like manner, the criteria listed above will serve as a touchstone for evaluating those instances in which the Commission is unlikely to proceed against advertisers for failure to have support for an advertisement. In the past, the Commission has recognized that there is a category of advertising themes, in the nature of puffing or other hyperbole, which do not amount to the type of affirmative product claims for which either the Commission or the consumer would expect documentation. In *Kirchner*,[17] we held that advertising an inflatable swimming aid as "invisible" is harmless hyperbole.

> "True, as has been reiterated many times, the Commission's responsibility is to prevent deception of the gullible and credulous, as well as the cautious and knowledgable (see *e. g., Charles of the Ritz Dist. Corp. v. F. T. C.* [1944-1945 TRADE CASES ¶ 57,267], 143 F. 2d 676 (2d Cir. 1944). This principle loses its validity, however, if it is applied uncritically or pushed to an absurd extreme in respect of every conceivable misconception, however outlandish, to which his representations might be subject among the foolish or feebleminded. Some people, because of ignorance or incomprehension, may be misled by even a scrupulously honest claim. Perhaps a few misguided souls believe, for example, that all 'Danish pastry' is made in Denmark. Is it, therefore, an actionable deception to advertise 'Danish pastry' when it is made in this country? Of course not. A representation does not become 'false and deceptive' merely because it will be unreasonably misunderstood by an insignificant and unrepresentative segment of the class of persons to whom the representation is addressed. If, however, advertising is aimed at a specially susceptible group of people (e. g., children), its truthfulness must be measured by the impact it will make on them, not other to whom it is not primarily directed."

In this case, complaint counsel apparently challenging the reasonableness of the basis for two specific affirmative product claims made for Un-Burn: (1) Un-Burn

---

[15] *All-State Industries,* Docket No. 8738 (slip opinion, pp. 13-14), *aff'd* [1970 TRADE CASES ¶ 73,112], 423 F. 2d 423 (1970), *cert. denied,* 400 U. S. 828 (1970).

[16] This standard pertains only to advertising representations, and does not deal with the question of whether the mere fact of marketing a product implies or requires that certain standards of safety and health must be met. *Cf. Chemway Corporation,* Docket C-1945 (June 14, 1971); *H. W. Kirchner,* 63 F. T. C. 1282 (1963).

[17] 63 F. T. C. at 1290.

actually anesthetizes nerves in sunburned skin,[18] and (2) Un-Burn stops pain fast.[19]

The Standard of Reasonableness

Complaint counsel's unfairness charge basically urges that the only reasonable basis for performance or effectiveness representations for a drug or medical product would be fully documented, adequate and well-controlled scientific studies or tests. Complaint counsel deny that a reasonable basis could be found in the medical literature, clinical experience, or general medical knowledge. Respondent on the other hand, argues that it possessed a reasonable basis to support its affirmative product claims, and therefore did not need to take the additional step of obtaining controlled scientific tests. Respondent rested its defense on the proposition that the complaint set forth too narrow a view of the type of support required to make affirmative product claims, and contended that there was in fact a reasonable basis for making the questioned claims for Un-Burn.

On appeal, complaint counsel argue that courts have held that the only form of evidence which is adequate and reliable to sustain claims for a drug such as Un-Burn is adequate and well-controlled studies or tests. In support of this proposition, complaint counsel cite cases which hold, based upon a reading of statutory language and the pertinent legislative history, that the Food and Drug Administration validly issued administrative regulations establishing criteria for adequate and well-controlled clinical investigations for determining drug efficacy.[20] Having disclaimed at trial any relationship between FDA standards of drug efficacy and the definition of "adequate and well-controlled scientific studies or tests" as set forth in their complaint, however, complaint counsel cannot now attempt to rely, directly or indirectly, on those FDA standards. Complaint counsel have rested their case squarely on the "ordinary dictionary definitions" of the words "adequate and well-controlled scientific studies or tests"—it is, accordingly, on this basis that the Commission must evaluate their argument and the record evidence.[21]

Adequate and Well-Controlled Scientific Studies or Tests

Complaint counsel argue that the only reasonable basis for making efficacy and performance claims for a drug such as Un-Burn would be adequate and well-controlled scientific studies or tests conducted prior to the marketing of the product. Thus, a primary issue at trial was the existence or non-existence of such studies or tests. It is clear that Pfizer's *safety* testing was not designed to, and did not in fact, support the affirmative *efficacy* representations made for the product (I.D., pp. 9-10). Respondent's pre-marketing tests consisting of *injections* of benzocaine could not indicate the probable anesthetic effect of a *topical* application of this substance (Tr. 259, 308, 344, 522). The tests for the product's *antiseptic* effects do not lend any support to the *anesthetic* effects claimed (Tr. 288, 311). Nor were the tests on guinea pigs sufficient to substantiate the efficacy of the product on human beings (Tr. 726). The hearing examiner found, and the record amply supports his determination, that Pfizer did not conduct adequate and well-controlled scientific studies or tests *prior* to marketing Un-Burn to substantiate the efficacy claims for Un-Burn (I. D., pp. 17, 35).

More generally, the record in this matter is clear that for a test, standing alone, to provide a reasonable basis for an affirmative product claim, the test should be an adequate and well-controlled scientific test (I. D., pp. 10-17; Tr. 330-331, 351-356). Such a test should be conducted on human beings, not on animals (Tr. 298, 343, 351, 509, 522). A pre-existing test protocol is usually essential to an adequate test (Tr. 296, 345, 1065). The record also indicated the strong desirability of double-blind scientific tests (Tr. 280, 370).

Some time *after* the present proceeding was instituted, respondent did undertake to conduct an adequate and well-controlled test of Un-Burn's efficacy (Tr. 676). This was the test conducted by Dr. Orentreich (Tr. 647; I. D. 30). While there was some argument as to whether this test actually met the standards of an adequate and well-controlled scientific test (O. A. 14-15),[22] it seems clear that it was designed to be such (Tr. 674-676, 864-865). The Orentreich test stands in marked comparison to the tests undertaken by respondents prior to marketing, and graphically demonstrates the insufficiency of such premarketing tests to support the efficacy claims made for the product (Tr. 716, 863, 1116, 1188, 1215, 1226). Even assuming that the Orentreich test did establish that Un-Burn actually anesthetizes nerves,[23] the fact that this test was not conducted *prior* to making the affirmative product claims for Un-Burn pre-

[18] Complaint, paragraph 4.

[19] CX 4-7; Complaint, paragraph 4.

[20] *PMA v. Richardson,* (D. Del. 1970). *Upjohn Co. v. Finch,* 422 F. 2d 944 (6th Cir. 1970).

[21] This precludes consideration, in connection with this particular case, of the FDA's activities in defining the scientific content, of "adequate and well-controlled clinical investigations." See HX-1; 35 Fed. Reg. 3073 (February 17, 1970), 35 Fed. Reg. 7250 (May 8, 1970).

[22] The nature and intricacy of the debate on the adequacy of this test leads to the view that the Commission's role should simply be one of attempting to determine the existence and general quality of the tests and a threshold determination as to the reasonableness of reliance thereon, rather than an attempt to conclusively determine the adequacy of the tests.

[23] One definite obstacle to such a finding is the fact that this test undertook to compare

cludes it from being considered as a defense to the violation charged in this complaint. In order to have had a reasonable basis, the tests must have been conducted prior to, and actually relied upon in connection with, the marketing of the product in question. Nor does the fact that the product subsequently performed as advertised indicate that there is a lack of public interest in the matter.[24] The fundamental unfairness results from imposing on the consumer the unavoidable economic risk that the product may not perform as advertised; that is, at the time of sale, neither the consumer nor the vendor have a reasonable basis for belief in the affirmative product claims.

It is thus clear that the tests conducted by Pfizer did not provide a reasonable basis for the making of these performance claims. The tests were not adequate and well-controlled scientific tests conducted prior to the making of the efficacy representations.

> "[T]o take the position that a particular type of test must be made, wholly disregards the value of the clinical experience of a number of experts in the dermatology field of medicine such as those called by respondent. Moreover, such a position would appear to repudiate clinical experience entirely and to insist that laboratory testing be substituted in all instances where advertising is involved." [25]

As a question of fact, based on the evidence in this record, the Commission finds that complaint counsel have failed to demonstrate that the only reasonable basis for these affirmative product claims would be adequate and well-controlled scientific studies or tests. It is accordingly necessary to consider, as a matter of fact, the other bases put forth by respondent in support of their "reasonable basis" defense.

Composition of Competing Products

As one of the factors in the argument that there existed a reasonable basis for the product claims in question, respondent alleges that it surveyed competing products on the market to determine (1) the ingredients in such products, and (2) the advertising claims which were being made for such products. Respondent apparently reasons that since the ingredients in Un-Burn are substantially identical to those competing products,[26] it is permissible to make the same advertising claims as are made for such competing products—or at least those which have not been challenged as false by a government agency (Tr. 1116, 1130, 1162). The restatement of this argument is sufficient to refute it. The Commission clearly can give no weight to this type of argument in evaluating whether there was a reasonable basis for respondent's claims.

The fact that apparently there did exist a valid efficacy test for a competing product of similar composition which was known to and verified by respondent, however, might have provided a reasonable basis for similar efficacy claims for Un-Burn (CX 99; Tr. 562-573; O. A. 24).[27] The evidence with regard to this particular test, however, falls substantially short of constituting an adequate test for the particular anesthetic claims made for Un-Burn. Nor is there sufficient evidence that Pfizer knew of, and relied upon, this test in marketing Un-Burn.

Medical Literature

Respondent urges that its search of the medical literature contained in Pfizer's library, prior to marketing Un-Burn, provided a reasonable basis for the Un-Burn efficacy representations. While complaint counsel do not meet this argument directly, their argument that the *only* reasonable basis would be scientific studies or tests encompasses this point. In oral argument, however, complaint counsel did concede that medical literature containing reports on adequate and well-controlled tests might be sufficient.

The record evidence is sufficient to demonstrate to the Commission that medical literature might, in some instances, be sufficient basis for making affirmative product claims (Tr. 671, 704, 713, 1054, 1108, 1118, 1128).

Closely allied with medical literature as a reasonable basis, would be the general state of medical knowledge at the time the claims were made, regardless of how that knowledge is ascertained (Tr. 1049, 1097, 1124; I. D. 20-23, 30-32). Thus, the examiner found that:

> "Recognized medical literature and the medical practice of dermatologists for between 50 and 70 years regarded the active ingredients in Un-Burn as effica-

---

the effectiveness of Un-Burn with the noneffectiveness of a placebo, rather than to compare Un-Burn's effectiveness with the level of effectiveness claimed by Pfizer's advertising (See, Tr. 680-682, 1215).

[24] Compare *FTC v. Colgate-Palmolive Co.* [1965 TRADE CASES ¶ 71,409], 380 U. S. 374, 388 (1965). A false representation violates § 5 even if the misstatement in no way affects the qualities of the product. The concern is "with methods designed to get a consumer to purchase a product, not with whether the product, when purchased, will perform up to expectations." In short, the focus in upon the method of marketing. See also, *Philip Morris, Inc.*, Docket 8838 (March 12, 1971) (marketing practices which allegedly constitute safety hazards are challenged as allegedly unfair); *FTC v. Algoma Lumber Co.* [1932-1939 TRADE CASES ¶ 55,041], 291 U. S. 67 (1934).

[25] I. D., p. 35:

[26] This argument is weakened by the fact that apparently no scienitific analysis was made to determine whether the competing products had the same formula as Un-Burn (Tr. 703).

[27] Such claims, of course, can not imply that respondent's product is unique or different from the competing product in question.

cious for the relief of sunburn pain." (I. D. 32.)

Persuasive in this regard is the fact that the NAS-NRC panels utilized by the Food and Drug Administration were permitted to recognize as probative reports on studies contained in the medical and scientific literature (RX 110, p. 5; HX 1; Tr. 369, 371, 535).

The guidelines for these NAS-NRC panels[28] set forth the following basis for judgments as to drug efficacy:

> "The judgments of the Panels will be based on the following criteria: (1) factual information that is freely available in the scientific literature, (2) factual information that is available from the FDA, from the manufacturer or other sources, or (3) on the experience and informed judgment of the members of the Panels." (See also, Tr. 535).

These Guidelines later discuss one instance where scientific literature alone could provide the basis for a judgment as to effectiveness:

> "It is anticipated that substantial evidence for the effectiveness of many of the drugs assigned to a Panel will be found to be well-documented in the scientific literature familiar to the members of the Panel. In these cases, the Panel may be prepared to make its recommendations and to support them by citations from the scientific literature alone."

In a later section, the Guidelines discuss other types of evidence of effectiveness:

> "IX. *Some Special Considerations*
>
> "In the deliberations of the Panels, issues will almost certainly arise as to considerations, other than factual evidence, that should be weighed in arriving at judgments on effectiveness. The significance of many of these factors will vary widely in different classes of drugs and of the indications. No general guidelines for these can be offered. As these questions arise, however, Panel chairmen are invited to present them to the Policy Advisory Committee together with any suggestions as to the manner in which they might be resolved.
>
> "A few general issues can, however, be anticipated.
>
> * * *
>
> "D. *Wide Usage*
>
> There will likely be cases in which a Panel is in doubt as to the sufficiency of evidence of effectiveness of a drug that has gained repute among practicing physicians or that has been in wide use for a period of years. It will be quite in order for the Panel to draw attention to these facts in recording its judgment as to effectiveness.
>
> * * *
>
> "F. *Subjective Evaluations*
>
> "The informed judgment and experience of the members of the Panels in valid evidence contributory to the final decision on the efficacy of a drug for the indications presented. In justifying its decision, however, the Panel is expected to delineate the extent to which it is supported by the substantive evidence available for its review."

Complaint counsel's burden in this proceeding is that of demonstrating that respondent's actions in reliance upon the medical literature did not provide a reasonable basis for the affirmative product claims. Complaint counsel, for example, could have offered evidence or argument that: (1) respondent's search of the medical literature was of such a limited scope that it was unreasonable, or (2) the conclusions drawn by respondent from the medical literature actually reviewed were unreasonable, or (3) the "testimonial" quality of the medical literature was not sufficient basis for the product claims.[29] Complaint counsel's insistence that the medical literature specifically report on actual *tests* fails to address itself to, or satisfy, their burden in this regard.[30] Complaint counsel's primary evidence on this point was the rebuttal testimony of Dr. Beaver, who basically showed a possible conflict in the medical literature. This does not satisfy the burden of proof resting on complaint counsel on this issue.

Clinical Experience

Respondent's final argument is that the clinical experience of the medical profession in itself provides a reasonable basis for making efficacy claims for Un-Burn. Again, in view of complaint counsel's primary focus on the necessity for scientific tests, the Commission is not in a position to definitely evaluate whether clinical experience as to benzocaine and menthol would provide a reasonable basis for assuming its efficacy. It was clear from the evidence of record,

[28] Guidelines for the Drug Efficacy Study of the National Academy of Sciences-National Research Council, August 1966 (RX 110; I. D., p. 30.).

[29] Complaint counsel's argument was misdirected to some degree, to any medical literature which a witness may have reviewed (Tr. 1312; CCRB 2; *Compare I. D.*, p. 19).

[30] Thus, we do not reach several significant issues pertinent to this point, *e. g.*, did the medical literature deal with the Un-Burn ingredients in the same combination and amounts as they appear in the final formulation of Un-Burn (O. A., 4. 16); is chemical equivalence sufficiently indicative of therapeutical equivalence (Tr. 1081, 1116, 1117, O. A. 12); are authors' opinions and conclusions sufficient, or must the actual underlying tests be described; or whether the medical literature will ever be capable of supporting product claims which relate to a condition which varies so widely among the people it affects as does sunburn.

however, the "clinical experience" covers a wide range of circumstances and must be carefully analyzed and evaluated, including consideration of the type of ailment being treated. Accordingly, the reasonableness of clinical experience must be evaluated as a factual issue in each case (Tr. 1083, 1097, 1108, 1122, 1185, 1253, 1258, 1263, 1300). In this regard, the relevant inquiry is into a respondent's knowledge of, and reliance upon, clinical experience *prior* to making the product claims in question. Thus, Pfizer's witnesses as to clinical experience, who were contacted by Pfizer only in preparation for trial, are irrelevant to the issue (*See I. D.*, pp. 20-23).

Respondent's Efforts to Provide a Reasonable Basis for Affirmative

Pfizer's Director of Marketing testified that he took three measures to satisfy himself as to the efficacy of the product Un-Burn. First, he received "complete assurance" from Pfizer's medical people that the claims he planned to use for Un-Burn could be supported by the two active ingredients in the quantities in which they were to be used in the product. He was assured that the way a topical anesthetic works is to anesthetize nerves and thereby stop pain (Tr. 605). He was also assured by the "medical people" that the product was patterned very closely after the market leader, Solarcaine. Secondly, he was assured that all available literature or information on these two active ingredients had been thoroughly reviewed and favorable conclusions derived from this review as to the efficacy of the ingredients as topical anesthetics. Finally, he personally reviewed all competitive advertising to satisfy himself that Pfizer would not be claiming anything more than other products with the same active ingredients. The Director of Marketing testified that Pfizer did not conduct tests on humans to determine whether the efficacy claims could be supported, but consciously "accepted another method of satisfying" themselves by going over the history of the ingredients. No specific tests were conducted on human beings to prove that Un-Burn anesthetizes nerve ends (*I. D.*, p. 10, 19; Tr. 623-624).

The Pfizer medical official responsible for testing all new Pfizer products, testified that two efficacy tests were run on Un-Burn:

1. Testing with regard to the antibacterial properties of the product, and

2. The guinea pig wheal tests.

These latter tests involved the injection of Un-Burn into guinea pigs. His conclusions as to the results of Pfizer's testing on Un-Burn were as follows:

"[T]he products passed the safety and efficacy tests. The tests demonstrated that there were no safety hazards pertaining to the products, and that the antibacterial activity of the product would support the antiseptic claim, and finally, the guinea wheal test demonstrated to us that the active ingredient, one of the active ingredients, benzocaine, was not inactivated by anything in the formulations." (Tr. 668.)

As a result of the safety and other tests, his review of the literature, and his discussions with Dr. Carlozzi, the Medical Director of Pfizer, Dr. Jenkins gave his opinion that the testing done was sufficient to establish the safety and efficacy of Un-Burn (*I. D.*, p. 20; Tr. 672-673).

Inasmuch as complaint counsel's argument did not go directly to the reasonableness of these actions, we lack a sufficient basis for a finding in this regard. In future cases, we would be interested in both the qualifications of the medical and scientific advisors, and some showing that their judgments were rendered on an informed and unbiased basis. Also properly considered here would be the issue of whether reliance upon medical literature and clinical evidence as to the separate ingredients in Un-Burn is appropriate, or whether additional consideration must be given to (1) the combination of ingredients as they appear in the final product, and (2) the various conditions of use to which the product can reasonably be expected to be subjected, including variations as to skin types and degrees of sunburn. The Commission is not, moreover, convinced of the reasonableness of respondent's attempts to rely upon clinical experience as to the efficacy of benzocaine and menthol in general, to support the specific degree of efficacy ("anesthetizes" nerves, "stops" sunburn) claimed for Un-Burn.[31]

Evidently respondent made no written report setting forth the actions which were taken to support the existence of a reasonable basis for its advertising claims. Such a report, if made in good faith prior to marketing, if reasonable in scope and approach,[32] and if reasonably clear as to the evidentiary basis for the specific claims in question (be they scientific tests, specified medical references, or specific clinical evidence), would certainly have, in itself, gone a considerable distance in demonstrating the existence of a reasonable basis for their affirmative product claims.

---

[31] The Orentreich test evaluated the efficacy of Un-Burn only in comparison to a placebo—it did not attempt to determine whether nerves were "actually anesthetized" or sunburn pain had in fact "stopped." (CCRB 3-4.)

[32] The issue of whether an advertisement has appropriately formulated the standard of what constitutes a "reasonable basis" remains a separate question of fact. See discussion at pp. 16-17, *supra*.

CODE
NEWS
THE CODE AUTHORITY OF THE NATIONAL ASSOCIATION OF BROADCASTERS
VOLUME 12/NUMBER 11/NOVEMBER 1979

"Balanced Regimen" Requirement Clarified, "Sweepstakes" Policy Established in Q&As Released By TV Code Board Children's Advertising Committee

The NAB Television Code Board's Children's Advertising Committee has issued 12 Q&As designed to clarify Children's Television Advertising Guideline (CTAG) II-C-2 ("balanced regimen" requirement), and a Q&A establishing a new policy for sweepstakes advertising to children.

The Q&As came after nearly a year-and-a-half of formal study which began in March 1978 when the Television Code Board directed its Children's Advertising Committee and the Code Authority to conduct a review of the Children's Television Advertising Guidelines and their interpretation and implementation. Later that year, when the Board was advised of the results of the review, it directed the Code Authority to recommend specific policies in the two areas. After additional reviews of the Code Authority's recommendations, the Board agreed upon a revised general approach and authorized the Children's Advertising Committee to complete and issue the Q&As.

The Q&As, which stem from CTAG II-C-2, specifically address the types of audio references to and video depictions of a balanced regimen that would be acceptable in children's commercials for breakfast-type products. They also deal with the applicability of II-C-2, and are responsive to other questions that have arisen regarding that guideline.

The Q&A regarding sweepstakes advertised to children both establishes a new policy that requires such sweepstakes commercials to give a realistic estimate of a child's chances of winning the contest, and reminds subscribers to give consideration to the appropriateness of the prize(s) being offered to children when reviewing such commericals.

The effective date of the Q&As is October 15, 1979 for new commercials, with March 1, 1980 being designated as the point at which all children's commercials must be compliant with them.

The members of the Children's Advertising Committee are: Michael McCormick (chairman), president, WTMJ-TV Milwaukee, Wis.; Alvina Britz, general manager, KTVO(TV) Kirksville, Mo.; Donn H. O'Brien, vice president, program practices, CBS Broadcast Group, New York, N.Y.; Leavitt J. Pope, president, WPIX-TV New York, N.Y.; Alfred R. Schneider, vice president, American Broadcasting Companies Inc., New York, N.Y., and Herminio Traviesas, vice president, broadcast standards policy, National Broadcasting Company, New York, N.Y.

Balanced Regimen

Q. Is the Guideline applicable to food products, other than cereals, which are advertised or positioned

Published by The Code Authority of The National Association of Broadcasters. Reprinted with permission.

in a breakfast context?

A. Yes. For example, Children's Television Advertising Guideline (CTAG) II-C-2 would be applicable to a commercial for an orange juice product if the commercial promotes use of the product at breakfast time. However, if the orange juice product is advertised for use at any time during the day/evening and the primary reference or depiction is not of its use at breakfast time, CTAG II-C-2 would not apply. (Please refer to paragraph 3 of the introduction to the CTAG for a general statement regarding the applicablity of the Guidelines. Copies of the Guidelines may be obtained free of charge from any Code Authority office.)

Q. Is it the intent of the Guideline to require a specific reference to the desirability of eating a complete/nutritionally balanced breakfast (e.g., "You should have a complete breakfast" or "You need a complete breakfast")?

A. No. While advertisers are encouraged to include such type statements in affected advertising, the basic purpose of the Guideline is to help create an awareness, or reinforce the existing awareness, in children of a balanced breakfast.

Q. Are phrases such as "complete breakfast," "nutritious breakfast," "balanced breakfast," and "nutritionally balanced breakfast" acceptable in the audio reference requirement of CTAG II-C-2?

A. Yes. In order to help achieve compliance with the Guideline, a statement including but not limited to a phrase such as indicated above is required in the commercial. On a related point, an advertiser must be able to document that the particular phrase used is an accurate description of the breakfast shown in the video.

Q. Is the phrase "good breakfast" also acceptable to convey the idea of a complete/nutritionally balanced breakfast?

A. Yes, provided it is used in a properly qualified context in which the idea of a "complete breakfast" is clearly established. For example, the term "good breakfast" would be acceptable in contexts such as the following:

"You need a good breakfast that's a fact. What's a good breakfast? Oh, different kinds of foods like juice, toast, milk, a fortified cereal. . ."

"Product X can be part of a good breakfast like this," in which "like this" clearly refers to a video depiction of the complete breakfast.

"Good" as a modifier of "complete breakfast," "nutritious breakfast," etc. would also be acceptable, i.e., "good complete breakfast"; "good nutritious breakfast." Further, the term "good breakfast" would be acceptable if it is tied into an immediately following or preceding reference to "complete breakfast," "nutritious breakfast," etc.

The term "good breakfast" would be unacceptable in the following context: "Product X can be part of a good breakfast" if there is no accompanying establishment in the audio of the complete/nutritionally balanced breakfast concept.

Q. Is it necessary to reference the particular foods that are shown as constituting a complete/nutritious breakfast?

A. No. While advertisers are encouraged to reference the particular foods depicted, such a reference is not mandatory.

Q. Does the Guideline require that the audio reference and video depiction be made simultaneously?

A. A simultaneous reference is preferred. A contiguous reference may be substituted for a simultaneous reference if other elements in the commercial are present and believed adequate to justify a contiguous reference, e.g., overall duration of the video depiction(s) of the complete breakfast, clarity of the complete breakfast depiction(s), whether particular foods constituting a complete breakfast are in fact referenced, the absence of copy language which may go counter to the intent of referencing and depicting a balanced breakfast, etc. In such situations, the audio reference to a "complete breakfast" may be made contiguous to the video depiction of the breakfast.

Q. May descriptive words be used in connection with the advertised product's .name or the phrase within the balanced breakfast statement?

A. A descriptive word may be used within the entire balanced breakfast statement in connection with either the advertised product's name or phrase, assuming it is an accurate description of the product or breakfast. The following examples are indicative of acceptable ways in which a descriptive may be used:
1. "*Crisp* Product X is part of this complete breakfast."
2. "Product X can be part of a *tasty* balanced breakfast."
3. "Product X can be a *chocolatey* part of this complete breakfast."
4. "Product X is part of this *good* nutritious breakfast."

Q. May the advertised product's brand name be referenced in the audio of the balanced breakfast statement?

A. Yes. An audio reference to the advertised product's brand name is acceptable.

Q. May the product package be displayed as part of the complete breakfast depiction?

A. Yes, provided it does not obscure or otherwise detract from the display of other foods that are shown as part of the complete breakfast.

Q. May breakfast-type product commercials state or use language which created the impression that it is necessary to use the advertised product in order to have a complete breakfast?

A. No. Commercials for breakfast-type products shall avoid ascribing essentiality to the advertised product While it is acceptable to say that the advertised product "may be", or "can be" part of a complete breakfast, the following type copy is believed to indicate that the advertised product is necessary to have a complete breakfast and would be unacceptable:
1. "Product X will give me a complete breakfast."
2. "Only *Brand Name* breakfast is a nutritious breakfast."
3. "Product X must (or should) be part of a complete breakfast."

However, it is acceptable to refer to the advertised product as an important or integral part of the specific complete breakfast which is shown in the video portion. The following examples are indicative of copy which may be used:

"Product X is an important part of *this* complete breakfast."

"You can enjoy *this* good, nourishing Product X breakfast."

Q Is an animated depiction of foods comprising the complete breakfast segment acceptable?

A. Yes. However, special care should be exercised to assure that the individual foods in the animated depiction are clear, realistic and easily recognized by children. The foods should not be drawn in an unrealistic manner. Colors should not be washed out. Contrast and lighting that minimizes the visibility of the foods should be avoided.

As with all complete breakfast segments, any action that may take place during the display of the foods shall not obscure or detract from the depiction of the foods.

Q. What factors should be taken into account to help assure that the video depiction of a complete breakfast is adequate to meet the objective of CTAG II-C-2?

A. Three factors are believed to be basic considerations in determining the adequacy of the video depiction of a complete breakfast. The manner in which they interrelate or are balanced is relevant to the sufficiency and appropriateness of the depiction under CTAG II-C-2. All factors are considered important in helping achieve the goal of prompt and easy recognition of the complete breakfast and its component parts by children.

The three factors are the video depiction's distance, clarity and duration, and the simultaneity or contiguity of the audio reference to the video depiction:

1. An establishing shot must be used to assure that the complete breakfast and its individual foods are highly visible and easily recognized by children. Foods in the establishing shot must be displayed in an uncluttered environment and the "real-life" color of the foods must be used. The video depiction of a balanced breakfast may contain action or movement provided it does not detract or distract from the foods shown.

2. In instances in which a complete breakfast is discussed, depicted or referred to throughout a commercial *or* interwoven within a commerical *or* in instances in which the commercial's setting is a breakfast table, a combination of various shots (close-up, medium, long) would be acceptable, provided one of them is an establishing shot of the complete breakfast which meets all of the requirements of Point 1.

3. A simultaneous or contiguous audio reference (Q&A #6) may be used in relationship to any of the complete breakfast video shots, although advertisers are encouraged to use it with the establishing shot.

Sweepstakes

Q. May sweepstakes be advertised to children?

A. Yes, provided the sweepstakes commercial contains a clear statement in which a realistic estimate of a child's chance of winning the sweepstakes is given. Also, Code subscribers should take into account the appropriateness of the prize(s) being offered to children when reviewing sweepstakes commercials.

United States of America

Congressional Record

PROCEEDINGS AND DEBATES OF THE 97th CONGRESS, SECOND SESSION

Vol. 128 WASHINGTON, TUESDAY, FEBRUARY 9, 1982 No. 10

Senate

(Legislative day of Monday, January 25, 1982)

SELF-REGULATORY PROCESS FOR ADVERTISING

• Mr. KASTEN. Mr. President, 10 years ago, the American Association of Advertising Agencies, American Advertising Federation, the Association of National Advertisers, and the Council of Better Business Bureaus established a self-regulatory process for advertising. While I am sure that the vast majority of advertising agencies and the vast majority of advertisers consider truthful advertising to be in their own best interest, the advertising industry has chosen not to trust matters of truth and accuracy to the individual conscience.

Instead, the three major advertising associations and the Council of Better Business Bureaus have worked together and developed a series of codes and the mechanisms to enforce them. The two principal administrative bodies in this self-regulatory process, the National Advertising Division of the Council of Better Business Bureaus and the National Advertising Review Board, have just completed their first decade of service with a notable record of success.

According to a recent presentation given by these groups to the Commerce Committee and staff, since 1971, NAD has processed some 6,000 matters, of which 1,860 were full-fledged investigations or cases. In 98 percent of the cases the issue was resolved either by voluntary compliance on the part of the advertisers or dismissal of the complaint. In only 2 percent of all cases has it been necessary to appeal to higher authority, the NARB. In no case has an advertiser refused to abide by the final decision of these bodies.

The NAD initiates about 45 percent of its cases from its own monitoring, with another 37 percent being competitor challenges. The remainder are consumer complaints—either directly to the NAD or to the 151 local Better Business Bureaus. (Children's advertising is treated as a special category requiring specialized expertise in the area of children's developing perceptions. A special section within the NAD, the Children's Advertising Review Unit monitors children's advertising, both broadcast and print, with particular care.)

When the NAD concludes that a claim or an advertising approach is questionable, they work with the advertiser at the top management level to find an acceptable solution. The NAD relies on the advertiser to cooperate voluntarily by setting straight anything judged to be misleading. In the vast majority of cases, the matter is resolved here.

A very few cases, however, are appealed to the NARB Chairman, who appoints a 5-member panel from the 50-member board of industry, consumer, and academic leaders and holds hearings on the matter. An advertiser's refusal to comply with an adverse decision of the NARB would result in the matter being forwarded to the appropriate Government enforcement agency for further action.

Advertiser acceptance of NARB decisions to date has made this final step unnecessary in any instance. Over 10 years, the NAD—NARB system has become an accepted force for the betterment of advertising, benefiting both the consumer and the industry.

Mr. President, I am pleased to see workable programs for industry self-regulation, because they often obviate the need for Government intrusion into the marketplace. In the case of the Consumer Product Safety Commission, Congress went so far as to require the agency to defer to voluntary consumer product safety standards rather than issuing mandatory standards when voluntary standards were effective. I commend the advertising industry for its efforts, and I look forward to working with them and other self-regulatory groups in the future.•

STATISTICAL REVIEW OF NAD/NARB CASEWORK
(to Dec. 31, 1981)

NAD Sources	1981	1971-1981
NAD Monitoring	62	711
Competitors	51	409
Local BBB's*	17	331
Consumer Complaints	11	244
Others	3	236
Total Cases Opened	144	1,931

*Half of all local BBB referrals are estimated to be consumer-initiated

NAD Disposition of Cases	1981	1971-1981
Substantiated	67	750
Claims Modified or Withdrawn	78	801
Referred to NARB	1	15*
Terminated for Other Reasons	9	324
Suspended	1	1
Total Cases Closed	156	1,891**

*An additional 22 cases were appealed to NARB after publication of NAD's disposition

**An additional 40 NAD cases were still under investigation as of 12/31/81

NARB Decisions	1971-1981
Cases Handled	37
NAD Upheld	25
NAD Reversed/Modified	8
Dismissed	4

MEDIA BREAKDOWN OF NAD CASES
(of 1,931 Cases Opened in period 1971-1981)

Media	#	%
Television	776	30
Radio	83	3
Magazine	741	28
Newspaper	543	21
Comic Book	52	2
Direct Mail	87	4
Other:		
Catalog	38	2
Sales Brochure	102	4
Labeling	84	4
Miscellaneous	57	2
Total	2,563*	100

*Cases frequently involve advertising in more than one medium

PRINCIPAL PRODUCT CATEGORIES OF NAD CASES
(of 1,931 Cases Opened in period 1971-1981)

More than 250

Foods & Beverages

201 to 250

Cosmetics & Toiletries
Automotive Products & Services

151 to 200

Household Products
Sports & Hobbies
Drugs & Health Aids

101 to 150

Appliances

51 to 100

Travel
Clothing

STATEMENT

OF

ORGANIZATION AND PROCEDURES

OF THE

NATIONAL ADVERTISING REVIEW BOARD

(As Amended to June 19, 1980)

ORGANIZATION

1.1 Purpose

The National Advertising Review Board (NARB) is a body of industry and public persons as herein defined sponsored by the National Advertising Review Council, Inc. (NARC) for the purpose of sustaining high standards of truth and accuracy in national advertising.

1.2 Structure of the NARB

The National Advertising Review Board shall be composed of a Chairman, fifty members, and as many alternate members as the Chairman may specify, all elected by the NARC Board of Directors. Thirty members of the NARB shall be persons whose principal affiliation is with an advertiser; ten members shall be persons whose principal affiliation is with an advertising agency; and ten members shall be public members. If any member's principal affiliation changes, his eligibility to serve as a member will be reconsidered by NARC. The status and privileges of alternate members shall be the same as the status and privileges of regular members except that alternate members are not qualified to vote upon any matter which comes before the full NARB. No member of the NARC Board of Directors, while so serving, shall be eligible to be a member or alternate member of the NARB.

1.3 Terms of Office

The term of office for NARB members shall be two years except that the terms of one-half of the members of the original NARB (fifteen advertiser members, five advertising agency members and five public members) shall be for one year. A member is eligible for reappointment for one additional term. An eligible member may be removed from office by a

1.3 (Continued)

two-thirds majority of the total membership of the NARB and by no other means. A member elected to fill a vacancy on the National Advertising Review Board between annual meetings shall serve for the remainder of the vacated term and be eligible for reappointment to one additional two year term.

1.4 Compensation

Advertiser and advertising agency members and alternates of the NARB shall receive no salary. Nonindustry members shall receive per diem compensation in such amount as shall be determined by the NARC Board of Directors and shall be entitled to reimbursement for such out-of-pocket expenses as they shall incur in connection with the performance of their duties on the NARB.

1.5 The NARB Chairman

There shall be a Chairman of the NARB who shall be elected by the NARC Board of Directors for a term of one year and who shall be eligible for re-election. The Chairman shall receive such compensation for his services as shall be determined by the NARC Board of Directors.

1.6 Duties of the Chairman

The NARB Chairman shall be the overall coordinator of the activities of NARB and shall be its public spokesman. He shall appoint a panel composed of five NARB members to hear and decide each case which is brought before the NARB. In the event the Chairman is unable to appoint a qualified panel from among the regular membership of the NARB, he shall appoint the necessary number of qualified alternate members to fill the panel. The Chairman shall also act as Chairman of the NARB's Steering Committee and shall perform such other duties as may be directed by the NARB.

1.7 The NARB Executive Director

There shall be an Executive Director of the NARB who shall be appointed by the Chairman to serve as the Staff Executive.

1.8 Duties of the Executive Director

The Executive Director shall assist the Chairman in carrying out his duties. He shall also be responsible for managing the NARB office, maintaining liaison with NAD and other organizations and such other duties or projects as assigned by the Chairman.

1.9 The Steering Committee

At its first meeting and at each annual meeting thereafter, the NARB shall elect from among its members a Steering Committee composed of four members affiliated with advertisers, two members affiliated with an advertising agency and two members who are public members, plus the Chairman (ex-officio). The Steering Committee shall act as liaison and spokesman for the NARB in its contacts with the NARC Board of Directors.

It shall survey and review the operations of the NARB (except that it shall have no authority with regard to individual cases which are being, have been, or may be considered by the NARB), and shall make recommendations thereon to the full NARB or to the NARC Board of Directors. It shall oversee the preparation and issuance of reports on NARB operations, or any other matters properly within the NARB's purview for submission to the members of the NARB.

1.10 Annual and Interim Reports

By March 31 of each year, the NARB Steering Committee shall cause to be prepared a report of the proceedings of the NARB during the preceding calendar year and shall submit such report to the NARB. The Steering Committee may direct the preparation and publication of such interim reports as the Committee deems necessary. Reports may be in such detail as the Steering Committee shall consider reasonably necessary to provide information to the public concerning the activities of the NARB, but under no circumstances shall any report disclose information on any proceeding currently being considered by the NARB. Reports may be published by the Chairman following their adoption, by majority, through a mail ballot by the NARB.

1.11 Meetings

As soon as practical after formation of the original NARB, the Chairman shall call a meeting of the full NARB. Thereafter, there shall be at least one annual meeting and such special meetings as the Steering Committee, in consultation with the Chairman, deems necessary. NARB members shall be given at least fifteen days' notice of annual and special meetings. At the original, and at each subsequent annual meeting, the NARB shall conduct such organizational and other business as may come before it.

1.12 Standards

The NARB shall promulgate, adopt, amend and publish, with the advice and counsel of the NARC Board of Directors, advertising standards to aid in its evaluation of the truth and accuracy of national advertising.

1.13 Autonomy of NARB

In the review and disposition of all cases coming before it, the NARB shall be completely autonomous and independent of any and all other persons and organizations. It shall conduct its business and issue its reports and opinions with full regard for the public interest. The individual members of the NARB shall be answerable to no one for the decisions reached and actions taken by the NARB or any panel thereof.

1.14 Definitions

The term "national advertising" shall mean advertising disseminated in all of the United States or in a substantial section thereof. The term "advertiser" shall mean any seller who uses "national advertising" in the sale of goods or services or for other purposes, and the term "advertising agency" shall mean any organization engaged in the creation and placement of "national advertising." The term "public or nonindustry member" shall mean any person who has a reputation for achievements in the public interest.

PROCEDURES

2.1 Function of the NAD

The National Advertising Division of the Council of Better Business Bureaus (hereinafter NAD) shall be responsible for receiving or initiating, evaluating, investigating, analyzing, and holding initial negotiations with an advertiser on complaints or questions from any source involving the truth or accuracy of national advertising.

The NAD shall make public a report on a monthly basis concerning all matters concluded during the month. These reports shall identify each advertiser, product, and subject matter reviewed, the NAD decision and its rationale or the fact the case is on appeal to the NARB. If the advertiser desires, a concise statement of his views shall be included. The complainant in each case shall be supplied with a copy of the report.

2.1 (Continued)

Complainants to NAD are required to provide their complete data at the outset to NAD with the understanding that NAD, if it believes that the advertising may be deceptive to the public, will have unrestricted use of the complainant's data and the right to share it with the advertiser. NAD cannot make a determination or seek an advertiser's cooperation to correct advertising based upon evidence submitted by a complainant which NAD is precluded from presenting to the advertiser for his comment and rebuttal. The complainant is not a party to this procedure, but merely a source of information to NAD. The parties to the dispute are NAD acting in the public interest and the advertiser acting in its own interest. The complainant, therefore, is not automatically entitled to review the advertiser's substantiation nor to condition the submission of its data to reciprocity on the part of the advertiser. NAD recognizes, however, that the complainant may be a highly qualified source which could provide valuable expertise in evaluating the advertiser's substantiation. NAD believes it desirable if the advertiser consents (and NAD will strongly urge advertiser consent) to seek the complainant's expertise in evaluating the advertiser's substantiation. But if the advertiser declines to permit the complainant to review his substantiation, NAD will honor that restriction.

While complainants will be urged to abide by these procedures, NAD will not refuse a valid complaint which involves issues of public interest on the grounds that the complainant objects to sharing proprietary data with its competitor. However, in placing limitations on the use of supporting data, the complainant not only weakens its own argument but may not thereafter change its mind and submit the data once the investigation is underway.

2.1A <u>Advertiser's Refusal to Cooperate</u>

Where, despite the best efforts of NAD, an advertiser refuses to participate in the self-regulatory process, or engages in outright fraud, or where an advertiser professes to cooperate but persistently continues a pattern of misleading and deceptive advertising, NAD may make a finding that such advertiser is not amenable to the self-regulatory process.

In that event NAD shall prepare a written statement setting forth all of the facts with appropriate exhibits, if any, leading to that conclusion and the statement shall be submitted for review to the Chairman of NARB.

2.1A (Continued)

If the Chairman of NARB concurs in the finding, he shall return the statement to NAD with the request that NAD file a complaint with an appropriate law enforcement agency.

If the Chairman of NARB concludes that further efforts may produce a willingness to participate in the self-regulatory process, he shall enter the negotiating process and may contact the advertiser and/or consult with the Steering Committee. If, thereafter, he concludes that the advertiser remains not amenable to self-regulation, he will advise the NAD to file a complaint with an appropriate law enforcement agency.

No public disclosure shall be made of referral to a law enforcement agency in cases in which the advertiser has not participated in the NAD/NARB self-regulatory process.

2.2 Requests for Review by the Advertiser or NAD

When an advertiser does not agree with a NAD decision, the NAD shall inform it that it has ten days to request an appeal of the NARB. Similarly, the NAD at that time may request review by the NARB. In such cases, the NAD or the advertiser shall prepare a Request for Review and mail one copy to the other party and a copy to the Executive Director of the NARB. The Request for Review shall contain: (1) a statement of facts supported by attached documentary and physical exhibits including any significant exculpatory material previously supplied by either party, and (2) an analysis of the facts giving reasons, conclusions and recommendations. The other party upon whom such Request for Review is served may submit to the Executive Director of the NARB within ten days any requests as to procedure or dates for meetings or hearings as well as any documents he wishes the Executive Director to submit to the panel.

2.3 Requests for Review by Complainant

Any complainant may request review of a prior NAD decision by filing a Request for Review with the Executive Director of NARB for transmittal to the Chairman of NARB within ten days after notification of the NAD decision. Such a request need not follow any particular form but should contain sufficient information to support a decision as to whether the matter is appropriate for NARB consideration.

If the Chairman decides that the complainant's request for review will be granted, he shall disseminate the Request for Review to the parties to the case in conformity with Section 2.2 of these Procedures.

2.4 <u>Appointment of Review Panel</u>

The Chairman, upon notification of a Request for Review from NAD or the advertiser by the Executive Director, or upon acceptance of a Request for Review by a complainant shall appoint a panel of qualified NARB members and designate the panel member who will serve as panel chairman.

2.5 <u>Eligibility of Panelists</u>

An "advertiser" NARB member will be considered as not qualified if his employing company manufactures or sells a product or service which directly competes with a product or service sold by the advertiser involved in the proceeding. An "agency" NARB member will be considered as not qualified if his employing advertising agency represents a client which sells a product or service which directly competes with the product or service involved in the proceeding. A NARB member, including a non-industry member, shall consider himself as disqualified if for any reason arising out of past or present employment or affiliation he believes that he cannot reach a completely unbiased decision. If the Chairman is unable to appoint a qualified panel; he shall complete the panel by appointing an alternate NARB member.

2.6 <u>Composition of Review Panel</u>

Each panel shall be composed of one "public" member, one "advertising agency" member, and three "advertiser" members. Alternates may be used where required. It will meet at the call of its Chairman, who will preside over its meetings, hearings and deliberations. A majority of the panel will constitute a quorum, but the concurring vote of three members is required to decide any substantive question before the panel.

2.7 <u>Procedures of Review Panel</u>

As soon as the panel has been selected, the Executive Director will inform all parties as to the identity of the panel members and will mail copies of the Request for Review and, upon receipt, any response or request submitted by the other party or parties to each of the panel members. Within ten days after receipt of the Request for Review, the panel members shall confer and decide and fix the procedure and time schedule which they will follow in resolving the matter. In reaching a decision as to procedure, the panel should aim for informality and speed. If any party has requested an opportunity to appear and offer testimony or argument, he shall be accommodated and shall submit to cross-questioning. All evidentiary material and oral testimony introduced in any matter before the NARB

2.7 (Continued)

shall be available for inspection by the NAD and the advertiser who is a party to such matter. All parties to a matter before the NARB shall be given ten days' notice of any hearing or meeting in which evidence or argument will be received. Such notice shall set out the date, place and procedure of the meeting or hearing.

Cases before a NARB panel will be limited to the material submitted by NAD to the advertiser and by the advertiser to NAD. The panel's review will be based on that record, and no other evidence will be considered. However, in the event that newly discovered evidence germane to the panel's decision becomes available, the panel may remand the case back to NAD for consideration and discussion with the advertiser. The advertiser's request for confidentiality of his substantiation and his request not to share that material with the complainant will be honored by the panel even though the complainant may have instituted the appeal.

2.8 Reporting of Panel Decisions

When the panel has reached a decision, it shall notify the Chairman of its decision and the rationale behind it in writing.

The Chairman, upon receipt of a panel's decision will transmit such decision and rationale to the advertiser who is party to the case, providing him with ten days to respond indicating his acceptance, rejection or any comments he may wish to make on the panel's decision. Thereafter, the Chairman will notify other parties to the Case of the panel's decision, incorporating therein the response from the advertiser, and make such report public.

In the event that a panel has determined that an advertisement is misleading or deceptive and the advertiser either fails to indicate that the specific advertisement(s) will be withdrawn or modified in accordance with the panel's findings within a time period appropriate to the circumstances of the case, the Chairman will issue a Notice of Intent to the advertiser that the full record on the case will be referred to the appropriate government agency. If the advertiser fails to respond or does not agree to comply with the decision of the panel within ten days of the issuance of the Notice of Intent, the Chairman shall so inform the appropriate government agency by letter, shall offer the complete NARB file upon request to such government agency, and shall publicly release his letter.

2.9 Closing a Case

When a panel has turned over a decision to the Chairman, and when the Chairman has executed the procedures in Section 2.8 of these "Procedures," the case will be closed and no further materially similar complaints on the advertising in question will be accepted by NAD or NARB.

2.10 Confidentiality of Panel Procedures

All panels, through the Executive Director, shall maintain a complete record of their proceedings, but a verbatim record is not required except to preserve the oral testimony of a witness. All deliberations, meetings, proceedings and writings of a panel other than the written statement of its conclusions and the rationales behind them shall be confidential, with the sole exception of those which the Chairman determines must be made available to an agency of the government.

GENERAL PROVISIONS

3.1 Amendment of Standards

Any proposals to amend the advertising standards which may be adopted by NARB may be acted on a majority vote of the entire membership of the NARB at any special or regular meeting or by written ballot distributed through the United States mails, provided that the text of the proposed amendment shall have been given to the members thirty days in advance of the voting date and provided further that the Board of Directors of the National Advertising Review Council, Inc., shall have been given notice of such proposed amendment at least sixty days in advance of the voting date to afford said Board of Directors the opportunity to render advice and counsel to the NARB members on the proposal and to make such other proposals and recommendations as it deems necessary and appropriate.

The Use of Consultive Panels for

Complaints Other Than Truth and Accuracy

Recognizing that, from time to time, NARB will be asked to consider content of advertising messages in controversy for reasons other than truth and accuracy, the following procedures shall be employed to deal with such complaints:

4.1 Acknowledgment

If the complaint is directed to NARB, that organization will acknowledge its receipt and forward it to NAD. If the complaint has been directed to NAD, it will acknowledge its receipt. The acknowledgment will include a brief explanation informing the complainant that all complaints are first processed by NAD which will determine whether the question is a matter of truth and accuracy or a matter of social responsibility. In either case, an explanation of the procedures to handle such matters will be provided to the complainant.

4.2 Nature of Complaints

Complaints other than truth and accuracy, to be considered, should be broadly applicable or involve techniques or concepts in frequent use. Complaints addressed to very limited kinds of advertising or involving idiosyncratic concepts shall not be processed.

4.3 Classification

When such complaints have been received from NAD, the Chairman and his staff shall quantify and classify them. The Chairman may consult with the NARB Steering Committee for assistance and guidance in this process.

4.4 Consultive Panels

The Chairman may consult with the NARB Steering Committee periodically when the volume and nature of such complaints justifies the convening of a consultive panel of five NARB members which will be comprised in the same ratio as the NARB.

4.5 Panel Procedures

Consultive panels shall review all matters referred to them by the Chairman and may consult other sources to develop data to assist in the evaluation of the broad questions under consideration. No formal inquiry should be directed to advertisers nor should the individual complainant be contacted.

4.6 Confidentiality

All investigations, consultations and inquiries shall be conducted in complete confidence.

4.7 Position Paper

If a panel concludes that the preparation of a position paper is desirable, the writing should be done by the panel and the conclusions should represent the thinking of the entire panel.

4.8 Voting on Publication

Such papers will be submitted to the Chairman for distribution to the full NARB for a vote. The vote to publish or not to publish may be filed by a member at any time during a three week period following the distribution by the Chairman to the full Board.

4.9 Publication

If a majority of the Board vote for publication, the paper will be published promptly with appropriate publicity.

***This opinion modifies the rule on Multiple Product Announcements

UNITED STATES DISTRICT COURT
FOR THE DISTRICT OF COLUMBIA

UNITED STATES OF AMERICA, Plaintiff, v. NATIONAL ASSOCIATION OF BROADCASTERS, Defendant.	Civil Action No. 79-1549 FILED MAR 3 - 1982 JAMES F. DAVEY, Clerk

Excerpt from OPINION

V

Different considerations dictate a different result with regard to the multiple product standard. That standard prohibits

---

36/ It is important to recognize that this action does not represent a complaint by a competitor that an industry established by its other competitors has adversely affected its product. See, e.g., Structural Laminates, Inc. v. Douglas Fir Plywood Ass'n, 261 F. Supp. 154 (D. Ore. 1966), aff'd per curiam, 399 F.2d 155 (9th Cir. 1968). Rather, it is alleged in this case that the standardization agreement adversely affects the customers of television stations that is, their advertisers and viewers.

37/ For example, under the Code a station could probably not choose to designate one hour as commercial-free, moving additional commercials to another hour in the broadcast day. Similarly, it would be difficult for an independent station to broadcast a sixty-minute program during prime time with only a single interruption for commercials while still selling the maximum amount of time permitted by the time standards. An independent station may broadcast fourteen minutes of commercials in sixty minutes of prime time, but only seven commercials may be broadcast during any single interruption. Advertising Standards, XV §§ 2, 4. Thus, each commercial would have to be atypically long, two minutes, in order for the station to sell the maximum amount of commercial time permitted by the Code. Similar difficulties may be encountered with respect to programs of different lengths and those broadcast in non-prime time. (Network-affiliated stations are apparently not subject to this limitation. Regulations XIV § 5.) It might be possible in theory for a station to sell fewer commercials and charge a higher price, but the Code appears to preclude some of the stations' options in this regard and to foster a standard arrangement.

38/ See Nixon v. Freeman, supra.

the advertisement of more than one product in a commercial lasting less than sixty seconds.[39/] It is apparent from the face of this standard that it has the effect of compelling some, perhaps many, advertisers to purchase more commercial time than their economic interests might dictate. In thus artifically increasing the demand for commercial time -- and perhaps limiting its supply as well (see <u>infra</u>) -- the standard raises both the price of time and the revenues of the broadcasters, to the detriment of the users of the broadcast medium and the consumers of their products.

An advertiser is not free, under the multiple product standard, to purchase one thirty-second spot to advertise two products; if he wishes to promote more than one item, he must purchase at least sixty seconds of time -- twice as much as he may actually want or need. The distinction is by no means trivial, just as the difference in cost between a single thirty-second spot and a sixty-second spot is not: on a highly-rated network program it can apparently run into well over $100,000.[40/] Translated into lengthy advertising campaigns, that difference might conceivably add up to millions of dollars in revenues to the broadcasters and in costs to the advertisers -- and indirectly to the consumers of the products these advertisers sell.

The burden of this standard falls especially heavily upon smaller enterprises. A relatively small business which is able to promote one successful product in a series of thirty-second commercials is precluded by the standard from using any portion of that thirty seconds to launch a second product the sales of

---

39/ Advertising Standards, IX § 5. The Code further provides that this provision does not apply if the commercials are "integrated so as to appear to the viewer as a single message." Retail and service establishments are exempt from this provision.

40/ N.Y. Times, Dec. 8, 1981, § 4 at p. 24 col. 3; <u>id</u>., Jan. 29, 1980, § 4, at p. 16 col. 4.

which will not, or not yet, support a commercial of its own.[41] Yet its larger competitor, with the resources to purchase sixty seconds of time, is free to use any part of that period to advertise a number of different products (some of which may be in direct competition with the smaller firm's product kept off the air by NAB's rule). For a discussion of NAB's defense of this policy, see note 73 infra.

The history of the standard bears out the conclusion that its effect is anticompetitive.[42] In 1964, NAB considered a proposal to prohibit "piggyback" commercials.[43] Various advertisers objected on economic grounds,[44] and, instead of an outright ban on piggybacks, NAB adopted the present standard. There again were protests, some claiming illegality under the Sherman Act, but the standard has remained in effect.

The multiple product standard may be regarded as an artifical device to enhance the demand for commercial time, as a means to limit the supply of such time,[45] or as a practice akin to a tying arrangement. Regardless of the label that is applied, the provision per se violates the antitrust laws.

41/ The commercial would be acceptable only if it was "integrated" so as to fall into the exception to this rule. See note 39, supra.

42/ NAB claims that the Court may not rely upon some of the documentary evidence submitted by the government. See Defendant's Supplemental Reply Brief at p. 29 n. 44. None of these exhibits provide information crucial to the Court's decision. They are discussed only to illuminate that decision by providing examples, and to give guidance to the parties in their preparation for trial. See also note 40, supra; notes 43-44, infra; pp. 26-27 infra.

43/ Piggybacks are advertisements containing messages for two or more products in a single commercial.

44/ The chief counsel of Helene Curtis Industries, Inc. stated that the proposal would penalize the small television advertiser, and the president of Alberto-Culver Company likewise noted that it would end the participation of many small advertisers in the medium. The Alberto-Culver witness further commented that multi-product commercials permit an advertiser to use an already profitable product to support much of the expense of introducing a new product, and he unfavorably compared the piggyback rule with newspaper and magazine practice (which do not require advertisers to restrict their advertisements to a single product).

45/ The government has labelled all of the Code provisions at issue in this case as supply restrictions. Plaintiff's Memorandum in Opposition to Motion to Dismiss at p. 11.

The standard, as indicated *supra*, is an artificial rule, adopted by the broadcasters acting in concert, which requires advertisers to purchase more commercial television time than they might wish and in excess of what they would be able to purchase if free market conditions prevailed.[46/] Its effect on a single advertiser is to increase his demand for commercial time, and its overall effect on broadcast industry-advertising industry relations is to enhance the aggregate demand for such time.

On this basis, the multiple product standard bears a strong conceptual resemblance to the agreement involved in *National Macaroni Manufacturers Ass'n* v. *FTC*, 345 F.2d 421 (7th Cir. 1965). In that case, manufacturers agreed upon a standard formula for the ingredients to be used in their macaroni and spaghetti products. The court found that the agreement had the purpose and effect of depressing demand for, and therefore the price of, durum wheat (a raw material used in the manufacture of macaroni and spaghetti), and it held such a standardization agreement to constitute a *per se* violation of the antitrust laws.[47/]

46/ In a free market, absent the NAB Code, there would be no obstacle to the promotion by an advertiser of several of his products in a shorter, and necessarily less expensive, period of time.

47/ Agreements affecting demand fall within the *per se* rule against price fixing for the same reasons as agreements artifically affecting supply: absent special circumstances, both "interfere with the setting of price by free market forces." *United States* v. *Container Corp. of America*, *supra*, 393 U.S. at p. 337. See pp. 6-7, *supra*.

Defendant has presented no valid reasons for not applying the *per se* rule of *National Macaroni* in this case,[48/] and none occurs to the Court. The agreement there fixed the composition of the members' product so as to reduce the demand for, and therefore the price of, a raw material they were using. The agreement here prescribes a rule for subscribers which necessarily has the effect of increasing the demand for, and therefore the price of, commercial time. The result is the same,[49/] and so are the legal consequences.[50/]

Nor does the reasoning which led the Court to decline in Part III *supra* to hold that the *per se* rule does not apply to the Code's time standards help the defendant on this aspect of the

---

48/ Defendant would distinguish *National Macaroni* on three bases. It argues, first, that the court in that case found both an anticompetitive purpose and an anticompetitive effect. Subsequent decisional law establishes that only one of these is necessary for an antitrust violation. See Part VII *infra*. Second, defendant asserts that the Code is not broadly applicable. However, it is clear that the NAB Code has the same dominance in the broadcasting industry that the trade association agreement had in *National Macaroni*. Code subscribers have eighty-five percent of the television viewers in the United States, and in addition, as NAB has conceded, the Code has a significant spillover effect which causes many non-subscribers to adhere to its provisions. NAB Comments before the Federal Trade Commission, *In the Matter of Proposed Trade Regulation Rule: Children's Advertising, supra*, at p. 10; Testimony of Stockton Helffrich before the Federal Communications Commission, *In the Matter of a Petition of Action for Children's Television*, Docket No. 19143, at p. 709. Third, defendant claims that the Code has procompetitive effects in that the supposed alternative -- government regulation -- would apply to all television stations while the Code applies only to subscribers. But if Congress chose to impose standards, either directly or through the Federal Communications Commission, compliance with the congressional directive would obviously not be an antitrust violation. In any event, the agreement's procompetitive effects must be assessed by examining the state of the industry in the absence of the challenged agreement rather than on the basis of hypotheticals.

49/ To be sure, in *National Macaroni* it was the defendants' demand for products that was being affected by the offending practice while in the instant case it is the demand of third parties. But as the discussion of tying arrangements *infra* demonstrates, in appropriate circumstances the antitrust laws are violated in the latter situation as well as the former.

50/ Manufacturers and other sellers may obviously use advertising and other forms of persuasion to increase the demand for their products, and they might even be free to do so on the basis of concerted action. But the multiple product standard is not a form of persuasion but a coercive device which leaves an advertiser with no option with respect to his demand for commercial time: if he desires to promote more than one product he must increase his demand for such time to sixty seconds per commercial announcement.

case. As indicated above, it is possible that the intrinsic characteristics of the broadcasting industry rather than the Code's time standards are instrumental in limiting the overall supply of commercial time, and for that reason these standards might not be found to have the specific effect on supply that is presumed by the general rule against supply restrictions. But the industry's characteristics are not relevant to the _National Macaroni_ principle; the only significant consideration under the branch of the _per se_ rule it represents is whether the agreement tampers with demand. Demand results directly from advertisers' need for commercial time; their need for time is not affected by various inherent limits on broadcast time or governmental rules against overcommercialization. Even when supply remains constant, it is clear that, in a free market, an increase in demand will lead to an increase in price.

If the multiple product standard is viewed as a supply limitation, on the theory that it limits the number of commercials possible in a given amount of time, the same result obtains. For the reasons cited above, the total supply of commercial time may be presumed to be limited, as a consequence either of the special characteristics of the industry, or of the Code's time standards, or both. Upon this limited amount of time the television broadcasters have imposed through NAB an additional restriction in the form of the multiple product standard. That standard makes commercial time available to the advertisers in such a manner, _i.e._, in segments of a particular size, as to reduce the supply of time even further.[51/] When producers combine to impose a rule that so

---

51/ The effect, if any, of the special characteristics of the industry would be to reduce the _total_ supply of commercial time. These characteristics do not impact upon the operation of a rule which further reduces the availability of this supply to consumers.

limits supply they artificially inflate price and act _per se_ in an anticompetitive manner. See pp. 6-7 _supra_.[52/]

Finally, as indicated above, the multiple product standard is in significant respects analogous to the practice of tying -- also a _per se_ violation of the Sherman Act. _Northern Pacific Railway Co._ v. _United States_, _supra_. See generally, L. Sullivan, _Antitrust_, _supra_, at §§ 150-162. Tying occurs when a seller requires purchasers of one product to purchase also a second product which the purchaesr does not or may not want. The rationale of the prohibition against tying is that it

> den[ies] competitors free access to the market for the tied product, not because the party imposing the tying requirements has a better product or a lower price but because of his power or leverage in another market. . . . [B]uyers are forced to forego their free choice between competing products.

Northern Pacific Railway Co. v. _United States_, _supra_, 356 U.S. at 6.

The tying cases, to be sure, are not technically applicable in this instance because the additional amount of commercial time advertisers are required to purchase under the multiple product standard does not represent a "different product" from the time the advertisers actually desire to purchase.[53/] However, the rationale underlying the rule against tying -- that sellers should be precluded from using their market power to force a buyer to purchase and to pay for something he does not want -- applies precisely in this case. NAB has used its dominance in the television industry to require companies who desire to advertise more than one product on television to buy more than they wish to purchase. Thus, the coercive use of market power to restrict buyers' decision-making which is at the heart of tying is also

---

52/ Even in an industry with unusual or special characteristics, a court is not precluded from finding a _per se_ violation where, as here, the practice under scrutiny is itself clearly anticompetitive and where, again as here, the industry's features do not vitiate the anticompetitive effect.

53/ See L. Sullivan, _Antitrust_, _supra_, at § 155.

present in the provision at issue here. See P. Areeda, Antitrust Analysis ¶ 541 (1981).[54/]

The Court concludes that for these reasons, both individually and on the basis of their interrelationship, NAB's multiple product standard falls within the *per se* rule and is violative of the Sherman Act. It follows that the conduct it represents must conclusively be presumed to be unreasonable, and defenses available in a Rule of Reason context (Parts VI through IX) are foreclosed. Broadcast Music, Inc. v. Columbia Broadcasting System, Inc., *supra*, 441 U.S. at 8; Klor's Inc. v. Broadway-Hale Stores, Inc., 359 U.S. 207, 211-12 (1959); Northern Pacific Railway Co. v. United States, *supra*, 356 U.S. at 5.

54/ The antitrust laws might not prohibit an individual television station from requiring advertisers to purchase a minimum amount of time, for such a requirement, to the extent that it is unreasonable, could be rectified by market forces. NAB's concerted action prevents these market forces from operating.

5

GOVERNMENTAL CONTROLS OF ADVERTISING

Thomas R. Hillhouse

February 12, 1982

GOVERNMENTAL CONTROLS OF ADVERTISING

1. Sources of Controls

A. Federal Level

1. Federal Trade Commission

a. Government control over advertising is vested primarily in the Federal Trade Commission. Section 5(b) of the Federal Trade Commission Act empowers the Commission to issue orders requiring any "person, partnership or corporation" to "cease and desist" from "using any unfair method of competition or unfair or deceptive act or practice in commerce." 15 U.S.C. 45.

(1) The role of the FTC in guarding consumers as well as competitors was given express Congressional sanction by the Wheeler Lea Act of 1938 which added to the Section 5 prohibition of "unfair methods of competition" the category of "unfair or deceptive acts or practices in commerce."

(a) Commission orders are self-executing with civil penalties of up to $10,000 for violation of a final order. 15 U.S.C. 45(g)(1). Each broadcast of a commercial can be a separate violation. U.S. v. J. B. Williams Co., Inc. 498 F.2d 414 (1974). Also, each separate dissemination to each consumer in violation of a consent order can be subject to a fine of up to $10M. U.S. vs. Readers Digest, 1981 ATRR No. 1029 (8/24/81). Cert. filed 10/22/81. Cert denied January 1982. Fine of $1,750,000 for violation of 1971 consent order.

Also <u>RJR Foods Inc.</u> CCH TRR ¶21,889 (1981). $70M fine to settle charges it violated a 1973 consent order by failure to disclose percent of fruit juice. See also STP reference <u>infra</u> - pays $700M for alleged violations of previous consent order.

(b) Injunctive remedy has not yet been used with great frequency but probably will be. <u>Travel King, Inc.</u> 1973-1976 CCH Transfer Binder ¶20,502 (1974) and CCH 1977-1 Trade Cases ¶61,419; <u>Southwest Sunsites, Inc.</u>, 3 CCH Trade Regulation Reporter ¶21,667 and ¶21,683 (1980).

(c) Section 5(m), added by the 1975 FTC Improvement Act, permits the Commission to proceed directly against a party for a civil penalty of up to $10,000 in two situations: a) when there is an alleged violation of a trade regulation rule with constructive knowledge, or (b) when there is an alleged violation of a final cease and desist order issued against <u>another</u> party with actual knowledge.

b. The FTC has greater powers in connection with its special jurisdiction over food, drugs, medical devices and cosmetics. 15 U.S.C. 52. See generally 2 CCH Trade Reg. Rep. ¶7880 <u>et seq</u>, also 75 <u>Mich. L. Rev.</u> 745 (1977)

(1) The Commission may, upon a proper showing of reason to believe that the practice is deceptive, obtain a preliminary injunction from a district court prohibiting the use

of the advertising pending adjudication of the merits. 15 U.S.C. 53(a).

(a) The proceeding before the agency itself follows the Sec. 5 format.

(b) Violation of these sections is a misdemeanor if the commodity advertising may be injurious to health when the product is employed as described or as ordinariy used or when the violation is with intent to defraud or mislead. 15 U.S.C. 54(a).

2. Food & Drug Administration

a. The FDA was given the power to regulate labels and labeling accompanying foods, drugs and cosmetics.

(1) Authority is derived from the Federal Food, Drug and Cosmetic Act of 1938. 21 U.S.C. 301-392.

(2) Some decisions have broadly interpreted labeling, thereby extending the FDA's jurisdiction to material which would commonly be thought of as advertising -- e.g., pamphlets.

(3) OTC Drug Review 21 CFR 330.10

(a) FTC "Claims" TRR - Proposed 40 FR 52631 (11/11/75), Terminated 46 FR 24584 (5/1/81)

(b) FTC Antacid Warnings TRR - proposed 41 FR 14534 (4/6/76)

(c) FDA "Exclusivity" Policy - 40 FR 11718 (1975)

(d) FTC "stockpiling" of claims - Aspercreme Investigation, Wall Street Journal 2/11/81

3. Environmental Protection Agency (FIFRA; 7 USC 135 et seq.)

   a. FTC effort to establish an industry warning requirement in pesticide advertising. (1968-1977) 33 FR 918 (1/2/68) 42 FR 62146 (12/9/77)

   b. FTC has forbidden advertising that is inconsistent or distracts from any warning or caution or direction for use found on the labeling of EPA registered products. Union Carbide Corp. v. Hercules Inc., 1973-1976 CCH Transfer Binder ¶20,584 (1974), modified 3 TRR ¶21,634 (1979); Farnam Companies, Inc., 3 TRR ¶21,758 (1980).

   c. Sterling Drug Inc. Docket No. 8899 (Lysol) 84 FTC 547 (1974).

4. Post Office Department

   a. Authority to enforce postal fraud statutes and federal anti-lottery laws. Will render advisory opinions concerning sweepstakes and lotteries.

   b. With growing popularity of instant winner games, USPS advisory opinions are cautioning that free entry should be readily available.

5. Federal Communications Commission

   a. FCC's stated position: "The main thrust" in the field of deceptive advertising must continue to come from the FTC which "has the capacity to formulate standards of deceptive advertising which are applicable to the various media."

   b. Product commercials may or may not be subject to the Fairness Doctrine depending on whether the commercial raises a controversial issue of public importance for which there is an opposing point of view.

B. State Level

1. States have accumulated a large number of civil and criminal statutes concerned with the advertising of a specific product, service or profession.

   a. Many of these involve limitations based on considerations of good taste and morality rather than on the dangers of deception.

   b. At least 22 states have adopted in some form the Printer's Ink model penal statute which punishes as a misdemeanor placing before the public deceptive or misleading statements.

2. Remedies Sought

   a. State regulation of advertising has been substantially increased with the passage of civil remedial statutes enforced statewide by the Attorney General and by the establishment by many attorneys general of specialized additions within the departments to deal exclusively with consumer law problems.

      (1) Normally, after a complaint is received, the state bureau informs the businessman involved and asks for an explanation.

         (a) The consumers who file complaints often wish to obtain some form of restitution and state bureaus, using implicit or explicit threats of prosecution or public exposure, are able to satisfy the complainant's desire in many cases.

         (b) State bureaus have instituted relatively few injunction proceedings in part because of the high priority given to collection of refunds.

b. Assurances of discontinuance are used in New York, whereby the Attorney General is authorized to accept a written assurance from a violator that he will discontinue a specific deceptive practice.

(1) A violation of the assurance constitutes prima facie proof for the State in a subsequent injunction proceeding.

3. As evidence of greater state activity consider the General Motors engine switching case. Total liability to GM was in the millions of dollars.

4. Outlook.

C. <u>Local Level</u>

1. Consumer fraud divisions have been established in a few large cities to proceed against major instances of false advertising. The offense must, of course, be proven beyond a reasonable doubt.

II. <u>FTC Activities</u>

A. Section 5 proceedings for false, deceptive and unfair advertising -- Basic principles;

1. The Commission need not show that there has been actual deception. It must establish only that the advertisement has a capacity to deceive.

a. Many courts have said that the relevant interpretation is the one that would be made by an average individual or by the buying public generally.

b. Action against advertisements which might not deceive a typical consumer is sometimes based on the advertisement's probable impact on the specific type of person to whom it is addressed.

(1) In considering advertisements for toys, the Commission has found a violation where it believes that

children could be misled even though adults might not be. Stupell Originals, Inc., 1963-1965 CCH Transfer Binder, ¶17,208, (1965). See also Topper FTC C-2073 and Mattel, FTC C-2071, 1970-1973 CCH Transfer Binder ¶19,735, (1971). Also consider the "Spider Man" vitamins case, Hudson Pharmaceutical Corp., 1976-1979 CCH Transfer Binder, ¶21,191 (1976); Tomy Corp., 42 FR 42681 (1981).

(2) Consider also the basis underlying the now terminated Children's Advertising TRR. (46 FR 21099, 48710) (1981).

c. For an extended discussion of the concept of "tendency to deceive" see Chapter 18 in Vol. 2 of The Law of Advertising, Rosden, 1974.

2. Interpreting the advertisement: Normally, the representation which is relevant in determining the legality of the advertisement is the general impression given by the advertisement read as a whole. Charles of the Ritz Distributors Corp. vs. FTC, 143 F.2d 676 (2d. Cir. 1944).

a. The literal truth of the individual assertions is not defense if they are so combined as to convey a misleading representation on a casual reading. Kalwajtys v. FTC, 237 F.2d 654 (1956). Deception may be by innuendo rather than outright false statements. National Bakers Service, Inc. v. FTC, 1964 Trade Cases, ¶71,061.

b. The ambiguous statement: An advertisement may be found unlawful if it is capable of being read in a misleading way, even though other non-misleading interpretations may also be possible or even likely. Murray Shoe Corp. v. FTC, 304 F.2d 270 (2d Cir. 1962).

(1) Secondary meaning: The FTC requires a "high degree of proof" that the word in fact has a secondary meaning to the general

public. Even if this burden is met, the Commission requires that it be carefully qualified to prevent consumers from inferring the primary meaning.

c. The truth of the representation:

(1) The product may not be represented as different from what it actually is even though the product itself may be better.

(a) The consumer is considered to have been wronged and the act violated if the buyer does not get what the advertisement leads him to expect, even if he in fact gets something "better." See discussion in FTC v. Colgate-Palmolive Company, 380 U.S. 374 at 388 (1965).

(2) Exaggeration: Some courts and the Commission itself have referred to terms such as "amazing" and "perfect" as puffing and have held that they are to be interpreted only as general recommendations not to be taken literally.

(3) Studies: A critical issue will be whether advertisements summarize an independent study in such a way as to suggest that the study was more favorable to the advertised product that it really was.

(4) Materiality: The FTC's prohibition of unfair or deceptive practices has been interpreted as barring only material untruths in advertising -- thus capable of affecting purchasing decisions. FTC v. Colgate-Palmolive Company, 380 U.S. 374, 386 (1965).

(5) "First contact" theory: The Commission has established the principle that the prohibition

against unfair or deceptive practices embraces misrepresentations used to make initial contact with the prospective customer even though the misrepresentations may not affect the final decision to buy.

(6) Consumer Research: The use of consumer research to support advertising claims is an area that has not been extensively discussed in the cases. Any research results used should be statistically significant and the survey should have been conducted in accordance with accepted scientific principles. Further, the advertiser should be aware of the possibility that the Commission could reverse the results of the survey to "prove" a deception, i.e., 10% of the respondents had an opinion opposite to that represented in the ad.

(7) Surveys: Advertising claims must not misrepresent the contents, results or conclusions of such surveys. Litton Industries, Inc. 3 TRR ¶21,784, Standard Brands, Inc. 3 TRR ¶21,779, Teledyne, Inc. 3 TRR ¶21,780, Kroger "Price Patrol" 3 TRR ¶21,877 (9/25/81). Also consider possible 43(a) problems (Triumph cigarette cases). Philip Morris v. Loew's, 511 F. Supp. 855 and RJR v. Loew's, 511 F. Supp. 867 (S.D.N.Y. 1980).

d. Demonstrations and testimonials:

(1) See discussion of demonstrations in FTC v. Colgate-Palmolive Company, 380 U.S. 374 (1965). See also In re Colgate-Palmolive Co., et al. 1967-1970 CCH Transfer Binder ¶19,074, (1970) and In re American Home Products Corp., et al, 1970-1973 CCH Transfer Binder, ¶19,673 (1971).

(2) Testimonials and endorsements: See FTC's Guides Concerning Use of Endorsements and Testimonials in Advertising. 45 FR 3870 (1/18/80); 16 CFR 255.

e. Qualifications and limitations: In an advertisement a "concise statement of an established fact immediately thereafter expanded" should not be found misleading even when the concise statement taken alone would have deceptive implications. FTC v. Sterling Drug, Inc., 317 F.2d 669, 675 (2d Cir. 1963).

(1) A claim made in laymen's language is not effectively limited by a technically phrased qualification.

(2) The qualification must not directly contradict the original assertions or be so vaguely worded as to create further uncertainty.

(3) The manner of display must also be considered -- the qualification must at the very least be likely to come to the attention of any person who sees the basic claim. See for instance the FTC Statement of Enforcement Policy on the standards for determining whether a disclosure is "clear and conspicuous," 2 CCH Trade Reg. Rep. ¶7569.09.

f. Dry Ban Case: The 1975 Dry Ban case was perceived by some individuals in the advertising community as evidence that the Commission would not proceed against advertising for small-ticket items, unless health or safety was involved. This case certainly did not support this reaction -- the Commission merely determined that the alleged claims had not been made in the ads. However, the opinion was favorable to advertisers in general because it indicated an unwillingness by that Commission to support hyper-technical cases brought by the Staff. Bristol-Myers Co., CCH 1973-1976 Transfer Binder ¶20,900.

g. Current trends; With the recent changes in the Commission and the Enactment of the 1980 FTC Improvements Act, the Commission itself will probably be less aggressive in attacking implied or overall impact claims. However, the staff will probably continue to scrutinize such claims and an advertiser should not rely upon what might appear to be temporary changes of direction in this area.

3. Implied uniqueness - When does the truth become unfair?

   a. ITT Continental Baking (Wonder Bread), Commission decision at 1973-1976 CCH Transfer Binder, ¶20,464 (1973).

   b. The complaint alleged that Wonder Bread advertising was false because the commercials implied that Wonder Bread was more nutritious than other breads even though no express claims of nutritional superiority were made. The Commission decided, based in part on survey evidence, that it was unable to conclude that the specific representation of nutritional superiority was contained in the advertisement.

   c. The Commission decided against Wonder Bread, however, on the charge that the commercials implied Wonder Bread was "an extraordinary food for producing dramatic growth in children." Although the representation was not expressly made by the advertisements in the precise language of the complaint, the Commission believed that the ads falsely implied that Wonder Bread is an extraordinary food for producing dramatic growth in children when, in fact, it is no more nutritious than other enriched breads.

   d. See also In re The Coca Cola Company (Hi-C), 1973-1976 CCH Transfer Binder, ¶20,470 (1973) where the FTC dismissed charges that Hi-C advertisements misrepresented Hi-Ci's nature, content and nutritive value. Hi-C was left free to call attention to its merits as a source of vitamin C provided it kept its literal claims true.

e. Language in the Procter & Gamble (Crisco Oil) consent decree, 1970-1973 CCH Transfer Binder, ¶19,889 (1972) still seems to be a good expression of the state of the law: "A statement as to the qualities or attributes of a product can amount to an implied uniqueness claim if it is made in a context which conveys an impression of uniqueness for the product. However, statements as to the qualities or attributes of products covered by the order will not constitute a violation of this order for the sole reason that such statements could also be made with respect to similar products."

4. Remedies -- Beneficial case.

a. Beneficial was prohibited from using its copyrighted "instant tax refund" advertising term because of the false and misleading impression it conveyed.

b. The Court of Appeals agreed that the prior advertising had a tendency to deceive, but disagreed that the only appropriate remedy was a total ban on the use of the "instant tax refund" slogan. (See 542 F.2d 611 (1976).)

c. Because of the First Amendment protection of commercial speech, the Court of Appeals held that the remedy could go no further in imposing a prior restraint than is necessary to correct the abuse. Thus, the Commission was required to consider if the ads could be properly qualified to prevent the prior deception.

d. Beneficial has agreed to an FTC order barring the use of such terms as "Instant Tax Refund" without clearly disclosing that loans it offers have no relationship with the individual's tax refund. See Beneficial consent order, 1976-1979 CCH Transfer Binder, ¶21,583 (1979).

B. Expansion of FTC's authority to challenge "unfair" methods of competition.

1. FTC v. Sperry & Hutchinson, 405 U.S. 233 (1972)

a. Substantially broadened the Commission's authority to challenge allegedly unfair methods of competition and allegedly unfair trade practices which do not violate either the letter or the spirit of the antitrust laws.

(1) The Opinion expressly authorizes the FTC to function like a court of equity and to "consider public values beyond simply those enshrined in the letter or encompassed in the spirit of the antitrust laws," in determining whether a particular act or practice violates the illusive but congressionally mandated standard of fairness which is established by Section 5 of the Act.

b. Court approved factors which make a practice unfair even though it is not deceptive and does not violate the antitrust laws.

(1) Whether the practice "offends public policy" by violating "some common law, statutory or other established concept of fairness."

(2) Whether the practice is "immoral, unethical, oppressive or unscrupulous."

(3) Whether the practice causes "substantial injury to consumers or competitors or other businessmen."

(a) The latter seems the most significant. The concept is already playing a critical role in the Commission's consumer protection activities, especially with respect to advertising practices -- e.g., Pfizer "Unburn" case.

(i) A difficult question is whether the S&H decision will be deemed to justify holding that advertising which causes consumers to buy a product without regard to price or quality but merely by inducing an emotional reaction which one fTC official has characterized as "non-rational experience" is "unfair" to consumers and in violation of Section 5 of the FTC Act.

2. Reasonable Basis for making a Claim - Pfizer ("Unburn") Decision, 1970-1973 CCH Transfer Binder, ¶20,056 (1972).

   a. Chairman Kirkpatrick's decision established guidelines for advertisements that contain affirmative claims regarding product performance. In essence, the Commission held that Section 5 of the FTC Act prohibits as unfair to consumers and to competitors any advertising containing an affirmative product claim for which the advertiser does not have a reasonable basis -- whether or not the claim proves to be true.

      (1) An advertiser must have prior proof of advertising claims to escape a Section 5 violation, even if the claims are true.

      (2) According to that opinion, it is unfair for an advertiser to subject consumers to the risk that a product will not perform as advertised; it is also unfair to competitors for an advertiser to obtain business by

means of affirmative product claims which are not reasonably based.

(3) Cites S&H case.

b. The opinion also states that the question of whether an advertiser has a reasonable basis for making a particular affirmative advertising claim is a question of fact, to be determined on the basis of all relevant circumstances present in each individual case -- including such factors as the type and specificity of the claim made, type of product involved, extent to which consumers rely on the claim made, the possible adverse effect on consumers if the claim proves to be inaccurate, and the type and accessibility of evidence which might provide a basis for making the claim.

c. FTC Chairman Miller's Recent Remarks.

3. Also follow the Analgesics cases, Dockets 8917-8919 (1973), American Home Products Corp., Bristol-Myers Company, Sterling Drug, Inc.

a. The Commission alleged there are not substantial chemical and pharmaceutical differences between the various products in question and that it is therefore both unfair and deceptive for the companies to advertise any one of the products in a manner which suggests it is more effective and will provide quicker relief than competing products. Compare the Anacin/Tylenol cases. American Home Products Corp. v. Johnson & Johnson, 436 F. Supp. 785 (D.C.N.Y. 1977); McNeilab v. American Home Products, 501 F. Supp 517 (S.D.N.Y. 1980); McNeil v. Sterling Drug (Bayer), Advertising Age (11/9/81). Although not cases of government regulation, they are interesting because they illustrate the possible use of Section 43(a) of the Lanham Act to challenge competitor's advertising. This section provides for civil action "by any person who believes that he is or is likely to be damaged by the use of any such false description or representation."

b. ALJ has issued initial decisions in each of the 3 Analgesics cases.

(1) American Home Products: 1976-79 CCH Transfer Binder ¶21,465 (1978)

(a) Prohibited AHP from making comparative product claims unless supported by two (2) well-controlled clinicals or disclosure made that claim not proven;

(b) Required corrective ads regarding tension relief claims (This was deleted in the Commission's Final Order. See Infra);

(c) Restricted "special ingredient" claims;

(d) Required disclosure of common names, including aspirin;

(e) Restricted fast relief claims.

(2) Bristol-Myers: 3 TRR ¶21,618 (1979)

(a) Prohibited B-M from making comparative product claims unless supported by two (2) well-controlled clinicals, and required disclosure of "substantial question" even with such clinicals;

(b) Required "reasonable basis" for non-comparative claims as to all OTC drugs;

(c) Restricted "special ingredient" claims;

(d) Required disclosure of common names, including aspirin;

(e) Prohibited tension relief claims.

(3) Sterling Drug: 3 TRR ¶21,789 (1981)

(a) Prohibited S-D from making comparaitve product claims unless supported by two (2) well-controlled clinicals, and required disclosure of "substantial question" even with such clinicals;

(b) Required "reasonable basis" for non-comparative claims as to all OTC drugs;

(c) Set forth criteria for comparative pharmaceutical quality claims;

(d) Restricted "special ingredient" claims;

(e) Required disclosure of common names, including aspirin.

4. In Nagle, Spillman & Bergmann, consent order, 1976-1979 CCH Transfer Binder, ¶21157, the FTC requires that Adolph's Salt Substitute not be advertised as reducing sodium intake to a level low enough to prevent any disease or condition without a reasonable basis. Further, Nagle could not represent that the causal relationship between salt intake and hypertension is well-established or that its salt substitute tasted like table salt.

5. In re K Mart Enterprises, Inc., 1973-1976 CCH Transfer Binder, ¶20,661 (1974) requires not only competent scientific tests, but directs that the test must support the advertising claim at not less than the 95% confidence level.

a. For example, at the 95% confidence level, 19 out of 20 of the advertised tires could be expected to give better traction than one of the other tires.

6. See also Firestone Tire & Rubber Co. v. FTC, 481 F.2d 246 (1973) which applied the "substantial scientific test data" criterion.

7. Unsafe Practices: Recent consent orders require advertisers to avoid depicting unsafe or unlawful practices.

    a. AMF, Inc., 44 FR 40333 (1979); 45 FR 17953 (1980): advertiser prohibited from showing young children riding bicycles, tricycles, etc., in improper, unsafe, etc. circumstances. Prepare and make available a TV safety message.

    b. American Motors Corp. 3 TRR ¶21,890 (1981): Proposed consent order requires advertiser to attach warning stickers to new jeeps and mail such stickers to current owners.

III. FTC Procedures

A. Investigations

1. Most investigations result from public complaints or actions initiated by the Commission itself.

    a. The Commission has been assuming an increasing responsibility for actively locating the violations, relying heavily upon a monitoring unit which examines advertisements in various media as well as upon casual observation by staff attorneys.

    b. Investigations may also result from allegedly deceptive advertisements coming to the attention of the Commission through other government personnel.

2. Responsibility for investigations rests with the Bureau of Consumer Protection where information received is studied by a staff attorney to determine whether the matter warrants investigation.

    a. If investigation seems warranted, the first step is normally an informal request letter to the party under investigation asking for data.

b. If the party is unwilling to cooperate or if the material submitted in response to the informal request letter indicates likelihood of a violation, the staff attorney will normally obtain formal investigation authority from the Commission (the "seven-digit investigation") and obtain further information under the authority.

c. If it is necessary to conduct technical studies of products to determine the truth of false ad claims made, the matter may be referred to the Commission's Division of Scientific Opinions.

   (1) Also used are the National Bureau of Standards, the Food & Drug Administration and the Department of Agriculture.

d. Increasingly, the number of investigations originating with and complaints filed by FTC Regional Offices is growing. The violations are essentially local while those handled by the Bureau of Consumer Protection are normally of a national or broad regional character.

3. <u>FTC possesses broad investigatory powers</u>:

   a. Itemized in Section 6 of the Act and made effective in Sections 9 and 10 through the grant of subpoena powers and the imposition of penalties for non-compliance.

      (1) The Commission can employ its power to obtain a special report from a corporation "merely on suspicion that the law is being violated or even just because it wants assurance that it is not" so long as it has jurisdiction over the matter being investigated, the information sounds "reasonably relevant" and the request is reasonably clear. <u>U.S. v. Morton Salt Company</u>, 338 U.S. 632 (1950).

(2) The right of the FTC to investigate and demand information cannot be challenged in an injunction suit, but the Declaratory Judgment Act is available to test the validity of an FTC investigation. See St. Regis Paper Co. vs. U.S., 368 U.S. 208 (1961).

b. Section 408 of the 1973 Trans-Alaska Pipeline Authorization Act enlarges the investigation powers of the Commission in that it vests the Commission with authority to enforce its own subpoena.

c. Details of FTC investigations are covered in the Agency's Rules, 16 CFR 2.1 - 2.4.

d. Judicial decisions in the last two decades have clearly established that the investigatory process may be used in pre-litigation. FTC v. Harrell, 313 F.2d 854 (2d Cir. 1963).

e. The existence of these powers and the sanctions behind them often encourage advertisers to comply voluntarily with the initial request for information - but should you?

f. 1980 FTC Improvements Act require CID's to be signed by a Commissioner pursuant to a Commission Resolution.

B. Follow-up of Investigation

1. After investigation, the staff attorney will draft a memorandum to the Commission recommending a course of action: that the file be closed, that informal enforcement procedures be taken or that a complaint be issued.

a. The Commission must authorize any further action to be taken.

b. If the Commission finds "reason to believe" that an unlawful practice has been or is being employed, it may institute informal enforcement procedures which may take the form of an oral promise or an exchange of letters. (See 16 CFR 2.21)

2. If no agreement is reached during investigation, the complaint/consent order procedure is employed.

   a. More than 75% of the cases docketed by the Commission are concluded through the consent order procedure.

   b. Generally, see 16 C.F.R. 2.31 - 2.35 for Consent Order procedure.

   c. Opportunity for preparation of an "appropriate agreement."

      (1) Usually the respondent will be able to negotiate with staff counsel as to the adequacy of the allegation of the complaint and the wording of the order which will be entered.

   d. Adverse publicity as well as the desire to avoid costs of litigation are factors which may influence advertisers to accept a consent order even though they think their legal position is strong.

   e. Once entered, the consent order is in all other respects effective in the same manner as an order the Commission entered after adjudication.

   f. A rule, 16 CFR 2.34, adopted on July 27, 1977, provides that when a provisionally acceptable consent order is published for the 60-day comment period, it will be accompanied by "material submitted to the Commission reasonably related to the merits of the order that is not exempt from disclosure under the Freedom of Information Act."

C. <u>Adjudication</u> - If no agreement on consent order, complaint issues.

1. The Hearing: The hearing on an agency complaint is conducted before an Administrative Law Judge according to the

provisions of the Administrative Procedure Act and the rules and procedures promulgated by the Commission itself. (See 16 CFR 3.1 - 3.72)

a. The discovery rules, as of January 18, 1979, were amended to conform the provisions on discovery more closely to the Federal Rules of Civil Procedure. The scope of discovery generally follows the relevance standard in the Federal Rules and a rule on interrogatories has been modeled on Federal Rule 33 (see 16 CFR ¶3.31(b) and ¶3.35). In any case, these amendments were to assure the Administrative Law Judge effective control of the proceeding with substantial flexibility in determining the scope of discovery (see Staff Summary of Proposed Rules, 43 Fed. Reg. 56862).

b. At the end of taking evidence, any party can file proposed findings, conclusions and order.

2. The Administrative Law Judge himself must file the initial decision within 90 days after completion of the taking of evidence. That decision becomes the decision of the Commission 30 days later unless in the meantime:

   a. A party appeals to the Commission.

   b. The Commission orders a stay.

   c. The Commission issues an order to place the case on its own docket.

      (1) On review, the Commission may exercise all the powers which it could have exercised if it had made the initial decision.

3. The respondent has a right to judicial review of the Commission decision in the Court of Appeals.

4. Compliance with the order: When a cease and desist order issues, the respondent must within 60 days submit a compliance report "setting forth in detail the manner and form of its compliance with the order". 16 CFR 3.61.

   a. These reports are reviewed to determine whether his actions comport with the order, and the agency can refuse to accept the report if it deems his conduct unsatisfactory.

   b. The advertiser must also file other reports if the agency requests them.

   c. Parties:

      (1) Not only the corporation or individual whose advertisements are challenged, but also any agents, corporate officers, parent corporations, the advertising agency conducting the campaign and others -- who can be shown to have had control over or to have participated in the alleged deception -- can be sued.

      (2) An outstanding order against an advertising agency may control a much larger section of the total national advertising than one against a single corporation because it prohibits the agency from using the technique in the promotion of products of all manufacturers it represents.

   d. Abandonment of the challenged practice is not necessarily a defense to an FTC proceeding.

D. <u>Civil Penalties for Knowing Violations</u> -- FTC Act Section 5(m)

   1. The Commission may commence a civil action to recover a civil penalty in a district court against <u>any</u> person, partnership or corporation which engages in such act or practice <u>whether or not</u> such person was subject to such cease and desist order so

long as that person had actual knowledge that such act or practice was unfair.

2. Civil penalty of up to $10,000.

3. Has not been actively used by the Commission and, therefore, has not been extensively challenged in the courts.

   a. Not clear what constitutes "actual" knowledge, although the Commission has used the technique of mailing "synopses" of prior cease and desist orders to corporations and agencies.

   b. Section 5(m)(2) provides that issues of fact will be tried _de novo_ in the district court if a civil penalty action is initiated against a defendant who is not a party to the cease and desist order. This provision probably limits the district court's _de novo_ hearings to the facts (i.e., does the pending case fall within the acts prohibited by the earlier cease and desist order?) and would not permit the defendant to reargue the law.

   c. Does the amendment apply to pre-1975 cease and desist orders or does it speak prospectively only? Obviously, the Commision feels that it applies to all orders. Does this raise due process questions? Does a party who would be affected by a future cease and desist order have a right to intervene in a Commission proceeding?

   d. Doesn't this provision elevate cease and desist orders to the level of trade regulation rules, thereby authorizing rulemaking by adjudication without offering potentially affected parties the right to participate?

   e. A Section 5(m) proceeding can probably only be initiated with respect to a prior "litigated" cease and desist order, although the language of the Act would not rule out an attempt by the Commission to base a proceeding on a prior Consent Order.

f. The <u>"Block Drug Caper"</u> - Block allowed the administrative law judge to enter an order against it and did not appeal to the Commisison. Block announced it would mail the order to its competitors to make it applicable to them under Section 5(m).

g. <u>US vs. Braswell, Inc.</u> 1981-2 Trade Cases ¶64,325 (9/28/81), upholding constitutional due proceess challenge to Sec. 5(m).

h. See also <u>Ford Motor Co. vs. FTC</u>, 654 F.2d 599 (9th Cir. 1981).

E. <u>Non-Judicial Procedures</u>

1. Advisory Opinions: The FTC has long given staff level advice on the compatibility of proposed conduct with the statutes it administers.

a. Such advice is not binding on the agency in the sense of estopping it from future prosecutions inconsistent with the advice.

b. Although the advice may be unilaterally revoked at any time, Commission rules make it binding to the extent that no prosecution may be undertaken until notice or revocation is given the party and he is afforded an opportunity to promptly discontinue the conduct in question.

c. The agency will not cosider requests for advisory opinions where:

(1) The requesting party is already employing the practice.

(2) The practice is under investigation or involved in a proceeding which may subject an order against the requesting party.

(3) The efforts required to answer the request appear likely to be substantial.

d. Reasons not to seek advisory opinion.

(1) The long delays required to get staff advice normally make the advisory opinion route impractical in advertising matters.

(2) Future campaign strategies may inadvertently be disclosed in spite of best effort to insure confidentiality.

e. See Generally 16 CFR 1.1 - 1.4.

2. Industry Guides: Administrative interpretations of laws, administered by the Commission for the guidance of the public in conducting its affairs in conformity with legal requirements. See 16 CFR ¶1.5.

a. Failure to comply may result in corrective action by the Commission under statutory provisions.

b. Do not have the force of substantive law.

F. Exclusionary Rule -- Ad Substantiation Cases

1. Effective October 26, 1977, 16 CFR 3.40 requires advertisers to submit timely and complete substantiation materials in response to compulsory process demands or have the material excluded at trial if it is offered in defense of a charge that the advertiser lacked a reasonable basis for an advertising claim.

a. The one exception to the exclusionary rule permits the later introduction of material that could not have been timely submitted by the exercise of due diligence, provided the commission was notified of the existence of the material immediately upon its discovery.

b. The rule was adopted over the dissents of Commissioners Collier and Clanton.

c. FTC Chairman Miller's comments before American Advertising Federation 12/8/81.

2. The exclusionary rule will undoubtedly be attacked as unconstitutional because it denies respondents the opportunity to present evidence in their defense at trial.

3. The rule may not have much practical effect if the Commission permits respondents to submit explanatory and supplemental materials at a later date; however, if the Commission tries to exclude such materials, it will place a tremendous burden on respondents to determine "how much" material should be submitted originally. (The rule excludes "_any_ material of _any_ type whatsoever that was _required_ to be submitted.")

4. Another area of concern is the use of the exclusionary rule in connection with a Commission proceeding against an "implied" claim which the advertiser does not feel was made in the challenged ad. If the advertiser chooses to defend on the basis that the claim was not made, must he still submit all substantiating materials which he might have available to protect himself at a later trial?

G. _1980 FTC Improvements Act_

1. Suspension of Children's Advertising TRR as of May 28, 1980.

2. Prohibition against any Kid-Vid TRR based on unfairness only.

3. Three-year moratorium against _any_ advertising TRR based on unfairness only.

H. _Industry TRR proceedings_

1. Authorized by 1975 Magnuson-Moss Act.

2. _Ford Motor Co. v. FTC_, 654 F.2d 599 (8/24/81, 9th Cir.) rehearing requested by FTC.

3. Legislative veto -- 1980 Act

   (a) Publish advance notice of TRR and send to Congress.

   (b) Proposed TRR must be sent to Congress 30 days prior to FR publication.

(c) TRR not effective for 90 days after FR publication; Congress can kill by resolution

3. Limits on investigations or rules regarding insurance, funeral business, agricultural cooperatives.

IV. Types of Orders Issued by FTC

A. The formal procedure established by Section 5 of the Act for enforcing its prohibition against deceptive acts or practices is an administrative adjudication to obtain an order that the respondent "cease and desist" from employing the practices. U.S.C. 45(b).

1. The ordinary cease and desist order -- "Go and sin no more" -- has been and continues to be the most widely sought and imposed remedy for violation of the statutes that the FTC enforces.

B. Affirmative Disclosure

1. It is now well established that the FTC can prohibit future advertising claims unless certain affirmative disclosures are made.

a. "Cease and desist orders compelling affirmative disclosure are enforced by the courts when they are necessary to prevent deception." Keele Hair and Scalp Specialists, Inc. v. FTC, 275 F.2d 18, 23 (5th Cir. 1960).

(1) Required only if the respondent were to make claims in future advertisements similar to those which were found to be misleading absent the disclosure.

(2) The best known example of affirmative disclosure requirements is in cigarette advertising where the Surgeon General's warning is required to appear in all cigarette advertising under a consent order agreed to by the cigarette manufacturers. 1970-1973 CCH Transfer Binder, ¶19,902 (1972).

(a) Commission had announced that it intended to issue complaints alleging their advertising was unfair and deceptive to the extent that it failed to include a clear and conspicuous disclosure of the warning statement.

2. The Commission has required affirmative product performance disclosure statements in connection with the sale of certain products. Cf. Octane Posting Rule, 16 C.F.R. Part 422, and Light Bulb Rule, 16 C.F.R. Part 409.

3. Contraceptive Consent Orders. The advertisers were not only required to make affirmative disclosures but also to run print ads in professional journals and prepare and distribute an informational pamphlet approved by FTC staff containing the affirmative disclosures required by FTC staff as well as other information regarding the advantages and disadvantages of various OTC contraceptive methods. American Home Products, 45 FR 14218, 47420 (1980); Jordan-Simner 45 FR 14221, 45901 (1980); Morton-Norwich, 45 FR 14226, 46351 (1980).

4. Antacid Warnings TRR - proposal.

C. Corrective Advertising

1. Complaints request as a condition for further advertising that the company disclose in a clear and conspicuous manner that the FTC had alleged or had found that previous advertising of the product was false and deceptive.

   a. The relief sought generally follows the same general format. If the company continues to advertise its product, it must for a period of time -- generally one year -- devote a certain amount of its advertising space or budget -- generally 25% -- to a statement that the previous advertising for the product has been found to be deceptive by the FTC.

2. In 1971, the Commission obtained its first consent order requiring corrective advertising. ITT Continental Baking Company (Profile Bread), 1970-1973 CCH Transfer Binder, ¶19,681 (1971).

   a. The advertisements in question strongly implied that eating Profile bread would lead to weight reduction.

   b. ITT consented to a cease and desist order which, in addition to prohibiting future claims of weight reducing qualities, requires that 25% of all advertising purchased by the baker for one year be devoted to disclosing that Profile is not effective for weight reduction.

      (1) Sample copy: "I would like to clear up any misunderstanding you may have about Profile Bread from its advertising or even its name. Does Profile bread have fewer calories than other breads? No. Profile has about the same for an ounce as other breads. To be exact, Profile has 7 fewer calories per slice. That's because it is sliced thinner. But eating Profile will not cause you to lose weight. A reduction of 7 calories is insignificant."

   c. Similarly, in Ocean Spray Cranberries, Inc., the FTC accepted a consent decree, (1970-1973 CCH Transfer Binder, ¶19,981 (1972)) which required that for one year, one out of four ads or 25% of media expenditures be devoted to a prescribed advertising text stating the previous claims were possibly subject to misrepresentation. Again, however, no requirement that the company disclose that the FTC had challenged the previous advertising.

3. Sugar Institute Proceeding (1972):

   a. The final order requires two trade associations in the sugar industry to place a corrective ad in each publication in which its misleading ads appeared. See 1970-1973 CCH Transfer Binder ¶20,142 (1972).

b. Made compulsory even though respondent had not intended to advertise further.

4. The Listerine Case

In late 1974 an FTC Administrative Law Judge issued a decision requiring every Listerine ad for two years to carry a corrective advertising statement. 1973-1976 CCH Transfer Binder, ¶20,776 (1974).

a. That decision was essentially affirmed by the full Commission on December 9, 1975. 86 FTC 1938.

(1) Thus, Warner-Lambert was forbidden to advertise Listerine unless each advertisement included the following language:

> "Contrary to prior advertising, Listerine will not help prevent colds or sore throats or lessen their severity."

(2) This remedy was required to continue in effect until $10 million had been expended on Listerine advertising, an amount roughly equal to the average annual Listerine advertising budget for 1952-1972. (Consider the more drastic remedy suggested by Mr. Kramer in 848 ATRR AA-7, January 26, 1978: "We might want Warner-Lambert to spend on corrective ads until it could demonstrate that the measurable effects of its prior campaigns regarding the effectiveness of Listerine as a cold remedy had been erased.")

b. The Court of Appeals, 562 F.2d 749 (D.C. Cir. 1977) cert. denied 435 U.S. 950 (1978), affirmed the Commission decision on August 2, 1977, Judge Robb dissenting, but it deleted the "Contrary to prior advertising" preamble from the corrective advertising statement.

c. In a supplemental opinion, denying a petition for rehearing, 562 F.2d 768 (D.C. Cir. 1977), the Court of Appeals elaborated on the First Amendment ground, probably because it realized the weakness of its earlier opinion on this point.

    (1) In a more sophisticated argument, the court explained how, in its opinion, future advertising would be deceptive without the disclaimer:

    > "When viewed from this perspective (50 years of prior false advertising), advertising which fails to rebut the prior claims as to Listerine's efficacy inevitably builds upon those claims; advertising continues the deception, albeit implicitly rather than explicitly."

    (2) Thus, the Court of Appeals has ingeniously tried to convert Listerine to an affirmative disclosure case rather than a corrective advertising case:

    > "The Commission is not regulating truthful speech protected by the First Amendment, but is merely requiring certain statements which, if not present in current and future advertisements would render those advertisements themselves part of a continuing deception of the public."

(3) Does such an argument make it difficult for the Commission to justify future "corrective" orders if the questioned advertising campaign only ran for a reasonable period of time? Obviously, not many claims are used for anywhere near 50 years.

(4) The FTC appears to adopt a "lingering effect" standard in Warner-Lambert. If the ads played a substantial role in creating a false belief about a product and this belief lingered on after the advertising ceased, then this accumulated impact of past advertising necessitates disclosure in future advertising.

(5) See "The Effects of the FTC's Listerine Corrective Advertising Order," A Report to the FTC by M. B. Mazis, July, 1981.

(6) Administrative Law Judges continue to suggest corrective advertising as a remedy (see American Home Products Corp., 1976-1979 CCH Transfer Binder, ¶21,465 (1978) (Anacin) and Teledyne, Inc. 3 CCH Trade Reg. Rep. ¶21,626 (1979)). However, the Commission deleted the corrective advertising requirement in the Anacin final order, 3 TRR ¶21,874 (1981).

5. The Egg Nutrition Case

In 1976 the Commission ordered the National Commission on Egg Nutrition to cease advertising that "there is no evidence that eating eggs, even in quantity, increases the risk of heart attacks or heart disease." 1976-1979 CCH Transfer Binder, ¶21,184 (1976).

a. Because these ads denied the existence of contrary evidence, the Court of Appeals had earlier granted the Commission's request for a temporary injunction under Section 13(a) of the

FTC Act. However, the NCEN was not enjoined from presenting its side of the scientific controversy. 1975 Trade Cases ¶60,320 (7th Cir. 1977).

b. The Commission's 1976 order also provided that the NCEN's future advertising affirmatively disclose "that many medical experts believe that existing evidence indicates that consumption of dietary cholesterol, including that in eggs, may increase the risk of heart disease." At page 21,099 of 1976-1979 CCH Transfer Binder. (As indicated by <u>Listerine</u> and <u>Egg Nutrition</u>, there is little difference between some corrective advertising orders and affirmative disclosure orders.)

c. On appeal, the Commission's order was affirmed except as to the required additional statement. 1977-2 Trade Cases ¶61,751 (7th Cir. 1977).

    (1) A "corrective" order was not necessary because there was no long history of deception, unlike <u>Listerine</u>.

    (2) The additional statement violated the NCEN's First Amendment rights because it "would require NCEN to argue the other side of the controversy, thus interfering unnecessarily with the effective presentation of the pro-egg proceeding. The desired preventive effect can be achieved by requiring the disclosure that there is a controversy among the experts and NCEN is presenting its side of the controversy." Page 73,100. Compare the earlier discussion of <u>Beneficial Finance</u>.

d. The Commission's modified order was affirmed as a justifiable "limited corrective advertising order." 850 ATRR E-1, February 9, 1978. It incorporated the Seventh Circuit's prior instructions, although it did retain the original required additional statement if the NCEN's ads disclosed the existence of or described scientific evidence supporting the theory that egg consumption will not increase the risk of heart disease.

6. The STP Case

STP agreed to a corrective advertising order which peculiarly was not primarily directed at the consumers who would have allegedly been deceived by prior ads.

a. STP paid $200,000 to run the advertisement in several business oriented publications such as The Wall Street Journal and Forbes and a few consumer oriented publications such as The New York Times and Newsweek.

b. The impact of the ad was not agreed upon. Advertising Age, February 13, 1978.

(1) Mr. Kramer said knowledgeable consultants had agreed that consumers would pick up from the ad that STP had "violated the law" and made misrepresentations in its ads.

(2) STP Chairman Craig A. Nalen countered that the ad would have little impact on STP's business and that it merely questioned defective tests done years earlier.

7. Recent examples required by Consent Order

a. Hayoun Cosmetique, 3 TRR ¶21,660 (1980).

b. Terrance D. Lesko, M.D., 3 TRR ¶21,670 (1980).

c. American Home Products, 3 TRR ¶21,663 (1980).

d. AMF, Inc., 44 FR 40333 (1979), 45 FR 17953 (1980).

8. FTC may permit "flexibility" in developing affirmative disclosure/corrective advertising remedies. Ford Motor Co. D-9105, 45 FR 74714 (1980).

D. Restitution Orders:

1. Under the "Magnuson-Moss Warranty-FTC Improvements Act," the FTC has power to institute civil redress actions for consumers injured by unfair or deceptive acts or practices.

   a. Specifically included are actions for: recission or reformation of contract, the refund of money or return of property, the payment of damages and public notification respecting the rule violation or the unfair or deceptive act or practice.

   b. Exemplary or punitive damages are not included.

   c. New Section 19 of the FTC Act.

2. Overcomes problems of Heater v. FTC 503 F.2d 321 (1974) which held that while the Commission can order a businessman to cease and desist from using deceptive acts or practices, the Commision could not also order the restitution of money bilked from innocent consumers by the deceptive acts or practices.

3. See Horizon Corp, 1973-1976 CCH Transfer Binder ¶21,845 and AMREP Corp., 1973-1976 CCH Transfer Binder ¶20,846 in which the FTC indicated in its complaints that it would consider the use of its restitution power under Section 19(b).

4. Karr Preventive Medical Products, 44 FR 67981; San-Mar Laboratories, 44 FR 58518 (1979), 45 FR 8583 (1980). Karr established a fund of $250,000. Utility of remedy is still open to question.

E. Injunctive Orders

1. The FTC has authority to represent itself in civil action without first notifying the Justice Department when the actions relate to consumers redress, subpoenas, court rebuttal and injunctions.

V. Liability of Advertising Agencies

A. Imposition of Liability on Advertising Agencies

1. Advertising agencies have an affirmative duty to ensure the truthfulness of representations made in advertising they produce.

2. FTC will generally not charge an agency if deceptive advertising resulted from a good faith reliance on supplied data which later proves incorrect. (See Merck & Co., 69 FTC 526 (1966)).

3. FTC will impose liability, however, if faulty advertising results from the use an agency has made of such supplied data, i.e., the data itself is correct, but the use of the data creates half-truths or exaggerations. (See Merck & Co., 69 FTC 526 (1966); Grey Advertising, 1976-1979 CCH Transfer Binder ¶21,459 (1978)).

4. The FTC will also impose liability on advertising agencies for implied representation as well as explicit claims in advertisements. ITT Continental Baking Co., 83 FTC 865 (1973).

5. FTC will apply "know or had reason to know" standard. Standard Oil of Calif. v. FTC, 84 FTC 1401 (1974).

B. Defenses of Advertising Agencies

1. Advertising agencies have the same defenses available as their clients.

2. Advertising agencies have two important additional defenses:

a. The advertising agency may argue that it was not an active participant in the false advertising or that it was but a secondary factor in the creation of advertising (see Bristol-Myers Co. et al., 46 FTC 162, 176 (1949)).

b. The advertising agency neither knew nor had any reason to know of the falsity of the advertising. (See Carter Products, Inc. v. FTC, 323 F.2d 523, 534 (1963)).

(1) Advertising agency may rely on data which client has supplied provided that agency has no reason to suspect data is faulty and agency does not create advertising which makes the data appear more substantial than it actually is. Merck & Co., 69 FTC 526 (1966).

(2) If data later proves faulty, advertising agency should not be liable if there was good faith reliance on such data and created advertising accurately reflecting such data. (See Standard Oil of Calif. et al., 1973-1976 CCH Transfer Binder, ¶20,789 (1974).

c. Reliance on the neither knew nor had reason to know defense has not been well received by FTC. FTC presumes agency knew or had reason to know if agency was solely or primarily responsible for the advertising approach selected. See Sun Oil Co., 84 FTC 247 (1974) and ITT Continental Baking Co. v. FTC, 83 FTC 865 (1973) aff'd 532 F.2d 207 (1976).

C. Extent of Liability of Advertising Agencies

1. Advertising agencies can be subject to Commission orders to the same extent as their clients. The FTC is permitted wide discretion in structuring the appropriate remedies. See Jacob Siegel Co. v. FTC, 327 US 608 (1946).

2. The FTC has prohibited practices with respect to products or services not covered in initial proceeding thereby covering all products or a whole class of products handled

by the defendant. Carter Prod. Inc. v. FTC, 323 F.2d 523 (1963). An all products order would create a particularly difficult situation for an advertising agency which had diverse products. Ted Bates, 46 FR 2355, 21599 (1981) (All products order regarding tests and surveys.)

3. Courts have generally limited cease and desist orders to cover only products with similar physical properties.

   a. In Carter Prod. Inc. v. FTC, 323 F.2d 523, 534 (1963), court suggested that the effect of the order on the advertising agency be limited to Carter's products rather than all products of all the agency's clients.

   b. Real breakthrough came with Virginia State Bd. of Pharmacy v. Virginia Citizens Consumer Council, 425 US 748 (1976).

      (1) Extended First Amendment constitutional protection for truthful commercial advertising.

      (2) Although case dealt with state regulation of advertising, courts have applied its principles to the FTC.

   c. In Beneficial Finance Corp. v. FTC, 542 F.2d 611 (1976), the court held that a total ban of use of phrase "instant tax refund" was excessive and beyond what was necessary to prevent deception.

   d. In Standard Oil of Calif. v. FTC, 577 F.2d 653 (1978), the court held that an all-products order against the advertising agency and its client was excessive and unwarranted.

D. Civil Penalties

1. Advertising agencies are liable for civil penalties up to $10,000 for each violation of a final order.

2. The FTC may proceed under §5(l) of the Act, or, if appropriate, under §5(m).

   a. Under Section 5(l), the district court decides whether the advertising agency has violated the terms of a final order, and, if so, how much the agency should be fined up to $10,000 per day for each violation.

   b. If the advertising agency has knowingly violated a trade regulation rule or knowingly violated a cease and desist order, the FTC may proceed under 5(m) and seek fines of up to $10,000 per day for each violation.

VI. Conclusion/Summary

6

COPYRIGHT, MUSIC AND THE NEW TECHNOLOGY

Elizabeth Elster Granville

March 11, 1982

SPECIAL PROBLEMS IN COPYRIGHTING COMMERCIALS

I. Copyright Protection Accorded to Advertising

II. Copyright Formalities

A) On visually perceptible copies, appropriate notice is required: 17 USC §401 (a)

1) A notice must be affixed when work:

a) published by authority of copyright owner

b) on all publicly distributed copies

B) Form of notice: 17 USC §401 (b) -- completed notice is:
© name of copyright owner 198___.

1) © (or the word Copyright or Copr.)

2) The name of the owner of copyright

3) Year of first publication

C) Position of notice:

1) Commercials for television

a) for untitled motion pictures or audio visual works of sixty (60) seconds duration

i) notice must appear on leader or film or tape immediately preceding the beginning of the work

ii) see 37FR 58313 (12/1/81)

2) Commercials for cable, pay TV and those prepared for showing in movie theatres

a) generally 90-120 seconds duration

b) notice must appear with:

title,
cast and credits,
immediately after beginning of work or immediately preceding the end of the work.

3) Commercials for radio

a) although a mere broadcast is not publication, distribution of cassettes to radio station may be a publication

b) notice of copyright should appear on cassette housing audio tape

III. <u>Contributions to a Collective work: 17 USC §404</u>

Separate contribution to collective work consisting of advertisements on behalf of persons other than the owner of copyright in the collective work should bear own notice

D) Deposit of copies: 17 USC §§409-412

1) In General

2) Advertising Exemption

a) print

b) broadcast

E) Registration

1) Fee of $10.

2) Should register print advertising with original artwork or photographs

3) Should register radio & TV commercials -- especially if original music incorporated

4) Send 2 copies of work with application for registration to Copyright Office

5) Necessary prerequisite for infringement suit (See 17 USC §§409,410,411,412)

IV. <u>Rights Protected: 17 USC §§101,106</u>

A) Copy

B) Reproduce

C) Distribute

D) Perform

E) Display

V. Ownership

A) Author is initial copyright owner: 17 USC §201 (a)

B) Ownership is divisible: 17 USC §201 (d) (2)

C) Works made for hire: 17 USC §201 (b)

1) Employer is the author

a) philosophy is that employer is the proximate cause of the work coming into existence

b) no creative contribution from employer is necessary (See, Shapiro Bernstein & Co. v. Bryan, 123 F2d 697, 51 USPQ 422 (2nd Cir. 1941)).

2) It is a work prepared by employee within the scope of employment or it is a work specially ordered or commissioned

3) Nature of compensation paid is not absolute detriment:

a) a periodic salary (Tobani v. Carl Fischer, Inc., 98 F2d 57 (2nd Cir. 1938)).

b) fee or royalty basis (Fred Fisher Music Co. v. Leo Feist, Inc., 55 F.Supp 359 (S.D.N.Y. 1944) (advance payment against royalties))

4) Key factor is that employer has right to direct and control manner in which writer creates his work (Epoch Producing Corp. v. Killiam Shows Inc., 522 F2d 737 (2d Cir.1975) (employer control is hallmark of employment for hire relationship)); Cf. Murray v. Gelderman, 566 F2d 1307 (5th Cir.1978) may also apply to independent contractor.

5) Works prepared on special order or commission:

"for hire" status applies to works specially ordered or commissioned as, among other things, a part of a motion picture or other audio visual work, a supplementary work. See, 17 USC §101

a) only in special order or commission situation need there be a writing between the employer (Agency) and employee creating an express "for hire" relationship. Agreement should be signed by both parties

   i) protects duration of copyright of 75 years from date of first publication or 100 years from creation, whichever expires first

   ii) in case of freelance work, any grant, such as sale, made by creator of work is subject to certain termination rights giving creator a right to recapture ownership

   iii) initial term of copyright in special circumstances cited in (ii) above is 35 years

b) under the 1909 Copyright Act, rights of commissioning party were broader

   i) the commissioning party had rights even in absence of written agreement (common law copyright protection under Act of 1909 versus statutory copyright under Copyright Act of 1976)

   ii) commissioning party could claim copyright against independent contractor regardless of whether or not work was within specially prescribed categories (*May v. Morganelli - Heumann & Assoc.*, 618 F2d 1363 (9th Cir. 1980)- evidence of a custom or usage in a particular industry could, under 1909 Act, permit inference that copyright vested in independent contractor

c) works created on commission prior to effective date of current Act

   1) hypothetical: A commissions B to photograph A. B is commercial photographer. Neither writing nor discussions between A and B as to who owned copyright in photograph

      a) under 1909 Act, presumption that A owns photograph.

      b) under 1976 Act, since portraits are not included in category of commissioned works which can fall within "for hire" relationship (and even if included, there was no writing conferring right on commissioning party) the copyright resides in B.

      c) doubtful that 1976 Act will be given retroactive effect since U.S. Supreme Court expressed view that statutes be applied prospectively. Billings v. U.S., 232 U.S. 261,282 (1914).

      d) there may be express contractual provision reserving to employee (or commissioned party) rights in certain media, while conveying to employer (or commissioning party) rights in other media

         i) without such express reservation, employer is the author and acquires exclusive rights in all media

         ii) increasingly more common in case of music used in commercials for creator to reserve to himself rights of public performance.

a) licenses public performance rights to a performing rights licensing organization such as BMI, ASCAP or SESAC.

b) collects through such organization for broadcast performances of commercial.

VI. Public Performance Income for Broadcast Commercials

A) Who owns right of public performance for the author and publisher? Should be a contractual provision if the creator of music has reserved right of public performance.

B) Which performing rights licensing organization licenses rights BMI, ASCAP,SESAC?

C) What are standard performance fees for a commercial?

D) How are fees collected by author and publisher?

1) Provide contracts to performing rights licensing organization

2) Agency documentation

3) Audio copy of commercial tape

E) What effect, if any, do performance fees have on amount or negotiation of creative fee?

VII. Fair use is a limitation on the copyright owner's exclusive rights in his copywritten work

A) Copyright protection does not extend to ideas contained in copyrighted work. Mazer v. Stein, 347 U.S. 201 (1954)

B) Statutory definition of fair use: see, 17 USC §107

C) The test is primarily a functional one in terms of intent and of copied portion's effect fulfilling actual or potential consumer demand for copied material.

If the function of plaintiff's work is different from that of defendant, the borrowing is permissible. (Reproduction of chorus lyrics of songs held non-infringing fair use where such reproductions appeared in magazines (Shapiro, Bernstein & Co. v. P.F. Collier, 26 U.S.P.Q.40 (S.D.N.Y.1934)) but see Johns & Johns Printing Co. v. Paul-Pioneer Music Corp., 102 F2d 282 (8th Cir. 1939) defendant copied only chorus lyrics of plaintiff's song and reproduced them in songsheet pamphlet. Court held no fair use but an infringement.

1) Exceptions to functional test

   a) comparative advertising

      i) reproduction of cover of plaintiff's copyrighted magazine -- not the essence of the magazine (e.g. part of its content)-- in a comparative advertisement for defendant's magazine is a fair use; commercial motivations do not destroy defense of fair use. Triangle Publications Inc. v. Knight-Ridder Newspapers, Inc., 626 F2d 1171 (5th Cir. 1980).

   b) parody, satire, burlesque

      i) tests of amount of material permitted to be copied

         a) recall or conjure up (original work) test Berlin v. E.C. Publications, Inc. 329 F2d 541 (2d Cir. 1964); Elsmere Music, Inc. v. Nat'l Broadcasting Co., 482 F2d 741 (S.D.N.Y. 1980) affd. 623 F2d 252 (2d Cir.1980)

b) substantial similarity test (not only substantial similarity of ideas but also similarity of expression of ideas).

   i) Walt Disney Prods. v. Air Pirates 581 F2d 751 (9th Cir. 1978); copying Disney figures, such as Mickey Mouse and Donald Duck, in entirety;

   ii) Loew's Inc. v. Columbia Broadcasting Sys.Inc. 131 F.Supp.165 (S.D.Cal. 9th Cir. 1955) Gaslight case: No fair use where almost verbatim copying. Plaintiff's motion picture, a serious melodrama, was infringed by Jack Benny in a burlesqued TV program of same work - there was not only substantial similarity but also almost complete identity of content;

   iii) Sid & Marty Krofft Television v. McDonald's Corp. 562 F2d 1157 (9th Cir.1977) suggests for commercials a two-part test:

      a) dissection or featural analysis (comparing the different features of the works) Miller Brewing Co. v. Carling O'Keefe Brewery 452 F.Supp. 429 (W.D.N.Y. 1978); Warner Bros. Inc. v. American Broadcasting Cos. 211 U.S.P.Q. 51 (S.D.N.Y. 1981)affd. 1981 Copyright Law and Decisions §25,284 (CA 2d Cir)

b) has defendant "captured total concept and feel of copyrighted [audio-visual] work" so that lay observer would instantly identify defendant's commercial character with plaintiff's character where only change occurs when defendant's character announces his name and business purpose D. C. Comics Inc. v. Crazy Eddie Inc., 79 Civ. 3786 (unreported S.D.N.Y. 1979); Dr.Pepper Co. v. Sambo's Restaurants, 517 F.Supp. 1202 (D.C.N.D.Texas 1981) court found that conjure up test had been exceeded by defendant. Court did not apply the appropriate featural analysis test and only if necessary then the total concept and feel test.

c) First Amendment Constitutional considerations

VIII. Home Taping of Audio-Visual Works

Universal City Studios, Inc. et al, v. Sony Corp et al, 211 U.S.P.Q. 761 (U.S.C.A. 9th Cir.1981)

A) No exemption for home taping of audio-visual works whether or not taping for profit.

B) Statute does not list convenience (delayed viewing), entertainment, or increased access as a purpose within scope of fair use.

C) Off-air copying of audio-visual works by owners of video recorders for private use infringes copyrighted material.

D) Not necessary for plaintiff to prove actual damanges. Sufficient that plaintiff will have to take steps to compete with appropriated versions of their work.

E) Contributory infringers are those who, know of infringing activity and induce, cause or materially contribute to infringing conduct

F) Video tape recorders are manufactured, advertised and sold for primary purpose of reproducing television programming (virtually all of which is copyrighted material); such recorders are not suitable for substantial non-infringing use

G) The infringers include, but are not limited to: manufacturer of machine; stores selling machine; advertising agencies, etc.

H) Current legislation introduced in Congress

   1) To create a fair use exemption for non-commercial home taping (DeConcini, D'Amato Bills)

   2) To create a compulsory license for video hometaping (Mathias Bill)

IX. <u>Open question whether there is a fair use exemption for audio recording</u>

A) Legislation creating an exemption

B) Legislation creating a compulsory license

IX Appendices

Appendix 1. Contract between Agency and composer

a. "acquisition of music rights"

b. limited rights

c. all rights

d. general purchase order form

e. song publishing agreement

f. music license agreement

   a) long form
   b) short form

Appendix 2.

a. BMI writer affiliation contract

b. BMI publisher affiliation contract

c. BMI forms to register commercials

   i) commercials using original music

   ii) commercials using existing music

CONTRACT BETWEEN AGENCY AND COMPOSER

May 17, 1976

Appendix 1.

a. ACQUISITION OF MUSIC RIGHTS

Dear

The following constitutes our agreement:

1. You have created and written and/or have had created and written a certain "work" which is the ____music ____lyrics ____arrangement (check which is applicable) of a music jingle, a copy of which is annexed hereto.

2. Subject to the provisions of paragraph 6, you hereby sell, assign, transfer and deliver to us, our successors and assigns, all rights, title and interest throughout the world in and to said work created by you, including, but not limited to, the publication and allied rights (and the performing rights thereto) (strike balance of sentence if signator is a member of a performing rights society.) It is specifically understood that we have the right to alter, expand, adapt and make any arrangements of said work, and we shall have the sole right to decide whether and in what manner said work shall be published, advertised, publicized or exploited by us, our successors or assigns. We shall have the further right to secure a statutory copyright therein anywhere in the world in the name(s) of such persons, firms or corporations as we may elect, and we or our designees will have the right to secure extensions and renewals of such copyright registrations.

3. We agree to pay to you and you agree to accept in full consideration for all services rendered by you to us and for all rights transferred by you to us, the sum of $ ________________.

4. You represent and warrant to us that:

   (a) The work created is original.

   (b) It does not and will not infringe upon or violate the copyrights or any other rights whatsoever of any person or entity.

   (c) No adverse claim exists with respect to it.

   (d) It has not heretofore been published or exploited in any form anywhere in the world.

   (e) You own and control said work and all rights in it throughout the world. (Not applicable if a work made for hire).

   (f) You have the full and exclusive right and authority to enter into this agreement and to make the grant herein contained.

   (g) (Check one):

   _______ You are a member of ASCAP

   _______ You are a member of BMI

   _______ You are not affiliated with any performing rights organization.

   _______ If work is registered under name other than that appearing above, state here, ____________________________________.

(h) (Check one)

_____ This work was created at our request while in the regular course of your employment by us.

_____ This work was created by you as an independent contractor.

_____ This work was created by you and/or for you independently.

5. You will indemnify and save harmless us, our client and any other person, firm or corporation making use of such work from and against any and all loss, damage or expense, including reasonable attorneys' fees, resulting from or by reason of the breach or alleged breach of any representation or warranty herein made by you. If the above submitted composition is an arrangement of music provided by us or an arrangement of music in the public domain, then you give the above warranties and representations only as to the new material incorporated therein.

6. Notwithstanding anything to the contrary otherwise provided, it is understood if composer is a member of a performing rights society, it is agreed that the performance rights in and to the composition, lyrics and/or arrangement(s) produced hereunder are reserved by you/or the composer, it being understood, however, that we are under no obligation to actually perform the composition, lyrics and/or arrangement(s) in the aforesaid manner. You agree to assign to our ASCAP publisher designee the publisher performing rights in the composition and said ASCAP publisher designee shall have the sole right to collect publisher performing fees derived from the use of such composition.

Please evidence your acceptance hereof and agreement hereto by signing in the place indicated.

Very truly yours,

Accepted and Agreed:

As Agent for

______________________________ ______________________________

______________________________ By____________________________

Appendix 1. b. limited rights

TB - 3 A-11 MUSIC RIGHTS/LIMITED RIGHTS 10/9/80

ACQUISITION OF MUSIC RIGHTS
(LIMITED RIGHTS)

To:

Date: ____________________

The following constitutes the agreement between you and us on behalf of our client ____________________________.

1. You have created and written a certain "work" which is the ( ) music ( ) lyrics ( ) arrangement (check which is applicable) of a musical jingle, a copy of which is annexed hereto, for the purpose of advertising the products or services of our client.

2. You hereby agree that the "work" is a work made for hire and the sole property of ______________________ ("Agency") as agent for the above-named client. It is speciiically understood that we have the right to alter, expand, adapt and make any arrangements of said work, and we shall have the sole right to decide whether and in what manner said work shall be published, advertised, publicized, performed or exploited by us, our successors or assigns. We shall have the further right to secure a statutory copyright therein anywhere in the world in the name(s) of such person, firms or corporations as we may elect, and we or our designees will have the right to secure extensions and renewals of such copyright registrations.

3. We agree to pay to you and you agree to accept in full consideration for all services rendered by you to us and for all rights herein the sum of $__________________ to be paid by us within thirty (30) days following completion of your services and submission by you of appropriate invoice.

Appendix 1. b.

TB - 3 A-12 MUSIC RIGHTS/LIMITED RIGHTS 10/9/80

4. You represent and warrant to us that:

(a) The work created by you is original;

(b) It does not and will not infringe upon or violate the copyrights or any other rights whatsoever of any person or entity;

(c) No adverse claim exists with respect to it;

(d) It has not heretofore been puolished or exploited in any form anywhere in the world;

(e) You own and control said work and all rights in it throughout the world;

(f) You have the full and exclusive right and authority to enter into this agreement and to make the grant herein contained; and

(g) Any and all materials that are incorporated in the work are works made for hire and free from any reversionary rights therein.

5. You agree to hold us, our within named client and their assigns, and licensees, harmless from and against any loss, damage or expense, including court costs and reasonable attorneys' fees, that we, our within named client, and their assigns and licensees may suffer or incur as a result of any breach or alleged breach of the foregoing warranties.

6. We hereby grant back to you the performance rights to the work, subject, however, to the following conditions:

(a) You warrant and represent that you are a member of ASCAP or BMI;

(b) The performance rights to the work will not be licensed on behalf of any other advertiser;

(c) ASCAP or BMI, as the case may be, will license the use of the work on radio and TV stations and networks throughout the U.S.A., without any special compensation therefor by stations, networks or us, such rights to be granted under the blanket license agreements with stations and networks;

Appendix. 1.b.

TB - 3 A-13 MUSIC RIGHTS/LIMITED RIGHTS 10/9/80

(d) In the event we shall desire to use the composition on stations or networks which have not entered into a blanket license agreement with ASCAP or BMI, this agreement shall be deemed to constitute a license for such uses, without any limitation or further compensation; and

(e) Neither you nor anyone deriving any rights from you shall at any time interfere with or hold up the performance of the work in any manner whatsoever or for whatever reason.

Please evidence your acceptance hereof and agreement hereto by signing in the place indicated.

MUSIC SUPPLIER

By:____________________	By:____________________
Typed Name:________________	Typed Name:________________
Title:____________________	Title:____________________

Note: "Work" must be attached

Appendix 1. c. all rights

TB - 3 A-16 MUSIC RIGHTS/ALL RIGHTS 10/9/80 B

ACQUISITION OF MUSIC RIGHTS
(ALL RIGHTS)

To:

Date:_______________________

The following constitutes the agreement between you and us on behalf of our client ______________________________.

1. You have created and written a certain "work" which is the ( ) music ( ) lyrics ( ) arrangement (check which is applicable) of a musical jingle, a copy of which is annexed hereto, for the purpose of advertising the products or services of our client.

2. You hereby agree that the "work" is a work made for hire and the sole property of ___________________ It is specifically understood that we have the right to alter, expand, adapt and make any arrangements of said work, and we shall have the sole right to decide whether and in what manner said work shall be published, advertised, publicized, performed or exploited by us, our successors or assigns. We shall have the further right to secure a statutory copyright therein anywhere in the world in the name(s) of such person, firms or corporations as we may elect, and we or our designees will have the right to secure extensions and renewals of such copyright registrations.

3. We agree to pay to you and you agree to accept in full consideration for all services rendered by you to us and for all rights herein the sum of $__________________ to be paid by us within thirty (30) days following completion of your services and submission by you of appropriate invoice.

Appendix 1. c.

TB - 3 A-17 MUSIC RIGHTS/ALL RIGHTS 10/9/80 B

4. You represent and warrant to us that:

(a) The work created by you is original;

(b) It does not and will not infringe upon or violate the copyrights or any other rights whatsoever of any person or entity;

(c) No adverse claim exists with respect to it;

(d) It has not heretofore been published or exploited in any form anywhere in the world;

(e) You own and control said work and all rights in it throughout the world;

(f) You have the full and exclusive right and authority to enter into this agreement and to make the grant herein contained; and

(g) Any and all materials that are incorporated in the work are works made for hire and free from any reversionary rights therein.

5. You agree to hold us, our within named client and their assigns, and licensees, harmless from and against any loss, damage or expense, including court costs and reasonable attorneys' fees, that we, our within named client, and their assigns and licensees may suffer or incur as a result of any breach or alleged breach of the foregoing warranties.

Please evidence your acceptance hereof and agreement hereto by signing in the place indicated.

MUSIC SUPPLIER

By:______________________	By:______________________
Typed Name:______________	Typed Name:______________
Title:___________________	Title:___________________

Note: "Work" must be attached

Appendix 1. d. general purchase order form

GENERAL PURCHASE ORDER FORM PROVISIONS

[On the face of the order form, in bold type]:

> **SUPPLIER'S DEPOSIT OF PAYMENT HEREUNDER SHALL CONSTITUTE FULL ACCEPTANCE BY SUPPLIER OF ALL TERMS AND CONDITIONS CONTAINED HEREIN AND ON THE REVERSE SIDE HEREOF.**

[On the reverse side of the order form]:

1. For the purposes of this order and in the event that the work which is the subject of this order is copyrightable subject matter, supplier and ______________________ ("Agency") hereby agree that the material shall be a work made for hire and the property of Agency as agents for the within named client. In the event that the material which is the subject of this order is not copyrightable subject matter, or for any reason is determined not to be a work made for hire, then and in such event Supplier hereby grants all right, title and interest to said material to Agency as agent for their within name client.

2. The rights herein obtained, include, but are not limited to: (a) the right to use, publish, display or reproduce such material in advertising and for the purposes of trade; (b) the right to alter such material; (c) the right to secure copyright therein; (d) the right to license, exploit, sell, assign, or otherwise dispose of such material or any of the said rights included herein; and (e) any and all subsidiary rights therein.

3. Supplier hereby represents and warrants: (a) that no third party has any rights in, to, or arising out of, or in connection with the material supplied hereunder; (b) that Supplier has full right and power to enter into this agreement; (c) that all models and any other living persons and the owner of any unique or unusual inanimate objects, which are used and are identifiable in the material supplied, have each and all executed valid and adequate releases and that upon demand Supplier shall supply Agency with a copy of the said releases; (d) that any and all materials which are incorporated in the materials supplied hereunder are works madefor hire and free from any reversionary rights therein.

Appendix 1. d. general purchase order form

4. Supplier agrees to hold Agency, its within named client and their assigns and licensees, harmless from and against any loss, damage or expense, including court costs and reasonable attorneys' fees, that Agency, its within named client, and their assigns and licensees may suffer or incur as a result of any breach or alleged breach of the foregoing warranties.

5. The terms and conditions set forth herein constitute the entire agreement between the parties and said terms and conditions cannot be modified or amended, except by agreement in writing, signed by the parties hereto.

6. The order may be cancelled by Agency at any time prior to its acceptance of the material or work covered by this order, upon written notice to Supplier. In such event, Agency shall be liable to pay Supplier, in lieu of the price specified on the face of this order, the direct costs incurred by Supplier in the performance of its obligations hereunder prior to such cancellation, provided, however, that the total amount of such costs shall not exceed the price specified on the face of this order.

7. This order, or any sums payable hereunder, may not be assigned by Supplier without the prior written consent of Agency.

8. Timely delivery is of the essence.

9. All materials supplied hereunder must comply with Agency's specifications and are subject to its approval.

Appendix 1. e.

E/M -6 B-21 SONG PUBLISHING AGREEMENT 12/23/80

MUSIC LICENSE AGREEMENT
(Short Form)

AGREEMENT made this day of _________, 198_ by and between _________________________________, ("Publisher") located at ________________________________ _______________________________ and ____________________ _______________________ located at ___________________________ ____________________ ("Licensee") as agent for_____________ _____________________ (hereinafter referred to as the "Client").

In consideration of the sum of $________, paid by the Licensee to the Publisher, the undersigned agree as follows:

1. Licensee shall have the nonexclusive, irrevocable right and license to record the copyrighted musical composition entitled "______________________________" by ____________________ and ____________________ in synchronism for radio commercial purposes to advertise Client's ________ __________________.

2. Licensee may use parody lyrics, as submitted to and approved by Publisher. Any additional changes of lyrics shall be subject to the further approval of Publisher, which approval shall not be unreasonably withheld.

3. This license is granted upon the express condition that the said recording(s) are to be used solely for broadcast purposes, that no sound records produced pursuant to this license are to be manufactured, sold, licensed or used separately or apart from radio broadcasts.

4. This is a license to record only, and the exercise of the recording rights herein granted is conditioned upon the performance of the musical composition over radio stations having valid licenses from the person, firm, corporation or other entity having the legal right to issue performance right licenses on behalf of the owner of such rights in the respective territories in which the musical composition shall be performed hereunder.

5. This license is granted for the territory comprising the states of _______________________________ _____ and ________.

6. The term of this License shall be for one year commencing ______________. Licensee shall thereafter have an option to renew the term hereof for an additional year upon the same terms and conditions upon

the payment to Publisher of the sum of $_________ no later than ___________ (__) days preceeding the end of the first year of the term hereof. Upon termination any and all rights given and granted hereunder shall forthwith cease and terminate, including the right to make or authorize any use whatsoever of the musical composition in radio broadcasts.

7. Publisher hereby represents and warrants to Licensee that:

(a) the musical composition is original;

(b) it does not and will not infringe upon or violate the copyrights or any other rights whatsoever of any person or entity;

(c) no adverse claim exists with respect to it;

(d) Publisher owns and controls the musical composition and all rights in it throughout the territory covered by this agreement; and

(e) Publisher has the full and exclusive right and authority to enter into this agreement and to make the grant herein contained.

8. Publisher agrees to hold Licensee and its Client and their respective assigns and licensees, harmless from and against any loss, damage or expense, including court costs and reasonable attorneys' fees, that they and their assigns and licensees may suffer or incur as a result of any breach or alleged breach of the foregoing warranties.

In witness whereof, the parties have set their signatures hereto on the day and date as first appears above.

PUBLISHER:

____

By__________________________________

LICENSEE:

____
as agent for
____

By__________________________________

Appendix 1. f. a) long form

MUSIC LICENSE AGREEMENT
(LONG LETTER FORM)

Dated:

To:

RE: ______________________

Gentlemen:

This is to confirm the agreement between you acting as agent for ______________________ ("Licensee") and us concerning the musical composition "______________ ______________" (words by ______________, music by ______________ ______________) ("Composition").

1. a. Subject to the terms and conditions of this agreement and provided that you have fully complied with all the terms and conditions hereof, we grant to you during the Term, the non-exclusive right to arrange and record the music of the Composition in conjunction with the Approved Lyrics (as hereinafter defined) in synchronization with film or video tape to be used solely in connection with the production of __________ commercials advertising Licensee's product, __________ ("Product"), and to broadcast such commercials ("Commercials") throughout the following markets: ______________ ______________________, and ______________ ("Territory"). The parodied lyrics attached hereto and made a part hereof are hereby deemed approved by us for use by you during the Term ("Approved Lyrics"); and

b. Notwithstanding the above, we hereby acknowledge that we will not grant any license to use the Composition in the advertising, marketing or promotion of any products competitive with or to the product, i.e. __________, in any media throughout the Territory from the date hereof and continuing thereafter for the duration of the Term and any extensions thereof.

2. The Term of this license shall consist of an initial period of one (1) year commencing from the date hereof ("First Television Period"), plus any renewals or extensions thereof.

3. You shall have the option to extend the Term of this license for ____ additional periods of __________ year(s) each by notice in writing to us to such effect any time prior to thirty (30) days before expiration of the then current year of the Term of this license ("Television Option Periods").

4. In addition to the option(s) granted to you in paragraph 3 hereof, we hereby grant you the option to extend the rights granted to you pursuant to Paragraph 1(a) hereof, but subject to the restrictions applicable thereto, to include the arranging and recording of the music of the Composition in conjunction with the Approved Lyrics on audio tape for use by you solely in connection with the broadcast of the commercials on radio throughout the Territory ("Radio Option(s)") with respect to the First Television Period or Television Option Period(s), as applicable provided that such Radio Option(s) is coterminous with the First Television Period or Television Option Periods, respectively. It is understood that the Radio Options granted above are exercisable only if the First Television Period is in effect or in the event you have exercised the Television Option Period(s). Each option granted to you pursuant to this paragraph may be exercised independently of any other option granted in this paragraph and shall be exercised with respect to any Television Period(s) at any time prior to the expiration of such period.

EM/9 A-3 MUSIC LICENSE AGREEMENT 1/6/81

5. In consideration of the rights granted by us herewith, you agree to pay to us the following sums:

   a. With respect to the First Television Period of the term, the sum of ________ ________ ($______) dollars for each period, to be paid upon execution of this license;

   and

   b. With respect to the Television Option Period(s), if applicable, the sum of ________________ ($______) dollars to be paid upon exercise of each option; and

   c. With respect to the Radio Option(s), if any, the sum of ______________ ($_____) dollars for each period, to be paid upon exercise of said option(s). It is specifically understood that the sum set forth in this sub-paragraph shall be payable with respect to each period of the Term with respect to which the said option is exercised.

6. While you agree to use your best efforts to broadcast the composition only on ASCAP licensed facilities, your failure to do so shall not constitute a breach by you hereunder.

7. This license cannot be transferred or assigned by affirmative act or by operation of law, without our express written consent, which may be withheld for any reason.

8. You agree to use your best efforts to assure that any arrangements of the Composition prepared by you shall be created as a "Work Made for Hire" as such term is used in the United States Copyright Law. It is understood, however, that such arrangement cannot be used by us without your expressed written consent. The arranger shall not be entitled to authorship credit or status as a collaborator or any remuneration by way of royalty or otherwise from the authors of the Composition(s) or from us. No arrangement shall change the basic melody of the Composition.

9. It is specifically understood and agreed that all rights not specifically granted herein are reserved to us.

10. We warrant and represent that we have the right to enter into this agreement and to license all rights hereinafter set forth. Our liability for breach of said warranty shall not exceed the amount of consideration paid by you to us hereunder. You warrant and represent that you have the right to enter into this license and perform in accordance with the terms hereof.

11. Nothing herein shall create any association, partnership, joint venture or relationship of principal and agent between the parties hereof; it being understood that the parties hereto are with respect to each other independent contractors; and neither party shall have any authority to bind the other or other's representatives in any way and shall not hold itself out to any third party as having such authority.

12. A waiver by either party of any term or condition of this license, in any instance, shall not be deemed or construed as a waiver of such conditions for the future or of any subsequent breach thereof. All remedies, rights, undertakings, obligations and agreements contained in this license shall be cumulative, and none of them shall be in limitation of the other remedy, right, undertaking, obligation or agreement of either party.

13. This license has been entered in the State of __________, and the validity, interpretation and legal effect to this license shall be governed by the laws of the State of ______________ applicable to contracts entered into and performed entirely within the State of __________ with respect to the determination of any claim, dispute or disagreement which may arise out to the interpretation, performance or breach of this license.

14. Except as otherwise specifically provided herein, all notices hereunder shall be in

writing and shall be given by personal delivery, registered or certified mail or telegraph (prepaid), at the respective addresses set forth above or as may be designated by either party in a similar manner. Such notices shall be deemed given when mailed or delivered to a telegraph office, except that notice of change of address shall be effective only from the date of its receipt.

15. This license contains the entire understanding of the parties hereto relating to the subject matter hereof and cannot be changed or terminated orally.

Very truly yours,

____

By_____________________________

AGREED AND ACCEPTED:

____
as agent for ___________________________

By_____________________________

Title___________________________

E/M-10 A10 Appendix 1. f. b) short form
MUSIC LICENSE AGREEMENT #2

AGREEMENT made this ___ day of _______, 198_ by and between _______________________, ("Publisher") located at ____ and _______________ located at _____________________________ _____________________________ ("Licensee") as agent for _____________________ ("Client").

In consideration of the sum of $______, payable to Publisher by Licensee within thirty (30) days following Licensee's first air date of a commercial produced hereunder, the undersigned agree as follows:

1. During the "Term" hereof, Licensee shall have the non-exclusive, irrevocable right and license to record the copyrighted musical composition entitled "_______________________" ("Composition") by _____________ in synchronism for television and radio commercial purposes to advertise Client's _________ services. In this connection, such music may be used for commercials of varying lengths, including :30 and :60 second versions.

2. Notwithstanding the above, Publisher hereby acknowledges that it will not grant any license to use the Composition in the advertising, marketing or promotion of any services competitive with Client's _________________ services in any media throughout the Territory from the date hereof and continuing thereafter for the duration of the Term and any extensions hereof.

3. This license is granted upon the express condition that the said recording(s) are to be used solely for broadcast purposes, that no sound records produced pursuant to this license are to be manufactured, sold, licensed or used separately or apart from such broadcasts.

4. The exercise of the rights herein granted is conditioned upon the performance of the Composition over broadcast stations having valid licenses from the person, firm, corporation or other entity having the legal right to issue performance right licenses on behalf of the owner of such rights in the respective territories in which the Composition shall be performed hereunder. While Licensee agrees to use its best efforts to broadcast the Composition only on licensed facilities, its failure to do so shall not constitute a breach hereunder.

E/M-10 A-11 MUSIC LICENSE AGREEMENT #2

5. This license is granted for the "Territory" comprising the states of ________________________________ ________________ and ________.

6. The "Term" of this license shall be for ____ year(s) following Licensee's first air date of a commercial hereunder. Such air date is currently anticipated to be February 23, 1981. Licensee shall thereafter have an option to renew the Term hereof for an additional period of ______ year(s) upon the same terms and conditions upon notice of no less than _________(__) days preceeding the end of the First and upon the payment to Publisher of the sum of $______ no later than (__) days succeeding the end of the First Period of the Term hereof. Thereafter, Publisher agrees to negotiate in good faith with Licensee for compensation for use beyond the extension hereof; it being understood that Publisher shall make the Composition available for such use presumming Licensee and Publisher agree on a reasonable rate of compensation in connection therewith. Upon termination any and all rights given and granted hereunder shall forthwith cease and terminate, including the right to make or authorize any use whatsoever of the Composition for broadcast purposes.

7. Licensee shall have the right to make reasonable minor adaptations or editing of the Composition so as to adapt it for use in the commercials context. Such adaptation or editing, however, shall maintain the integrity of the Composition.

8. Publisher hereby represents and warrants to Licensee that:

(a) the Composition is original;

(b) it does not and will not infringe upon or violate the copyrights or any other rights whatsoever of any person or entity;

(c) no adverse claim exists with respect to it;

(d) Publisher owns and controls the Composition and all rights in it throughout the territory covered by this agreement; and

(e) Publisher has the full and exclusive right and authority to enter into this agreement and to make the grant herein contained.

9. Publisher agrees to hold Licensee and its Client and their respective assigns and licensees, harmless from and against any loss, damage or expense, including court costs and reasonable attorneys' fees, that they and their assigns and licensees may suffer or incur as a result of any breach or alleged breach of the foregoing warranties.

10. Licensee shall also have the right, if it so elects, to use a previously recorded version of the Composition for commercial use as specified herein. Such right, however, shall be contingent upon Licensee securing permission from any recording company owning such recording and Publisher shall have no responsibility in connection therewith.

11. This agreement shall be construed in accordance with the laws of the State of ____________.

In witness whereof, the parties have set their signatures hereto on the day and date as first appears above.

PUBLISHER:

____

By__________________________________

LICENSEE:

____
as agent for
____

By__________________________________

BMI CONTRACTS

Appendix 2. a. BMI writer affiliation contract

BMI

BROADCAST MUSIC, INC.

320 West 57th Street New York, N.Y. 10019

Date

Dear

The following shall constitute the agreement between us:

1. As used in this agreement:

(a) The word "period" shall mean the term from to , and continuing thereafter for additional terms of two years each unless terminated by either party at the end of said initial term or any additional term, upon notice by registered or certified mail not more than six months or less than sixty (60) days prior to the end of any such term.

(b) The word "works" shall mean:

(i) All musical compositions (including the musical segments and individual compositions written for a dramatic or dramatico-musical work) composed by you alone or with one or more collaborators during the period; and

(ii) All musical compositions (including the musical segments and individual compositions written for a dramatic or dramatico-musical work) composed by you alone or with one or more collaborators prior to the period, except those in which there is an outstanding grant of the right of public performance to a person other than a publisher affiliated with BMI.

2. You agree that:

(a) Within ten (10) days after the execution of this agreement you will furnish to us two copies of a completed clearance sheet in the form supplied by us with respect to each work heretofore composed by you which has been published in printed copies or recorded commercially or which is being currently performed or which you consider as likely to be performed.

(b) In each instance that a work for which clearance sheets have not been submitted to us pursuant to sub-paragraph (a) hereof is published in printed copies or recorded commercially or in synchronization with film or tape or is considered by you as likely to be performed, whether such work is composed prior to the execution of this agreement or hereafter during the period, you will promptly furnish to us two copies of a completed clearance sheet in the form supplied by us with respect to each such work.

(c) If requested by us in writing, you will promptly furnish to us a legible lead sheet or other written or printed copy of a work.

3. The submission of clearance sheets pursuant to paragraph 2 hereof shall constitute a warranty by you that all of the information contained thereon is true and correct and that no performing rights in such work have been granted to or reserved by others except as specifically set forth therein in connection with works heretofore written or co-written by you.

4. Except as otherwise provided herein, you hereby grant to us for the period:

(a) All the rights that you own or acquire publicly to perform, and to license others to perform, anywhere in the world, any part or all of the works.

(b) The non-exclusive right to record, and to license others to record, any part or all of any of the works on electrical transcriptions, wire, tape, film or otherwise, but only for the purpose of performing such work publicly by means of radio and television or for archive or audition purposes and not for sale to the public or for synchronization (i) with motion pictures intended primarily for theatrical exhibition or (ii) with programs distributed by means of syndication to broadcasting stations.

(c) The non-exclusive right to adapt or arrange any part or all of any of the works for performance purposes, and to license others to do so.

5. (a) The rights granted to us by sub-paragraph (a) of paragraph 4 hereof shall not include the right to perform or license the performance of more than one song or aria from a dramatic or dramatico-musical work which is an opera, operetta, or musical show or more than five minutes from a dramatic or dramatico-musical work which is a ballet if such performance is accompanied by the dramatic action, costumes or scenery of that dramatic or dramatico-musical work.

(b) You, together with the publisher and your collaborators, if any, shall have the right jointly, by written notice to us, to exclude from the grant made by sub-paragraph (a) of paragraph 4 hereof performances of works comprising more than thirty minutes of a dramatic or dramatico-musical work, but this right shall not apply to such performances from (i) a score originally written for and performed as part of a theatrical or television film, (ii) a score originally written for and performed as part of a radio or television program, or (iii) the original cast, sound track or similar album of a dramatic or dramatico-musical work.

(c) You retain the right to issue non-exclusive licenses for performances of a work or works (other than to another performing rights licensing organization), provided that within ten (10) days of the issuance of such license we are given written notice of the titles of the works and the nature of the performances so licensed by you.

6. (a) As full consideration for all rights granted to us hereunder and as security therefor, we agree to pay to you, with respect to each of the works in which we obtain and retain performing rights during the period:

(i) For performances of a work on broadcasting stations in the United States, its territories and possessions, amounts calculated pursuant to our then current standard practices upon the basis of the then current performance rates generally paid by us to our affiliated writers for similar performances of similar compositions. The number of performances for which you shall be entitled to payment shall be estimated by us in accordance with our then current system of computing the number of such performances.

It is acknowledged that we license the works of our affiliates for performance by non-broadcasting means, but that unless and until such time as feasible methods can be devised for tabulation of and payment for such performances, payment will be based solely on broadcast performances. In the event that during the period we shall establish a system of separate payment for non-broadcasting performances, we shall pay you upon the basis of the then current performance rates generally paid by us to our other affiliated writers for similar performances of similar compositions.

(ii) In the case of a work composed by you with one or more collaborators, the sum payable to you hereunder shall be a pro rata share, determined on the basis of the number of collaborators, unless you shall have transmitted to us a copy of an agreement between you and your collaborators providing for a different division of payment.

(iii) All monies received by us from any performing rights licensing organization outside of the United States, its territories and possessions, which are designated by such performing rights licensing organization as the author's share of foreign performance royalties earned by your works after the deduction of our then current handling charge applicable to our affiliated writers.

(b) We shall have no obligation to make payment hereunder with respect to (i) any performance of a work which occurs prior to the date on which we have received from you all of the information and material with respect to such work which is referred to in paragraphs 2 and 3 hereof, or (ii) any performance as to which a direct license as described in sub-paragraph (c) of paragraph 5 hereof has been granted by you, your collaborator or publisher.

7. We will furnish statements to you at least twice during each year of the period showing the number of performances as computed pursuant to sub-paragraph (a) (i) of paragraph 6 hereof and at least once during each year of the period showing the monies due pursuant to sub-paragraph (a) (iii) of paragraph 6 hereof. Each statement shall be accompanied by payment to you, subject to all proper deductions for advances, if any, of the sum thereby shown to be due for such performances.

8. (a) Nothing in this agreement requires us to continue to license the works subsequent to the termination of this agreement. In the event that we continue to license any or all of the works, however, we shall continue to make payments to you for so long as you do not make or purport to make directly or indirectly any grant of performing rights in such works to any other licensing organization. The amounts of such payments shall be calculated pursuant to our then current standard practices upon the basis of the then current performance rates generally paid by us to our affiliated writers for similar performances of similar compositions. You agree to notify us by registered or certified mail of any grant or purported grant by you directly or indirectly of performing rights to any other performing rights organization within ten (10) days from the making of such grant or purported grant and if you fail so to inform us thereof and we make payments to you for any period after the making of any such grant or purported grant, you agree to repay to us all amounts so paid by us promptly on demand. In addition, if we inquire of you by registered or certified mail, addressed to your last known address, whether you have made any such grant or purported grant and you fail to confirm to us by registered or certified mail within thirty (30) days of the mailing of such inquiry that you have not made any such grant or purported grant, we may, from and after such date, discontinue making any payments to you.

(b) Our obligation to continue payment to you after the termination of this agreement for performances outside of the United States, its territories and possessions shall be dependent upon our receipt in the United

States of payments designated by foreign performing rights organizations as the author's share of foreign performance royalties earned by your works. Payment of such foreign royalties shall be subject to deduction of our then current handling charge applicable to our affiliated writers.

(c) In the event that we have reason to believe that you will receive or are receiving payment from a performing rights licensing organization other than BMI for or based on United States performances of one or more of your works during a period when such works were licensed by us pursuant to this agreement, we shall have the right to withhold payment for such performances from you until receipt of evidence satisfactory to us of the amount so paid to you by such other organization or that you have not been so paid. In the event that you have been so paid, the monies payable by us to you for such performances during such period shall be reduced by the amount of the payment from such other organization. In the event that you do not supply such evidence within eighteen (18) months from the date of our request therefor, we shall be under no obligation to make any payment to you for performances of such works during such period.

9. In the event that this agreement shall terminate at a time when, after crediting all earnings reflected by statements rendered to you prior to the effective date of such termination, there remains an unearned balance of advances paid to you by us, such termination shall not be effective until the close of the calendar quarterly period during which (a) you shall repay such unearned balance of advances, or (b) you shall notify us by registered or certified mail that you have received a statement rendered by us at our normal accounting time showing that such unearned balance of advances has been fully recouped by us.

10. You warrant and represent that you have the right to enter into this agreement; that you are not bound by any prior commitments which conflict with your commitments hereunder; that each of the works, composed by you alone or with one or more collaborators, is original; and that exercise of the rights granted by you herein will not constitute an infringement of copyright or violation of any other right of, or unfair competition with, any person, firm or corporation. You agree to indemnify and hold harmless us and our licensees from and against any and all loss or damage resulting from any claim of whatever nature arising from or in connection with the exercise of any of the rights granted by you in this agreement. Upon notification to us or any of our licensees of a claim with respect to any of the works, we shall have the right to exclude such work from this agreement and/or to withhold payment of all sums which become due pursuant to this agreement or any modification thereof until receipt of satisfactory written evidence that such claim has been withdrawn, settled or adjudicated.

11. (a) We shall have the right, upon written notice to you, to exclude from this agreement, at any time, any work which in our opinion (i) is similar to a previously existing composition and might constitute a copyright infringement, or (ii) has a title or music or lyric similar to that of a previously existing composition and might lead to a claim of unfair competition, or (iii) is offensive, in bad taste or against public morals, or (iv) is not reasonably suitable for performance.

(b) In the case of works which in our opinion are based on compositions in the public domain, we shall have the right, upon written notice to you, either (i) to exclude any such work from this agreement, or (ii) to classify any such work as entitled to receive only a fraction of the full credit that would otherwise be given for performances thereof.

(c) In the event that any work is excluded from this agreement pursuant to paragraph 10 or sub-paragraph (a) or (b) of this paragraph 11, all rights in such work shall automatically revert to you ten (10) days after the date of our notice to you of such exclusion. In the event that a work is classified for less than full credit under sub-paragraph (b) (ii) of this paragraph 11, you shall have the right, by giving notice to us, within ten (10) days after the date of our letter advising you of the credit allocated to the work, to terminate our rights therein, and all rights in such work shall thereupon revert to you.

12. In each instance that you write, or are employed or commissioned by a motion picture producer to write, during the period, all or part of the score of a motion picture intended primarily for exhibition in theaters, or by the producer of a musical show or revue for the legitimate stage to write, during the period, all or part of the musical compositions contained therein, we agree to advise the producer of the film that such part of the score as is written by you may be performed as part of the exhibition of said film in theaters in the United States, its territories and possessions, without compensation to us, or to the producer of the musical show or revue that your compositions embodied therein may be performed on the stage with living artists as part of such musical show or revue, without compensation to us. In the event that we notify you that we have established a system for the collection of royalties for performance of the scores of motion picture films in theaters in the United States, its territories and possessions, we shall no longer be obligated to take such action with respect to motion picture scores.

13. You make, constitute and appoint us, or our nominee, your true and lawful attorney, irrevocably during the term hereof, in our name or that of our nominee, or in your name, or otherwise, to do all acts, take all proceedings, execute, acknowledge and deliver any and all instruments, papers, documents, process or pleadings that may be necessary, proper or expedient to restrain infringement of and/or to enforce and protect the rights granted by you hereunder, and to recover damages in respect to or for the infringement or other violation of the said rights, and in our sole judgment to join you and/or others in whose names the copyrights to any of the works may stand; to discontinue, compromise or refer to arbitration, any such actions or proceedings or to make any other disposition of the disputes in relation to the works, provided that any action or proceeding commenced by us pursuant to the provisions of this paragraph shall be at our sole expense and for our sole benefit.

14. You agree that you, your agents, employees or representatives will not, directly or indirectly, solicit or accept payment from writers for composing music for lyrics or writing lyrics to music or for reviewing, publishing, promoting, recording or rendering other services connected with the exploitation of any composition, or permit use of your name or your affiliation with us in connection with any of the foregoing. In the event of a violation of any of the provisions of this paragraph 14, we shall have the right, in our sole discretion, by giving you at least thirty (30) days' notice by registered or certified mail, to terminate this agreement. In the event of such termination no payments shall be due to you pursuant to paragraph 8 hereof.

15. No monies due or to become due to you shall be assignable, whether by way of assignment, sale or power granted to an attorney-in-fact, without our prior written consent. If any assignment of such monies is made by you without such prior written consent, no rights of any kind against us will be acquired by the assignee, purchaser or attorney-in-fact.

16. In the event that during the period (a) mail addressed to you at the last address furnished by you pursuant to paragraph 19 hereof shall be returned by the post office, or (b) monies shall not have been earned by you pursuant to paragraph 6 hereof for a period of two consecutive years or more, or (c) you shall die, BMI shall have the right to terminate this agreement on at least thirty (30) days' notice by registered or certified mail addressed to the last address furnished by you pursuant to paragraph 19 hereof and, in the case of your death, to the representative of your estate, if known to BMI. In the event of such termination no payments shall be due you pursuant to paragraph 8 hereof.

17. You acknowledge that the rights obtained by you pursuant to this agreement constitute rights to payment of money and that during the period we shall hold absolute title to the performing rights granted to us hereunder. In the event that during the period you shall file a petition in bankruptcy, such a petition shall be filed against you, you shall make an assignment for the benefit of creditors, you shall consent to the appointment of a receiver or trustee for all or part of your property, or you shall institute or shall have instituted against you any other insolvency proceeding under the United States bankruptcy laws or any other applicable law, we shall retain title to the performing rights in all works for which clearance sheets shall have theretofore been submitted to us and shall subrogate your trustee in bankruptcy or receiver and any subsequent purchasers from them to your right to payment of money for said works in accordance with the terms and conditions of this agreement.

18. Any controversy or claim arising out of, or relating to, this agreement or the breach thereof, shall be settled by arbitration in the City of New York, in accordance with the Rules of the American Arbitration Association, and judgment upon the award of the arbitrator may be entered in any Court having jurisdiction thereof. Such award shall include the fixing of the expenses of the arbitration, including reasonable attorney's fees, which shall be borne by the unsuccessful party.

19. You agree to notify our Department of Performing Rights Administration promptly in writing of any change in your address. Any notice sent to you pursuant to the terms of this agreement shall be valid if addressed to you at the last address so furnished by you.

20. This agreement cannot be changed orally and shall be governed and construed pursuant to the laws of the State of New York.

21. In the event that any part or parts of this agreement are found to be void by a court of competent jurisdiction, the remaining part or parts shall nevertheless be binding with the same force and effect as if the void part or parts were deleted from this agreement.

Very truly yours,

BROADCAST MUSIC, INC.

ACCEPTED AND AGREED TO:

By ....

....

AGREEMENT made on .... between BROADCAST MUSIC, INC. ("BMI"), a New York corporation, whose address is 320 West 57th Street, New York, N.Y. 10019 and

....,

a .... doing business as ....

.... ("Publisher"), whose address is...

....

WITNESSETH:

FIRST: The term of this agreement shall be the period from ....

to ...., and continuing thereafter for additional periods of five (5) years each unless terminated by either party at the end of such initial period, or any such additional five (5) year period, upon notice by registered or certified mail not more than six (6) months or less than three (3) months prior to the end of any such term.

SECOND: As used in this agreement, the word "works" shall mean:

A. All musical compositions (including the musical segments and individual compositions written for a dramatic or dramatico-musical work) whether published or unpublished, now owned or copyrighted by Publisher or in which Publisher owns or controls performing rights, and

B. All musical compositions (including the musical segments and individual compositions written for a dramatic or dramatico-musical work) whether published or unpublished, in which hereafter during the term Publisher acquires ownership or copyright or ownership or control of the performing rights, from and after the date of the acquisition by Publisher of such ownership or control.

THIRD: Except as otherwise provided herein, Publisher hereby sells, assigns and transfers to BMI, its successors or assigns, for the term of this agreement:

A. All the rights which Publisher owns or acquires publicly to perform, and to license others to perform, anywhere in the world, any part or all of the works.

B. The non-exclusive right to record, and to license others to record, any part or all of any of the works on electrical transcriptions, wire, tape, film or otherwise, but only for the purpose of performing such work publicly by means of radio and television or for archive or audition purposes and not for sale to the public or for synchronization (1) with motion pictures intended primarily for theatrical exhibition or (2) with programs distributed by means of syndication to broadcasting stations.

C. The non-exclusive right to adapt or arrange any part or all of any of the works for performance purposes, and to license others to do so.

FOURTH:

A. The rights granted to BMI by subparagraph A of paragraph THIRD hereof shall not include the right to perform or license the performance of more than one song or aria from a dramatic or dramatico-musical work which is an opera, operetta, or musical show or more than five (5) minutes from a dramatic or dramatico-musical work which is a ballet if such performance is accompanied by the dramatic action, costumes or scenery of that dramatic or dramatico-musical work.

B. Publisher, together with all the writers and co-publishers, if any, shall have the right jointly, by written notice to BMI, to exclude from the grant made by subparagraph A of paragraph THIRD hereof performances of works comprising more than thirty (30) minutes of a dramatic or dramatico-musical work, but this right shall not apply to such performances from (1) a score originally written for and performed as part of a theatrical or television film, (2) a score originally written for and performed as part of a radio or television program, or (3) the original cast, sound track or similar album of a dramatic or dramatico-musical work.

C. Publisher retains the right to issue non-exclusive licenses for performances of a work or works (other than to another performing rights licensing organization), provided that within ten (10) days of the issuance of such license BMI is given written notice of the titles of the works and the nature of the performances so licensed by Publisher.

FIFTH:

A. As full consideration for all rights granted to BMI hereunder and as security therefor, BMI agrees to make the following payments to Publisher with respect to each of the works in which BMI has performing rights:

(1) For performances of works on broadcasting stations in the United States, its territories and possessions BMI will pay amounts calculated pursuant to BMI's then standard practices upon the basis of the then current performance rates generally paid by BMI to its affiliated publishers for similar performances of similar compositions. The number of performances for which Publisher shall be entitled to payment shall be estimated by BMI in accordance with its then current system of computing the number of such performances.

It is acknowledged that BMI licenses the works of its affiliates for performance by non-broadcast ng means, but that unless and until such time as feasible methods can be devised for tabulation of and payment for such performances, payment will be based solely on broadcast performances. In the event that during the term of this agreement BMI shall es.ablish a system of separate payment for non-broadcasting performances, BMI shall pay Publisher upon the basis of the then current performance rates generally paid by BMI to its other affiliated publishers for similar performances of similar compositions.

(2) For performances of works outside of the United States, its territories and possessions BMI will pay to Publisher all monies received by BMI in the United States from any performing rights licensing organization which are designated by such organization as the publisher's share of foreign performance royalties earned by any of the works after the deduction of BMI's then current handling charge applicable to its affiliated publishers.

(3) In the case of works which, or rights in which, are owned by Publisher jointly with one or more other publishers who have granted performing rights therein to BMI, the sum payable to Publisher under this subparagraph A shall be a pro rata share determined on the basis of the number of publishers, unless BMI shall have received from Publisher a copy of an agreement or other document signed by all of the publishers providing for a different division of payment.

B. Notwithstanding the foregoing provisions of this paragraph FIFTH, BMI shall have no obligation to make payment hereunder with respect to (1) any performance of a work which occurs prior to the date on which BMI shall have received from Publisher ll of the material with respect to such work referred to in subparagraph A of paragraph TENTH hereof, and in the case of foreign performances, the information referred to in subparagraph B of paragraph FOURTEENTH hereof, or (2) any performance as to which a direct license as described in subparagraph C of paragraph FOURTH hereof has been granted by Publisher, its co-publisher or the writer.

SIXTH:. BMI will furnish statements to Publisher at least twice during each year of the term showing the number of performances of the works as computed pursuant to subparagraph A(1) of paragraph FIFTH hereof, and at least once during each year of the term showing the monies received by BMI referred to in subparagraph A(2) of paragraph FIFTH hereof. Each such statement shall be accompanied by payment of the sum thereby shown to be due to Publisher, subject to all proper deductions, if any, for advances or amounts due to BMI from Publisher.

SEVENTH:

A. Nothing in this agreement requires BMI to continue to license the works subsequent to the termination of this agreement. In the event that BMI continues to license any or all of the works, however, BMI shall continue to make payments to Publisher for so long as Publisher does not make or purport to make directly or indirectly any grant of performing rights in such works to any other licensing organization. The amounts of such payments shall be calculated pursuant to BMI's then current standard practices upon the basis of the then current performance rates generally paid by BMI to its affiliated publishers for similar performances of similar compositions. Publisher agrees to notify BMI by registered or certified mail of any grant or purported grant by Publisher directly or indirectly of performing rights to any other performing rights organization within ten (10) days from the making of such grant or purported grant and if Publisher fails so to inform BMI thereof and BMI makes payments to Publisher for any period after the making of any such grant or purported grant, Publisher agrees to repay to BMI all amounts so paid by BMI promptly on demand. In addition, if BMI inquires of Publisher by registered or certified mail, addressed to Publisher's last known address, whether Publisher has made any such grant or purported grant and Publisher fails to confirm to BMI by registered or certified mail within thirty (30) days of the mailing of such inquiry that Publisher has not made any such grant or purported grant, BMI may, from and after such date, discontinue making any payments to Publisher.

B. BMI's obligation to continue payment to Publisher after the termination of this agreement for performances outside of the United States, its territories and possessions shall be dependent upon BMI's receipt in the United States of payments designated by foreign performing rights licensing organizations as the publisher's share of foreign performance royalties earned by any of the works. Payment of such foreign royalties shall be subject to deduction of BMI's then current handling charge applicable to its affiliated publishers.

C. In the event that BMI has reason to believe that Publisher will receive or is receiving payment from a performing rights licensing organization other than BMI for or based on United States performances of one or more of the works during a period when such works were licensed by BMI pursuant to this agreement, BMI shall have the right to withhold payment for such performances from Publisher until receipt of evidence satisfactory to BMI of the amount so paid to Publisher by such other organization or that Publisher has not been so paid. In the event that Publisher has been so paid, the monies payable by BMI to Publisher for such performances during such period shall be reduced by the amount of the payment from such other organization. In the event that Publisher does not supply such evidence within eighteen (18) months from the date of BMI's request therefor, BMI shall be under no obligation to make any payment to Publisher for performances of such works during such period.

EIGHTH: In the event that this agreement shall terminate at a time when, after crediting all earnings reflected by statements rendered to Publisher prior to the effective date of such termination, there remains an unearned balance of advances paid to Publisher by BMI, such termination shall not be effective until the close of the calendar quarterly period during which (A) Publisher shall repay such unearned balance of advances, or (B) Publisher shall notify BMI by registered or certified mail that Publisher has received a statement rendered by BMI at its normal accounting time showing that such unearned balance of advances has been fully recouped by BMI.

NINTH:

A. BMI shall have the right, upon written notice to Publisher, to exclude from this agreement, at any time, any work which in BMI's opinion (1) is similar to a previously existing composition and might constitute a copyright infringement, or (2) has a title or music or lyric similar to that of a previously existing composition and might lead to a claim of unfair competition, or (3) is offensive, in bad taste or against public morals, or (4) is not reasonably suitable for performance.

B. In the case of works which in the opinion of BMI are based on compositions in the public domain, BMI shall have the right, at any time, upon written notice to Publisher, either (1) to exclude any such work from this agreement, or (2) to classify any such work as entitled to receive only a stated fraction of the full credit that would otherwise be given for performances thereof.

C. In the event that any work is excluded from this agreement pursuant to subparagraph A or B of this paragraph NINTH, or pursuant to subparagraph C of paragraph TWELFTH hereof, all rights of BMI in such work shall automatically revert to Publisher ten (10) days after the date of the notice of such exclusion given by BMI to Publisher. In the event that a work is classified for less than full credit under subparagraph B(2) of this paragraph NINTH, Publisher shall have the right, by giving notice to BMI within ten (10) days after the date of BMI's notice to Publisher of the credit allocated to such work, to terminate all rights in such work granted to BMI herein and all such rights of BMI in such work shall revert to Publisher thirty (30) days after the date of such notice from Publisher to BMI.

TENTH:

A. With respect to each of the works which has been or shall be published or recorded commercially or synchronized with motion picture or television film or tape or which Publisher considers likely to be performed, Publisher agrees to furnish to BMI:

(1) Two copies of a completed clearance sheet in the form supplied by BMI, unless a cue sheet with respect to such work is furnished pursuant to subparagraph A(3) of this paragraph TENTH.

(2) If such work is based on a composition in the public domain, a legible lead sheet or other written or printed copy of such work setting forth the lyrics, if any, and music correctly metered; provided that with respect to all other works, such copy need be furnished only if requested by BMI pursuant to subsection (c) of subparagraph D(2) of this paragraph TENTH.

(3) If such work has been or shall be synchronized with or otherwise used in connection with motion picture or television film or tape, a cue sheet showing the title, composers, publisher and nature and duration of the use of the work in such film or tape.

B. Publisher shall submit the material described in subparagraph A of this paragraph TENTH with respect to works heretofore published, recorded or synchronized within ten (10) days after the execution of this agreement and with respect to any of the works hereafter so published, recorded, synchronized or likely to be performed prior to the date of publication or release of the recording, film or tape or anticipated performance.

C. The submission of each clearance sheet or cue sheet shall constitute a warranty by Publisher that all of the information contained thereon is true and correct and that no performing rights in any of the works listed thereon has been granted to or reserved by others except as specifically set forth therein.

D. Publisher agrees:

(1) To secure and maintain copyright protection of the works pursuant to the Copyright Law of the United States and pursuant to the laws of such other nations of the world where such protection is

afforded; and to give BMI prompt written notice of the date and number of copyright registration and/or renewal of each work registered in the United States Copyright Office.

(2) At BMI's request:

(a) To register each unpublished and published work in the United States Copyright Office pursuant to the Copyright Law of the United States.

(b) To record in the United States Copyright Office in accordance with the Copyright Law of the United States any agreements, assignments, instruments or documents of any kind by which Publisher obtained the right to publicly perform and/or the right to publish, co-publish or sub-publish any of the works.

(c) To obtain and deliver to BMI copies of: unpublished and published works; copyright registration and/or renewal certificates issued by the United States Copyright Office; any of the documents referred to in sub-section (b) above.

E. Publisher agrees to give BMI prompt notice by registered or certified mail in each instance when, pursuant to the Copyright Law of the United States, (1) the rights granted to BMI by Publisher in any work shall revert to the writer or the writer's representative, or (2) copyright protection of any work shall terminate.

ELEVENTH: Publisher warrants and represents that:

A. Publisher has the right to enter into this agreement; Publisher is not bound by any prior commitments which conflict with its undertakings herein; the rights granted by Publisher to BMI herein are the sole and exclusive property of Publisher and are free from all encumbrances and claims; and exercise of such rights will not constitute infringement of copyright or violation of any right of, or unfair competition with, any person, firm, corporation or association.

B. Except with respect to works in which the possession of performing rights by another person, firm, corporation or association is specifically set forth on a clearance sheet or cue sheet submitted to BMI pursuant to subparagraph A of paragraph TENTH hereof, Publisher has exclusive performing rights in each of the works by virtue of written grants thereof to Publisher signed by all the authors and composers or other owners of such work.

TWELFTH:

A. Publisher agrees to defend, indemnify, save and hold BMI, its licensees, the advertisers of its licensees and their respective agents, servants and employees, free and harmless from and against any and all demands, loss, damage, suits, judgments, recoveries and costs, including counsel fees, resulting from any claim of whatever nature arising from or in connection with the exercise of any of the rights granted by Publisher in this agreement; provided, however, that the obligations of Publisher under this paragraph TWELFTH shall not apply to any matter added to, or changes made in, any work by BMI or its licensees.

B. Upon the receipt by any of the parties herein indemnified of any notice, demand, process, papers, writ or pleading, by which any such claim, demand, suit or proceeding is made or commenced against them, or any of them, which Publisher shall be obliged to defend hereunder, BMI shall, as soon as may be practicable, give Publisher notice thereof and deliver to Publisher such papers or true copies thereof, and BMI shall have the right to participate by counsel of its own choice, at its own expense. Publisher agrees to cooperate with BMI in all such matters.

C. In the event of such notification of claim or service of process on any of the parties herein indemnified, BMI shall have the right, from the date thereof, to exclude the work with respect to which a claim is made from this agreement and/or to withhold payment of all sums which may become due pursuant to this agreement or any modification thereof until receipt of satisfactory written evidence that such claim has been withdrawn, settled or adjudicated.

THIRTEENTH: Publisher makes, constitutes and appoints BMI, or its nominee, Publisher's true and lawful attorney, irrevocably during the term hereof, in the name of BMI or that of its nominee, or in Publisher's name, or otherwise, to do all acts, take all proceedings, and execute, acknowledge and deliver any and all instruments, papers, documents, process or pleadings that may be necessary, proper or expedient to restrain infringement of and/or to enforce and protect the rights granted by Publisher hereunder, and to recover damages in respect of or for the infringement or other violation of the said rights, and in BMI's sole judgment to join Publisher and/or others in whose names the copyrights to any of the works may stand, and to discontinue, compromise or refer to arbitration, any such actions or proceedings or to make any other disposition of the disputes in relation to the works; provided that any action or proceeding commenced by BMI pursuant to the provisions of this paragraph THIRTEENTH shall be at its sole expense and for its sole benefit.

FOURTEENTH:

A. It is acknowledged that BMI has heretofore entered into, and may during the term of this agreement enter into, contracts with performing rights licensing organizations for the licensing of public performing rights controlled by BMI in territories outside of the United States, its territories and possessions (hereinafter called "foreign territories"). Upon Publisher's written request, BMI agrees to permit Publisher to grant performing rights in any or all of the works for any foreign territory for which, at the time such request is received, BMI has not entered into any such contract with a performing rights licensing organization; provided, however, that any such grant of performing rights by Publisher shall terminate at such time when BMI shall have entered into such a contract with a performing rights licensing organization covering such foreign territory and shall have notified Publisher thereof. Nothing herein contained, however, shall be deemed to restrict Publisher from assigning to its foreign publisher or representative the right to collect a part or all of the publishers' performance royalties earned by any or all of the works in any foreign territory as part of an agreement for the publication, exploitation or representation of such works in such territory, whether or not BMI has entered into such a contract with a performing rights licensing organization covering such territory.

B. Publisher agrees to notify BMI promptly in writing in each instance when publication, exploitation or other rights in any or all of the works are granted for any foreign territory. Such notice shall set forth the title of the work, the country or countries involved, the period of such grant, the name of the person, firm, corporation or association entitled to collect performance royalties earned in the foreign territory and the amount of such share. Within ten (10) days after the execution of this agreement Publisher agrees to submit to BMI, in writing, a list of all works as to which Publisher has, prior to the effective date of this agreement, granted to any person, firm, corporation or association performing rights and/or the right to collect publisher performance royalties earned in any foreign territory.

C. In the event that BMI transmits to Publisher performance royalties designated as the writer's share of performance royalties earned by any of the works in any foreign territory, Publisher shall promptly pay such royalties to the writer or writers of the works involved. If Publisher is unable for any reason to locate and make payment to any of the writers involved within six (6) months from the date of receipt, the amounts due such writers shall be returned to BMI.

FIFTEENTH:

A. Publisher agrees that Publisher, its agents, employees, representatives or affiliated companies, will not directly or indirectly during the term of this agreement:

(1) Solicit or accept payment from or on behalf of authors for composing music for lyrics, or from or on behalf of composers for writing lyrics to music.

(2) Solicit or accept manuscripts from composers or authors in consideration of any payments to be made by or on behalf of such composers or authors for reviewing, arranging, promotion, publication, recording or any other services connected with the exploitation of any composition.

(3) Permit Publisher's name, or the fact of its affiliation with BMI, to be used by any other person, firm, corporation or association engaged in any of the practices described in subparagraphs A(1) and A(2) of this paragraph FIFTEENTH.

(4) Submit to BMI, as one of the works to come within this agreement, any musical composition with respect to which any payments described in subparagraphs A(1) and A(2) of this paragraph FIFTEENTH have been made by or on behalf of a composer or author to any person, firm, corporation or association.

B. Publisher agrees that Publisher, its agents, employees or representatives will not directly or indirectly during the term of this agreement make any effort to ascertain from, or offer any inducement or consideration to, anyone, including but not limited to any broadcasting licensee of BMI or to the agents, employees or representatives of BMI or of any such licensee, for information regarding the time or times when any such BMI licensee is to report its performances to BMI, or to attempt in any way to manipulate performances or affect the representative character or accuracy of BMI's system of sampling or logging performances.

C. Publisher agrees to notify BMI promptly in writing (1) of any change of firm name of Publisher, and (2) of any change of twenty percent (20%) or more in the ownership thereof.

D. In the event of the violation of any of the provisions of subparagraphs A, B or C of this paragraph FIFTEENTH, BMI shall have the right, in its sole discretion, to terminate this agreement by giving Publisher at least thirty (30) days' notice by registered or certified mail. In the event of such termination, no payments shall be due to Publisher pursuant to paragraph SEVENTH hereof.

SIXTEENTH: In the event that during the term of this agreement (1) mail addressed to Publisher at the last address furnished by it pursuant to paragraph TWENTIETH hereof shall be returned by the post office, or (2) monies shall not have been earned by Publisher pursuant to paragraph FIFTH hereof for a period of two consecutive years or more, or (3) the proprietor, if Publisher is a sole proprietorship, shall die, BMI shall have the right to terminate this agreement on at least thirty (30) days' notice by registered or certified mail addressed to the last address furnished by Publisher pursuant to paragraph TWENTIETH hereof and, in the case of the death of a sole proprietor, to the representative of said proprietor's estate, if known to BMI. In the event of such termination, no payments shall be due Publisher pursuant to paragraph SEVENTH hereof.

SEVENTEENTH: Publisher acknowledges that the rights obtained by it pursuant to this agreement constitute rights to payment of money and that during the term BMI shall hold absolute title to the performing rights granted to BMI hereunder. In the event that during the term Publisher shall file a petition in bankruptcy, such a petition shall be filed against Publisher, Publisher shall make an assignment for the benefit of creditors, Publisher shall consent to the appointment of a receiver or trustee for all or part of its property, Publisher shall file a petition for corporate reorganization or arrangement under the United States bankruptcy laws, Publisher shall institute or shall have instituted against it any other insolvency proceeding under the United States bankruptcy laws or any other applicable law, or, in the event Publisher is a partnership, all of the general partners of said partnership shall be adjudged bankrupts, BMI shall retain title to the performing rights in all works for which clearance sheets shall have theretofore been submitted to BMI and shall subrogate Publisher's trustee in bankruptcy or receiver and any subsequent purchasers from them to Publisher's right to payment of money for said works in accordance with the terms and conditions of this agreement.

EIGHTEENTH: Any controversy or claim arising out of, or relating to, this agreement or the breach thereof, shall be settled by arbitration in the City of New York, in accordance with the Rules of the American Arbitration Association, and judgment upon the award of the arbitrator may be entered in any court having jurisdiction thereof. Such award shall include the fixing of the expenses of the arbitration, including reasonable attorney's fees, which shall be borne by the unsuccessful party.

NINETEENTH: Publisher agrees that it shall not, without the written consent of BMI, assign any of its rights hereunder. No rights of any kind against BMI will be acquired by the assignee if any such purported assignment is made by Publisher without such written consent.

TWENTIETH: Publisher agrees to notify BMI's Department of Performing Rights Administration promptly in writing of any change in its address. Any notice sent to Publisher pursuant to the terms of this agreement shall be valid if addressed to Publisher at the last address so furnished by Publisher.

TWENTY-FIRST: This agreement cannot be changed orally and shall be governed and construed pursuant to the laws of the State of New York.

TWENTY-SECOND: In the event that any part or parts of this agreement are found to be void by a court of competent jurisdiction, the remaining part or parts shall nevertheless be binding with the same force and effect as if the void part or parts were deleted from this agreement.

IN WITNESS WHEREOF, the parties hereto have caused this agreement to be duly executed as of the day and year first above written.

BROADCAST MUSIC, INC.

By ______________________________

....

By ______________________________
(Title of Signer) ....

5/81

Appendix 2. c. BMI forms to register commercials
i) commercials using original music

BMI

NOTICE TO BMI REGARDING ORIGINAL COMMERCIAL

The undersigned warrant and represent as follows:

1. ______________________________, ______________________________ has
name(s) of composer(s)

(have) composed the music and ______________________, ______________________
name(s) of lyricist(s)

has(have) written the lyric for a musical work entitled ______________________

to be used as part of broadcast commercial announcements by ______________________
name of sponsor

for the product ____________________ (which announcements are herein called "the commercials")
name of product

and that ______________________________, ______________________________
name(s) of publisher(s)

is(are) the publisher(s) thereof.

2. The work has not been written as a "work made for hire" or pursuant to any other agreement which would prevent the licensing of performing rights in the work by BMI pursuant to the writer(s) and/or publisher(s) agreement(s) with BMI.

3. The agreement among the parties provides for the division of writer and publisher performance royalties as follows:

______________________ writer	_____% share	______________________ publisher	_____% share
______________________ writer	_____% share	______________________ publisher	_____% share
______________________ writer	_____% share		

4. The work is and will be used for at least 15 seconds or more as the sole auditory focus of audience attention in the course of the commercials.

5. Attached are a lead sheet and tape of the work as used in the commercials and an accurate list of broadcast time bought for the commercials by the sponsor or the undersigned agency on behalf of the sponsor for the period from ____________________ to ____________________.

6. It is understood by all parties that payments to the writer(s) and/or publisher(s) of the work will be made by BMI in reliance on the representations made in this notice and the documents attached hereto.

Dated: ____________________

____
Writer

____
Writer

____
Writer

____
Agency (or sponsor)

By____________________
(Title) __________

____
Publisher

By____________________
(Title) __________

____
Publisher

By____________________
(Title) __________

THIS DOCUMENT MUST BE SIGNED BY EACH WRITER AND PUBLISHER CLAIMING RIGHTS AND BY THE APPROPRIATE REPRESENTATIVE OF THE ADVERTISING AGENCY OR SPONSOR.

BMI

____
Name of Sponsor or Agency

By____________________
(Signature and Title)________

Address of Sponsor or Agency ____________________

REPORT OF STATION TIME BOUGHT FOR COMMERCIAL

Entitled ____________________ For ____________________
Name of Sponsor

Station or Network	Broadcast Dates	Number of Performances Per Day

BMI

Appendix 2. c. BMI forms to register commercials
ii) commercials using existing music

NOTICE TO BMI REGARDING COMMERCIAL USING EXISTING MUSIC

The undersigned warrant and represent as follows:

1. ______________________, ______________________ has
name(s) of lyricist(s)

(have) written a lyric set to the music of the composition ______________________
original title

______________________ written and composed by ______________________,
of composition — name(s) of original

______________________, which musical work (herein called "the new work")
lyricist(s) and composer(s)

is intended to be used as part of broadcast commercial announcements by __________
name

______________________ for the product ______________________ (which announce-
of sponsor — name of product

ments are herein called "the commercials") and that ______________________,
name(s) of

______________________ is(are) the publisher(s) thereof.
publisher(s)

2. Neither the music nor the lyric has been written as "works made for hire" or pursuant to any other agreement which would prevent the licensing of performing rights in the new work by BMI pursuant to the writer(s) and/or publisher(s) agreement(s) with BMI.

3. The agreement among the parties provides for the division of writer and publisher royalties for performance of the new work as a commercial as follows:

writer	share %	publisher	share %
______	____%	______	____%
______	____%	______	____%
______	____%		
______	____%		

4. The new work is and will be used for at least 15 seconds or more as the sole auditory focus of audience attention in the course of the commercials.

5. Attached are a lead sheet and tape of the new work as used in the commercials and an accurate list of the broadcast time bought for the commercials by the sponsor or the undersigned agency on behalf of the sponsor for the period from ______________________ to ________________________.

6. It is understood by all parties that payments to the writer(s) and/or publisher(s) of the new work will be made by BMI in reliance on the representations made in this notice and the documents attached hereto.

Dated: ___________________________

____
Writer

____
Writer

____
Writer

____
Writer

____
Agency (or sponsor)

By______________________________
(Title) ________

____
Publisher

By______________________________
(Title) ________

THIS DOCUMENT MUST BE SIGNED BY EACH WRITER AND PUBLISHER CLAIMING RIGHTS AND BY THE APPROPRIATE REPRESENTATIVE OF THE ADVERTISING AGENCY OR SPONSOR.

____
Publisher

By______________________________
(Title) ________

____
Name of Sponsor or Agency

By____________________________
(Signature and Title)________

Address of Sponsor or Agency ____________________________

____

REPORT OF STATION TIME BOUGHT FOR COMMERCIAL

Entitled ________________________ For ________________________
Name of Sponsor

Station or Network	Broadcast Dates	Number of Performances Per Day

NOTES

7

NONPRESCRIPTION DRUG ADVERTISING

Stuart Lee Friedel

March 11, 1982

NONPRESCRIPTION DRUG ADVERTISING

I. FEDERAL TRADE COMMISSION JURISDICTION

A. Section 12 of the Federal Trade Commission Act states:

(a) It shall be unlawful for any person, partnership or corporation to disseminate, or cause to be disseminated any false advertisement

(1) By U.S. mails or in commerce by any means, for the purpose of inducing, or which is likely to induce, directly or indirectly a purchase of drugs, . . . or

(2) By any means for the purpose of inducing, or which is likely to induce directly or indirectly the purchase in commerce of drugs,. . . .

(b) The dissemination or causing to be disseminated of any false advertisement within the provisions of subsection (a) of this section shall be an unfair or deceptive act or practice in commerce, within the meaning of Section 5.

B. Section 5 of the Federal Trade Commission Act states:

unfair methods of competition in commerce and unfair or deceptive practices in commerce are hereby declared unlawful.

II. FOOD AND DRUG JURISDICTION

A. Section 502 of the Federal Food, Drug and Cosmetic Act states that a drug shall be deemed to be misbranded if its labeling is false or misleading in any particular.

B. Section 201(m) of the Federal Food, Drug and Cosmetic Act defines the term "labeling" to mean all labels and other written, print, or graphic matter (1) upon any article or any of its containers or wrappers, or (2) accompanying such article.

III. MEMORANDUM OF UNDERSTANDING BETWEEN THE FEDERAL TRADE COMMISSION AND THE FOOD AND DRUG ADMINISTRATION ON NONPRESCRIPTION DRUG ADVERTISING

With the exception of prescription drugs, the Federal Trade Commission has primary responsibility with respect to the regulation of the truth or falsity of all advertising (other than labeling) of foods, drugs, devices, and cosmetics. In the absence of express agreement between the two agencies to the contrary, the Commission will exercise primary jurisdiction over all matters regulating the truth or falsity of advertising of food, drugs (with the exception of prescription drugs), devices, and cosmetics. 36 Fed. Reg. 18539.

A. The analgesic cases.

<u>FTC</u> v. <u>American Home Products</u>, Docket 8918;

<u>FTC</u> v. <u>Sterling Drug</u>, Docket 8919;

<u>FTC</u> v. <u>Bristol-Myers Company</u>, Docket 8917

<u>FTC</u> v. <u>Thompson Medical Company</u> (Aspercreme), Docket No. 9149.

In <u>FTC</u> v. <u>Pfizer, Inc</u>., the Commission established the principle that an advertiser must have a "reasonable basis" to support advertised representations, prior to the making of such claims. Reasonable basis was undefined and was to be determined on a case by case basis. In the analgesic cases, the FTC has now set forth the type of reasonable basis which is necessary for a comparative drug claim, i.e. adequate and well-controlled clinical studies.

B. "Claims" - TRR and Warnings "TRR"

1. FTC drops attempt to legislate rule that advertising claims must be identified in syntax, with labeling claims. Yet see, in the Matter of Mentholatum Company, File No. 792 3213.

2. FTC considers issuing rule to require antacid products to disclose labeling warnings in advertising.

V. <u>FOOD AND DRUG ADMINISTRATION MONOGRAPHS</u>

Review of drug efficacy will establish permissible statement of drug indication.

VI. <u>LANHAM ACT.</u>

15 U.S.C., Section 1125(a) states: Any person who shall . . . use in connection with any goods or service . . . any false description or representation, including words or other symbols containing false and/or representing the same, and shall cause such foods to enter into commerce shall be liable for damages to anyone damaged by the falsity.

See:

<u>American Home Products Corp</u>. v. <u>Abbott Laboratories</u> 83 Civil 4345.

<u>American Home Products Corp</u>. v. <u>Johnson & Johnson</u>, 436 F. Supp 785.

8

CONSTITUTIONAL PROTECTION OF ADVERTISING

Elhanan C. Stone

March 11, 1982

<u>Constitutional Protection of Advertising</u>

I. Excerpts from Virginia State Board of Pharmacy V. Virginia Citizens Consumer Council, 425 U.S. 748 (1976).

II. Proposed FTC rulemaking on children's advertising.

III. Linmark Associates, Inc. V. The Township of Willingsboro, 431 U.S. 85 (1977).

IV. Beneficial Finance, Co., V. FTC, 542 F. 2d 611 (CA-3 1976).

V. Texas Optometric Association, Inc., V. N. Jay Rogers, 440 U.S. 1 (1979) - (See case attached).

VI. Cablecom-General, Inc., et. al. V. Richard A. Crisp, Dir. Alcoholic Beverage Control Bd., USDC WD Oklahoma, Slip Opinion December 18, 1981.

VII. Central Hudson Gas and Electric Corp. V. Public Service Commission, 447 U.S. 557 (1980). (See excerpts attached)

The conventional wisdom among lawyers, until a few years ago, was that advertising, "mere commercial speech," was not entitled to First Amendment protection. Recent supreme court decisions cited above have made it clear that the First Amendment does apply to advertising. The court's rules are still evolutionary in manner. There are indications that there may be reasonable time, place and manner restrictions which may be applied to advertising which may not be applied to other forms of speech. It is clear that there is no First Amendment protection for misleading advertising and such advertising may be subject to prior restraint. The constitutional protection provided may conflict with FTC interpretations of what constitutes unfair advertising. There was an FTC rulemaking proceeding which would require that drug advertising be limited to claims and symptons in haec verba as they appear on the label. Obviously this constitutes a restraint on what otherwise might be truthful advertising.

An area which has not yet been clearly litigated but which would seem to be ripe for decision as constitutional protections evolve is the conflict between an individual's right of privacy or his property right in publicity and the advertiser's First Amendment right. C.F. However, a recent case involving the Marx Brothers and the imitation of their style and performance in a theatrical production entitled <u>A Day In Hollywood A Night In The Ukraine</u> indicates that courts might recognize some right of publicity in a style of performance. Groucho Marx's Productions Inc., et. al., USDC SDNY Number 80 Civ. 2310 Slip Opinion October 2, 1981.

The Willingsboro case cited above raises questions of conflict between a public policy which would discourage "block busting" by prohibiting for sales signs on real property and the right of a property owner to propose a commercial transaction - selling his property. It would seem that commercial speech will continue to be hemmed in by the rule of reason and a balancing test will continue to be applied to it.

The Oklahoma liquor control case cited above indicates that even though such matters as the control of alcoholic beverages is left to the state under the United States Constitution, there are overriding First Amendment interests in free speech and an overly broad restriction must give way to an advertisers right to speak.

A serious First Amendment question is also raised when the Federal Trade Commission attempts to impose a restraint upon unfair, as differentiated from misleading, advertising. An analysis of First Amendment cases going back to <u>Near V. Minnesota, 283 U.S. 697 (1931)</u> would seem to indicate that such a restraint are also impermissible. Questions as to prior restraint are also raised under FTC enforcement guides which require that proper substantiation be in the files of the advertiser prior to the publication of a claim. Would not such a requirement tend to prevent what could be truthful statements even though not fully substantiated? Does not that requirement address itself to administrative convience rather than truthfulness? Compare <u>Jay Norris, Inc. V. FTC, 598 F. 2d 1244 (CA-2, 1979)</u>. Query in light of current constitutional theory would the "reasonable basis" requirement set forth in the Pfizer Un-Burn case Paragraph 20056 CCH Trade Reg. Rep. be upheld as requiring that the "reasonable basis" be in hand at the time of making the claim?

Central Hudson Gas and Electric Corp.
v.
Public Service Commission

~~Opinion.~~

Mr. Justice Powell delivered the opinion of the Court.

This case presents the question whether a regulation of the Public Service Commission of the State of New York violates the First and Fourteenth Amendments because it completely bans promotional advertising by an electrical utility.

I

In December 1973, the Commission, appelle here, ordered electric utilities in New York State to cease all advertising that "promot[es] the use of electricity." App. to Juris. St., at 31a. The order was based on the Commission's finding that "the interconnected utility system in New York State does not have sufficient fuel stocks or sources of supply to continue furnishing all customer demands for the 1973-1974 winter." *Id.*, at 26a.

Three years later, when the fuel shortage had eased, the Commission requested comments from the public on its proposal to continue the ban on promotional advertising. Central Hudson Gas & Electric Corporation, the appellant in this case, opposed the ban on First Amendment grounds. App. A10. After reviewing the public comments, the Commission extended the prohibition in a Policy Statement issued on February 25, 1977.

The Policy Statement divided advertising expenses "into two broad categories: promotional — advertising intended to stimulate the purchase of utility services — and institutional and informational, a broad category inclusive of all advertising not clearly intended to promote sales."[1] App. to Juris. St., at 35a. The Commission declared all promotional advertising contrary to the national policy of conserving energy. It acknowledged that the ban is not a perfect vehicle for conserving energy. For example, the Commission's order prohibits promotional advertising to develop consumption during periods when demand for electricity is low. By limiting growth in "off-peak" consumption, the ban limits the "beneficial side effects" of such growth in terms of more efficient use of existing power plants.*Id.*, at 37a. And since oil dealers are not under the Commission's jurisdiction and thus remain free to advertise, it was recognized that the ban can achieve only "piecemeal conservationism." Still, the Commission adopted the restriction because it was deemed likely to "result in some dampening of unnecessary growth" in energy consumption. *Ibid.*

The Commission's order explicitly permitted "informational" advertising designed to encourage "*shifts* of consumption" from peak demand times to periods of low electricity demand. *Ibid.* (emphasis in orginal). Informational advertising would not seek to increase aggregate consumption, but would invite a leveling of demand throughout any given 24-hour period. The agency offered to review "specific proposals by the companies for specifically described [advertising] programs that meet these criteria." *Id.*, at 38a.

When it rejected requests for rehearing on the Policy Statement, the Commission supplemented its rationale for the advertising ban. The agency observed that additional electricity probably would be more expensive to produce than existing output. Because electricity rates in New York were not then based on marginal cost,[2] the Commission feared that additional power would be priced below the actual cost of generation. This aditional electricity would be subsidized by all consumers through generally higher rates. *Id.*, at 57a-58a. The state agency also thought that promotional advertising would give "misleading signals" to the public by appearing to encourage energy consumption at a time when conservation is needed. *Id.*, at 59a.

Appellant challenged the order in state court, arguing that the Commission had restrained commercial speech in violation of the First and Fourteenth Amendments.[3]

---

[1] The dissenting opinion attempts to construe the Policy Statement to authorize advertising that would result "in a net energy savings" even if the advertising encouraged consumption of additional electricity. *Post*, at 13. The attempted construction fails, however, since the Policy Statement is phrased only in terms of advertising that promotes "the purchase of utility services" and "sales" of electricity. Plainly, the Commission did not intend to permit advertising that would enhance net energy efficiency by increasing consumption of electrical services.

[2] "Marginal cost" has been defined as the "*extra* or incremental cost of producing an *extra* unit of output." P. Samuelson, Economics 463 (10th ed. 1976) (emphasis in original).

[3] Central Hudson also alleged that the Com-

The Commission's order was upheld by the trial court and at the intermediate appellate level.[4] The New York Court of Appeals affirmed. It found little value to advertising in "the non-competitive market in which electric corporations operate." 47 N.Y.2d 94, 110, 390 N.E. 2d 749, 757 (1979). Since consumers "have no choice regarding the source of their electric power," the court denied that "promotional advertising of electricity might contribute to society's interest in 'informed and reliable' economic decisionmaking."*Ibid.* The court also observed that by encouraging consumption, promotional advertising would only exacerbate the current energy situation. *Id.*, at 110, 390 N.E.2d, at 758. The court concluded that the governmental interest in the prohibition outweighed the limited constitutional value of the commercial speech at issue. We noted probable jurisdiction, — U.S. — (1979), and now reverse.

II

The Commission's order restricts only commercial speech, that is, expression related solely to the economic interests of the speaker and its audience. *Virginia State Board of Pharmacy v. Virginia Citizens Consumer Council, Inc.*, 425 U.S. 748, 762 [1 Med.L.Rptr. 1930] (1975); *Bates v. State Bar of Arizona*, 433 U.S. 350, 363-364 [1 Med.L.Rptr. 2097] (1977);*Friedman v. Rogers*, 436 U.S. 447, 456 (1979). The First Amendment, as applied to the States through the Fourteenth Amendment, protects commercial speech from unwarranted governmental regulation.*Virginia State Board of Pharmacy*, 425 U.S., at 761-762. Commercial expression not only serves the economic interest of the speaker, but also assists consumers and furthers the societal interest in the fullest possible dissemination of information. In applying the First Amendment to this area, we have rejected the "highly paternalistic" view that government has complete power to suppress or regulate commercial speech. "[P]eople will perceive their own best interests if only they are well enough informed and. . .the best means to that end is to open the channels of communication, rather than to close them . . . ." *Id.*, at 770; see *Linmark Associates, Inc.* v. *Township of Willingboro*, 431 U.S. 85, 92 (1977). Even when advertising communicates only an incomplete version of the relevant facts, the First Amendment presumes that some accurate information is better than no information at all.*Bates v. State Bar of Arizona, supra*, 433 U.S., at 374.

Nevertheless, our decisions have recognized "the 'commonsense' distinction between speech proposing a commercial transaction, which occurs in an area traditionally subject to government regulation, and other varieties of speech."*Ohralik v. Ohio State Bar Assn.*, 436 U.S. 447, 455-456 (1978); see *Bates v. State Bar of Arizona, supra*, at 381; see also Jackson & Jeffries, Commercial Speech: Economic Due Process and the First Amendment, 65 Va. L. Rev. 1, 38-39 (1979).[5] The Constitution

mission's order reaches beyond the agency's statutory powers. This argument was rejected by the New York Court of Appeals, 47 N.Y.2d 94, 102-104; 390 N.E.2d 749, 752-754 (1979), and was not argued to this Court.

[4] 63 App. Div. 2d 364 (1978) (Appellate Division of State Supreme Court); App. to Juris. St., at 22a (N.Y. Sup. Ct., Feb. 17, 1978).

[5] In an opinion concurring in the judgment, MR. JUSTICE STEVENS suggests that the Commission's order reaches beyond commercial speech to suppress expression that is entitled to the full protection of the First Amendment. See *Post*, at 3. We find no support for this claim in the record of this case. The Commission's Policy Statement excluded "institutional and informational" messages from the advertising ban, which was restricted to all advertising "clearly intended to promote sales." App. to Juris. St., at 35a. The complaint alleged only that the "prohibition of promotional advertising by Petitioner is not reasonable regulation of Petitioner's commercial speech. . . ."*Id.*, at 70a. Moreover, the state court opinions and the arguments of the parties before this Court also viewed this litigation as involving only commercial speech. Nevertheless, the concurring opinion of MR. JUSTICE STEVENS views the Commission's order as suppressing more than commercial speech because it would outlaw, for example, advertising that promoted electricity consumption by touting the environmental benefits of such uses. See*post*, at 3. Apparently the concurring opinion would accord full First Amendment protection to all promotional advertising that includes claims "relating to. . . questions frequently discussed and debated by our political leaders."*post*, at 3.

Although this approach responds to the serious issues surrounding our national energy policy as raised in this case, we think it would blur further the line the Court has sought to draw in commercial speech cases. It would grant broad constitutional protection to any advertising that links a product to a current public debate. But many, if not most, products may be tied to public concerns with the environment, energy, eco-

therefore accords a lesser protection to commercial speech than to other constitutionally guaranteed expression. *Id.*, at 456, 457. the protection available for particular commercial expression turns on the nature both of the expression and of the governmental interests served by its regulation.

The First Amendment's concern for commercial speech is based on the informational function of advertising. See*First National Bank of Boston v. Bellotti*, 435 U.S. 765, 783 [3 Med.L.Rptr. 2105] (1978). Consequently, there can be no constitutional objection to the suppression of commercial messages that do not accurately inform the public about lawful activity. The government may ban forms of communication more likely to deceive the public than to inform it,*Friedman v. Rogers*, 440 U.S. 1, 13, 15-16 (1979);*Ohralik v. Ohio State Bar Assn.*, 436 U.S., at 464-465, or commercial speech related to illegal activity, *Pittsburgh Press Co. v. Pittsburgh Comm'n on HUman Relations*, 413 U.S. 376, 388 [1 Med.L.Rptr. 1908] (1973).[6]

If the communication is neither misleading nor related to unlawful activity, the government's power is more circumscribed. The State must assert a substantial interest to be achieved by restrictions on commercial speech. Moreover, the regulatory technique must be in proportion to that interest.

Under the first criterion, the Court has declined to uphold regulations that only indirectly advance the state interest involved. In both Bates and Virginia Board of Pharmacy, the Court concluded that an advertising ban could not be imposed to protect the ethical or performance standards of a profession. The Court noted in Virginia Board of Pharmacy that "[t]he advertising ban does not directly affect professional standards one way or the other." 425 U.S., at 769. In Bates, the Court overturned an advertising prohibition that was designed to protect the "quality" of a lawyer's work. "Restraints on advertising . . . are an ineffective way of deterring shoddy work." 433 U.S., at 378.[7]

The second criterion recognizes that the First Amendment mandates that speech restrictions be "narrowly drawn." In re Primus, 436 U.S. 412, 438 (1978).[8] The

---

nomic policy, or individual health and safety. We rule today in*Consolidated Edison Co. v. Public Service Comm'n of New York. supra*, that utilities enjoy the full panoply of First Amendment protections for their direct comments on public issues. There is no reason for providing similar constitutional protection when such statements are made only in the context of commercial transactions. In that context, for example, the State retains the power to "insur[e] that the stream of commercial information flow[s] cleanly as well as freely."*Virginia State Board*, 425 U.S., at 772. This Court's decisions on commercial expression have rested on the premise that such speech, although meriting some protection, is of less constitutional moment than other forms of speech. As we stated in *Ohralik, supra*, the failure to distinguish between commercial and noncommercial speech "could invite dilution, simply by a leveling process, of the force of the [First] Amendment's guarantee to the latter kind of speech." 436 U.S., at 456.

[6] In most other contexts, the First Amendment prohibits regulation based on the content of the message.*Consolidated Edison Co. v. Public Service Comm'n of New York*, No. 79-134 (— , 1980) slip op., at 6-9. Two features of commercial speech permit regulation of its content. First, commercial speakers have extensive knowledge of both the market and their products. Thus, they are well-situated to evaluate the accuracy of their messages and the lawfulness of the underlying activity.*Bates v. State Bar of Arizona*,433 U.S., at 381 (1977). In addition, commercial speech, the offspring of economic self-interest, is a hardy breed of expression that is not "particularly susceptible to being crushed by overbroad regulation."*Ibid.* The limitation on expression must be designed carefully to achieve the State's goal. Compliance with this requirement may be measured by two criteria. First, the restriction must directly advance the state interest involved; the regulation may not be sustained if it provides only ineffective or remote support for the government's purpose. Second, if the governmental interest could be served as well by a more limited restriction on commercial speech, the excessive restrictions cannot survive.

[7] In *Linmark Associates v. Township of Willingboro, supra*, we observed that there was no definite connection between the township's goal of integrated housing and its ban on the use of "For Sale" signs in front of houses. 431 U.S., at 95-96.

[8] This analysis is not an application of the "overbreadth" doctrine. The latter theory permits the invalidation of regulations on First Amendment grounds even when the litigant challenging the regulation has engaged in no constitutionally protected activity. *E. g., Kunz v New York*, 340 U.S. 290 (1951). The overbreadth doctrine derives from the recognition that unconstitutional restriction of expression may deter protected speech by parties not before the court and thereby escape judicial review *Broadrick v. Oklahoma*, 413 U.S. 601, 612-613 (1973); see Note, The First Amendment Over-

regulatory technique may extend only as far as the interest it serves. The State cannot regulate speech that poses no danger to the asserted state interest, see First National Bank of Boston v. Bellotti, supra, 435 U.S., at 794-795, nor can it completely suppress information when narrower restrictions on expression would serve its interest as well. For example, in Bates the Court explicitly did not "foreclose the possibility that some limited supplementation, by way of warning or disclaimer or the like, might be required" in promotional materials. 433 U.S., at 384. See Virginia State Board of Pharmacy, supra, 425 U.S., at 773. And in Carey v. Population Services, International, 431 U.S. 678, 701-702 (1977), we held that the State's "arguments do not justify the total suppression of advertising concerning contraceptives." This holding left open the possibility that the State could implement more carefully drawn restrictions. See id., at 712 (POWELL, J., concurring in part and concurring in the judgment); id., at 716-717 (STEVENS, J., concurring).[9]

In commercial speech cases, then, a four-part analysis has developed. At the outset, we must determine whether the expression is protected by the First Amendment. For commercial speech to come within that provision, it at least must concern lawful activity and not be misleading. Next, we ask whether the asserted governmental interest is substantial. If both inquiries yield positive answers, we must determine whether the regulation directly advances the governmental interest asserted, and whether it is not more extensive than is necessary to serve that interest.

breadth Doctrine, 83 Harv. L. Rev. 844, 853-858 (1970). This restraint is less likely where the expression is linked to "commercial well-being" and therefore is not easily deterred by "overbroad regulation." *Bates v. State Bar of Arizona*, 433 U.S., at 381.

In this case, the Commission's prohibition acts directly against the promotional activities of Central Hudson, and to the extent the limitations are unnecessary to serve the State's interest, they are invalid.

[9] We review with special care regulations that entirely suppress commercial speech in order to pursue a nonspeech-related policy. In those circumstances, a ban on speech could screen from public view the underlying governmental policy. See *Virginia State Board of Pharmacy, supra*, 425 U.S., at 780, n. 8 (STEWART, J., concurring). Indeed, in recent years this Court has not approved a blanket ban on commercial speech unless the expression itself was flawed in some way, either because it was deceptive or related to unlawful activity.

III

We now apply this four-step analysis for commercial speech to the Commission's arguments in support of its ban on promotional advertising.

A

The Commission does not claim that the expression at issue either is inaccurate or relates to unlawful activity. Yet the New York Court of Appeals questioned whether Central Hudson's advertising is protected commercial speech. Because appellant holds a monopoly over the sale of electricity in its service area, the state court suggested that the Commission's order restricts no commercial speech of any worth. The court stated that advertising in a "noncompetitive market" could not improve the decisionmaking of consumers. 47 N.Y. 2d, at 110; 390 N.E. 2d, at 757. The court saw no constitutional problem with barring commercial speech that it viewed as conveying little useful information.

This reasoning falls short of establishing that appellant's advertising is not commercial speech protected by the First Amendment. Monopoly over the supply of a product provides no protection from competition with substitutes for that product. Electric utilities compete with suppliers of fuel oil and natural gas in several markets, such as those for home heating and industrial power. This Court noted the existence of interfuel competition 45 years ago, see West Ohio Gas Co. v. Public Utilities Comm'n, 294 U.S. 63, 72 (1935). Each energy source continues to offer peculiar advantages and disadvantages that may influence consumer choice. For consumers in those competitive markets, advertising by utilities is just as valuable as advertising by unregulated firms.[10]

Even in monopoly markets, the suppression of advertising reduces the information available for consumer decisions and thereby defeats the purpose of the First Amendment. The New York court's argu-

[10] Several commercial speech decisions have involved enterprises subject to extensive state regulation. *E. g., Friedman v. Rogers*, 440 U.S. 1, 4-5 (1979) (optometrists); *Bates v. Arizona State Bar*, 433 U.S. 350 (1977) (lawyers); *Virginia State Bd. of Pharmacy v. Virginia Citizens Consumer Council, Inc.*, 425 U.S. 748, 750-752 (1976) (pharmacists).

ment appears to assume that the providers of a monopoly service or product are willing to pay for wholly ineffective advertising. Most businesses — even regulated monopolies — are unlikely to underwrite promotional advertising that is of no interest or use to consumers. Indeed, a monopoly enterprise legitimately may wish to inform the public that it has developed new services or terms of doing business. A consumer may need information to aid his decision whether or not to use the monopoly service at all, or how much of the service he should purchase. In the absence of factors that would distort the decision to advertise, we may assume that the willingness of a business to promote its products reflects a belief that consumers are interested in the advertising.[11] Since no such extraordinary conditions have been identified in this case, appellant's monopoly position does not alter the First Amendment's protection for its commercial speech.

B

The Commission offers two state interests as justifications for the ban on promotional advertising. The first concerns energy conservation. Any increase in demand for electricity — during peak or off-peak periods — means greater consumption of energy. The Commission argues, and the New York court agreed, that the State's interest in conserving energy is sufficient to support suppression of advertising designed to increase consumption of electricity. In view of our country's dependence on energy resources beyond our control, no one can doubt the importance of energy conservation. Plainly, therefore, the state interest asserted is substantial.

The Commission also argues that promotional advertising will aggravate inequities caused by the failure to base the utility's rates on marginal cost. The utilities argued to the Commission that if they could promote the use of electricity in periods of low demand, they would improve their utilization of generating capacity. The Commission responded that promotion of off-peak consumption also would increase consumption during peak periods. If peak demand were to rise, the absence of marginal cost rates would mean that the rates charged for the additional power would not reflect the true costs of expanding production. Instead, the extra costs would be borne by all consumers through higher overall rates. Without promotional advertising, the Commission stated, this inequitable turn of events would be less likely to occur. The choice among rate structures involves difficult and important questions of economic supply and distributional fairness.[12] The State's concern that rates be fair and efficient represents a clear and substantial governmental interest.

C

Next, we focus on the relationship between the State's interests and the advertising ban. Under this criterion, the Commission's laudable concern over the equity and efficiency of appellant's rates does not provide a constitutionally adequate reason for restricting protected speech. The link between the advertising prohibition and appellant's rate structure is, at most, tenuous. The impact of promotional advertising on the equity of appellant's rates is highly speculative. Advertising to increase off-peak usage would have to increase peak usage, while other factors that directly affect the fairness and efficiency of appellant's rates remained constant. Such conditional and remote eventualities simply cannot justify silencing appellant's promotional advertising.

In contrast, the State's interest in energy conservation is directly advanced by the Commission order at issue here. There is an immediate connection between advertising and demand for electricity. Central Hudson would not contest the advertising ban unless it believed that promotion would increase its sales. Thus, we find a direct link between the state interest in conservation and the Commission's order.

D

We come finally to the critical inquiry in this case: whether the Commission's com-

[11] There may be a greater incentive for a utility to advertise if it can use promotional expenses in determining its rate of return, rather than pass those costs on solely to shareholders. That practice, however, hardly distorts the economic decision whether to advertise. Unregulated businesses pass on promotional costs to consumers, and this Court expressly approved the practice for utilities in *West Ohio Gas Co. v. Public Utilities Comm'n*, 294 U.S. 63, 72 (1935).

[12] See W. Jones, Regulated Industries 191-287 (2d ed. 1976).

plete suppression of speech ordinarily protected by the First Amendment is no more extensive than necessary to further the State's interest in energy conservation. The Commission's order reaches all promotional advertising, regardless of the impact of the touted service on overall energy use. But the energy conservation rationale, as important as it is, cannot justify suppressing information about electric devices or services that would cause no net increase in total energy use. In addition, no showing has been made that a more limited restriction on the content of promotional advertising would not serve adequately the State's interests.

Appellant insists that but for the ban, it would advertise products and services that use energy efficiently. These include the "heat pump," which both parties acknowledge to be a major improvement in electric heating, and the use of electric heat as a "back-up" to solar and other heat sources. Although the Commission has questioned the efficiency of electric heating before this Court, neither the Commission's Policy Statement nor its order denying rehearing made findings on this issue. In the absence of authoritative findings to the contrary, we must credit as within the realm of possibility the claim that electric heat can be an efficient alternative in some circumstances.

The Commission's order prevents appellant from promoting electric services that would reduce energy use by diverting demand from less efficient sources, or that would consume roughly the same amount of energy as do alternative sources. In neither situation would the utility's advertising endanger conservation or mislead the public. To the extent that the Commission's order suppresses speech that in no way impairs the State's interest in energy conservation, the Commission's order violates the First and Fourteenth Amendments and must be invalidated. See *First National Bank of Boston v. Belotti, supra.*

The Commission also has not demonstrated that its interest in conservation cannot be protected adequately by more limited regulation of appellant's commercial expression. To further its policy of conservation, the Commission could attempt to restrict the format and content of Central Hudson's advertising. It might, for example, require that the advertisements include information about the relative efficiency and expense of the offered service, both under current conditions and for the foreseeable future. Cf. *Banzhaf v. FCC,* — U.S. App. D.C. — 405 F.2d 1082 [1 Med.L.Rptr. 2037] (1968), cert. denied, 396 U.S. 842 (1969).[13] In the absence of a showing that more limited speech regulation would be ineffective, we cannot approve the complete suppression of Central Hudson's advertising.[14]

IV

Our decision today in no way disparages the national interest in energy conservation. We accept without reservation the argument that conservation, as well as the development of alternate energy sources, is an imperative national goal. Administrative bodies empowered to regulate electric utilities have the authority — and indeed the duty — to take appropriate action to further this goal. When, however, such action involves the suppression of speech, the First and Fourteenth Amendments require that the restriction be no more extensive than is necessary to serve the state interest. In this case, the record before us fails to show that the total ban on promotional advertising meets this requirement.[15]

---

[13] The Commission also might consider a system of previewing advertising campaigns to insure that they will not defeat conservation policy. It has instituted such a program for approving "informational" advertising under the Policy Statement challenged in this case. See p. 2, *supra.* We have observed that commercial speech is such a sturdy brand of expression that traditional prior restraint doctrine may not apply to it. *Virginia State Board of Pharmacy v. Virginia Citizens Consumer Council, Inc., supra,* 425 U.S., at 771, n. 24. And in other areas of speech regulation, such as obscenity, we have recognized that a prescreening arrangement can pass constitutional muster if it includes adequate procedural safeguards. *Freedman v. Maryland,* 380 U.S. 51 (1965).

[14] In view of our conclusion that the Commission's advertising policy violates the First and Fourteenth Amendments, we do not reach appellant's claims that the agency's order also violated the Equal Protection Clause of the Fourteenth Amendment, and that it is both overbroad and vague.

[15] The Commission order at issue here was not promulgated in response to an emergency situation. Although the advertising ban initially was prompted by critical fuel shortage in 1973, the Commission makes no claim that an emergency now exists. We do not consider the powers that the State might have over utility advertising in emergency circumstances. See *State v. Oklahoma Gas & Electric Co.,* 536 P. 2d 887, 895-896 (Okla. 1977).

OKLAHOMA TELECASTERS ASSOCIATION v. CRISP

**U.S. District Court
Western District of Oklahoma**

OKLAHOMA TELECASTERS ASSOCIATION, et al., v. RICHARD A. CRISP, Director, Alcoholic Beverage Control Board, No. Civ-81-139-W, February 10, 1982

REGULATION OF MEDIA CONTENT

Commercial speech/advertising — Commercial advertising (§15.03)

Oklahoma's constitutional and statutory prohibition against advertising of alcoholic beverages, which is at best only indirect method of advancing state's legitimate and substantial interest in preventing alcoholism and alcohol abuse, and which is more extensive than necessary to further state's interest in health and welfare of its citizens, violates First Amendment.

Plaintiffs sought injunctive and declaratory relief against enforcement of Oklahoma constitutional and statutory provisions that prohibit plaintiffs from broadcasting advertisements for alcoholic beverages. On December 18, 1981, the court issued an opinion granting plaintiff's motion for summary judgment (7 Med.L. Rptr. 2490). The court now orders that opinion withdrawn and the following opinion substituted for it.

Full Text of Order and Opinion

West, J.

ORDER

The Memorandum Opinion filed December 18,1981, [7 Med.L.Rptr. 2490] is withdrawn and the following Memorandum Opinion shall be substituted for it nunc pro tunc.

DATED this 10th day of February, 1982.

Memorandum Opinion
Introduction

Plaintiffs, Oklahoma Telecasters Association and several Oklahoma telecasting companies, have sued Richard A. Crisp, Director of the Alcoholic Beverage Control Board. Plaintiffs seek injunctive and declaratory relief alleging that the Oklahoma constitutional and statutory provisions which prohibit Plaintiffs from broadcasting advertisements for alcoholic beverages originating outside Oklahoma and from soliciting and accepting advertisements for alcoholic beverages are violative of Plaintiffs' Constitutional rights.

Plaintiffs have moved for summary judgment pursuant to Rule 56, F.R.Civ.P., on the grounds that the constitutional and statutory ban on advertising violates the plaintiffs' First Amendment right to freedom of speech. Plaintiffs also contend the ban is a violation of Plaintiffs' right to equal protection under the law. The Oklahoma Press Association has filed an amicus curiae brief in support of Plaintiffs' Motion for Summary Judgment.

Defendant has filed a Motion to Dismiss pursuant to Rule 12(b)(6), *supra*. Defendant contends that because the Twenty-first Amendment grants a broad sweep of power to Defendant to regulate the liquor industry, the passage of Okla. Const., art. 27, §5 and the enactment of 37 O.S. §516 (1971) do not violate the freedom of speech protection of the First Amendment Defendant further contends that no equal protection violation is manifest in the laws in question because they bear a rational relationship to the legitimate government goal of protecting the health, safety, and welfare of the people of Oklahoma. Defendant contends that quasi-judicial and prosecutorial immunity of Richard A. Crisp bars a claim under 42 U.S.C. §1983. S.A.N.E., Inc., has filed an amicus curiae brief in support of Defendant's Motion to Dismiss.

District Court Jurisdiction

The plaintiffs invoke the jurisdiction of this Court pursuant to 28 U.S.C. §§1331, 1343, 2201, and 42 U.S.C. §1983. Defendant in its answer denies jurisdiction, claiming that the Court should abstain because no federal question is presented and because the Supreme Court of Oklahoma has ruled upon the questions presented here and has declared the constitutional provisions and statute in question to be constitutionally valid.

Defendant does not address these jurisdictional issues in its brief in support of its Motion to Dismiss other than to assert that Defendant is immune from suit pursuant to 42 U.S.C. §1983 because of the doctrine of quasi-judicial and prosecutorial immunity. Nevertheless, the Court is aware of Defendant's position and authorities from contentions in other briefs and oral arguments presented to the Court. Accordingly, the Court has considered the threshold issue of jurisdiction.

Title 28 U.S.C. §1343 provides in relevant part:

> The district court shall have original jurisdiction of any civil action authorized by law to be commenced by any person:
>
> * * * *
>
> (3) To redress the deprivation under color of any . . . statute, ordinance . . . of any right, privilege or immunity secured by the Constitution of the United States, ...
>
> (4) To recover damages or to secure equitable or other relief under any Act of Congress providing for the protection of civil rights . . . .

Title 42 U.S.C. §1983 provides in relevant part:

> Every person who, under color of any statute, ordinance . . . of any state . . . subjects or causes to be subjected, any citizen of the United States . . . to the deprivation of any rights, privileges, or immunities secured by the Constitution and laws, shall be liable to the party injured in an action at law, suit in equity, or other proper proceeding for redress.

The doctrine of quasi-judicial or prosecutorial immunity might be relevant if this were a suit for damages pursuant to 42 U.S.C. §1983; however, Defendant cites no authority in support of application of the doctrine to a suit such as this one for declaratory or injunctive relief. Neither section 1983 itself nor the Eleventh Amendment presents a bar to a suit for prospective injunctive relief against a state official acting in his official capacity. See, *Acha v. Beame*, 438 F.Supp. 70, 77 (S.D. N.Y. 1977), *aff'd*, 570 F.2d 57 (1978), and cases cited therein.

The federal court has a duty to give due respect to a suitor's choice of a federal forum for the hearing and decision of his federal constitutional claims. *Zwickler v. Koota*, 389 U.S. 241 (1967).

The Court is not called upon to give relief that may relate in any way to a pending state criminal proceeding. Accordingly, the type of abstention called for by *Younger v. Harris*, 401 U.S. 37 (1971), would not be appropriate. Neither is the Court dealing with an ambiguous state statute which might require abstention under the Pullman Doctrine. *Railroad Commission of Texas v. Pullman Co.*, 312 U.S. 496 (1941). See generally, Wright, Miller & Cooper, *Federal Practice and Procedure:* Jurisdiction §4242 at 456.

Furthermore, the issues before this Court have not been decided by the Oklahoma Supreme Court. In *Oklahoma Alcoholic Beverage Control Board v. Heublein Wines International*, 566 P.2d 1158 (Okla. 1977), the Oklahoma Supreme Court held that Oklahoma's prohibition on the advertisement of alcoholic beverages did not violate the Commerce Clause. In *Oklahoma Alcoholic Beverage Control Board v. Burris*, 626 P.2d 1316 (1980), the Oklahoma Supreme Court held that the First Amendment rights of a retail seller of alcoholic beverages were not violated by Oklahoma's laws with respect to liquor advertising. Retail sellers are permitted to place a sign outside their retail outlets and are permitted to advertise in the Yellow Pages of the telephone directory. Those cases are distinguishable from this case where Plaintiffs are prohibited from rebroadcasting alcoholic beverage advertisements which originate outside Oklahoma and from accepting and soliciting any alcoholic beverage advertisements.

The plaintiffs in this case have demonstrated a genuine threat of enforcement of the constitutionally contested laws and the Court finds that it has jurisdiction of the case pursuant pursuant to 42 U.S.C. §1983, 28 U.S.C. §§1331, 1343, and 2201.

Motion for Summary Judgment
Motion to Dismiss

The standard for consideration of cross-motions was recently reiterated in *Harrison Western Corporation v. Gulf Oil Co.*, 662 F.2d 690 (1981) at 691:

> We are fully aware of the fundamental principle that summary judgment is not to be granted unless the pleadings, depositions, answers to interrogatories and admissions on file, together with the affidavits, if any, show that there exists no genuine issue as to any material fact and that the moving party is entitled to judgment as a matter of law. *Coyce v. Carter Oil Co.*, 618 F.2d 669, 672 (10th Cir. 1980); Rule 56(c), F.R.Civ.P. It is also settled doctrine that the fact that both parties have moved for summary judgment does not permit the entry of a summary judgment if disputes remain as to material facts. *Buell Cabinet Co., Inc. v. Sudduth*, 608 F.2d 431 (10th Cir. 1979); *Securities*

and Exchange Commission v. American Commodity Exchange, Inc., 546 F.2d 1361 (10th Cir. 1976); *Rains v. Cascade Industries, Inc.*, 402 F.2d 241 (3rd Cir. 1968). However, cross motions for summary judgment do authorize the Court to assume that there is no evidence which needs to be considered other than that which has been filed by the parties. *Securities & Exchange Commission v. American Commodity Exchange, Inc., supra; H.B. Zachry Co. v. O'Brien*, 378 F.2d 423 (10th Cir. 1967).

Cross-motions have been filed by the parties. In this case the Court is not only legally authorized to assume that there is no evidence which needs to be considered other than that which has been presented by the parties (*Securities & Exchange Commission v. American Commodity Exchange, Inc., supra*), but the parties have assured the Court both in pretrial conference and in their briefs that irrespective of any factual disputes with respect to other issues in the case, there are no genuine issues of material fact with respect to the issues raised by the motions before the Court. Neither side wishes further evidentiary hearing, and the Court is asked by both parties to decide as a matter of law whether upon the undisputed facts before the Court, Plaintiffs' constitutional rights are violated because they are prohibited by Oklahoma law from rebroadcasting alcoholic beverage advertisements originating outside Oklahoma and from soliciting and accepting such advertisements.

The Court has given careful consideration to the well reasoned arguments of both parties, to the amicus curiae briefs on behalf of each side to the dispute, and to the legal authorities cited in support of the various contentions. Careful analysis of the pertinent legal authorities demonstrates conclusively that the laws in question, as applied to Plaintiffs, are violative of Plaintiffs' First Amendment rights and that Plaintiffs are entitled to the declaratory and injunctive relief they seek. Because the laws are unconstitutional as applied to Plaintiffs, the Court need not consider whether the laws are unconstitutional on their face and/or whether they are unconstitutional on equal protection grounds.

The following facts have been stipulated by the parties:

1. This Court has personal jurisdiction over the parties.

2. The telecasting of advertisements for alcoholic beverages or the solicitation or acceptance of such advertisements by Oklahoma telecasters is prohibited by the Oklahoma Constitution, art. 27, §5 and by 37 O.S. §§501 et seq.

3. Richard A. Crisp, in his capacity as Director of the Alcoholic Beverage Control Board, is authorized to refer criminal charges against telecasters who telecast advertisements for alcoholic beverages or who solicit or accept advertisements for alcoholic beverages.

Additionally, the following facts which are material to the issue before the Court are uncontroverted:

1. The Oklahoma Telecasters Association is an unincorporated association comprised of the captioned corporations and partnerships, all licensed and engaged in the business of television broadcasting in the state of Oklahoma.

2. The programming broadcast by the plaintiffs is supported to a great extent by commercial advertising sold by the plaintiffs to private businesses, individuals, and others.

3. Network programming transmitted to the plaintiffs for rebroadcast has included advertisements for alcoholic beverages, particularly wine. Such advertising is lawful where it is originated and in most states where it is rebroadcast by network affiliates, but plaintiffs are required to "block out" network advertising of alcoholic beverages.

4. The stated purpose of the advertising ban is to reduce consumption of alcoholic beverages.

5. Consumption of alcoholic beverages in Oklahoma has increased substantially in the last 20 years despite the ban on advertising of such beverages.

6. The sale, purchase, and consumption of alcoholic beverages is, subject to certain limitations not material to this action, lawful in Oklahoma.

The State of Oklahoma can, under the Twenty-first Amendment totally prohibit the sale of alcoholic beverages within the state of Oklahoma. The question before the Court is whether having legalized the sale of alcoholic beverages, the State can totally prohibit advertising of alcoholic beverages except for one sign at the retail outlet and a listing of wholesalers and retailers of alcoholic beverages in the Yellow Pages of the telephone directory.

There is no question that Plaintiffs have a speech interest protected by the First Amendment to the United States Constitution. *Virginia State Board of Pharmacy v. Virginia Citizens Consumer Council, Inc.*, 425

U.S. 748, 773 [1 Med.L.Rptr. 1930] (1976); *Bigelow v. Virginia*, 421 U.S. 809 (1975); *Bates v. State Bar of Arizona*, 433 U.S. 350 [2 Med.L.Rptr. 2097] (1977); *Ohralik v. Ohio State Bar Association*, 436 U.S. 447 (1978).

The Supreme Court traced the recent development in the protection of commercial speech in *Metromedia, Inc. v. City of San Diego*, 49 U.S.L.W. 4925 (1980), as follows:

> The extension of First Amendment protection to purely commercial speech is a relatively recent development in First Amendment jurisprudence. Prior to 1975, purely commercial advertisements and services or goods for sale were considered to be outside the protection of the First Amendment. *Valentine v. Chrestensen*, 316 U.S. 52 (1942). That construction of the First Amendment was severely cut back in *Bigelow v. Virginia*, 421 U.S. 809 (1975). In *Virginia Pharmacy Board v. Virginia Consumer Council*, 425 U.S. 748 (1976), we plainly held that speech proposing no more than a commercial transaction enjoys a substantial degree of First Amendment protection: A state may not completely suppress the dissemination of truthful information about an entirely lawful activity merely because it is fearful of that information's effect upon its disseminators and its recipients

49 U.S.L.W. at 4929.

In applying the First Amendment to commercial speech, the Supreme Court rejected the "highly paternalistic" approach that the State's protectiveness of its citizens rests in large measure on the advantages of their being kept in ignorance. Instead, it noted the presence of a potent alternative — "that alternative is to assume that this information is not in itself harmful, that people will perceive their own best interests if only they are well enough informed, and that the best means to that end is to open the channels of communication rather than to close them." *Virginia State Board of Pharmacy v. Virginia Citizens Consumer Council, Inc., supra*, at 770.

Such commercial expression not only serves the economic interest of the speaker but also assists the consumers and furthers the societal interest in the fullest possible dissemination of information. *Virginia Board of Pharmacy v. Virginia Consumer Council, Inc., supra; Bates v. State Bar of Arizona*, 433 U.S. 350, 365 (1977). See also, *Linmark Associates, Inc. v. Township of Willingboro*, 431 U.S. 85, 92 (1977).

Recently, the Supreme Court has found unconstitutional a blanket prohibition of price advertising by pharmacists, a blanket suppression of advertising by attorneys, and a blanket prohibition of advertising carrying information about the availability and price of contraceptives. *Virginia Board of Pharmacy v. Virginia Consumer Council, supra; Bates v. State Bar of Arizona*, 433 U.S. 350, 383 (1977); *Carey v. Population Services International*, 431 U.S. 678 [2 Med.L.Rptr. 1935] (1977).

Of course misleading advertising may be prohibited entirely. *Ohralic v. Ohio State Bar Association, supra, Friedman v. Rogers*, 440 U.S. 1 [4 Med.L.Rptr. 2213] (1979). And even when advertising is not misleading, the State retains some authority to regulate if the restriction is narrowly drawn and the regulation furthers the State's substantial interest. *Central Hudson Gas Co. v. Public Service Commission*, 447 U.S. 557 [6 Med.L.Rptr. 1497] (1980).

Article 27, §5 of the Constitution of Oklahoma makes it "unlawful for any person, firm or corporation to advertise the sale of alcoholic beverage within the State of Oklahoma, except one sign at the retail outlet bearing the words 'Retail Alcoholic Liquor Store.' " The Oklahoma Statutes provide:

> It shall be unlawful for any person, firm or corporation to advertise any alcoholic beverages or the sale of same within the State of Oklahoma, except one sign at the retail outlet bearing the words 'Retail Alcoholic Liquor Store.' or any combination of such words, or any of them, and no letter in any such sign shall be more than four (4) inches in height, or more than three (3) inches in width, and if more than one line is used, the lines shall not be more than one (1) inch apart.

37 O.S. (1971) §516.

The defendant claims that the Twenty-first Amendment overrides any First and Fourteenth Amendment rights of the plaintiffs.

The Twenty-first Amendment, §2, provides:

> The transportation or importation into any State, Territory, or possession of the United States for delivery or use therein of intoxicating liquors, in violation of the laws thereof is hereby prohibited. U.S.Const. amend. XXI, §2.

Defendant relies upon *California v. LaRue*, 409 U.S. 109 (1972), in urging the proposition that any speech which is used in connection with the sale of alcoholic beverages may be proscribed by a state under the broad grant of power to the states by the Twenty-first Amendment.

The circumstances of the present case are distinguishable from *California v. LaRue, supra.* In that case the California Department of Alcoholic Beverage Control regulations prohibited certain sexually explicit live entertainment or films in establishments licensed to sell liquor by the drink. The regulations prohibited the performance of specific acts including sexual intercourse, masturbation, sexual acts prohibited by law, touching or fondling of breasts or genitals, displaying of genitals, or films depicting such prohibited acts. The Supreme Court found that the State's interest outweighed the challenger's First Amendment rights and that the State had chosen a reasonable means to attain its interests since it had not totally prohibited the performances in question but had merely proscribed such performances in establishments licensed to sell liquor by the drink.

In this case, the plaintiffs are prohibited from disseminating advertisements of something the public already knows from experience and from reading newspaper and magazine advertising - that alcoholic beverages exist and are for sale at certain prices.

A careful reading of *California v. LaRue, supra,* reveals that the decision "did not go so far as to hold or say that the Twenty-first Amendment supersedes all other provisions of the United States Constitution in the area of liquor regulations." *Id.* at 115.

The Supreme Court recently addressed the power of the states under the Twenty-first Amendment in deciding that a California state plan for wine pricing was subject to the federal antitrust laws despite the state's power to regulate importation and transportion of liquor under the Twenty-first Amendment. *California Liquor Dealers v. Midcal Aluminum,* 445 U.S. 97 (1980). The Supreme Court points out that in determining state powers under the Twenty-first Amendment, the focus has been largely on the language of the provision rather than the history behind it. ". . . Even when the states had acted under the explicit terms of the Amendment the Court resisted the contention that §2 'freed the states from all restrictions upon the police power to be found in other provisions of the Constitution . . . .' " *Id.* at 108. The Supreme Court states that important federal interests in liquor matters survived the ratification of the Twenty-first Amendment including the equal protection requirements of the Fourteenth Amendment (citing to *Craig v. Boren,* 429 U.S. 190, 204-209 (1976)) and due process requirements (citing to *Wisconsin v. Constantineau,* 400 U.S. 433, 436 (1971)).

The Supreme Court has decided that fundamental constitutional rights such as due process, equal protection, and freedom of speech are not swallowed up by the Twenty-first Amendment. Accordingly, we are required to consider each part of the constitution in light of the other and in the context of the issues and interests at stake in the case before us.

Applying the legal propositions that the State cannot totally prohibit the dissemination of truthful information about a lawful activity; that the State has broad power under the Twenty-first Amendment to regulate the sale of alcoholic beverages; and that the State retains the authority to regulate advertising if the interference is in proportion to the interests served to the undisputed facts before us, is it constitutional for the State of Oklahoma to totally prohibit the advertising of alcoholic beverages except for one sign at the retail outlet and a listing of outlets in the Yellow Pages of the telephone directory?

The four-part inquiry in *Central Hudson Gas and Electric Corp. v. Public Service Commission, supra,* provides a means of balancing the constitutional rights of the parties. The analysis turns on the nature of the expression sought to be suppressed and the government interests served by the regulation in question.

The test is as follows: First, the expression must be protected by the First Amendment; that is, it must concern lawful activity and not be misleading. Second, the asserted government interest must be substantial. Third, the regulation in question must directly advance the governmental interest asserted; and fourth, the regulation must not be more extensive than is necessary to serve that interest.

In applying the test to this case, first, we are dealing with protected speech because there is no claim that the communications suppressed are either misleading or related to unlawful activity.

Second, the asserted government interest is substantial. Promotion of temperance is the State interest cited in the Opinion of the Attorney General as justification for the ban. Atty.Gen.Op.No. 77-244 (September 19, 1977). Another stated goal of the Oklahoma Alcoholic Beverage Control Act as stated in the briefs is "an exercise of the police power of the State of Oklahoma for the protection of the welfare, health, peace, temperance, and safety of the people of the State. . . ." The State of Oklahoma has a substantial interest in the health and welfare of its people. The Twenty-first Amendment gives it a substantial amount of control over the sale of alcoholic beverages. The Court recognizes the legitimacy and importance of the State's goals of protecting its citizens. The disease of alcoholism and the deaths and injuries caused by the abuse of alcohol are very real concerns to the people and the government of this state.

Third, the Court finds that under the undisputed facts, the ban on advertising is at best an indirect means of advancing the State's interest in temperance for the following reasons. There is no evidence before the Court that Oklahoma's ban on advertising is a direct means of preventing alcohol abuse or protecting the health, safety, or welfare of Oklahomans. It is uncontroverted that consumption of alcoholic beverages in Oklahoma has increased substantially in the last twenty years despite the ban on advertising of such beverages. Of course, the argument can be made that an even greater increase would have occurred but for the ban. The realities of the situation are that beer commercials have been permitted despite the ban; wine commercials are heard in Oklahoma on radio broadcasts which originate outside the state; beer, wine, and distilled spirits advertisements in magazines originating outside Oklahoma are permitted. The Court finds it hard to believe that the prohibition of advertising by Oklahoma media is a direct means of achieving temperance.

There are other means available to the State which are more direct means of combating Oklahoma's alcohol abuse problems. Some of these were recommended by the Task Force on Alcohol Abuse after several months of study and interchange on the issue. The highest priority was given to early and continuing education about the biological and psychological effects of alcohol and its potential for personal and social harm. See, "Alcohol Abuse in Oklahoma," Report and Recommendation of the Task Force on Alcohol Abuse. Such an approach would be in keeping with the Supreme Court's view that the best means to help people to perceive their best interests is to open the channels of communication rather than to close them.

Fourth, the State's attempted regulation is more extensive than necessary to serve the State's interest.

Defendant contends that it is important for the Court to note that Oklahoma has not denied the liquor industry all means of advertising its product, noting that retail liquor establishments are permitted one sign and a listing in the Yellow Pages of the telephone directory.

The plaintiffs in this case, however, are telecasters and are totally prohibited from rebroadcasting advertisements for alcoholic beverages which originate in other states and from soliciting and accepting advertisements for alcoholic beverages. As to these plaintiffs, the regulation is not one of time, place, and manner but is a total prohibition of the dissemination of all information on the subject of alcoholic beverages.

A means less restrictive than blanket suppression has not been tried. For example, the State might appropriately require warnings of health hazards. It is not clear that an absolute prohibition of advertising is the only solution.

Weighing all of the rights and interests involved, the State of Oklahoma has a substantial interest in the health and welfare of its citizens and broad power to regulate the sale of alcoholic beverages under the Twenty-first Amendment. The State has the authority to regulate advertising that is inherently misleading or is misleading in practice. The State's power under the Twenty-first Amendment will likely support carefully drawn restrictions of advertising which are short of a total prohibition of advertising. But Plaintiffs enjoy a substantial degree of First Amendment protection which requires that the State's regulation of commercial speech, even with the added weight of the Twenty-first Amendment, be carefully drawn to directly further the State's interest and that it be no more extensive than reasonably necessary to further the State's interest. In the absence of any allegations that the prohibited advertising is misleading, the Court finds that a total prohibition of all advertising by the plaintiffs fails to meet these requirements.

Accordingly, Defendant is hereby permanently enjoined from enforcing Article 27, §5, of the Oklahoma Constitution and 37 O.S. §516 (1971) against the plaintiffs and a declaratory judgment shall be entered that enforcement of these laws would violate Plaintiffs' rights under the First Amendment as guaranteed to the states by the Fourteenth Amendment to the United States Constitution.

Defendant's Motion to Dismiss is DENIED in all respects. Plaintiffs' Motion for Summary Judgment is GRANTED.

IT IS SO ORDERED this 10th day of February, 1982, NUNC PRO TUNC December 18, 1981; the Memorandum Opinion entered December 18, 1981, is withdrawn and this Memorandum Opinion is substituted therefor.

NOTES

9

COMPARATIVE ADVERTISING

Felix H. Kent

SPECIAL NOTE TO EXHIBIT A:

As of March 10, 1982 the advertising standards of the NAB Radio and Television Codes (including guidelines, interpretations, policies, etc.) have been cancelled and enforcement thereof terminated until the conclusion of litigation in which the NAB is currently involved or until further notice. This action was taken by the NAB Executive Committee on March 10, 1982.

March 11, 1982

COMPARATIVE ADVERTISING

Until the early 1970's, comparative advertising was virtually unknown. The practice of naming competitors was "taboo" with advertisers and with media. In 1971 the Federal Trade Commission encouraged the networks to accept comparative advertising for the sake of greater disclosure to the consumer, so that the consumer may make "rational purchase decisions."

Comparative advertising has become a highly popular form of advertising and, naturally, has led to disputes among advertisers, and to regulation by government, the courts and self-reulatory bodies.

I. Self-Regulation

   A. Networks

   B. The National Association of Broadcasters

   C. Council of Better Business Bureaus; NAD and NARB

   D. Individual media.

The principles of self-regulation, generally, are that comparative advertising must be accurate, fair and not disparaging. Comparisons must be material, relate to specified product characteristics or properties and any differences must be significant. Proper support, such as clinical tests, market surveys, research, etc. must be supplied. (See NAB Comparative Advertising Guidelines attached as Exhibit "A".)

Self-regulation offers many advantages in costs, procedures and lack of publicity, but (except for networks) is not quick in resolving disputes. Further, self-regulation presumes voluntary submission by advertisers to the jurisdiction of the self-regulatory bodies.

II. Federal Trade Commission

Deceptive comparative advertising can be a violation of Section 5 of the Federal Trade Commission Act and has been adjudicated in a number of cases such as: _In the Matter of American Home Products Corp._, 81 FTC 579; _In the Matter of the Mennen Company_ 58 FTC 676; _FTC v. Carter Products, Inc._, et al 1963 Trade Cases 70,902; _In the Matter of Eversharp, Inc._, et al 57 FTC 841.

The FTC may act upon the complaint of an advertiser but is not obligated to do so. Further, FTC actions move slowly and do not provide a quick remedy for comparative advertising abuses.

III. Judicial Remedies

Section 43(a) of the Lanham Act, which

originally was only interpreted to apply to trademark infringements and "palming off" of products, has been interpreted to apply to advertising in a number of recent cases. It has become the most powerful weapon for an advertiser to contest a competitor's advertising claims.

The continued evolution of Section 43(a) can be traced as follows:

THE LANHAM ACT - Sec 43(a)

> "(a) Any person who shall affix, apply or annex, or use in connection with any goods or services, or any container or containers for goods, a false designation of origin, <u>or any false description or representation</u>, including the words or other symbols <u>tending falsely to describe or represent the same</u>, and shall cause such goods or services to enter into commerce, <u>shall be liable to a civil action</u> by any person <u>doing business in the locality</u> falsely indicated as that of origin or in the region in which said locality is situated, or <u>by any person who believes that he is or is likely to be damaged by the use of any such false description or representation.</u>"
> (Emphasis added.)

1. <u>L'Aiglon Apparel, Inc.</u> v. <u>Lana Lobell, Inc.</u>, 214 F.2d 649 (3rd Cir. 1954). - Departure from "palming off".

2. <u>Skil Corp.</u> v. <u>Rockwell International</u>, 375 F.Supp. 777 (N.D.Ill. 1974). - Established criteria for injunctive case:

(a) The defendant must make a false statement about its own product (not just the competitor's product).

(b) A substantial segment of the audience must actually be deceived or there must be a tendency to deceive a substantial segment of the audience.

(c) The deception must be material and must be likely to influence the purchase decision.

(d) The goods must be in interstate commerce.

(e) The plaintiff must be likely to be injured as a result of the false advertising or he must show that he has been injured.

Only a likelihood of deception must be shown for injunctive action.

3. Subsequent cases expand upon Skil criteria; analogy to FTC interpretations of deceptive advertising.

4. American Brands, Inc. v. R.J. Reynolds and L.K.P. International Limited, 413 F.Supp. 1352 (S.D.N.Y. 1976).
   "Low-tar" claims not false on face. Must have consumer reaction.

5. American Home Products Corp. v. Johnson & Johnson, 436 F.Supp. 785 (S.D.N.Y. August 29, 1977) aff'd 577 F.2d 160 (2d Cir. May 1, 1978).
   Court will consider use of "innuendo, intimations, ambiguous suggestions" in advertising.

6. Injunctions granted were advertising false on its face:

   Philip Morris Incorporated v. Loew's Theatres, Inc. (Lorillard), 511 F.Supp. 855 (S.D.N.Y. July 26, 1980). Misleading use of statistics in claiming "National Test Winner"

   Quaker State Oil Refining Corporation v. Burmah-Castrol, Inc., 504 F.Supp. 178 (S.D.N.Y. October 10, 1980). - Irrelevant performance claim

7. McNeilab, Inc. v. American Home Products Corp., 501 F.Supp. 517 (S.D.N.Y. November 21, 1980).
False claim that Extra Strength Anacin was a stronger analgesic than Extra Strength Tylenol. Effective use of consumer surveys.
No intent to deceive is necessary. If intent can be shown, then less consumer research may be required.

8. Vidal Sassoon, Inc. v. Bristol-Myers Company, 661 F.2d 272 (2d Cir. 1981).
The questioned advertising claim does not have to relate to "inherent quality or characteristic" of product. Monadic blind tests led to false statement about product.

There are still substantial questions to be answered in cases under 43(a):

(a) Money Damages

Require proof of deception.
Measure of damages: Alberto-Culver v. Gillette and J. Walter Thompson

(b) Misrepresentation of Competitor's Product

Statute requires misrepresentation of defendant's own product. Did Sassoon expand meaning? Would an action lie if there was only a misrepresentation of the competitor's product?

(c) Who has standing to sue?

"Any injured person". Competitor only?
Does he have to be named?
Consumer Class Action?
Note references in decisions to "public interest".

(d) Constitutional Restraints

Constitution does not protect false claims but may serve to limit extent of injunctive relief.

(e) Advertising Agency's Liability

Not determined. Probably immaterial in injunctive action, but may have effect in damage action.

The application of 43(a) gives the aggrieved advertiser the opportunity for injunctive relief which he needs to avoid loss of market share. This section may become increasingly important during a period in which the FTC is expected to be "low profile".

EXHIBIT "A"

National Association of Broadcasters Code Authority
Comparative Advertising Guidelines

Effective April 1, 1975

The Code Authority believes that comparative advertising only when used truthfully and fairly can provide the consumer with useful information and be of some aid in making an informed choice between/among competitive products and services.

The following Guidelines are, therefore, intended to assist advertisers and broadcasters, respectively, in their preparation and evaluation of commercials which name or otherwise directly identify competitive products and services.

1) Identification

The identification of competitors shall be in accordance with the following Guidelines:

A. Competitors shall be accurately and clearly identified.

B. Identification shall be for comparison purposes only. It shall not be used solely to upgrade the advertised product(s) by association with the competitor(s).

C. Disparagement of competitors, competing products or services shall not be used.

D. When aspects of products/services are compared they must be significant and meaningful to the overall performance of the product.

2) Claims

A. Comparisons and demonstrations thereof shall be based on specified product/service differences directly related to the product's use comparing similar properties or ingredients, dimension to dimension, feature to feature.

B. Comparative or superlative claims based solely on consumer or professional preference or on sales data shall not be made in a manner which implies universally superior effectiveness or performance. Such claims may be made provided they are supportable by adequate substantiation.

C. Claims, demonstrations and other representations shall include all information necessary for their proper understanding by the average consumer. Inadequately qualified language, "dangling comparatives" and similar references shall not be permitted.

D. The overall impression created by advertising shall be accurate.

3) Support of Claims

A. Product testing and survey evaluation germane to the comparative claims shall be conducted in accord with generally accepted scientific and technical procedures.

B. The advertiser shall have the burden of establishing that he/she has exercised diligence to determine that the test used in support of any superiority claimed over competitors is fair and accurate.

C. Where applicable, government, industry or other established standards shall be used to determine the appropriateness of material used as substantiation.

D. Competitive tests or surveys should be conducted by an objective source, preferably an independent one.

E. For claims based upon differences in performance, substantiation shall demonstrate that these differences provide material benefit to the consumer.

F. Material used as substantiation shall take into account: 1) the purpose for which products/services are intended; 2) the manner in which they are normally used by the consumer; and 3) individual label instructions.

G. Where applicable, test findings shall be based on statistical tests of significance in accordance with recognized standards of statistical validity.

NOTES

10

LITIGATION AGAINST ADVERTISER AND AGENCY

Robert M. Callagy

March 9, 1982

A. Litigation Against Advertiser and Agency

This survey will review legal principles applicable to libel, invasion of privacy, right of publicity, copyright infringement, unfair competition and related federal and state common law claims. It will also highlight current trends in the law applicable to such claims and discuss available defenses and copy clearance strategy.

I. Defamation

As an initial matter, the most common types of defamation claims against advertiser or agency are those involving:

1. individuals or companies which claim to be identifiable in disparaging copy or in an unflattering picture,

2. coincidental use of a real name in a context calculated to injure reputation and

3. product disparagement.

The elements of a cause of action for libel are:

1. As to the material -- statement, photograph, innuendo or inference, description, etc. --

   a. is it untrue,

   b. is it defamatory -- injurious to reputation - diminishing the esteem, respect, goodwill or confidence in which plaintiff is held, or exciting adverse or derogatory feelings or opinions against plaintiff (Mencher v. Chesley, 297 N.Y.94 (1947), Street v. N.B.C., 645 F.2d 1227 512 F. Supp. 398 (6th Cir. 1981); Rudin v. Dow Jones, 510 F. Supp. 210 (S.D.N.Y. 1981); Raymer v. Doubleday, 615 F.2d 241 (5th Cir. 1980); or does it falsely charge, for example, that a pure food product contains poisonous substances. Potentially libelous statements would fall into the following general categories:

(1) commission of a crime - Fitzgerald v. Penthouse, 639 F.2d 1076 (4th Cir. 1981).

(2) moral delinquency,

(3) suffering from a mental or serious physical disease,

(4) unfavorable status such as being an illegal alien,

(5) association -- that the person maintains unpopular beliefs or is associated with disreputable groups or causes such as communism or McCarthyism, Stripling v. Literary Guild, et al., (U.S. Ct. of Appeals, 5th Cir).

(6) misconduct in one's business, profession or finances, being dishonest, incompetent, a shyster, quack, plagiarist, insolvent or bankrupt.

(7) product is worthless, fails to comply with federal standards.

(c) is it defamatory. . .

(1) on its face (libel per se)? or

(2) by extrinsic facts - requiring reference to extrinsic facts to establish defamatory meaning (libel per quod)? (Hinsdale v. Orange County Publishing Corp., 17 N.Y.2d 284 (1966) or

(3) by omission (Rinaldi v. Holt, Rinehart & Winston, Inc., 53 App. Div.2d 839, 386 N.Y.S.2d 818 (1st Dept. 1976), rev'd, 42 N.Y.2d 369 (1977), cert. denied, 434 U.S. 969 (1977).

2. Is the defamatory character of the material established or precluded by. . .

(a) contemporary opinions? (e.g., what would have been considered libelous years ago is not libelous now, and vice-versa; e.g., one's involvement with the CIA; Oliver v. The Village Voice, Inc., 417 F. Supp. 235 (S.D.N.Y. 1976); or

(b) the particular context in which the material is presented? (i.e., what is libelous of A is not libelous of B; James v. Gannet Co., Inc., 40 N.Y.2d 415 (1976); Blouin v. Anton, 638 F.2d 1272 (Vermont Sup. Ct. 1981); Church of Scientology v. Cazares, 455 F. Supp. 420 (5th Cir. 1981); or

(c) because the plaintiff is libel proof? (e.g., a criminal with no reputation to protect - Cardillo v. Doubleday Co. Inc., 518 F.2d 638 (2d Cir. 1957). The "libel proof" doctrine may be expanding.

3. Is the material a statement of fact which may be true or false (thus precluding or establishing liability, as the case may be) (e.g., calling a judge "probably corrupt"' Rinaldi v. Holt, Rinehart & Winston, Inc., supra), or an expression of opinion, or fair comment and criticism on matters of public concern (which requires further examination) (Buckley v. Littell, 539 F.2d 882 (2d Cir. 1976)?

4. If the latter,

(a) unless the latter is pure comment or opinion (whether or not justified), which is not susceptible to proof of truth or falsity and which does not require substantiating facts, and which precludes liability (Stripling v. Literary Guild, et al., supra; Hotchner v. Castillo-Puche, 551 F.2d 910 (2d Cir. 1977), cert. denied,

434 U.S. 834 (1977); Buckley v. Littell, supra; labelling William F. Buckley a "fellow traveller" of "fascism").

(b) are the actual and true supporting facts, basis and/or reasons for the opinion set forth, (so that liability is precluded) (Dolcin Corp. v. Reader's Digest Association, Inc., 7 App. Div. 2d 449, 183 N.Y.S.2d 3412 (1st Dept. 1959); supra; Unification Church v. Harper & Row, 420 N.Y.S.2d 56 (1979, aff'd without op., Vol. 188 N.Y.L.J. No. 19, at 6 (Jan. 28, 1980); Holy Spirit Assoc. v. Sequoia Elsevier et al., 4 Med. L. Rptr. 1744 (1978), (Unification Church-facist or anti-Semitic).

The material must not be a negative characterization. . .

(1) which is published without the purpose at least in part of informing the public of a newsworthy matter, or

(2) which is supported by false facts (New York Times v. Sullivan, 376 U.S. 254 (1964), or

(3) which is coupled with a clear but false implication that the author is privy to facts about plaintiff which are unknown to the general public (Hotchner v. Castillo-Puche, supra), or

(4) which is unfair, not because it is immoderate or because some people might disagree with it, but because the conclusions do not logically follow from the premises, or because they go beyond the premises? (Unification Church v. Sequoia Elsevier, et al., supra)

B. <u>An Identifiable, Living Plaintiff</u>

1. Is the material (fiction or non-fiction, or a photograph or illustration). . .

a. "of or concerning" plaintiff, who is. . .

(1) an individual, or

(2) an organization, whether business (corporation, unincorporated association, partnership, etc.) or otherwise (society or labor union), or

(3) the owner of a place or manufacturer of a product? (*i.e.*, comparative advertisements)

(a) To be actionable, the statement or picture complained of must be false and must reflect adversely on the owner's or manufacturer's integrity. (*El Meson Espanol v. NYM Corp.*, 521 F.2d 737 (2d Cir. 1975) (a restaurant); *Harwood Pharmacal Co. v. National Broadcasting Co., Inc.* 9 N.Y.2d 460.

(b) When the disparagement does *not* reflect adversely on the integrity of the owner or manufacturer, plaintiff may recover only upon proof of falsity, actual malice (as defined below) and special damages (actual pecuniary loss). (*Drug Research Corp. v. Curtis Publishing Co.*, 7 N.Y.2d 435 (1960).

b. That is, is plaintiff or the place or product identifiable --

(1) as an individual or entity? (*Bindrim v. Mitchell, et al.*, 92 C.A.2d 861 (1979), *cert. denied* 48 U.S.L.W. 3343)

(Nov. 20, 1979); (1979); Lyons v. New American Library, et al., No. 80-11 (Sup. Ct. Franklin Cty.) (Dec. 19, 1979) 78 A.D.2d 723 (1980).; Marios Enterprises v. Morton Norwich, 6 Med. L.Rptr. 1651 (W.D. Kan. 1980)

(2) as a member of a group, when the defamatory material refers to. . .

all members of a small group? (Bornmann v. Star Co., 174 N.Y. 213 (1903)) or

"some members" of a small group, Nieman-Marcus v. Lait, 13 F.R.D. 311 (S.D.N.Y. 1932)

(3) No defamation, when statement refers to all members of a larger group. (Gross v. Cantor, 270 N.Y. 93 (1930); Neiman-Marcus v. Lait, supra, New York Hearing Aid Dealers Guild, Inc. v. Stossel, 63 App. Div. 2d 894, 405 N.Y.S.2d 1017 (1st Dept. 1978)) --

c. so that a reasonable viewer would understand the material as referring to plaintiff? (Note also that a disclaimer that a fictitious character or corporation does not represent a living person or corporation is ineffective, if the viewer can identify the individual or corporation to be a prototype of the character or corporation mentioned).

2. If so, is plaintiff alive? (Rose v. Daily Mirror, Inc., 284 N.Y. 335 (1940). The states' laws vary as to whether a cause of action for defamation of a living person survives the person's death; by statute in New York, the cause of action does not survive.

C. Standards of Liability: There Is No Liability For Publication of Misstatements of Fact Defamatory on Their Face. . .

1. As to a public official,

   a. with respect to his or her public activities or capacity, or anything that might touch on his or her fitness for office,

   b. unless publication is with "actual malice" (New York Times v. Sullivan, supra); i.e.,

      (1) knowing falsity (to be established by plaintiff with clear and convincing clarity -- a higher burden of proof than the burden applicable in the normal civil case) or

      (2) reckless disregard for truth or falsity (the evidence must establish with convincing clarity that defendant had a high degree of awareness of probable falsity, or entertained serious doubts as to the truth; St. Amant v. Thompson, 390 U.S. 727 (1968); Garrison v. Louisiana, 379 U.S. 64 (1964)).

   c. No liability for publication with common law malice, i.e. ill will, spite, hatred hostility, deliberate intention to harm, or sinister or corrupt motives.

2. As to a public figure,

   a. who is such as a. . .

      (1) "pervasive public figure," one for all purposes and in all contexts, by virtue of fame and influence in public matters? (e.g., celebrities, well-known entertainers, ex-politicians, Mafia figures). Curtis Publishing Co. v. Butts, 388 U.S. 130 (1967);

Associated Press v. Walker, 388 U.S. 130 (1967); Carson v. Allied News Co., 529 F.2d 206 (7th Cir. 1976); Buckley v. Littell, supra; but see Hutchinson v. Proxmire, 431 F.Supp. 1311 U.S.D.C. W.D. Wis. (1977)

(2) "vortex public figure," one for a limited range of issues - in the vortex of a public controversy or particular matter of public interest, whether. . .

(a) voluntarily, having thrust oneself into the vortex of a public controversy, to influence its outcome (Gertz v. Robert Welch, Inc., 418 U.S. 323 (1974); but see Wolston v. Reader's Digest Association, Inc., 99 S. Ct. 2701 (1979); Waldbaum v. Fairchild Publications, 627 F.2d 1287 (U.S. Ct. of App, D.C. (1980); Brewer v. Memphis Pub. Co., Inc. 626 F.2d 1238 (U.S.C.A. 5th Cir. (1980) cert. denied 101 S.C. 3112; Midwife v. Copley, 7 Med. L. Rptr. (Cal. Ct. of App. 1981).

(b) involuntarily, by events (e.g., the Rosenberg children, Meeropol v. Nizer, 381 F. Supp. 29 (S.D.-N.Y. 1974), aff'd, 560 F.2d 1061 (2d Cir. 1977), cert. denied, 434 U.S. 1013 (1978); but see Pring v. Penthouse, 7 Med. L. Rptr. (D.C. Wyo. 1981); Dresbach v. Doubleday, 518 F. Supp. 1285 (D.D.C. 1981).

b. unless publication is with actual malice.

3. As to a private individual in a matter of legitimate public interest and concern (Gertz v. Robert Welch, Inc. supra).

a. fault must be established by a preponderance of the evidence,

b. (in all states) so long as liability without fault is precluded, and

   (1) at least in New York (Chapadeau v. Utica Observer-Dispatch, Inc., supra, unless publication is with gross negligence; and

   (2) depending on the particular state, unless publicaton is with actual malice, ordinary negligence or some intermediate standard.

c. Although not settled, the law may be that when the statement at issue is libelous per quod, and the subject matter is of a general or public interest, even private plaintiffs may have to prove actual malice to recover. (Gertz v. Robert Welch, Inc., supra, 418 U.S. at 348).

4. In a private matter, not of legitimate public interest,

   a. as to a --

      (1) "vortex" public official (i.e., re matters not concerning one's public activities or fitness for office), or

      (2) "vortex" public figure (one who is not a public figure for all purposes, or for the issue which is the subject of the action), or

      (3) private individual (Time, Inc. v. Firestone, 424 U.S. 448 (1976).

   b. at least in New York, unless publication is with negligence (Gertz and Chapadeau did not consider this issue).

5. Fictional use -- plaintiff must establish that a reasonable number of people failed to appreciate fictional nature of material, that plaintiff was identifiable, and that defendant either knew that material referred to plaintiff or should have suspected that material referred to plaintiff.

6. Subsequent action or failure to act, after notice of claim, could impose a new duty to investigate and a basis for possible liability.

D. <u>Defense to Liability</u>

1. Full defenses:

   a. truth (in most defamation actions it would be either difficult or extremely expensive to prove the truth and therefore, in view of the constitutional and other defenses available, this defense should be avoided unless documentary evidence is available to substantiate the statement); or

   b. pure opinion or fair comment on matters of public interest; or

   c. no "fault" -- whether . . .

      (1) no "actual malice", as to public officials and public figures, or

      (2) in general, no gross or ordinary negligence, as to private individuals; acted in the usual and customary manner employed to develop, screen and air commercials in the advertising industry.

   d. consent (<u>Teichner v. Bellans</u>, 181 N.Y.S.2d 842 (1959); or

   e. the right of reply (<u>Shenkman v. O'Malley</u>, 2 App. Div.2d 567 N.Y.S.2d 290 (1st Dept. 1936)), -- <u>i</u>.<u>e</u>., "self defense to a defamatory attack, which defense is. . .

(1) conducted in good faith and

(2) limited to the scope of the attack; or

f. the statute of limitations has run.

(1) The statutes of limitations vary among the states, generally in the range of one-half to two years; in New York, as in most states, the statute of limitations is one year. CPLR 215.

(2) Generally, the statute of limitations starts to run when the material is made available for public consumption. Sorge v. Parade Publications, Inc. 20 App. Div. 2d 338, 247 N.Y.S.2d 317 (1st Dept. 1964); Gregoire v. G.P. Putnam's Sons, 298 N.Y.2d 119 (1948), although certain recent California decisions have delayed commencement of statute of limitations until date of discovery. (Fluery v. Harper & Row, 7 Med. L. Rptr. 1795 (S.D. Cal. 1981).

(3) New York (although not every state) has the "single publication" rule -- running identical successive print ads or commercials gives rise to only one cause of action and that cause of action accrues at the time of first release to the public. (But see Rinaldi v. Viking Penguin, 7 Med. L. Rptr. 1202 (N.Y. Ct. of App. 1981)

2. No defense to liability: repetition of a libel (including "it is alleged that. . .") which. .

a. is also libel, but not if it is the repetition of what would be libelous material but for the existence of an absolute privilege which precludes liability.

b. Such a privilege exists for full, fair, impartial and accurate reports of statements made in open, public. .

   (1) judicial or quasi-judicial proceedings,

   (2) legislative proceedings,

   (3) executive proceedings,

   (4) administrative proceedings and/or

   (5) reports of all such proceedings, as well as of official public records. (New York Civil Rights Law Section 74).

c. Material may also be protected by the neutral reporting privilege (Edwards v. National Audubon Society, Inc., 556 F.2d 13 (2d Cir. 1977), cert. denied, 434 U.S. 1002 (1978), which applies. . .

   (1) to protect accurate and disinterested reporting of reputation -- damaging allegations or charges which are newsworthy merely by having been made,

   (2) which allegations relate to. . .

      (a) public figures,

      (b) but not to private individuals (Dixson v. Newsweek, Inc., 562 F.2d 626 (10th Cir. 1977)).

3. Not defense to liability, but may mitigate damages:

   a. partial truth (Crane v. New York World Telegram, 308 N.Y. 470 (1955)),

   b. no malice (New York Civil Rights Law Section 78),

c. retraction or apology,

d. innocent republication,

e. anger or provocation,

f. plaintiff's bad reputation, and/or

g. plaintiff sustained no damage.

E. Potential Liability for Libel

1. Compensatory damages (Gertz v. Robert Welch, Inc., supra), which measure the. . .

   a. injury to plaintiff's reputation,

   b. plaintiff's mental suffering and/or

   c. plaintiff's out-of-pocket money losses; and

2. Punitive damages, upon a showing of actual malice. Gertz v. Robert Welch, Inc., supra; Appleyard v. Transamerican Press, Inc., 539 F.2d 1026 (4th Cir. 1976), cert. denied, 429 U.S. 1041 (1977); Maheu v. Hughes Tool Co., 569 F.2d 459 (9th Cir. 1978).

II. INVASION OF PRIVACY

A. "The Right of Privacy" - Roberson v. Rochester Folding Box Co., 171 N.Y. 538, 64 N.E. 442, 1902

- The New York Right of Privacy statute (Sec. 51 N.Y. Civil Rights Law)
- The development of the right of privacy by statute and decisions.
- Differences between invasion of privacy/publicity and libel.

B. <u>False Light Invasion of Privacy</u>.

1. Does the material -- statements, impressions, accounts of incidents, dialogue, emotions or beliefs attributed to the character, picture, poses -

2. even though the basic underlying facts may be true and even laudatory,

3. place a living individual in a false light in the public eye (<u>Time, Inc. v. Hill</u>, 385 U.S 374 (1967); <u>Spahn v. Julian Messner</u>, 18 N.Y.2d 324 (1966), 21 N.Y.2d 124 (1967)); <u>Cantrell v. Forest City Publishing Co</u>., 419 U.S. 245 (6th Cir. (1974)); <u>Pring v. Penthouse</u>, 7 Med. L. Rptr. (D.C. Wyo. 1981) -whether through . . .

   (a) material and substantial fictionalization expansion, embellishment of the truth; or

   (b) factual omissions or errors in context (<u>Varnish v. Best Medium Publishing Co</u>., 405 F.2d 608 (2d Cir. 1968), <u>cert. denied</u>, 394 U.S. 957 (1969), <u>reh. denied</u>, 395 U.S. 931 (1969)); or

   (c) deceptive, grotesque or unnatural poses in photographs or drawings. . .

4. so as to give a false impression of the character or the subject matter?

5. Advice -- if the answer to the above is yes, do not publish without substantiation to confirm that there is no false light.

6. Where the false material concerns a matter of public interest, a plaintiff must prove actual malice. Most lower courts have imposed <u>New York Times</u> rule on all plaintiffs.

C. <u>Publication of Embarrassing Private Facts</u>

1. Does the material (text or picture), even though it may be truthful,

2. contain embarrassing, intimate private facts about a living individual? (Time, Inc. v. Hill, supra; Virgil v. Time. Inc. 527 F.2d 1122 (9th Cir. 1975), cert. denied, 425 U.S. 998 (1976).

3. That is, is the material. . .

   a. highly offensive to the reasonable person (one of ordinary sensibilities), or outrage the community's notions of decency, and

   b. in which the public has no legitimate interest (i.e., matters which are not newsworthy, but rather are being published for their own sake, and for the sake of sensationalism), and

   c. which are not a matter of public knowledge, and have not been previously published so long ago as no longer to be newsworthy?

4. As to the latter, is the potential plaintiff . . .

   a. a public official or public figure whose identity, and the accompanying facts, remain public (Sidis v. F-R Publishing Corp., 113 F.2d 806 (2d Cir. 1940), cert. denied, 311 U.S. 711 (1940)), or

   b. is he or she rehabilitated by the passage of time from his or her former notorious life, such that the privacy claim may prevail over the assertion of newsworthiness, to preclude publication of present identity? Briscoe v. Reader's Digest Association, Inc., 4 Cal. 3d 524, 483 P.2d 34 (1971)

5. The court may take into consideration whether the private material was secured openly or surreptitiously.

6. There may be no cause of action in New York under the New York Civil Rights Law.

7. Advice - if the answers to the above are yes, do not publish without securing consent to publication.

8. There is no invasion of privacy if the facts already

   a. are known to the public; or

   b. are available in public records; or

   c. are matters of public interest or concern.

D. <u>Invasion by Physical Intrusion on Privacy</u>

1. Was the material (text or picture) obtained by conduct which could amount totortious intrusion --

   a. that is, unlawful or excessive, intentionally intrusive methods, <u>e.g.</u>,

      (1) trespass (<u>Florida Publishing Co. v. Fletcher</u>, 340 So.2d 914 (Fla. Sup. Ct. 1976), or

      (2) surreptitious surveillance, wiretapping, eavesdropping or "hidden photography" (<u>Dieteman v. Time, Inc.</u>, 449 F.2d 245 (9th Cir. 1971); or

      (3) exceeding the bounds of consent (<u>LeMistral, Inc. v. Columbia Broadcasting System</u>, 61 App. Div. 2d 491, 402 N.Y.S.2d 815 (1st Dept. 1978); <u>Pearson v. Dodd</u>; <u>Anderson v. WROC TV</u>, 441 N.Y.S.2d 220 (1981).

   b. which is an intrusion into something intended to be private, <u>Falwell v. Penthouse</u> and

   c. which methods are highly offensive or objectionable to the reasonable person?

2. Advice - if so, do not publish without obtaining appropriate consents.

E. Statutory Right of Privacy (Misappropriation) New York Civil Rights Law §§ 50-51)

1. Is the material a misappropriation to one's own use or benefit of

2. a living individual's (not a corporation or partnership)

3. name or recognizable portrait or picture, including any sufficiently clear representation of the individual,

4. without his or her written consent.

5. for advertising purposes or purposes of trade, rather than "incidentally"? (Brinkley v. Casablances, 7 Med. L. Rptr. 1457 (N.Y. Sup. Ct. App. Div. 1st Dept. 1981); Pagan v. New York Herald Tribune, Inc., 32 App. Div. 2d 341, 301 N.Y.S.2d 120 (1st Dept. 1969), aff'd, 26 N.Y.2d 941 (1970); Booth v. Curtis Publishing Co., 15 App. Div. 2d 343, 223 N.Y.S.2d 737 (1st Dept. 1962); aff'd, 11 N.Y.2d 907 (1962); Murray v. New York Magazine Co., 27 N.Y.2d 406 (1971); Namath v. Sports Illustrated, 48 App. Div. 2d 487, 371 N.Y.S.2d 10 (1st Dept. 1975); i.e., as. . .

   a. a legitimate subject for news, informative presentation, fair comment or public interest; or

   b. where an advertisement merely republishes news previously published in a news medium (Friedan v. Friedan, 414 F. Supp. 723 (S.D.N.Y. 1978)); or

   c. where the name, portrait or picture bears some relationship to, or is a mere background element of the material, such that the use is incidental; McManaman v. Daily Freeman Newspaper, et al., N.Y.L.J. September 24, 1981; Leviston et al. v. Korvettes, et al., N.Y.L.J. October 14, 1981, p. 13, col. 4; Fox v. Fixx et al., 183 N.Y.L.J., p.6, col.3 (Feb. 20, 1980)

(N.Y. Cty. Sup. Ct.); (Metzger v. Dell Publishing Co., 207 Misc. 182, 136 N.Y.S.2d 888 (Sup. Ct. N.Y. Co. 1955) and/or is not there merely to attract attention (i.e., an advertisement in disguise) (Dallesandro v. Henry Holt & Co., Inc., 4 App. Div.2d 470, 166 N.Y.S.2d 805 (1st Dept. 1957), appeal conditionally dismissed, 7 N.Y.2d 735 (1959)); Ali v. Playgril, Inc., 447 F. Supp. 723 (S.D.N.Y. 1978); or

d. is biographical material about a public figure, unless

   (1) it is fictionalized, or

   (2) it contains false material represented to be true and published with actual malice (Spahn v. Julian Messner, supra).

F. Common Law Right of Publicity (Misappropriation)

1. Has a person's (living or dead) -- Factors, Etc. v. ProArts, Inc., 444 F. Supp. 279 (S.D.N.Y. 1977), aff'd, 579 F.2d 215, (2d Cir. 1978), Factors Etc. v. ProArts, Inc. rev'd on rehearing, 579 F.2d 215 (1981); Price v. Hal Roach Studios, Inc. 400 F. Supp. 836 (S.D.N.Y. 1975); Hicks v. Casablanca Records, 464 F. Supp. 426 (S.D.N.Y. 1978); Lugosi v. Universal Pictures, 139 Cal. Rptr. 35 (1977); Marx Bros. v. Day and Night Company, 7 Med. L. Rptr. 2030 (S.D.N.Y. 1981) --

2. name. likeness and/or distinguishing characteristics

3. been exploited commercially by him or her during his or her lifetime (probably an element of proof), and

4. are they now being used commercially in the questioned material, which. . .

a. does not concern the person as a public figure and

b. is not connected with a newsworthy matter or a matter of public interest (Paulsen v. Personality Posters, Inc., 59 Misc. 2d 444, 299 N.Y.S.2d 501 (Sup. Ct. N.Y. Co. 1968)),

5. without his or her consent, or the consent of the heirs of the person? (Marx Productions v. Day and Night Company, 7 Med. L. Rptr. 2030 (S.D.N.Y. 1981); Zacchini v. Scripps-Howard Broadcasting Co., 433 U.S. 562 (1977); see, Lugosi v. Universal Pictures, 139 Cal. Rptr. 35 (1977).

6. There is no liability, however, for biographical material of a celebrity who (or whose heirs) may have rights of publicity, which material contains an openly fictionalized account of incidents or events (Hicks v. Casablanca Records, 464 F. Supp. 426 (S.D.N.Y. 1978) (plaitiffs were the heirs of Agatha Christie).

7. Does the right of publicity survive death.

   a. Difference from Rights of Privacy.

      Rights are personal, cannot be assigned. Andretti v. Rolex; Brinkley v. Casablancas; cannot survive death. Right of Publicity is assignable during life.

   b. Cases holding right of publicity survives death and is descendible.

      Factors I and II; Hicks v. Casablanca.

   c. Cases holding right does not survive death.

Memphis - Presley

Lugosi v. Universal Pictures and Guglielmi v. Spelling-Goldberg.

d. Does right of publicity under New York law survive?

Andretti and Brinkley suggest it may not, because is subsumed under statutory right of privacy.

e. Which state's law governs in determining if right of publicity survives or expires at death.

Marx Productions v. Cohen, et al.

8. Advice - if so, do not use without consent.

G. Potential Liability for Invasion of Privacy

1. Injunctive relief,

2. Actual damages for mental distress and injury to property (under libel, damages are easier to prove because testimony of third parties not critical), and/or

3. Compensatory damages limited to amount of compensation plaintiff should have received for publicity value. (Guccione v. Hustler, 7 Med. L. Rptr. 2077 (Ohio Ct. App. 1981).

4. Punitive damges, for knowing misconduct or bad faith. Cohen v. Hallmark Cards, Inc. 58 App. Div. 2d 770, 397 N.Y.S.2d 899 (1st Dept. 1977).

III. COPYRIGHT, INFRINGEMENT - PLAGIARISM

A. A plaintiff alleging copyright infringement or plagiarism, (under Copyright Act, also receives statutory protection for material not previously copyrighted) must show:

1. Ownership of material,

2. Copying (which is shown by direct or indirect evidence of access to the allegedly infringed work; indirect access is proved by evidence of substantial similarity which is so striking that there must have been copying), and

3. Substantial similarity between the two works in question (usually the converse of the third element of the "fair use" determination) (see below), as judged by the "ordinary viewer."

4. Novelty Textile Mills v. Joan Fabrics Corp., 558 F.2d 1090, 1092 (2d Cir. 1977); Reyher v. Children's Television Workshop, 387 F. Supp. 869 (S.D.N.Y. 1975), aff'd, 533 F.2d 87 (2d Cir. 1976).

B. Subject Matter

1. What may be protected, such that use may not be made without the owner's consent:

a. Original works of authorship fixed in any tangible medium of expression (§102 of the Copyright Act, including published or unpublished (§104(a)). . .

(1) literary works (most often: advertising, materials, catalogues, books, including fiction and non-fiction works and their translations; letters; diaries; scripts prepared for oral delivery by lecture, sermon, and address.

(2) musical works, including any accompanying words;

(3) dramatic works, including any accompanying music;

(4) pictorial, graphic and sculptural works (most often: prints, photo-

graphs, illustrations, drawings, maps, and their reproductions; color arrangements);

(5) motion pictures and other audiovisual works;

(6) sound recordings; and

(7) compilations and derivative works, but only to the extent of the material contributed by the author of such a work, as distinguished from the preexisting material employed in the work (most often" periodicals, newspapers, pamphlets and their component parts, automatically; composite and cyclopedic works, annotations, commentaries, directories) (§103 of the Copyright Act).

b. Definitions for most of these terms are contained in §101 of the Copyright Act.

2. What may <u>not</u> be protected, and thus <u>may</u> be used without consent:

a. Ideas (although the means of expression of ideas may be copyrighted), procedures, processes, systems, methods of operation, concepts, principles or discoveries, regardless of the form in which they are described, explained, illustrated or embodied in an original work of authorship (§102(b) of the Copyright Act).

b. Protection for the use of ideas also carries over to protect the author's use of. . .

(1) Scenes a faire -- plots, incidents or language which follow a common theme -- and

the general public, or when an authorized offer is made to dispose of the work in any such manner even if a sale or other such disposition does not in fact occur.

c. Publication does not occur when it is "limited" -

(1) communicated to a definitely selected group, and

(2) for a limited purpose, without the right of diffusion, reproduction, distribution or sale;

(3) _e.g._, submission of material for approval or sale.

C. _Fair Use May Be Made of Others' Works_

1. Even without the copyright owner's consent, "fair use" may be made of a copyrighted work for purposes such as criticism, news reporting, teaching, scholarship or research.

2. Fair use is determined in accordance with the following factors: (§107 of the Copyright Act; _see also_ 23 A.L.R. 3d 139)

a. the purpose and character of the use, including whether such use is of a commercial nature or is for nonprofit educational purposes (look also for scholarly, scientific and historical purposes);

b. the nature of the copyrighted work (generally, its availability, and thus a very limited defense for unpublished works, _e.g._, letters and diaries);

c. the amount and substantiality of the portion used in relation to the copyrighted work as a whole (look for copying of the structure or pattern of a work (_e.g._, plot, incidents) or of the specific elements (e.g., lines, words, paraphrasing)); and

d. the effect of the use upon the potential market for and value of the copyrighted work (look to see if the two works would compete in the market place, and look for defenses based on the functions of criticism and review, and satire, burlesque and parody).

D. Potential Liability for Copyright Infringement and Plagiarism

1. Injunctive relief (§502 of the Copyright Act); and/or

2. Impounding and destruction or other disposition of infringing materials (§503); and/or

3. A monetary award, consisting of. . .

   a. plaintiff's actual damages, plus defendant's profits which are attributable to the infringement (§504(b)); or

   b. statutory or "in lieu" damages (§504(c)):

      (1) a minimum award of $250 and a maximum award of $10,000, but only one award regardless of the number of infringing copies published, but

      (2) if infringement was willful, a maximum award of $50,000, and

      (3) if infringement was innocent, as little as $100; and/or

4. In the discretion of the Court, full statutory costs and attorney's fees may be awarded (§505); and/or

5. Criminal penalties for willful infringement for commercial or private financial gain (§506).

E. <u>Advice</u>

1. Use of particular materials may not be made without consent of the copyright proprietor, unless the material is not copyrightable or is in the public domain, or the use is "fair use".

2. As to this latter, review the origins of the creator's ideas, sources, research, experience in the field, and his or her own ideas as to permissible use of other's material.

IV. <u>UNFAIR COMPETITION</u>

A. 1. <u>Elements</u> - difficult to abstractly define - Courts refer, on a case by case basis, to anything from "the rules of fair play" to "means which shock judicial sensibilities." Includes such practices as:

a. Palming off one's goods or products as those of another

b. Tortious interference with business

c. Misappropriation of secondary meaning

2. Actual competition not an indispensable prerequisite - Courts look to injury suffeed by the complaining party or the public due to an infringers acts.

B. <u>Statutory Protection - Lanham Act §43(a) 15 U.S.C. 1125(a)</u>

1. has there been a use of a name or mark in connection with goods or services in interstate commerce

2. that is likely to confuse (<u>Dallas Cowboys Cheerleaders, Inc. v. Pussycat Cinema, Ltd.</u>, 604 F.2d 200 (2d Cir. 1979)) or deceive (<u>S.K.& F. Co. v. Premo Pharmaceutical Laboratories</u>,

625 F.2d 1055 (3d Cir. 1980)) purchasers into believing the source of the goods or services

3. is that of a competitor who has a protectable interest in a similar name or mark. . .

   a. is the name or mark strong or 'fanciful" such that it is entitled to protection (Russ Berrie & Co., Inc. v. Jerry Elsner Co. Inc. 482 F. Supp. 980 (S.D.N.Y. 1980)), or

   b. has the name or mark been registered, or

   c. has the name or mark acquired a secondary meaning, (Carter-Wallce, Inc. v. Proctor & Gamble Company, 434 F.2d 794 (9th Cir. 1970)).

C. 1. Leading U.S. Supreme Court Cases

   a. Sears, Roebuck & Co. v. Stiffel Co., 376 U.S.s. 225, 140 U.S.P.Q. 524 (1964) (state unfair competition law may not prohibit copying of a pole lamp unprotected by a federal patent or copyright).

   b. Compco Corp. v. Day-Brite Lighting, Inc. 376 U.S. 234, 140 U.S.P.Q. 528 (1964) (state unfair competition law may not be used to give relief against copying the design of a lighting fixture which was the subject of an invalid federal design patent).

2. Post Sears and Compco Cases Permitting Recovery on Unfair Competition Grounds

   a. Sterling House, Inc. v. Dell Publishing Co., Inc., 174 U.S.P.Q. 299 (S.D.N.Y. 1972) (plaintiff granted relief against copying of format of its magazine cover);

   b. Robert Stigwood Group Ltd. v. Sperber, 457 F.2d 50, 173 U.S.P.Q. 258 (2nd Cir. 1972) (even if title "Jesus Christ Superstar" is uncopyrightable "writing," no bar to protection against deception);

c. Orion Pictures v. Dell Publishing, 471 F. Supp. 392 (U.S.D.C., S.D.N.Y.) (1979) (injunctive relief granted on "passing off" and inference of secondary meaning" grounds regarding overstatement of relationship of paperback book with movie "A Little Romance")

3. Post Sears and Compco Cases Denying Recovery on Unfair Competition Grounds

a. Booth v. Colgate-Palmolive Co., 362 F. Supp. 343 (S.D.N.Y. 1973) (Shirley Booth denied relief for claimed imitation of her voice in a television commercial depicting the copyrighted cartoon character "Hazel," portrayed on television by Ms. Booth.)

b. United Artists Corporation, et al. v. Ford Motor Company, et al., 76 Civ. 4444 (USDC, S.D.N.Y. 483 F. Supp. 89) (1980) (relief denied on allegations of passing off, misrepresentation and misappropriation of secondary meaning of the "Pink Panther" animated character).

V. COMPARATIVE ADVERTISING

A. Definition -

1. Advertisements which, explicitly or implicitly, direct a prospective customer's attention to similarities or differences between an advertised product and the product of one or more competitors.

2. Truthful comparative advertising generally regarded as lawful.

B. Main Problems

1. False unsupportible statements about one's own product (Lanham Act and state statutes)

2. Disparagement - Untrue or misleading statements about a competitors goods which influence, or tend to influence the public not to buy.

VI. ADVERTISERS AND AGENCY LIABILITY INSURANCE COVERAGE

A. Setting out rights and obligations among advertisers, agencies and third party defendants.

B. Coverage (Copies of a sample Coverage Description and Sample Advertiser and Advertising Agency Insurance Policies are annexed in the Appendix.)

C. Insurance Policy exclusions and reservations of rights.

D. Defense strategy for advertiser and agency defendants.

ADVERTISERS AND ADVERTISING

AGENCY LIABILITY

SEABOARD SURETY COMPANY
90 William Street, New York 10038

SEABOARD SURETY COMPANY

HOME OFFICE

90 WILLIAM STREET, NEW YORK, N. Y. 10038

ADVERTISERS AND ADVERTISING AGENCY LIABILITY

Seaboard Surety Company entered the Advertisers and Advertising Agency Liability Insurance field in 1950 to fill the void left after four successive insurers discontinued writing this technical coverage. During the past twenty-three years our approach to underwriting, claim and legal matters has earned us the respect of Advertisers, Advertising Agencies, Broadcasters and Program Producers who have availed themselves of our Legal Liability Policies.

Seaboard issues a separate Policy for the Advertiser and for the Advertising Agency with each being designed to meet their specific needs. Under these contracts, Seaboard agrees (subject, of course, to the conditions, limitations, and exclusions set forth therein), to defend at its cost any suit brought against the Insured, and to pay any final judgment rendered therein, claiming damages as a result of:

(A) Libel, slander, defamation or,

(B) Any infringement of copyright or of title or of slogan or,

(C) Piracy, plagiarism, or idea misappropriation under implied contract or,

(D) Any invasion of rights of privacy.

Policy Limits

The Advertisers and Advertising Agency Policy forms are single limit contracts available at a minimum $100,000 limit of liability. The Policy limit applies to all claims involving one occurrence regardless of the frequency of repetition, or the number or kind of media used and whether the claim is made by one or more persons.

The premium for the Advertising Agency Policy is based on the gross annual billings; the premium for the Advertisers Policy is based on annual advertising expenditures. Policies can be issued for periods of either one or three years. The premium for a three year Policy is 2½ times the annual. One claim payment or the cost of defending one suit could more than offset the total premiums paid over a period of years.

Seaboard Surety Company is authorized to do business throughout the United States and Canada, and policies can be arranged by any licensed Agent or Broker. Specimen Policies and application forms may be obtained from any Seaboard Branch Office.

Importance of Insurance

Invested capital, surplus and future profits can be placed in serious jeopardy by reason of a substantial uninsured claim and/or legal expenses. Our Policy helps to preserve assets and at the same time is a valuable protector of "Agency-Client" relationships, particularly when both parties are named defendants and "grey areas" exist as to the ultimate responsibility.

Many Advertisers insist their Agencies carry this insurance and some Agencies strongly recommend that their accounts purchase similar protection. Product defamation, idea misappropriation and copyright suits are common examples of losses. Invasion of privacy claims arising out of unauthorized use of pictures and names are also a source of claims.

First notice of claim is usually the serving of a summons and complaint requiring immediate attention and answer by qualified attorneys. Seaboard's legal staff has more than twenty years experience in this field. Without defense coverage, the Insured must locate and engage competent attorneys to protect their interests in these delicate areas. Approximately 82% of our overall claim costs are legal defense costs. Thus, the coverage of defense costs in Seaboard's Advertisers and Advertising Agency Liability Policies is probably their most important feature. Litigation costs, even to defend groundless claims, generally are substantial.

Both policies also cover liability assumed by either the Advertiser or Advertising Agency under contracts with other parties to hold such parties harmless from loss and/or expense resulting from claims, falling within the perils enumerated hereinbefore and arising out of matter or material furnished by the Insured. On the other hand, uninsured third party hold harmless or indemnity agreements given to our Insured are worthless if the indemnitor is insolvent, has ceased operations or cannot be located when claim is made.

BRANCH OFFICES

Atlanta, Georgia
3445 Peachtree Road, N. E. — Room 950
404-237-3334

Baltimore, Maryland
Hampton Plaza
300 East Joppa Road, Suite 408
301-828-0737

Boston, Massachusetts
Three Center Plaza, Suite 500
617-227-9200

Chicago, Illinois
A-1820 175 West Jackson Boulevard
312-922-2486

Columbus, Ohio
250 East Broad Street, Suite 903
614-224-9727

Dallas, Texas
211 North Ervay Building
214-747-1875

Detroit, Michigan
211 Fort Street, West — Room 1011
313-961-5933

Honolulu, Hawaii
841 Bishop Street, Suite 1610
808-538-3874

Indianapolis, Indiana
3901 No. Meridian Street, Suite 406
317-923-3396

Kansas City, Missouri
Commerce Tower, Suite 904
P.O. Box 13144
816-421-1616

London
Plantation House
31 Fenchurch Street
London, EC3M 3DX, England

Los Angeles, California
3810 Wilshire Boulevard, Suite 1220
213-381-3741

New York, New York
90 William Street
212-943-7440

Orlando, Florida
3191 Maguire Boulevard
P. O. Box 20354
305-894-7221

Richmond, Virginia
4905 Radford Avenue
P.O. Box 8664
703-359-0265

San Francisco, California
100 Pine Street, Suite 375
415-981-7581

Seattle, Washington
Seattle First National Bank Building
1001 Fourth Avenue, Room 3206
206-622-2590

Smithtown, New York
Smithtown Executive Plaza
222 Middle Country Road
Jericho Turnpike
516-979-8484

Springfield, New Jersey
Independence Plaza
500 Morris Avenue
201- 467-1141

Syracuse, New York
Monroe Building
333 East Onondaga Street
315-471-0154

LIBEL, SLANDER, COPYRIGHT, PIRACY, PLAGIARISM, AND PRIVACY LIABILITY POLICY
(ADVERTISERS' FORM)

Seaboard Surety Company

A STOCK COMPANY

HOME OFFICE: NEW YORK, NEW YORK

Policy No. ALP

SCHEDULE OF STATEMENTS

1. Name and Principal Address of Insured:

2. Policy Period:
From ... to ...
12:01 A. M., standard time at the address of the named Insured as stated herein.

3. The advertising expenditures of the Insured in its latest completed fiscal year were $. The premium, predicated upon the aforementioned advertising expenditures, is $. The minimum premium for this policy is $, and is not subject to short rate adjustment.
4. The Company's liability for the Indemnity in Paragraph 1 of the Insuring Agreements, whether for one Insured or more than one Insured, is limited to Dollars ($) for any advertisement, publicity article, broadcast or telecast or any combination thereof involving the same injurious material or act, regardless of the frequency of repetition thereof or the number or kind of media used, whether claim is made by one or more persons.
5. The Insured represents that no other similar insurance is carried, except

SEABOARD SURETY COMPANY

(A stock insurance company, herein called the Company)

In consideration of the premium named herein and of the representations set forth in the Schedule of Statements, DOES HEREBY AGREE with the Insured, named in such Schedule of Statements, which is made a part hereof, as follows:

INSURING AGREEMENTS

Indemnity 1. To pay on behalf of the Insured all sums which the Insured shall become obligated to pay by reason of the liability imposed upon him by law, or assumed by him under contract as defined herein, as the result of any final judgment for money damages resulting from

(a) libel, slander, defamation or

(b) any infringement of copyright or of title or of slogan or

(c) piracy, plagiarism, or unfair competition or idea misappropriation under implied contract or

(d) any invasion of rights of privacy

committed or alleged to have been committed in any advertisement, publicity article, broadcast or telecast and arising out of the Insured's advertising activities.

Service 2. To defend, in the name and on behalf of the Insured, any suit seeking damages for any of the above causes, even if such suit is groundless, false or fraudulent. The Company shall have the right to make such investigation, negotiation and settlement of any claim or suit as it may deem expedient, or may permit the Insured to make any such investigation, negotiation and settlement as may be approved by the Company in writing.

In the event that in any suit which the Company has agreed to defend, as provided for in Paragraph 2 hereof, any application for an injunction or injunctive relief shall be made by the plaintiff, the Company agrees to defend, in the name and on behalf of the Insured, against such application for an injunction or injunctive relief; but the obligation of the Company so to defend against such application for an injunction or injunctive relief shall not extend beyond the determination of the court of first instance.

Countersigned at this day of 19

Countersigned by

Authorized Representative

Form 6045D (Rev. 8-74)

Expense 3. To pay all premiums on bonds to release attachments for an amount not in excess of the applicable limit of this Policy and all premiums on appeal bonds required in the defense of any suit, but without any obligation to apply for or furnish such bonds; all costs taxed against the Insured in any such suit, all expenses incurred by the Company and all interest accruing after entry of judgment until the Company has paid, tendered or deposited in court such part of such judgment as does not exceed the limit of the Company's liability thereon.

The Company agrees to pay the amounts incurred under Paragraphs 2 and 3 in addition to the applicable limits of liability of this Policy.

Territory 4. This Policy applies only to legal proceedings brought in the Courts of the United States or its possessions or of the District of Columbia, or the Courts of any of the states of the United States, or of the Dominion of Canada.

DEFINITIONS

Definition of Insured 1. The unqualified word "Insured" wherever used in this Policy, includes not only the named Insured or employee thereof, but also any partner, executive officer or director thereof, while acting within the scope of his duties as such.

Definition of Contract 2. The word "contract", wherever used in this Policy, shall mean the liability assumed or agreed upon by the Insured with any party, including but not limited to advertising agencies, broadcasting companies, publishers and other media for advertising, to hold said parties harmless from loss and/or expense resulting from claims for damages on account of violation, or alleged violation, of the rights of others, arising from the broadcasting, or telecasting, or the publication for the Insured of any advertising matter including copy, portraits, pictures or other material for use in connection therewith, furnished by the Insured, but only in so far as such liability pertains to the hazards set forth in sections (a), (b), (c), or (d) of Paragraph 1 Indemnity, of this Policy.

Nothing in this Policy shall be construed to cover any liability for the negligence of said parties in their handling, use or publication of any advertising matter or material furnished by the Insured, regardless of such assumption or agreement by the Insured.

Definition of Damages 3. The term "damages" or "money damages" wherever used in this policy shall not include fines or penalties. The Company's liability for punitive or exemplary damages awarded against any Insured shall not exceed one-half of such damages but in no event more than a sum equal to ten percent (10%) of the policy limit, or $50,000, whichever is less. The Company's liability for punitive or exemplary damages as provided for herein shall be part of and not in addition to the policy limit. The Company shall have no liability for punitive or exemplary damages awarded against any Insured in any jurisdiction in which insurance against such damages is prohibited.

THIS AGREEMENT IS SUBJECT TO THE FOLLOWING CONDITIONS:

Exclusions A. This Policy does not cover any liability for:

1. Failure of performance of contract, but this shall not relate to claims for the unauthorized appropriation of ideas based upon the alleged breach of an implied contract;
2. Physical property damage or for damages which may be attributed to, or are a direct or consequential result of bodily injury to or death of any person, whatever the cause of such injury or death;
3. Infringement of trade mark, service mark or trade name, nor shall this policy cover any claims or suit for unfair competition based upon infringement of trade mark, service mark, or trade name;
4. Incorrect description of any article or commodity or any mistake in advertised price or any claim or suit based upon or arising out of alleged false, misleading, deceptive, fraudulent or misrepresenting advertising or to any claim or suit for unfair competition based thereon;
5. Liability of others assumed by the Insured under any contract or agreement except a contract as defined herein;
6. Any claim, suit or action brought against the Insured because of an act committed by that Insured with knowledge that the same constituted any of the hazards insured by this policy;

Limits B. The Company's liability for the Indemnity provided in Paragraph 1 of the Insuring Agreements is limited to the amount as expressed in Statement 4 of the Schedule of Statements, and such amount shall not be cumulative from year to year or from period to period. In the event such amount is increased during the term of this Policy, such increased amount shall apply only in respect of acts or events first committed after the effective date of such increase. The inclusion herein of more than one Insured shall not operate to increase the limit of the Company's liability.

Cancelation C. This Policy may be canceled by the named Insured by mailing to the Company written notice stating when thereafter such cancelation shall be effective. This Policy may be canceled by the Company by mailing to the named Insured at the address shown in Statement 1 of the Schedule of Statements written notice stating when, not less than ten days thereafter, such cancelation shall be effective. The mailing of notice, as aforesaid, shall be sufficient proof of notice and the effective date and hour of cancelation stated in the notice shall become the end of the Policy Period. Delivery of such written notice, either by the named Insured or by the Company, shall be equivalent to mailing. If the named Insured cancels, earned premium shall be computed in accordance with the customary short rate table and procedure, but shall not be less than the minimum premium set forth in the Schedule of Statements. If the Company cancels, earned premium shall be computed pro rata. Premium adjustment may be made at the time cancelation is effected, and if not then made, shall be made as soon as practicable after cancelation becomes effective. The Company's check or the check of its representative mailed or delivered as aforesaid, shall be sufficient tender of any refund of premium due the named Insured.

ENDORSEMENT NO.__________

It is hereby understood and agreed that Exclusions Section A of the Policy to which this endorsement is attached is amended to include the following:

7. Any claim unless resulting from events occurring during the effective period of this policy. If such events shall have occurred or have been initiated prior to the effective date hereof and shall have been repeated or continued during the Policy period, or shall be repeated or continued, thereafter, then the Company's liability shall be limited to that proportion of the total claim or judgement which the number of events during the Policy Period upon which the claim is based, bears to the total number of events upon which such claim is based.

Effective Date .... 19.......

Nothing herein contained shall be held to vary, alter, waive or extend any of the terms, conditions, agreements or limitations of this policy other than as above stated.

Attached to and forming part of Policy No.............................. issued to ....

.... of ....

by SEABOARD SURETY COMPANY.

Countersigned by ....
Authorized Representative.

Form 6210

President.

APPLICATION FOR ADVERTISERS
LIBEL AND SLANDER, COPYRIGHT, PIRACY, PLAGIARISM, AND PRIVACY INSURANCE

Subject to Acceptance By

SEABOARD SURETY COMPANY

New York, New York

1. Name of Insured ....
2. Address ....
3. Corporation, Partnership or Individual (indicate which) ....
   Date Formed ....
4. Names of controlled, affiliated or subsidiary companies to be included as Insureds ....
5. Describe the nature of your operation (including affiliates and subsidiaries) ....
6. Do you use Comparative Advertisements? . . . Yes .... No ....
   A) If your answer to the foregoing is yes, describe the nature and extent of the Advertisements ....
      a) affirmative statements and claims concerning your own advertised products or services ....
      b) a depiction or identification of a competitor and/or his product or service ....
7. Advertising Agency(s) which create(s) your Advertisements (including affiliates and subsidiaries) ....
8. Number of LIBEL, SLANDER, COPYRIGHT, PIRACY, PLAGIARISM OR PRIVACY SUITS in past ten years ....
9. Number of judgements rendered .... Amount of each judgement ....
10. Number of settlements before trial .... Amount of each settlement ....
11. Do you have any such suits pending .... State details ....
12. Describe each program(s) which is self produced ....
13. Total Advertising expenditures of insured (including affiliates and subsidiaries listed above) in latest completed fiscal year were $ ....
14. If foreign advertising done, list countries and amount of expenditures in each ....
    a) These expenditures are ☐ / are not ☐ included in above total expenditure figures
15. The policy period is from .... 19 .... to .... 19 ....
16. Limits of coverage desired $ ....
17. a) Do you presently carry an Umbrella Liability Policy that includes Advertiser's Liability? Yes ☐ No ☐
    b) If yes, state amount of coverage and limit at which the Umbrella attaches ....

Name of Insured

....

By ....

NAME AND TITLE

*IF ADDITIONAL SPACE IS NEEDED USE BACK OR ATTACH SEPARATE RESPONSE.

Form 853A - Rev. 12/78

(ATTACH ENDORSEMENTS HERE)

Notices D. Upon receipt by the Insured of information relating to an act or event which might result in a claim or claims under this Policy, written notice thereof shall be given by or on behalf of the Insured to the Company or its authorized agent as soon as practicable. Such notice shall contain particulars of the thing or act that is the subject of the claim as well as copy of the claim. If suit is brought against the Insured to enforce such claim, the Insured shall forward to the Company with reasonable promptness every summons, notice, or other process that may be served upon him.

Co-operation of Insured E. The Insured shall not make any admission of liability, nor shall he authorize any officer, employee or other person to make any admission of liability, either before or after a claim is made; nor shall he, except at his own cost, incur any expense, make any payment or settle any claim; nor shall he interfere in any negotiations for settlement or in any legal proceeding with respect to any claim hereunder without, in each case, the written consent of the Company. In the event the Insured shall settle or defend any claim or suit without the written approval of the Company, any amount which the Insured shall pay or become liable to pay, including expenses, on account of such claim or suit shall not be recoverable under this Policy. The defense by the Company of any suit or the prosecution of any appeal shall not operate as a waiver by the Company of any of its defenses to any claim by the Insured, should the Insured fail to comply with any of the terms or conditions of the Policy.

Whenever required by the Company, the Insured shall aid in securing information and evidence and the attendance of witnesses, and shall co-operate with the Company in the defense of any claim or suit or in the prosecution of any appeal; and the Company shall reimburse the Insured for expenses, other than loss of earnings, incurred at the Company's request.

Subrogation F. In the event of any payment under this Policy, and to the extent of such payment, the Company shall be subrogated to all the Insured's rights of recovery therefor against any person or organization, other than an advertising agency for the Insured also insured by this Company; and the Insured shall execute all papers required and shall co-operate with the Company to secure to it such rights.

Other Insurance G. If the Insured carries other insurance or indemnity not designated in Statement 5, of the Schedule of Statements covered by the terms of this Policy, the Company shall be liable hereunder for only that proportion of the loss that the amount of this Policy bears to the total of this Policy and such other insurance regardless of whether such other insurance shall be deemed excess only, contributing or otherwise.

Changes H. Notice to any agent or knowledge possessed by any agent or by any other person shall not effect a waiver or a change in any part of this Policy or estop the Company from asserting any right under the terms of this Policy; nor shall the terms of this Policy be waived or changed, except by endorsement issued to form a part of this Policy, signed by the President, a Vice-President, Secretary or an Assistant Secretary and countersigned by a duly Authorized Representative of the Company.

Statutory Provisions I. If any condition of this Policy is at variance with any specific statutory provision applicable thereto, such specific statutory provision shall supersede the condition inconsistent therewith.

Statements J. The Statements contained in the Schedule forming a part of the Policy are made by the Insured and, by the acceptance of this Policy, the Insured represents the same to be true.

Action Against Company K. No action shall lie against the Company to recover for any loss under this Policy unless brought within two years after the amount of such loss is made certain either by judgment against the Insured, after trial of the issue, or by agreement between the parties with the consent of the Company. Bankruptcy or insolvency of the Insured shall not relieve the Company of any of its obligations hereunder.

Assignment L. Any assignment or change of interest hereunder, whether voluntary or involuntary, shall render the Policy void unless such assignment of change is consented to in writing by the President, a Vice-President, a Secretary or an Assistant Secretary of the Company.

IN WITNESS WHEREOF, the SEABOARD SURETY COMPANY has caused this Policy to be signed by its President and Secretary and countersigned by a duly Authorized Representative of the Company.

Secretary

President

LIBEL, SLANDER, COPYRIGHT, PIRACY, PLAGIARISM, AND PRIVACY LIABILITY POLICY
(AGENCY FORM)

Seaboard Surety Company

A STOCK COMPANY
HOME OFFICE: NEW YORK, NEW YORK

Policy No. AP.................................

SCHEDULE OF STATEMENTS

1. Name and Principal Address of Insured:

2. Policy Period:
From.............................to.............................
12:01 A. M., standard time at the address of the named insured as stated herein.

3. The gross billings of the Insured in its latest completed fiscal year were $................................ The premium, predicated upon the aforementioned gross billings, is $................................
The minimum premium for this policy is $................................, and is not subject to short rate adjustment.

4. The Company's liability for the indemnity provided in Paragraph (1) of the Insuring Agreements, whether for one Insured or more than one Insured, is limited to .... Dollars ($................................) for any advertisement, publicity article, broadcast or telecast or any combination thereof involving the same injurious material or act, regardless of the number or kind of media used, or frequency of repetition thereof, whether claim is made by one or more persons.

5. The Insured represents that no other similar insurance is carried, except................................

SEABOARD SURETY COMPANY

(A stock insurance company, herein called the Company)

In consideration of the premium named herein and of the representations set forth in the Schedule of Statements, DOES HEREBY AGREE with the Insured, named in such Schedule of Statements, which are made a part hereof, as follows:

INSURING AGREEMENTS

Indemnity

1. To pay on behalf of the Insured all sums which the Insured shall become obligated to pay by reason of the liability imposed upon him by law, or assumed by him under contract as defined herein, as the result of any final judgment for money damages resulting from
   (a) libel, slander, defamation or
   (b) any infringement of copyright or of title or of slogan or
   (c) piracy, plagiarism, or unfair competition or idea misappropriation under implied contract or
   (d) any invasion of rights of privacy
committed or alleged to have been committed in any advertisement, publicity article, broadcast or telecast and arising out of the Insured's business of Advertising Agents.

Service

2. To defend, in the name and on behalf of the Insured, any suit seeking damages for any of the above causes, even if such suit is groundless, false or fraudulent. The Company shall have the right to make such investigation, negotiation and settlement of any claim or suit as it may deem expedient, or may permit the Insured to make any such investigation, negotiation and settlement as may be approved by the Company in writing.

In the event that in any suit which the Company has agreed to defend, as provided for in Paragraph (2) above, any application for an injunction or injunctive relief shall be made by the plaintiff, the Company agrees to defend, in the name and on behalf of the Insured, against such application for an injunction or injunctive relief; but the obligation of the Company so to defend against such application for an injunction or injunctive relief shall not extend beyond the determination of the court of first instance.

Countersigned at .... this.............. day of.............................. 19........

Countersigned by ....
Authorized Representative

Form 6043D (Rev. 9-72)

Expense

3. To pay all premiums on bonds to release attachments for an amount not in excess of the applicable limit of this Policy and all premiums on appeal bonds required in the defense of any suit, but without any obligation to apply for or furnish such bonds; all costs taxed against the Insured in any such suit, all expenses incurred by the Company and all interest accruing after entry of judgment until the Company has paid, tendered or deposited in court such part of such judgment as does not exceed the limit of the Company's liability thereon.

The Company agrees to pay the amounts incurred under Paragraphs (2) and (3) in addition to the applicable limit of liability of this Policy.

Territory

4. This Policy applies only to legal proceedings brought in the Courts of the United States or its possessions or of the District of Columbia, or Courts of any of the states of the United States, or of the Dominion of Canada.

DEFINITIONS

Definition of Insured

1. The unqualified word "Insured" wherever used, includes not only the named Insured or employee thereof, but also any partner, executive officer, or director thereof, while acting within the scope of his duties as such.

Definition of Contract

2. The word "contract", wherever used in this Policy, shall mean the liability assumed or agreed upon by the Insured with any party, including but not limited to clients, broadcasting companies, publishers and other media for advertising, to hold said parties harmless from loss and/or expense resulting from claims for damages on account of violation, or alleged violation, of the rights of others, arising from the broadcasting, or telecasting, or the publication for the Insured of any advertising matter including copy, portraits, pictures or other material for use in connection therewith, furnished by the Insured, but only in so far as such liability pertains to the hazards set forth in sections (a), (b), (c), or (d) of Paragraph (1) Indemnity, of this Policy.

Nothing in this Policy shall be construed to cover any liability for the negligence of said parties, in their handling, use or publication of any advertising matter or material furnished by the Insured, regardless of such assumption or agreement by the Insured.

Definition of Damages

3. The term "damages" or "money damages" wherever used in this policy shall not include fines or penalties, nor shall they include punitive or exemplary damages awarded against any Insured in a jurisdiction in which insurance against such damage is prohibited.

THIS AGREEMENT IS SUBJECT TO THE FOLLOWING CONDITIONS:

Exclusions

A. This Policy does not cover any liability for:

1. Failure of performance of contract but this shall not relate to claims for the unauthorized appropriation of ideas based upon the alleged breach of an implied contract;
2. Physical property damage or for damages which may be attributed to, or are a direct or consequential result of bodily injury to or death of any person, whatever the cause of such injury or death.
3. Bodily injuries, death or physical property damage;
4. Infringement of trade mark, service mark or trade name, nor shall this policy cover any claim or suit for unfair competition based upon infringement of trade mark, service mark, or trade name.
5. Incorrect description of any article or commodity;
6. Mistake in advertised price;
7. Liability of others assumed by the Insured under any contract or agreement except a contract as defined herein;
8. Any claim unless resulting from events occurring during the effective period of this Policy. If such events shall have occurred or have been initiated prior to the effective date hereof and shall have been repeated or continued during the Policy Period, or shall be repeated or continued thereafter, then the Company's liability shall be limited to that proportion of the total claim or judgment which the number of events during the Policy Period, upon which the claim is based, bears to the total number of events upon which such claim is based.
9. Any claim, suit or action brought against the Insured because of an act committed by that Insured with knowledge that the same constituted any of the hazards insured by this policy.

Limits

B. The Company's liability for the Indemnity provided in Paragraph (1) of the Insuring Agreements is limited to the amount as expressed in Statement 4 of the Schedule of Statements. In the event such amount is increased during the term of this Policy, such increased amount shall apply only in respect of acts or events first committed after the effective date of such increase. The inclusion herein of more than one Insured shall not operate to increase the limit of the Company's liability.

ENDORSEMENT NO.________________

The attached policy is amended as follows:

1. By deleting therefrom Definition 3 "Definition of Damages" and substituting the following in lieu thereof:

"Definition of Damages" 3. The term "damages" or "money damages" wherever used in this policy shall not include fines or penalties. The Company's liability for punitive or exemplary damages awarded against any insured shall not exceed one-half of such damages, but in no event more than a sum equal to ten percent (10%) of the policy limit, or $50,000., whichever is less. The Company's liability for punitive or exemplary damages as provided for herein shall be part of and not in addition to the policy. The Company shall have no liability for punitive or exemplary damages awarded against any insured in any jurisdiction in which insurance against such damages is prohibited."

2. CONDITIONS, Exclusions, A., 5. is hereby deleted in its entirety and the following substituted in lieu thereof:

"5. Incorrect description or any article or commodity, or any claim or suit based upon or arising out of alleged false, misleading, deceptive, fraudulent or misrepresenting advertising or to any claim or suit for unfair competition based thereon."

Effective Date________________19____

Nothing herein contained shall be held to vary, alter, waive or extend any of the terms, conditions, agreements or limitations of this policy other than as above stated.

Attached to and forming part of Policy No.____________issued to________________

________________________of________________________

by SEABOARD SURETY COMPANY.

Countersigned by ________________________
Authorized Representative.

Form 6211

President

DEDUCTIBLE ENDORSEMENT NO. ____________

In consideration of the premium charged for the attached policy, it is hereby understood and agreed as follows:

(1) $5000.00 for each claim shall be deducted from the total amount of all sums which the Company agrees to pay on account of indemnity and services under Insuring Agreements 1 and 2 of the policy.

(2) The terms of the policy, including those with respect to notices, Insured's cooperation, and the Company's right to investigate, negotiate and settle any claim or suit, apply irrespective of the application of the deductible amount.

(3) The Company may incur expense and may pay any part or all of the deductible amount to effect settlement of any claim or suit and, upon notification of the action taken, the Insured shall promptly reimburse the Company for its loss and expense payments up to the full amount of the deductible on each claim.

(4) If the Company is satisfied with the judgement of the Trial Court, or with any settlement which is offered, and the Insured either desires to appeal or to litigate the suit, and said judgement or settlement is in excess of the Insured's retention, the Company reserves the right to settle with the Insured for the difference between the amount of said settlement, or judgement and the Insured's retention, and upon doing so, shall be relieved of any further liability to or on behalf of the Insured.

(5) In the event that any claim covered by this policy or any suit which the Company has agreed to defend, as provided for herein can be settled for a sum within the Insured's retention the Company agrees that it will not settle such suit without the consent of the Insured provided, however, that if the Insured shall refuse to consent to such settlement, the Company shall have no liability for any loss in excess of the retention with respect to such claim or suit, and the obligation of the Company to defend the Insured in such claim or suit shall thereupon terminate.

Effective Date.................................19........

Nothing herein contained shall be held to vary, alter, waive or extend any of the terms, conditions, agreements or limitations of this policy other than as above stated.

Attached to and forming part of Policy No.....................issued to..............................

....of..

by SEABOARD SURETY COMPANY.

Countersigned by ....
Authorized Representative.

Form 6211

President

APPLICATION FOR ADVERTISING AGENCY
LIBEL AND SLANDER, COPYRIGHT, PIRACY, PLAGIARISM, AND PRIVACY INSURANCE

Subject to Acceptance By

SEABOARD SURETY COMPANY

New York, New York

1. Name of Advertising Agency ....
2. Address..........
3. Agency is Corporation, Partnership or Individual (indicate which) ....
   Date Formed ....
4. Do you create Comparative Advertisements ....
   a) If so, list accounts, types and description of Advertising ....
   ....
5. Number of LIBEL, SLANDER, COPYRIGHT, PIRACY, PLAGIARISM OR PRIVACY SUITS in past ten years ....
   ....
6. Number of judgements rendered.......... Amount of each judgement ....
   ....
7. Number and amount of settlements before trial..........
8. Do you have any such suits pending.......... State details..........
   ....
   ....
9. Latest fiscal year was completed .... 19..........
10. What were agencies gross billings in latest completed fiscal year:

	DOMESTIC	FOREIGN
a) Excluding capitalized and service fees	$	....
b) Capitalized and service fees $	....	....
projected into gross billings @ 6-2/3 times	$	....
TOTAL GROSS BILLINGS..........	$	....

11. List foreign countries with an approximate breakdown of total Gross Billings for each..........
    ....
    ....
12. Does Agency act as producer of any radio or television programs ....
13. If so, list name and details of each program presently on air ....
    ....
14. The policy period is from ...., 19 ...... to .... 19 .....
15. Limits of coverage desired $..........
16. List similar insurance carried including excess ....

Name of Agency ....

By ....
Name and Title

*IF ADDITIONAL SPACE IS NEEDED USE BACK OR ATTACH SEPARATE RESPONSE.

Form 854 Rev. 12/78

(ATTACH ENDORSEMENTS HERE)

Cancelation C. This Policy may be canceled by the named Insured by mailing to the Company written notice stating when thereafter such cancelation shall be effective. This Policy may be canceled by the Company by mailing to the named Insured at the address shown in Statement 1 of the Schedule of Statements written notice stating when, not less than ten days thereafter, such cancelation shall be effective. The mailing of notice, as aforesaid, shall be sufficient proof of notice and the effective date and hour of cancelation stated in the notice shall become the end of the Policy Period. Delivery of such written notice, either by the named Insured or by the Company, shall be equivalent to mailing. If the named Insured cancels, earned premium shall be computed in accordance with the customary short rate table and procedure, but shall not be less than the minimum premium set forth in the Schedule of Statements. If the Company cancels, earned premium shall be computed pro rata. Premium adjustment may be made at the time cancelation is effected, and if not then made, shall be made as soon as practicable after cancelation becomes effective. The Company's check or the check of its representative mailed or delivered as aforesaid, shall be sufficient tender of any refund of premium due to the named Insured.

Notices D. Upon receipt by the Insured of information relating to an act or event which might result in a claim or claims under this Policy, written notice thereof shall be given by or on behalf of the Insured to the Company or its authorized agent as soon as practicable. Such notice shall contain particulars of the thing or act that is the subject of the claim as well as copy of the claim. If suit is brought against the Insured to enforce such claim, the Insured shall forward to the Company with reasonable promptness every summons, notice, or other process that may be served upon him.

Co-operation of Insured E. The Insured shall not make any admission of liability, nor shall he authorize any officer, employee or other person to make any admission of liability, either before or after a claim is made; nor shall he, except at his own cost, incur any expense, make any payment or settle any claim; nor shall he interfere in any negotiations for settlement or in any legal proceeding with respect to any claim hereunder without, in each case, the written consent of the Company. In the event the Insured shall settle or defend any claim or suit without the written approval of the Company, any amount which the Insured shall pay or become liable to pay, including expenses, on account of such claim or suit shall not be recoverable under this Policy. The defense by the Company of any suit or the prosecution of any appeal shall not operate as a waiver by the Company of any of its defenses to any claim by the Insured, should the Insured fail to comply with any of the terms or conditions of the Policy.

Whenever required by the Company, the Insured shall aid in securing information and evidence and the attendance of witnesses, and shall co-operate with the Company in the defense of any claim or suit or in the prosecution of any appeal; and the Company shall reimburse the Insured for expenses, other than loss of earnings, incurred at the Company's request.

Subrogation F. In the event of any payment under this Policy, and to the extent of such payment, the Company shall be subrogated to all the Insured's rights of recovery therefor against any person or organization, other than the client of the insured agency; and the Insured shall execute all papers required and shall co-operate with the Company to secure to it such rights.

Other Insurance G. If the Insured carries other insurance or indemnity not designated in Statement 5, of the Schedule of Statements, covered by the terms of this Policy, the Company shall be liable hereunder for only that proportion of the loss that the amount of this Policy bears to the total of this Policy and such other insurance regardless of whether such other insurance shall be deemed excess only, contributing or otherwise.

Changes H. Notice to any agent or knowledge possessed by any agent or by any other person shall not effect a waiver or a change in any part of this Policy or estop the Company from asserting any right under the terms of this Policy; nor shall the terms of this Policy be waived or changed, except by endorsement issued to form a part of this Policy, signed by the President, a Vice-President, Secretary or an Assistant Secretary and countersigned by a duly Authorized Representative of the Company.

Statutory Provisions I. If any condition of this Policy is at variance with any specific statutory provision applicable thereto, such specific statutory provision shall supersede the condition inconsistent therewith.

Statements J. The Statements contained in the Schedule forming a part of the Policy are made by the Insured and, by the acceptance of this Policy, the Insured represents the same to be true.

Action Against Company K. No action shall lie against the Company to recover for any loss under this Policy unless brought within two years after the amount of such loss is made certain either by judgment against the Insured, after trial of the issue, or by agreement between the parties with the written consent of the Company. Bankruptcy or insolvency of the Insured shall not relieve the Company of its obligations hereunder.

Assignment L. Any assignment or change of interest hereunder, whether voluntary or involuntary, shall render the Policy void unless such assignment or change is consented to in writing by the President, a Vice-President, a Secretary or an Assistant Secretary of the Company.

IN WITNESS WHEREOF, the SEABOARD SURETY COMPANY has caused this policy to be signed by its President and Secretary and countersigned by a duly Authorized Representative of the Company.

Secretary

President

11

LABOR PROBLEMS AFFECTING THE ADVERTISING INDUSTRY

Elhanan C. Stone

March 11, 1982

Labor Problems Affecting the Advertising Industry

A. Screen Actors Guild

1. Scope of Contract
2. Persons Covered
3. Still Photographs
4. Exclusivity
5. Restrictions on Use
6. Alternate Scenes or Lines
7. Indemnification
8. Arbitration
9. Union Security
10. Preference of Employment
11. Right to Work States

B. A.F.T.R.A.

C. Screen Extras Guild

D. American Federation of Musicians

SAG has jurisdiction over filmed television commercials and television commercials produced on tape in SAG production facilities. AFTRA has jurisdiction over live television and radio commercials, recorded radio commercials and recorded television commercials produced in AFTRA facilities. Where there is overlapping jurisdiction, the producer may choose which union he wishes to work under. Caveat. If AFTRA talent is hired at scale, an agent will demand an extra 10% because he cannot take his commission from the actor's scale payment. The jurisdiction of both unions is national in scope. Although preference of employment applies in only the preference zones (schedule B II SAG contract) union security and all other terms and conditions of the contract apply nationally. Production in a right to work state exempts a producer only from the union security requirement that an actor be a member of the union prior to employment. No other term or condition of the contract is affected by right to work legislation.

The arbitration clause of both SAG and AFTRA contracts is very broad. Exclusive jurisdiction over all controversies arising under those contracts is vested in an arbitration panel. The arbitration is tried under the voluntary arbitration rules of the American Arbitration Association unless both the union and producer agree to a different forum. The 1982 SAG and AFTRA contracts provide for a permanent panel of arbitrators. The single arbitrator for any case will be chosen at random. The AAA arbitration rules and the previous proceedure will remain in effect until the permanent panel is agreed upon by the contracting parties.

SEG has jurisdiction over all filmed extras work in television commercials. SAG has jurisdiction over extras work performed within a 300 mile radius of New York. AFTRA commercials have extra work covered under the AFTRA television recorded commercials contract. However, when work is performed outside of the preference zones established in the SEG contract, the rates set forth in the contract for extra work are not applicable.

The contractual right to use a television commercial under both AFTRA and SAG is granted to the producer and is limited by the respective contracts. No additional right accrues to the producer unless it is bargained for. Even though the producer might have had the right under the common law, he loses any such common law right under the union contracts. For instance, a deceased actor might no longer have a right ot privacy and his name or likeness could freely be used in a commercial with no liability for payment. However, if the commercial was produced under the union contract his right to payment is a vested property interest which descends to his estate.

4. DEFINITIONS

Commercials are short advertising or commercial messages made as motion pictures, 3 minutes or less in length, and intended for showing over television. Advertising or commercial messages include any narration, dialogue, songs, jingles or other matter which depict or mention the advertiser's name, product or service. They include program openings and closings which mention the advertiser's name, product or service. Advertising and commercial messages over 3 minutes in length shall be subject to separate negotiations between the Guild and Producer.

5. SCOPE OF CONTRACT

A. The terms and conditions of this Contract apply to commercials produced by Producer in the United States, which includes its commonwealths, territories and possessions, and to commercials for which Producer engages players within such territorial areas wherever such commercials are made.

B. The showing of commercials anywhere within the United States, its commonwealths, territories and possessions, Canada and Mexico, shall be included in determining use fees.

C. The parties to this Contract agree that every effort will be made to encourage advertisers to produce TV commercials within the geographic scope of this Contract. As part of this objective Producers agree that they will not produce commercials outside the geographic scope of this Contract engaging entirely non-Guild players primarily for reasons of economy or economic advantages in the engagement of players.

On request Producer will supply the Guild with complete records and reports of commercials which were made outside the geographic scope of this Contract. In the event such material discloses production outside the geographic scope of this Contract in violation of the intent and spirit of Section 5 C, the Guild may require advance notice of all future production outside of the geographic scope of this Contract.

6. PERSONS COVERED

The following classifications of persons are included in the term "player" and are covered by this Contract:

A. Anyone who is seen and who speaks a line or lines of dialogue, whether directly employed for such work, or after being hired as an extra player, as provided in paragraph 26 of Schedule A of the Producer-Screen Actors Guild Codified Basic Agreement of 1967 as amended;

B. Anyone whose face appears silent, alone in a stationary camera shot, and is identified with the product or service;

C. Anyone whose face appears silent and is identifiable and whose foreground performance demonstrates or illustrates a product or service, or illustrates or reacts to the on or off-camera narration or commercial message. Persons appearing in the foreground solely as atmosphere and not otherwise covered by the foregoing shall be deemed extra players;

D. Notwithstanding any of the provisions of subsections A, B or C hereof, anyone who is the subject of a closeup and who is identifiable shall be deemed a "player". A "closeup" is defined as that term is understood in motion picture photography.

E. Stunt players are included in the term "player" if they perform an identifiable stunt which demonstrates or illustrates a product or service or illustrates or reacts to the on or off-camera narration or commercial message. Stunt players need not be identifiable per se; only the stunt performed need be identifiable;

F. Specialty dancers and specialty acts are included in the term "player" if the requirements of this Section 6 are otherwise fulfilled;

G. Anyone whose voice is used off camera, except "omnies";

H. Persons appearing in "stop action," "squeeze action" or still photographs as defined in and subject to the limitations of Section 7 hereof;

I. Puppeteers are defined as those who operate hand or string-manipulated puppets. Such player shall be paid compensation for services and for use as follows:

1. Where the puppets are owned by a producer, advertiser or advertising agency, a player engaged to manipulate such puppets shall be employed in accordance with the provisions of subsection A of Section 19, and shall be paid the on-camera rates therein provided for services in making each commercial. For uses beyond the first 13-week cycle, an additional on-camera session fee shall be due and payable within 15 working days after the commencement of the second cycle of use of each commercial. However, if such player speaks any line or lines, in addition to the payments above provided, he shall be paid the applicable off-camera rates for the use of commercials, and in such case the sums paid under the first sentence of this subsection I shall be credited against such use payments.

2. Where the puppets are identified with the player as a specialty act or are owned by the player, such player shall be employed in accordance with the provisions of subsection A of Section 19, and shall be paid the on-camera rates therein provided for services in making each commercial and shall be further paid for the use thereof the applicable on-camera rates.

J. Airplane or helicopter pilots are included in the term "player" if, at the direction of Producer, their flying or taxiing demonstrates or illustrates a product or service or illustrates or reacts to the on or off-camera narration or commercial message;

K. A featured foreground performance by specialty acts, specialty dancers or stunt players in a commercial shall be covered for all purposes, including residuals, whether or not their performance demonstrates or illustrates a product or service, or illustrates or reacts to the on or off-camera narration or commercial message;

L. Anyone who speaks lines or performs a stunt for a commercial and whose performance is not utilized in a commercial so as to qualify such person as a player under the provisions of this Section 6 shall, nevertheless, receive the applicable session fee provided hereunder and all working conditions applicable to players;

M. The application of this Contract to persons fulfilling the requirements of this Section 6 is limited only by the provisions of Section 8. Members of the public who appear in testimonial or hidden camera commercials, non-professionals, minors, etc., shall receive the wages, working conditions and other benefits provided by this Contract.

N. The rates set forth herein for group players shall also apply to group dancers who are within the jurisdiction of the Screen Actors Guild in New York and Screen Extras Guild elsewhere in the United States.

7. STILL PHOTOGRAPHS

Persons appearing in television commercials in "stop action" photographs, "squeeze action" photographs or in photographs involving similar techniques or results, and persons appearing in television commercials in still photographs made for any advertising purpose, which photographs as used in the commercial would bring such persons within the definition of the term "player" as provided in Section 6, shall be entitled to sums equal to session and use fees as provided herein.

However, the following types of uses of still photographs are not covered by this Contract:

A. Photographs which appear in a casual leafing through of an album, book, magazine or newspaper;

B. Photographs of trademarks and service marks (registered and unregistered);

C. Photographs of packaging and labeling;

D. Actual print where a photograph appears incidentally and is not highlighted or featured;

E. Billboards, displays and point-of-sale items which appear incidentally and are not highlighted or featured;

15. EXCLUSIVITY

A. The exclusivity to which scale players may agree shall be limited to an agreement not to accept employment in commercials advertising any competitive product. Only players receiving scale plus 50% for the employment and use payments may agree not to accept employment in commercials advertising non-competitive products, but may not agree to grant complete exclusivity. Only a player who has entered into a term contract to perform services on a continuing basis for a guaranteed amount may agree to grant complete exclusivity. The contract or memorandum thereof shall be submitted to the Guild for its consent to the granting of complete exclusivity, the granting of which consent shall not be unreasonably withheld or delayed.

B. A product or service shall not be deemed competitive with another product or service solely because both are made or offered by the same advertiser, nor shall a product or service be deemed competitive with another product or service merely because it is manufactured or offered by another advertiser competitive in some other product or service area.

C. Exclusivity may not be required of players engaged to portray non-identifiable voices (disguised voices, dialects, cartoon voices, etc.) or for lip sync.

D. No exclusivity agreement may be made which extends beyond the maximum periods of use provided in Section 29 hereof, subject to the provisions for renewals thereof.

E. Player shall not be required to grant warranties or exclusivity of any kind with respect to any work performed or to be performed in other commercials as an extra player, nor may any player be required to grant any warranties with respect to any commercial, except within the area of exclusivity permitted by subsection A hereof.

F. No exclusivity rights may be required by Producer with respect to off-camera group players, other than "name" groups.

G. No exclusivity rights may be acquired by Producer with respect to players who perform in Seasonal Commercials.

H. Producer and player agree that exclusivity is one of the fundamental aspects of this Contract and is one of the foundations for use fees. Therefore, any breach of exclusivity by a player must be considered a serious breach of his agreement with Producer and may lead to substantial damages being assessed against player. The Guild agrees that it shall be a policy of the Guild to make members aware of their professional responsibility to live up to exclusivity agreements and to encourage adherence thereto.

I. Exclusivity agreements apply with respect to employment in television commercials made under both the Guild's Collective Bargaining Agreement and under the Collective Bargaining Agreement of the American Federation of Television and Radio Artists (AFTRA).

16. RESTRICTIONS ON USE OF COMMERCIALS; ADDITIONAL SERVICES

A. The rights granted to Producer in commercials shall be limited to the right to use, distribute, reproduce and/or exhibit such commercials over television. Producer shall have the right to use the name and likeness of the player and his acts, poses and appearances in such commercials, in trade publications for the purpose of publicizing the business of Producer.

B. Producer agrees that no part of the photography or sound track of a player made for a commercial shall be used other than in commercials as provided hereunder, without separately bargaining with the player and reaching an agreement regarding such use. The foregoing requirement of separate bargaining applies to reuse in other commercials after the maximum period of use has expired pursuant to Section 29, reuse in theatrical or television motion pictures, or use or reuse in any other field or medium. Such separate bargaining shall take place prior to the time of such proposed reuse but the player may not agree to such reuse at the time of original employment except as follows:

1. Bargaining for the right to use the player's sound track in radio may take place at the time of employment, provided that additional payment is made for such use at the time of such employment.

2. Bargaining for the right to use the player's photography or sound track in any other field or medium may take place at the time of employment, provided the specific nature and extent of such use is specified and proper payment is made at such time.

All such bargaining shall be subject to the minimum wages and use fees, if any, provided for in the collective bargaining agreement, if any, applicable to the field in which the photography or sound track is used. If Producer is unable to find the player within a reasonable time, it shall notify the Guild, and if the Guild is unable to find the player within a reasonable time, Producer may reuse the photography or sound track without penalty.

If Producer fails to separately bargain with the player as provided above, or if Producer and the player bargain but are unable to reach an agreement, Producer shall be prohibited from making such use of the material. In case of violation of the foregoing, the player shall be entitled to damages for such unauthorized use equivalent to three times the amount originally paid the player for the number of days of work covered by the material used. In addition, minimum use fees, if any, applicable to the field in which the material is used, shall be paid. However, the player may, in lieu of accepting such damages, elect to arbitrate his claim or bring an individual legal action in a court of competent jurisdiction to enjoin such use and recover such damages as the court may fix in such action.

The provisions of this subsection B shall not be applicable to unidentifiable off-camera group players. With respect to on-camera players, the provisions of this subsection B shall apply only if the player is recognizable and, with respect to stunt players, only if the stunt is identifiable.

C. If Producer wishes to use the player's sound track in a simulcast, the individual player's contract shall contain a provision requiring additional compensation payable at the time of such simulcast. Such additional compensation shall be no less than the rates provided for in the applicable collective bargaining agreement for radio.

D. No service of the player is contracted for except as specified in this collective bargaining agreement. This paragraph is not intended to prevent a player from contracting for services of a kind not covered by this Contract by individual contract at such rates of pay and under such conditions as Producer and the player shall agree, subject only to the fact that it shall not be in conflict with this collective bargaining agreement.

19. E. **Alternate Scenes or Lines**

1. Session

Notwithstanding anything contained in this Section 19 to the contrary, alternate scenes photographed or lines recorded for legal or continuity clearance reasons for a specific single commercial during a session, whether or not pre-scripted, shall not be considered new or additional commercials for purposes of session fee payments subject to both the following conditions:

(a) The alternate scene or line changes are variations in dialogue or action within the basic theme, creative concept and background as indicated by the specific script or storyboard.

(b) Such changes are within the player's role in the commercial.

2. Use

The following shall apply with respect to the use of alternate scenes photographed or lines recorded which are permitted under Paragraph 1 above.

(a) The definition of a new or additional commercial remains subject to the editing provisions of Section 25, Editing of Commercials, for the purpose of computing use payments for commercials in which such alternate scenes and lines are used.

(b) When the alternate scenes or lines are incorporated into a commercial which does not constitute a new or additional commercial under the provisions of Section 25:

(i) if such commercial is telecast within 26 weeks after the session date of the basic commercial for which the alternate scenes or lines were produced, then an amount equivalent to a session fee, which may not be credited against use, shall be paid to each player directly involved in making the alternate scenes or lines so used;

(ii) if such commercial is telecast more than 26 weeks after the session date of the basic commercial for which the alternate scenes or lines were produced, then an amount equivalent to two session fees, neither of which may be credited against use, shall be paid to each player directly involved in making the alternate scenes or lines so used.

(c) When the alternate scenes or lines are incorporated into a commercial which constitutes a new or additional commercial under the provisions of Section 25:

(i) if such commercial is telecast within 26 weeks after the session date of the basic commercial for which the alternate scenes or lines were produced, then an amount equivalent to a session fee, which may be credited against use shall be paid to each player in that commercial;

(ii) if such commercial is telecast more than 26 weeks after the session date of the basic commercial for which the alternate scenes or lines were produced, then an amount equivalent to two session fees, one of which may be credited against use, shall be paid to each player in that commercial.

(d) The maximum period of use of any commercial into which the alternate scenes or lines are incorporated shall be limited to the same period during which the basic commercial may be used as provided in Section 29, Maximum Period of Use.

57. **INDEMNIFICATION**

A. Subject to the provisions of D, E and F hereof, in the event any other member of the cast, production staff, crew or any other person, firm or corporation shall suffer injury to his or her person and/or property, of any kind whatsoever by reason of, or as a result of, the performance by any actor or stunt player (hereinafter in this paragraph called "performer") of a stunt or act in the course and scope of his employment under this collective bargaining agreement, under the direction and control of the Producer, Producer shall at all times indemnify and save the performer harmless from and against all liability, loss, damages and costs, including reasonable counsel fees, which the performer may for any cause at any time sustain or incur by reason of such performance. In the event legal action is taken against the performer, either jointly with the Producer or alone, the Producer shall at his own cost and expense and without undue delay provide the defense of the performer in all such litigations.

B. In the event any legal action in the courts or before Administrative bodies results by reason of, or as a result of, any material or action of a performer included in a commercial in the scope and course of his employment under this collective bargaining agreement, under the direction and control of the Producer, Producer shall at all times indemnify and save the player harmless from and against all liability, loss, damages and costs, including reasonable counsel fees, which the performer may for any cause at any time sustain by reason of such performance. In the event legal action, in the courts or administratively is taken against the player, either jointly with Producer or alone, Producer shall at his own cost and expense and without undue delay provide the defense of the player in all such litigation.

C. The indemnity provided for in A and B above shall be limited to actions of the performer which he takes pursuant to the direction, control or request of the Producer or the Producer's designee, or material provided to the performer by the Producer or his designee. The performer shall similarly indemnify the Producer against any liability, loss, damages and costs, including reasonable counsel fees, which the Producer may at any time sustain or incur by reason of any action taken by the performer contrary to the direction of the Producer or outside the course and scope of his employment or by reason of any fraudulent material provided by the performer.

D. The indemnitee shall notify the indemnitor promptly in writing in case knowledge shall come to the indemnitee of any claim or litigation arising out of such performance and thereafter deliver to the indemnitor every demand, notice, summons, complaint or other process received by him or his representative relating thereto.

E. The indemnitee shall cooperate fully in the defense so provided by indemnitor of such claim or action, and upon the indemnitor's request, shall attend hearings and trials and whenever possible, assist in (i) securing and giving evidence; and (ii) obtaining the attendance of witnesses at such hearings and trials

F. The indemnitee shall not make any settlement or compromises of any such claim or litigation without the prior written consent of the indemnitor. Any settlement or compromise by the indemnitee without indemnitor's prior consent of any such claim or litigations shall nullify indemnitor's obligation under A or B above.

G. If the indemnitee has reason to believe that any indemnitor does not have financial resources sufficient to cover its indemnity under this agreement, then the indemnitee may require that insurance be provided so as to cover any reasonable liability which the indemnitor may incur. When the indemnitee is a performer, the Guild may act on his behalf in making a reasonable determination of financial responsibility.

H. Nothing herein contained shall be construed to: (i) deprive indemnitor of any lawful defense to such claim or action including the defense that such claim arose by reason of indemnitee's acts outside the scope of his employment; or (ii) expand Producer's liability to any person under the applicable Workmen's Compensation Law.

ARBITRATION

All disputes and controversies of every kind and nature whatsoever between any Producer and the Guild or between any Producer and any player arising out of or in connection with this Contract, and any contract or engagement (whether overscale or not and whether at the minimum terms and conditions of this Contract or better) in the field covered by this Contract as to the existence, validity, construction, meaning, interpretation, performance, non-performance, enforcement, operation, breach, continuance, or termination of this Contract and/or such contract or engagement, shall be submitted to arbitration in accordance with the following procedure:

A. The Guild, acting on its own behalf or on behalf of any person employed under this Contract, or the Producer concerned, may demand such arbitration in writing. The parties shall thereupon endeavor to agree upon a single qualified arbitrator acceptable to them both. If the parties cannot agree upon a single qualified person within 5 working days after the demand for arbitration, the party demanding arbitration shall serve upon the other a notice which shall include the name of the arbitrator appointed by the party demanding arbitration. Within 3 working days after such notice, the other party shall name its arbitrator, or in default of such appointment, such arbitrator shall be named forthwith by the Arbitration Committee of the American Arbitration Association and the 2 arbitrators so selected shall name a third within a period of 5 working days, and in lieu of their agreement upon such third arbitrator, he shall be appointed by the Arbitration Committee of the American Arbitration Association. Each party shall bear its own arbitration expenses.

B. The hearing shall be held on 2 days' notice and shall be concluded within 14 days unless otherwise ordered by the arbitrator(s). The arbitration award shall be made within 7 days after the close of the submission of evidence, shall be final and binding upon all parties to the proceeding, and judgment upon such award may be entered by any party in the highest court of the forum, state or federal, having jurisdiction.

C. The word "Producer" as used in this Contract includes any third person to whom a commercial has been sold, assigned, transferred, leased or otherwise disposed of. Any Producer including such third party "Producer" may file with the Guild the name and address of an available person in New York City, or in Los Angeles, upon whom service of a demand for arbitration and other notices and papers under this paragraph may be made. If such name and address is not on file with the Guild, or if although on file the named person is not available, the Producer irrevocably appoints the Secretary of the American Arbitration Association as his agent to accept service and receive all notices, demands for arbitration and service of process in actions on the award in any suit by the Guild or Guild members. Producer further agrees that such notices, demands for arbitration and other process or papers may be served on the foregoing persons by registered mail sent to their last known address with the same force and effect as if the same had been personally served.

D. The parties agree that the provisions of this paragraph shall be a complete defense to any suit, action or proceeding instituted in any federal, state or local court or before any administrative tribunal with respect to any controversy or dispute which arises during the period of this Contract and which is therefor arbitrable as set forth above. The arbitration provisions of this Contract shall, with respect to such controversy or dispute, survive the termination or expiration of this Contract.

E. The Guild shall be an ex-officio party to all arbitration proceedings hereunder in which any artist is involved and may do anything which an artist named in such proceeding might do. Copies of all notices, demands, and other papers filed by any party in arbitration proceedings and copies of all motions, actions or proceedings in court following the award, shall be promptly filed with the Guild.

F. Nothing herein contained shall be deemed to give the arbitrator(s) the authority, power or right to alter, amend, change, modify, add to or subtract from any of the provisions of this Contract.

G. It is the policy of the Guild not to process unduly late claims.

SCHEDULE B

I. UNION SECURITY

A. Every player hereafter employed by any Producer, whether by contract or otherwise, or who acts before the camera, or who makes sound track within the Guild's jurisdiction for any Producer shall be a member of the Guild in good standing.

The Guild may waive, in its discretion, the provisions of this Section with respect to prominent persons appearing as themselves, other than professional entertainers; provided, however, that all other terms and conditions of this Contract shall apply to the engagement of such persons.

B. Each Producer shall give the Guild full opportunity to check performance by such Producer of its agreement under this Section including access to sets, but the Guild's checking shall be done in such a manner as not to interfere with production. The Guild agrees that with respect to the admission of persons as members of the Guild, it will comply with applicable law. The Guild reserves the right to adopt reasonable and legal requirements for membership. The Guild may refuse admission or, if it sees fit, admit on terms, players suspended or expelled by the Guild or by any branch of the Associated Actors and Artistes of America, or by any other actors' union in the United States. Nothing herein shall limit the right of the Guild to discipline, suspend, or expel a member or to refuse to re-admit him. The Guild agrees, however, that if it suspends or expels a member who is under contract to a Producer, or if a member resigns, the suspension, expulsion, or resignation shall not affect the player's obligation to perform any existing contract or contracts with such Producer or such Producer's right to demand performance, unless the Producer otherwise consents. Subject to the qualifications hereinafter set forth, the Producer agrees that in every future contract it enters into with a player, the player shall agree that the player shall be a member of the Guild in good standing and shall remain so for the duration of the contract. Any non-member of the Guild and any suspended or expelled member whom the Producer may be lawfully entitled to employ under this Contract shall be paid the same minimum salary and shall be given the same working conditions as are provided in this Contract. No breach by a member of the Guild of his obligation to the Guild shall give such member a defense to any Producer's right to enforce an existing contract against such member.

C. The foregoing subsections A and B, requiring as a condition of employment membership in the Guild, shall not apply until on or after the 30th day following the beginning of such employment or the effective date of this Contract, whichever is the later; the Guild and the Producers interpret this sentence to mean that membership in the Guild cannot be required of a player by a Producer as a condition of employment until 30 days after his first employment as an actor in the motion picture Industry; "first employment" meaning the first employment as an actor in the motion picture Industry on or after August 10, 1948. The foregoing sentence shall be deemed inoperative if any of the following events shall occur:

1. If the Labor Management Act of 1947 is repealed; or
2. If the provision of such Act to which the foregoing sentence has reference is repealed or modified so the foregoing sentence is unnecessary to comply with such Act; or
3. If such Act or such provision is held unconstitutional by the Supreme Court of the United States.

The Producer shall not be held to have violated this subsection if it employs a player who is not a member of the Guild in good standing, if the Producer has reasonable grounds for believing that membership in the Guild was not available to such player on the same terms and conditions generally applicable to other members, or if the Producer has reasonable grounds for believing that membership in the Guild was denied to such player or such player's membership in the Guild was terminated for reasons other than the failure of the player to tender the periodic dues and the initiation fee uniformly required as a condition of acquiring or retaining membership in the Guild; provided, however, the Producer shall not be deemed to have such reasonable grounds for believing until he has made inquiry of the Guild as to the facts. The preceding sentence shall be deemed inoperative if any of the following events shall occur: (1) if the Labor Management Act of 1947 is repealed; or (2) if the provision of such Act to which the preceding sentence has reference is repealed or modified so the preceding sentence is unnecessary to comply with such Act; or (3) if such Act or such provision is held unconstitutional by the Supreme Court of the United States.

D. The Producer agrees to report to the Guild in writing within 15 days of the first employment of a non-member of the Guild, giving the non-member's name, Social Security number, and his first date of employment. An inquiry by any Producer to the Guild as to the first date on which a player has been employed in the Industry shall be answered by the Guild, and its answer shall bind the Guild, and the Producer if it acts in good faith shall not be liable for acting on such answer, but the Producer who failed to report shall be liable to the Guild for such failure to report.

E. The interpretation contained in the first sentence of subsection C of this Section I has been approved by an advisory opinion of the general counsel of the National Labor Relations Board. If such approval of such sentence is changed by a ruling of such general counsel, then the new ruling of such general counsel shall prevail, until the same is overruled by the Board or a court of competent jurisdiction. If the Board or a court of competent jurisdiction shall change said ruling in a proceeding in which the Guild is a party, then the new ruling or opinion shall prevail, until the same is reversed by a court of competent jurisdiction.

F. The Guild agrees that it will not impose unreasonable dues or assessments. If Producer claims a violation by the Guild of the provisions of this subsection F, such question shall be handled by conciliation and, if necessary, by arbitration hereunder. It is the intention of the parties to prevent the Guild from closing its books so as to prevent any person who wishes to act in motion pictures from joining the Guild. Nothing in the preceding sentence shall limit the right of the Guild to discipline or suspend or expel a member or to refuse to re-admit him.

G. The Guild recognizes the fact that it no longer has jurisdiction over extra work performed in and around the County of Los Angeles, State of California. The jurisdiction of Screen Actors Guild, Inc., over extras in the City of New York is the subject matter of a separate agreement. Nothing herein contained shall prevent any member of Screen Actors Guild, Inc., from joining and maintaining membership in any union representing extra players.

H. Children under 14 years of age shall be included hereunder.

I. Whenever any Producer is entitled hereunder to a permit or waiver from the Guild, the Guild agrees to issue the same without cost.

J. It is understood that it would be impossible to accurately fix the actual damages suffered by the Guild by reason of a breach by a Producer of the Union Security provisions of this Section. It is therefore agreed that the Producer will pay to the Guild, as liquidated damages, the sum of $320 for each breach by the Producer of the Union Security provisions of this Section. The hiring by the Producer of a player in violation of the provisions hereof shall be deemed a single breach, regardless of the number of days of employment involved in the hiring; but each separate hiring of the same person in violation hereof shall be deemed a separate breach.

K. Any breach of the provisions of this Section shall be subject to arbitration between the Guild and the Producer.

II. PROFESSIONAL RECOGNITION – PREFERENCE OF EMPLOYMENT

A. In recognition of the services performed by professional players, Producer agrees that in the hiring of players, for work to be performed within the applicable zone (referred to in subsection C hereof), preference will be given to qualified professional actors. A "qualified professional actor," for the purpose of this Section, is a person who has had prior employment as a motion picture actor at least once during the period of 3 years prior to the date of the proposed employment; however, employment under the exceptions provided in D 1-4 of this Section or D 1-5 of prior Guild Commercials Contracts, or employment under comparable exemptions of the Guild's past or present Theatrical, Television or Industrial Agreements shall not constitute prior employment for this purpose.

B. The obligation of the Producer to give preference to qualified professional actors shall require the employment of a qualified professional actor, unless no qualified professional actor of the type required is reasonably and readily available to the Producer through the use of the present hiring practices generally and customarily followed by the motion picture Industry in the employment of such players. If a qualified professional actor is reasonably and readily available to the Producer for employment in the locality where the Producer's studio is based, he shall be deemed available regardless of the place within the applicable zone at which the services are to be performed.

C. The provisions of this Section shall not apply where services are performed at locations beyond the following preference zones in areas where the Guild maintains offices:

Los Angeles, California	– 300 miles from the corner of Beverly and La Cienega Blvds.
New York, New York	– 100 miles from the center of Columbus Circle

Florida	– 100 miles from the center of Coral Gables, Florida and 50 miles from the center of Orlando, Florida
San Francisco, California	– 100 miles from the intersection of Powell and Market Streets; the zone expressly includes Lake Tahoe
Chicago, Illinois	– 100 miles from the center of the city
Boston, Massachusetts	– 100 miles from the center of the city
Detroit, Michigan	– 100 miles from the center of the city
Denver, Colorado	– 100 miles from the center of the city
Dallas, Texas	– 100 miles from the center of the city
Phoenix, Arizona	– 100 miles from the center of the city
Tucson, Arizona	– 100 miles from the center of the city
Washington, D.C.	– 100 miles from the center of the city
Philadelphia, Pa.	– 100 miles from the center of the city
Atlanta, Georgia	– 100 miles from the center of the city
San Diego, California	– 100 miles from the center of the city
Seattle, Washington	– 100 miles from the center of the city
Minneapolis, Minnesota	– 100 miles from the center of the city
Cleveland, Ohio	– 100 miles from the center of the city
St. Louis, Missouri	– 100 miles from the center of the city

A preference zone of 100 miles from the center of any other city where the Guild maintains an office shall apply.

In the event the Guild establishes offices in cities other than those listed above and Producer claims that there is not a sufficiently large professional talent pool in the area of any office hereafter established by the Guild to warrant application of Preference of Employment, or if Producer so claims with respect to any of the ten last cities (listed above) starting with the city of Phoenix, Arizona, the matter shall be submitted to the Industry-Guild Standing Committee for determination.

D. There shall be automatically excluded from the provisions of this Section the following:

1. Persons who portray themselves who by words or actions participate in the giving of a testimonial or endorsement;

2. Extras who are adjusted for non-script lines;

3. Military personnel where governmental restrictions prevent use of civilian personnel in restricted areas or in the handling of governmental property or equipment; however, the use of military pilots or military aircraft shall not be the subject of an automatic waiver but the facts shall be presented to the Guild and waivers will be granted in accordance with the previously established custom in the motion picture Industry;

4. Persons having special skills or abilities, or special or unusual physical appearance where such skills, abilities or appearance are required by and are used in a commercial, if professional actors having such required skills or physical appearance are not reasonably and readily available to the Producer through the use of the hiring practices generally and customarily followed by the motion picture Industry in the employment of such players;

5. The first employment within the studio zone of a person with respect to whom the Producer presents in writing to the Guild facts showing (a) that the person has had sufficent training and/or experience so as to qualify for a career as a professional motion picture actor, and (b) that such person intends to pursue currently the career of a motion picture actor and intends to be available currently for employment in the motion picture Industry;

6. Children under the age of 7 years.

Producer agrees to promptly report to the Guild each hiring under the provisions of this subsection D, together with the reasons why the person so employed comes within the provisions of this subsection.

If a player is employed under one or more of the exceptions provided in subparagraphs 1-4, the obligation to give preference to qualified professional players shall nevertheless be applicable to any subsequent employment of such player by Producer.

E. It is expressly understood and agreed that nothing in this Section contained shall alter or modify Producer's exclusive right to cast any and all players performing services for Producer.

F. It is understood that it would be impossible to accurately fix the actual damages suffered by the Guild by reason of a breach by the Producer of the provisions of this Section. It is therefore agreed that the Producer will pay to the Guild, as liquidated damages the sum of $300 for each breach by the Producer of any of the provisions of this Section. The hiring by a Producer of a person other than a qualified professional actor, in violation of the provisions hereof, shall be deemed a single breach, regardless of the number of days of employment involved in the hiring; but each separate hiring of the same person in violation hereof shall be deemed a separate breach.

G. All disputes under this Section shall be determined by arbitration.

H. Employment of a player who is ineligible to work in the United States by reason of visa status shall be a violation of the provisions of this Section and the penalties provided in subsection F shall be applicable.

III. STRIKES

A. No-Strike Clause

The Guild agrees that, during the effective term hereof, it will not call or engage in a strike affecting production of commercials against any Producer signatory hereto.

B. Limitation on Liability

The Guild is a corporation. Nothing in this Section shall enlarge the liability of its officers, directors, agents, and members, this Section being an additional limitation thereon. The Guild will not be held liable for unauthorized acts of its officers, agents, directors, or members; neither the Guild nor its officers, directors, agents, or members not participating in the actions hereinafter mentioned, shall be liable for any strike, slowdown, or work stoppage, unless the same be authorized by the Guild in accordance with its By-Laws, but the foregoing exemption of this sentence shall not apply unless the Guild, upon request from the Producer affected thereby, shall proclaim promptly and publicly that such strike, slowdown or work stoppage is unauthorized, and follows such pronouncement within a reasonable time thereafter, if requested so to do by the Producer affected, with disciplinary proceedings in accordance with its By-Laws against the participants in such unauthorized action.

C. The Guild hereby notifies Producer that under Guild rules, in the event of a duly authorized strike by a performers' union having jurisdiction over television commercials in a foreign country, players may not perform services in, or grant Producer any foreign rights in, commercials where such commercials are to be used for the purpose of strike breaking. The normal supply of commercials to such foreign country shall not be considered strike breaking. Producers are not bound by such rules of the Guild, but neither the Guild nor any Guild members shall be subject to action for breach of contract or otherwise for complying with or enforcing such rule.

STANDARD SCREEN ACTORS GUILD EMPLOYMENT CONTRACT FOR TELEVISION COMMERCIALS

Date____________________, 19____

Between____________________________, Producer, and____________________________, Player.

Producer engages Player and Player agrees to perform services for Producer in television commercials as follows:

Date of Engagement____________________________

Time and Place of Engagement____________________________

For____________________ (Advertising Agency) and____________________ (Advertiser)

Address____________________________

PRODUCT____________________ NO. OF COMMERCIALS__________

Check if Applicable:
- ☐ Dealer Commercial(s)
  - ☐ Type A
  - ☐ Type B
- ☐ Seasonal Commercial(s)
- ☐ Test Market Commercial(s)
- ☐ Non-Air Commercial(s)

Commercial ID____________________

☐ Player does not consent to the use of his services in commercials made hereunder as dealer commercials payable at dealer commercial rates.

☐ Player does not consent to the use of his services in commercials made hereunder on a simulcast.

CLASSIFICATION: ( ) On Camera ( ) Off Camera

( ) Player	( ) Singer-solo or duo	( ) Singer-Signature-solo or duo
( ) Stunt Player	( ) Group-3-5	( ) Group-Signature-3-5
( ) Puppeteer	( ) Group-6-8	( ) Group-Signature-6-8
( ) Specialty Act	( ) Group-9 or more	( ) Group-Signature-9 or more
	( ) Contractor	( ) Pilot

	Session Fee (On-Camera Player)	Session Fee (Off-Camera Player)
Compensation:	$	$

Check if: Flight Insurance ($10) Payable ☐ $__________

Wardrobe to be furnished by Producer ☐ by Player ☐

If furnished by Player, No. of Garments ;

Non-evening wear @ $7.50 ;

Evening wear @ $15.00 ; Total Wardrobe Fee $__________

The standard provisions printed on the reverse side hereof are a part of this contract. If this contract provides for compensation at minimum SAG scale, no addition, changes or alterations may be made in this form other than those which are more favorable to the Player than herein provided.

If this contract provides for compensation above minimum SAG scale, additions may be agreed to between Producer and Player which do not conflict with the provisions of the SAG Commercials Contract; provided that such additional provisions are separately set forth under "Special Provisions" hereof and signed by the Player.

Until Player shall otherwise direct in writing, Player authorizes Producer to make all payments to which Player may be entitled hereunder as follows:

☐ To Player at____________________ (Address)

☐ To Player c/o____________________ at____________________ (Address)

All notices to Player shall be sent to the address designated above for payments and, if Player desires, to one other address as follows:

To____________________ (Name) at____________________ (Address)

All notices to Producer shall be addressed as follows:

To Producer at____________________ (Address)

This contract is subject to all of the terms and conditions of the SAG Commercials Contract.

Producer____________________ Player____________________

By____________________

Player hereby certifies that he is 21 years of age or over. (If under 21 years of age this contract must be signed below by a parent or guardian.)

I, the undersigned, hereby state that I am the____________________ (Mother, Father, Guardian) of the above named Player and do hereby consent and give my permission to this agreement.

Special Provisions: ____________________ (Signature of Parent or Guardian)

Player acknowledges that he has read all the terms and conditions in the Special Provisions section above and hereby agrees thereto.

Player____________________ Social Security Number____________________

(W-4 form is attached here.)

STANDARD PROVISIONS

1. RIGHT TO CONTRACT

Player states that to the best of his knowledge, he has not authorized the use of his name, likeness or identifiable voice in any commercial advertising any competitive product or service during the term of permissible use of commercial(s) hereunder and that he is free to enter into this contract and to grant the rights and uses herein set forth.

2. EXCLUSIVITY

Player states that since accepting employment in the commercial(s) covered by this contract, he has not accepted employment in nor authorized the use of his name or likeness or identifiable voice in any commercial(s) advertising any competitive product or service and that he will not hereafter, during the term of permissible use of the commercial(s) for which he is employed hereunder, accept employment in or authorize the use of his name or likeness or identifiable voice in any commercial(s) advertising any competitive product or service. This paragraph shall not apply to off-camera group players (other than name groups) or to players employed in seasonal commercials.

3. OTHER USES (Strike "a" or "b" if such rights not granted by Player)

(a) Foreign Use

Producer shall have the right to the foreign use of the commercial(s) produced hereunder, for which Producer agrees to pay player not less than the additional compensation provided for in the SAG Commercials Contract. Producer agrees to notify SAG in writing promptly of any such foreign use.

(b) Theatrical & Industrial Use

Producer shall have the right to the commercial(s) produced hereunder for theatrical and industrial use as defined and for the period permitted in the SAG Commercials Contract, for which Producer shall pay player not less than the additional compensation therein provided.

4. ARBITRATION

All disputes and controversies of every kind and nature arising out of or in connection with this contract shall be subject to arbitration as provided in Section 55 of the SAG Commercials Contract.

5. PRODUCER'S RIGHTS

Player acknowledges that player has no right, title or interest of any kind or nature whatsoever in or to the commercial(s). A role owned or created by Producer belongs to Producer and not to player.

RIGHT TO WORK STATES (All other states allow a union security provision)

PREFERENCE ZONES IN RIGHT TO WORK STATES

		AFTRA miles from center of city	SAG miles from center of city	SEG miles from center of city
1.	Alabama	*	*	
2.	Arizona		Tucson 100 mi Phoenix 100 mi	Tucson 100 mi Phoenix 100 mi
3.	Arkansas			
4.	Florida	Orlando 50 mi. Coral Gables-Miami 100 mi	Coral Gables 100 mi Orlando 50 mi	Coral Gables 100 mi Orlando 50 mi
5.	Georgia	Atlanta 100 mi	Atlanta 100 mi	Atlanta 100 mi
6.	Iowa			
7.	Kansas			
8.	Louisiana	New Orleans 100 mi		New Orleans 50 mi
9.	Mississippi			
10.	Montana			
11.	Nebraska			
12.	Nevada	**Las Vegas	**Las Vegas	**Las Vegas
13.	North Carolina			
14.	North Dakota			
15.	South Carolina			
16.	South Dakota			
17.	Tennesse	Nashville 100 mi	Nashville 100 mi	Nashville 50 mi
18.	Texas	Dallas-Ft.Worth 100 mi	Dallas-Ft.Worth 100mi	Dallas-Ft.Worth 100mi
19.	Utah			
20.	Virginia	***	***	***
21.	Wyoming			

* The Atlanta 100 mile zone covers a portion of Alabama

** The Los Angeles 300 mile zone covers a portion of Nevada including Las Vegas

*** The Washington, D.C. 100 mile zone covers a portion of Virginia

NOTES

Program Schedule and Faculty

LEGAL AND BUSINESS ASPECTS OF THE ADVERTISING INDUSTRY

New York City, April 22-23, 1982

PROGRAM SCHEDULE:

Registration is thirty minutes before each morning session. Coffee will be available at that time.

FIRST DAY: 9:30 a.m.-4:30 p.m.
Morning Session: 9:30 a.m.-12:30 p.m.

Agreements between agencies and clients

Services the agency is to supply.
Ownership of ideas. Commissions on termination. Agency's position in different types of lawsuits. Does agency indemnify client?
Liabilities of advertiser and agency. Bankruptcy of agency. Bankruptcy of client. Single and double liability.
Forms of agency-client relationships: house agencies; "a la carte" service; media-buying services.

Basic copy rules

Use of names, photographs, titles, and excerpts from literary materials. Use of imitations. Use of trademarks.
Releases required for: testimonial advertising; acquisition of music; use of stock photos, flags, money, and stamps.
Use of guarantees, sweepstakes, contests, and the terms "new," "free offer," and "cents off."

Industry self-policing

NAB Code Authority network review. NARB and legal issues. Questions of taste. Special problems of children.

Afternoon Session: 2:00 p.m.-4:30 p.m.

Governmental controls of advertising

Sources of federal, state, and local controls.

Pressures on advertisers: consumer groups; class actions; fairness doctrine; proposed legislation.

Federal Trade Commission activities; expansion of the "unfairness" doctrine. Trends in section 5 enforcement for false and deceptive advertising. Enforcement of existing orders under Magnuson-Moss Warranty. FTC Improvement Act procedures.

FTC procedures: investigation; complaint; negotiations; hearing.

Advertising substantiation; adoption of evidentiary rules.

Copyrights and the new technology

Special problems in copyrighting commercials, cable programming, videodiscs, and videocassettes.

Home taping: *Universal City Studios Inc. v. Sony Corporation of America.*

Fair use of music. Other recent cases.

SECOND DAY: 9:30 a.m.-4:30 p.m.

Morning Session: 9:30 a.m.-12:30 p.m.

Nonprescription drug advertising

Jurisdiction of FDA; overlapping jurisdiction with FTC.

Over-the-counter drug advertising.

Analgesic cases and the *Block Drug* case.

Trade regulation rules as a means to regulate; drug label claims – OTC review; *Tylenol v. Bayer;* OTC monographs as standards of parity; self-regulation.

Constitutional protection of advertising

Effects of the Supreme Court decision in *Virginia Board of Pharmacy;* self-regulation. Substantiation and requirements.

Comparative advertising

Increased popularity of comparative advertising and legal consequences. Private actions among advertisers. Network and NAB Rules on comparative advertising; Lanham Act section 43.

Afternoon Session: 2:30 p.m.-4:30 p.m.

Advertising litigation

Libel, invasion of privacy, right of publicity, copyright infringement, unfair competition, and plagiarism; injunction actions. Advertiser's and agency's liability policies. Advertiser liability; agency liability; joint liability.

Labor and contract problems affecting the advertising industry

Contracts with media and suppliers; contracts with talent.

FACULTY:

CO-CHAIRMEN:

Felix H. Kent
Hall, Dickler, Lawler, Kent
and Howley
New York City

Elhanan C. Stone
Senior Vice President – General Counsel
Ted Bates Advertising/New York
New York City

Robert M. Callagy
Satterlee and Stephens
New York City

Stuart Lee Friedel
Davis and Gilbert
New York City

Elizabeth Elster Granville
Assistant Vice President
– Public Relations
Broadcast Music, Inc.;
Chair
Committee on Copyright
and Literary Property of the
Association of the Bar
New York City

Thomas R. Hillhouse
Division Counsel
The Procter & Gamble Company
Cincinnati

Marylou Jennerjahn
Vice President – Commercial
Clearance
Columbia Broadcasting Company
New York City

Raphael G. Scobey
Battle, Fowler, Joffin
and Kheel
New York City

Ronald Smithies
National Advertising
Division
Council of Better Business
Bureaus, Inc.
New York City

PLI PROGRAM ATTORNEY:
Ruth Druss